W9-CNI-292

Global Sociology
Introducing Five Contemporary Societies

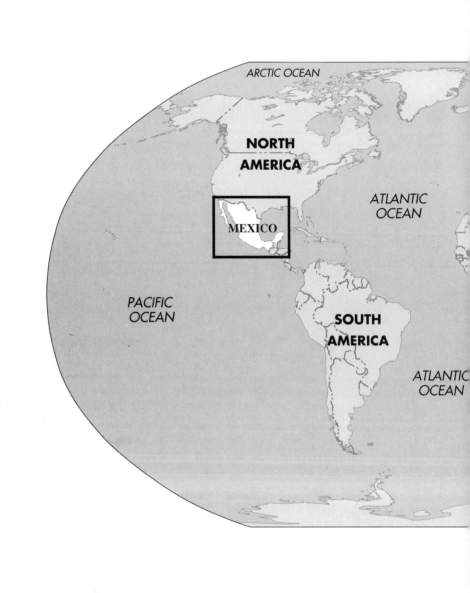

ARCTIC OCEAN

NORTH
AMERICA

ATLANTIC
OCEAN

MEXICO

PACIFIC
OCEAN

SOUTH

AMERICA

ATLANTIC
OCEAN

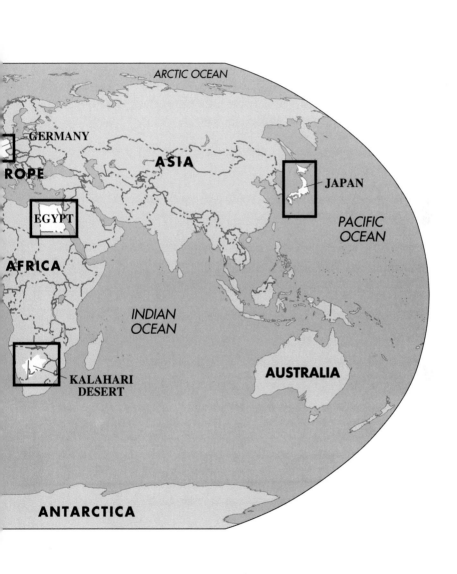

ARCTIC OCEAN

GERMANY

ASIA

ROPE

JAPAN

EGYPT

PACIFIC
OCEAN

AFRICA

INDIAN
OCEAN

AUSTRALIA

KALAHARI
DESERT

ANTARCTICA

CARNEGIE LIBRARY
LIVINGSTONE COLLEGE
SALISBURY, NC 28144

Global Sociology

Introducing Five Contemporary Societies

Linda Schneider

Nassau Community College

Arnold Silverman

Nassau Community College

WCB McGraw-Hill

Boston, Massachusetts   Burr Ridge, Illinois   Dubuque, Iowa
Madison, Wisconsin   New York, New York   San Francisco, California
St. Louis, Missouri

WCB/McGraw-Hill

A Division of The **McGraw·Hill** Companies

GLOBAL SOCIOLOGY
Introducing Five Contemporary Societies

Copyright © 1997 by The McGraw-Hill Companies, Inc. All rights reserved. Printed in the United States of America. Except as permitted under the United States Copyright Act of 1976, no part of this publication may be reproduced or distributed in any form or by any means, or stored in a data base or retrieval system, without the prior written permission of the publisher.

This book is printed on acid-free paper.

3 4 5 6 7 8 9 0 DOC DOC 9 0 9 8 7

ISBN 0-07-057018-3

This book was set in Times Roman by Graphic World, Inc.
The editors were Jill S. Gordon and Katherine Blake;
the production supervisor was Richard A. Ausburn.
The cover was designed by Charles A. Carson.
Cover photo: Bachmann/Photo Researchers, Inc., Native Woman/Mr. Sakkara, Egypt.
The photo editor was Anne Manning.
Project supervision was done by The Total Book.
R.R. Donnelley & Sons Company was printer and binder.

Library of Congress Cataloging-in-Publication Data

Schneider, Linda.
    Global sociology: introducing five contemporary societies / Linda
Schneider. Arnold Silverman.

        p.   cm.
    Includes bibliographical references and index.
    ISBN 0-07-057018-3 (pbk.)
    1. Sociology.   2. Sociology—Cross-cultural studies.
I. Silverman, Arnold R., (date).   II. Title.
HM51.S3488   1997
301—dc20   96-20151

About The Authors

LINDA SCHNEIDER is Professor of Sociology at SUNY–Nassau Community College. She received her Ph.D. in Sociology from Columbia University. Professor Schneider has for many years enjoyed teaching introductory sociology and has long been involved in activities related to undergraduate instruction. She has published in the ASA journal *Teaching Sociology,* contributed to panels about teaching at conferences of the Eastern Sociological Society, the Community College Humanities Association, the Community College General Education Association and the American Association of Community Colleges. Professor Schneider has directed several grants from the National Endowment for the Humanities, the Fund for the Improvement of Postsecondary Education, and the National Science Foundation for multidisciplinary and global curriculum development.

ARNOLD SILVERMAN is Professor of Sociology at SUNY–Nassau Community College. He received his Ph.D. in Sociology from the University of Wisconsin, Madison. Professor Silverman has published widely, and his articles appear in the *American Sociological Review, Built Environment, Contemporary Sociology, Social Service Review,* and elsewhere. He is the co-author of *Chosen Children,* a longitudinal study of American adopting families. Professor Silverman has also been active in efforts to improve the quality of undergraduate instruction. He co-directed a faculty development effort financed by the Fund for the Improvement of Postsecondary Education to encourage active learning in undergraduate teaching. He has been chair of the Eastern Sociological Society's Committee on Community Colleges, and he is currently the coordinator of Nassau Community College's Freshman Learning Communities program.

This book is dedicated to the peoples of Egypt, Germany, Mexico, and Japan, and the ¡Kung Bushmen, with whom we share a mutual human history and a common future.

Photo Credits

Contents

Chapter 3.   The iKung: Bushmen of Southern Africa   108

List of Tables

Introduction: To the Student

Global Sociology

Today, no one can afford to ignore the variety of the world's societies. If you go to work in the business world, it is very likely that in selling your products, or buying supplies, or even in managing your company's factories, you will need to deal with people from other societies. The better you understand cultures that differ from your own, the more likely it is that you will be successful. When you go on vacation or listen to music, you may come in contact with unfamiliar cultures. You will enjoy yourself more if you are comfortable with diversity. You may even find that you are a soldier in some distant society, since more and more nations are sending United Nations "peacekeeper" troops to troublespots around the world. *Global Sociology* is a sociological introduction to the diversity of the world's societies.

Sociology has an important message for you: there are many ways to arrange group life; many different kinds of families, economies, and governments; endlessly varied values, beliefs, attitudes, and customs. Until very recently in human history, most people lived quite isolated lives, seldom meeting people from other societies. People readily believed that their own way of life was the only way, or the best way, and that other societies were strange or evil. In today's global world, condemning other societies leads to misunderstanding and violence. The world's peoples need to learn about each other. We believe that the more you know about different ways of life, the more profoundly you will appreciate how much all humans have in common.

We chose five societies to include in this book:

Japan: A Conforming Culture

Mexico: Social Groups in a Diverse Society

The !Kung: Bushmen of Southern Africa

Egypt: Faith, Gender, and Class

Germany: Social Institutions and Social Change in a Modern Western Society

It was hard to choose just five societies from all the hundreds in the world today. First of all, we chose societies from different parts of the world and different cultural regions. One society in this book is in Asia, one in Latin America, one in Europe, and two in Africa, though one of these, Egypt, is culturally part of the Middle East. Japan and Germany are rich, industrialized nations. Mexico and Egypt are "developing" nations, struggling with poverty, and the iKung Bushmen are not a nation at all.

We looked for societies very different from your own, to illustrate the range of the world's social diversity. Egypt is an Islamic society, where five times a day, the call to prayer penetrates every street and house. Many people pray at every call and strive to follow the laws of Islam. In Japan, people enjoy celebrating the holidays of many religions. At Christmas, Japanese people give each other presents and eat take-out fried chicken. Afterwards, they attend a ceremony in a Buddhist temple. But only 10 percent of Japanese people consider themselves religious.

The Germans and the iKung Bushmen could not be more different peoples, but they have in common the experience of rapid social change. The iKung Bushmen are one of the last peoples on earth who live by gathering wild food. They are now losing their land and their way of life, marking the end of a major chapter in the story of humanity. With reunification, east Germans have abandoned socialism and are struggling to adapt to capitalist values and institutions.

Egyptians and Mexicans live with tremendous contrasts of wealth and poverty, and protest often breaks into violence. Rich Egyptians have made their country the world's largest importer of German luxury cars, but poor Egyptians, desperate for housing, have taken to living in cemeteries. Indian peasants in Chiapas, Mexico, took up arms against local landowners and the government, and their rebellion touched off a major decline in the international value of the peso, and a domestic economic crisis.

Learning Sociology from Diversity

Learning about many different societies will help you deepen your understanding of sociological concepts. Sociology textbooks teach concepts like values, norms, roles, socialization, deviance, social stratification, modernization, etc. The five societies in this book were chosen to illustrate these and other important sociological concepts. When you understand how sociological concepts can be applied to diverse societies, you will understand the concepts much better.

Let's take an example: the concept of social stratification. We have chosen societies for this book with very varied forms of social stratification. The iKung Bushmen are an almost entirely egalitarian society: no one has any more possessions or any more power than anyone else. Learning about the iKung will sharpen your ability to see inequalities in other societies, including your own. In Egypt, there are very sharp inequalities between men and women. In Japan, people pay close attention to status differences in age, gender, education, and occupation, but income inequalities are quite minimal. In Mexico, millions of people earn the minimum wage of under $4 a day, while the richest Mexicans have imported cars and air-conditioned houses and send their children to college abroad. When you learn about many different systems of social stratification, you will understand the concept better.

In order to help you understand what life is like in different societies, we have included in each chapter a number of *vignettes:* short, fictional sketches of individuals, their life situations, and their feelings. None of the characters in the vignettes are real people. We made them up, inspired by people we read about and people we met.

Learning through Comparison

Comparison and contrast are very powerful means of learning. The iKung Bushmen spend all their lives in groups of 15 to 40 people, related by kinship. Imagine how hard it would be to teach them the concept of "bureaucracy." They have never waited on line at the Department of Motor Vehicles or filled out forms for registration at college. When you study the iKung Bushmen, you will learn how new and unusual bureaucracies are in human experience.

Comparison has always been the essence of sociology. Sociologists know that when you are immersed in your own society, you take it for granted and assume that its ways are part of human nature, universal and unchanging. We most easily discover what our own society is like when we learn about a different society. As sociologists say, "the fish is the last to discover water."

Comparison is a wonderful means of applying concepts and theories and deepening your understanding of their meaning. Comparison is also a challenge to intolerance. Studying world societies shows us that there is no one right way to live, and that the most fundamental characteristic of "human nature" is our tremendous flexibility in creating diverse cultures.

Active Learning

Suppose you wanted to learn to play basketball and someone told you to listen to another person talk about the game, and then watch other people play it. You would be disgusted with this advice, because you know that in order to learn basketball, you must play the game yourself and then practice, practice, practice. If you have a coach or someone else to watch you and give you pointers, you will learn even faster.

Will you be surprised to hear that learning sociology (or any other college subject) works the same way? Just reading or hearing someone else present sociological ideas isn't enough. You must practice your own sociological reasoning, out loud and in writing and have others coach you in your work in order to learn the subject.

Global Sociology is designed so that you can practice applying sociological concepts to a descriptive "data base" of information about five different societies. As you read this book, ask yourself: can I talk about these societies using the language of sociology? Try to describe the values of each society, or the roles they expect men and women to play. Think about how family life is organized in each society, or what social groups are most important in peoples' lives. Questions at the end of each chapter will help you put your knowledge of sociology to active use.

One of the best ways of practicing sociological thinking is by making comparisons. We invite you to compare each of these societies to your own society: what similarities and what differences can you see? You can also compare the societies in this book with each other. In writing the book, we have been greatly tempted to make comparisons ourselves, but we have tried to discipline ourselves and stick to description. We wanted to leave the work and play of comparison to the students and instructors who use *Global Sociology.*

Preface: To the Instructor

We wrote this book to give students a broader context for understanding both sociology and their own society. For several years both authors had assigned William Kephart's *Extraordinary Groups* when teaching Introductory Sociology. We liked Kephart's case study approach. Reading his descriptions of a variety of American religious groups, students were exposed to diverse cultures and social structures. Despite these advantages, we were unhappy confining our comparisons to religious sects. Linda's student Mike Godino put it nicely when he told us, "You know, Introductory Sociology is great. I'm learning about ways of life I never imagined, and it makes me see my own society so much more clearly by contrast. But I'm not sure I want to know this much about these little religious groups. Isn't there a book that does the same thing for different countries, important countries that we should understand?" Mike's comment crystallized our desire to extend the range of comparisons, and we searched around, but there wasn't such a book. There were ethnographies, but these were anthropological rather than sociological. Then there were "global" textbooks. We liked these texts, but we were looking for a supplement with indepth case studies.

Finally we decided to write the book ourselves: *Global Sociology* is a softcover supplement to any standard sociology text, providing broad and comprehensive **sociological** description of five diverse contemporary societies. We aimed for wide geographic distribution: we chose one Asian society—Japan; one Latin American society—Mexico; one European society—Germany; and two African societies—Egypt and the ¡Kung Bushmen. Two of the societies are wealthy and industrial, and two are poor "developing" nations. For contrast, we included a non-national society—the hunting and gathering ¡Kung Bushmen.

One of our concerns in writing *Global Sociology* has been to create a text that instructors can use without being specialists in the study of Japan, Mexico, Egypt, Germany, or the ¡Kung Bushmen. General knowledge and a sociologist's understanding of how societies work is ample background for using *Global Sociology*. We are confident that you will see how *Global Sociology* can easily be introduced into your courses. Although it is interesting to read some of the more specialized studies we have recommended, it is by no means a require-ment for the effective use of *Global Sociology.*

The five societies described here vary in many ways: in their definitions of male and female roles, in their degree of inequality, in the salience of religious values and norms in their cultures, and in their population dynamics. *Global So-ciology* includes two different socialist societies: East Germany and Egypt, and it examines the post-socialist transformation of East Germany. The book also examines two different capitalist societies: West Germany and Japan, whose styles of capitalism contrast with that of the United States.

Global Sociology is structured so as to parallel the major sections of a stan-dard sociology text. Each chapter is organized around basic sociological top-ics: culture, social structure, and group life, socialization, deviance, social in-stitutions, social stratification, and social change. Earlier chapters place more emphasis on topics usually introduced first in Introductory Sociology. Chap-ters on Japan, Mexico, and the ¡Kung Bushmen provide much discussion of culture, social structure, socialization, and deviance, though they include other topics too. Later chapters on Egypt and Germany touch more briefly on beginning concepts and emphasize social stratification, social institutions, and social change.

Global Sociology will help bring to life abstract textbook presentations of concepts with a wealth of vivid illustrations. Reading about Japanese greeting norms, or Mexican patronage politics, or the effects of population growth in Egypt, or East Germans' first encounters with capitalism, or how the ¡Kung Bushmen avoid conflict, students will see the universal relevance of sociologi-cal ideas. Questions posed at the end of each chapter lead students to make so-ciological comparisons and to apply sociological concepts to descriptive knowl-edge.

Comparison is one of the great strengths of sociology. By comparing other societies with their own, students learn about the range of social variation, and they learn what makes their own society distinctive. Reading *Global Sociology,* students will spontaneously make comparisons with their own society, and they can be encouraged to compare the diverse societies described in the book. To aid in this effort, the text provides a variety of tables, summarizing impor-tant comparative data for Japan, Mexico, Egypt, Germany, and the United States.

Although most of our students were born and raised in the United States, an increasing number are from countries as diverse as El Salvador, Haiti, Ja-maica, Iran, China, Greece, and the former Soviet Union. It is exciting to see that these students can use *Global Sociology* to make meaningful comparisons with the societies and cultures they have been born and raised in. *Global Sociol-ogy* doesn't require that students carry the assumptions, insights, and values of an American childhood and schooling.

Learning about other societies helps all students become aware of their eth-nocentrism and reach beyond it. Students develop a sense of attachment to the societies they study, even when some of what they read disturbs them. To help students use their imaginations in picturing unfamiliar societies, we have included fictional vignettes of individuals in each society. Vignettes help students make human connections across cultural divides.

We have found that reading *Global Sociology* heightens student interest in other societies. News from abroad becomes absorbing when students have a framework in which to place it. *Global Sociology* presents societies that are often in the news, and our own students have become alert to news coverage about the societies they study. When an earthquake shook Japan and a revolutionary movement riveted Mexico, students brought in news clippings and compared Japanese, Mexican, and American responses to crises. When they read about Egypt, our students noticed for the first time that Muslims in their community and their college were observing Ramadan.

Global Sociology is a new approach to making Introductory Sociology global. Our students have enjoyed "field-testing" the book. We hope you and your students will enjoy it too.

Acknowledgments

We would like to acknowledge the help that so many people gave us throughout the writing of this book. First we need to thank our students whose response led us to this effort and who "field tested" earlier drafts of *Global Sociology*. Teresa Sala Imhof of McGraw Hill offered the initial enthusiasm that led us to transform a "good idea" into a coherent proposal. Phil Butcher—also of McGraw-Hill—convinced us that our idea was both viable and appreciated by a potential publisher. Kathy Blake, of McGraw Hill's College Division, did a great deal to expedite the development process. Kathy helped us keep the entire project in perspective as we wrestled with the details of Egyptian population dynamics and Mexican credit cooperatives.

A panel of reviewers gave us useful insights and generously shared their knowledge of the societies described in *Global Sociology*. They include Karen Lynch Frederick of Saint Anselm College, Peter Kivisto of Augustana College, David Maines of Wayne State University, Jon Schlenker of the University of Maine-Augusta, Theodore H. Tsoukalas of the University of Nebraska–Omaha, Pelgy Vaz of Fort Hays State University and Theodore Wattron of Florida Community College–Jacksonville. Special thanks go to Brenda Phillips of Texas Woman's University. Our reviewers' grasp of the teaching process has helped to make this book a more useful classroom document.

Janet Abu-Lughod of the New School for Social Research and Lila Abu-Lughod of New York University helped us develop a broader and better understanding of contemporary Egypt. Their direction in terms of sources and ideas was invaluable.

Marilyn Rosenthal and her colleagues at the Nassau Community College Library worked hard to find the monographs, articles, and government documents on which our work is based. They were more than ably assisted by the staffs of the community libraries of Rochester, Vermont and Merrick, New York. We thank Heather Masterson of Clovis Point in Rochester, Vermont for solving many of our word processing problems.

We also appreciate the comments of William Feigelman, our departmental colleague and chair, who shared with us his considerable expertise as an academic author.

Finally, we recognize our debts to our respective spouses and children who encouraged us and endured our preoccupation with researching and writing *Global Sociology.*

Linda Schneider

Arnold Silverman

Global Sociology
Introducing Five Contemporary Societies

JAPAN

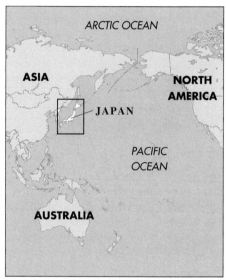

To reach Japan from the United States or Canada you would need to fly across the North Pacific almost to Siberia. Air traffic to Tokyo is so busy you might need to fly to nearby Korea and take a shuttle. Rising from defeat in World War II, Japan has become one of the world's most productive economies.

LOCATION: Japan is located on the eastern edge of Asia, 200 miles from Korea and across the Sea of Japan from China and Russia. East of Japan lies the Pacific Ocean.

AREA: Japan consists of four large islands of Hokkaido, Honshu, Shikoku, and Kyushu (145,000 square miles or 420,000 square kilometers). Together they are the size of California or Newfoundland. Honshu is largest and the site of Tokyo and many of Japan's cities.

LAND: A rugged hilly landscape; Mt. Fuji, a dormant volcano is 12,000 feet high. Less than 1 acre in 6 is flat; most of this is along the coasts where cities compete with farms for space.

CLIMATE: Similar to the east coast of the United States. It is colder on Hokkaido and nearly subtropical in southern Kyushu. Japan receives 50 inches of rain a year, much of it falling as snow.

POPULATION: In 1995, 125 million people; in 2025 the population should be virtually the same.

INCOME: U.S. $31,450 per capita per year.

EDUCATION: An average adult completes eleven years of schooling.

RELIGION: 75% combine Buddhism and Shinto, a unique Japanese religion; less than 2% Christian.

MINORITIES: Korean Japanese, Ainu, Burakumin.

CHAPTER 1

Japan: A Conforming Culture

INTRODUCTION

Of all the societies in this book, Japan is perhaps the one most widely known, and most surrounded by controversy. Especially in the United States, media coverage on Japan is constant. News articles, murder mysteries, plays, and movies take advantage of the public preoccupation with Japan as an economic rival. Much description of Japan is negative: the Japanese are portrayed as mindless drones, frantically working to outstrip the United States; skilled copyists incapable of original, independent thought. But there is also a great deal of admiration for Japan: study after study examines the effectiveness of Japanese elementary education, Japanese corporate management, Japanese factory organization, and the merits of adopting or adapting these practices in the West are intensely debated. Also, thousands of westerners practice Japanese martial arts, or Japanese meditation techniques, and learn to admire ancient Japanese cultural traditions.

Will the real Japan please stand up? Spiritual culture? Unscrupulous economic rival? Empire of conformity? Paradise of order, efficiency, and technology? Controversy about Japan and Japanese institutions will doubtless continue, but there are some strikingly important aspects of Japanese society you should know about in order to understand Japan's rise to economic power and world importance.

A Sense of "Peoplehood"

The Japanese believe that you cannot understand their society unless you know that they are a unique people, physically and mentally different from all the rest of the world's peoples. Tradition holds that the Japanese people are a single family, all descended from a common ancestor, the sun goddess Amaterasu. Many Japanese people believe that their society's economic success, low crime rate, and high level of education are the result of its people's distinct racial stock.

But Japanese racial identity is in reality a social belief, not a physical fact. Anthropologists tell us that the Japanese people are part of the Mongoloid group of peoples, which includes the Koreans and the Han Chinese. There is some variety, too, in the appearance of the Japanese people—different shades of skin color, and hair and eyes ranging from black to brown reflect a heritage of Polynesian, Chinese, and East Asian ancestry. And while they believe that Koreans are physically distinctive, the Japanese are unable to identify Japanese-born Koreans by their appearance (Tasker, pp. 15–16, 34; Feiler, p. 135).

3

Although it is not a physical fact, the Japanese sense of "peoplehood" has a firm social foundation. Japan, like most other societies, is inhabited by people whose ancestors came from many places. Japan is a chain of islands, about 200 miles off the coast of Korea. The most ancient people to arrive in Japan were the Ainu, a distinctive race which dates back thousands of years into prehistory. After the Ainu, other peoples came to Japan from southern and northern Asia. But it is important to know that there has been no significant immigration into Japan for more than a thousand years. For all that time, the peoples of Japan mingled, until they developed the world's most racially and culturally unified society. There are in fact some minority groups in Japan (which we will examine later), but they are few and small in size. The Japanese sense of distinctiveness is reinforced by language: unlike the rest of the world's major languages, Japanese is spoken by only one ethnic group, and by relatively few foreigners (Tasker, p. 26).

While the Japanese people are not the separate race they believe themselves to be, they are indeed an unusually homogeneous people, much more so than the people of other societies. Their sense of peoplehood has given them unique advantages that other societies don't have. They are able to merge the concepts of racial and national identity, and their acute sense of distinctiveness, carefully cultivated by Japan's leaders, helps foster an unusually strong feeling of group solidarity and national purpose in Japanese society.

"An Island Nation"

"Japan is an island nation," schoolchildren are repeatedly told, "surrounded by seas and enemies, so we must depend on each other." Though their country is perceived by others as a giant power in the global economy, the Japanese people share a sense of national vulnerability. Many Japanese think of their country as small, even weak, unprotected from assault by outside forces. They are acutely aware that Japan, though self-sufficient up to the twentieth century, is now highly dependent on the world economy, more so than any other major power. Japan has no oil, almost no raw materials, and must import much of its meat and grain. Since the land is very mountainous, only a small portion is suitable for agriculture, and almost the entire population is squeezed into only one-fifth of the total area. The Japanese play down their early twentieth-century history as an aggressive imperial power, which invaded China and other Asian nations and provoked the United States to war (Tasker, pp. 8–10; Feiler, pp. 88, 141).

JAPAN'S HISTORY

The Japanese sense of vulnerability to external powers, with its accompanying feeling of loyalty and obligation to the nation, is not of recent origin. Japan's history can best be understood as a sequence of eras in which the nation alternately isolated itself from, or eagerly absorbed, foreign influences. Geography gave Japan a choice about its relation to the outside world. Two hundred miles of stormy seas protected the country from invasion by foreign forces, but permitted contact with the great mainland Asian cultures through travel and trade. In the modern era, Japan was one of the last Asian cultures to face western colonizers, and had the opportunity to study the effects of western domination elsewhere.

Contact with China

The first great turning point in Japanese history happened over a thousand years ago, in the seventh century. Japan was at that time a tribal society in which people lived by gardening and fishing, without cities, with only a weak national government and a ruling family whose importance was largely symbolic. But early in the seventh century, a prince of the ruling family, Prince Shotoku, began to import cultural practices from China, at that time the world's most advanced nation. Prince Shotoku began by importing Chinese Buddhism and Buddhist art. For the next three centuries, Japan's rulers continued to study China and adopt Chinese institutions, arts, and technology, deliberately "improving" Japanese society. Japan adopted China's courtly manners and arts, its centralized government and elaborate bureaucracy, its tax system, and its system of writing. The Japanese even built elaborate Chinese-style capital cities, remarkable in a society which previously had lacked even towns! But it is important to understand that then, and later, all of Japan's foreign borrowings were voluntary. Japan never had another culture imposed on it by force. In fact, after the ninth century, Japan retreated into isolation and slowly digested all its borrowed Chinese culture, blending it with native ways, and finally producing a new, distinctly Japanese culture (Reischauer, 1977, pp. 41–51).

The Tokugawa Era

In the sixteenth century, a dramatic first contact with the West was greeted with intense opposition and renewed isolation. Portuguese missionaries and traders reached Japan in the late fifteenth century, and in the next 100 years converted more than 300,000 Japanese to Christianity. Japan's rulers responded ferociously. They forced thousands of Japanese Christians to renounce their religion or face execution. By 1638, they had completely sealed off Japan from the outside world. Laws forbade the Japanese from building ocean-going ships or traveling abroad, and only a few foreign traders—Koreans, Chinese, and Dutch—were allowed to enter Japan. During two centuries of isolation (known as the Tokugawa Era, 1635–1853, after the leading line of *shoguns,* or rulers of the period) Japan was peaceful and stable. Important changes took place, though, including the development of a class of entrepreneurs, the rise of a centralized government, and the forging of a strong sense of national identity. A few Japanese scholars read Dutch books and kept up with news of the scientific and political revolutions taking place in the West (Christopher, pp. 47–48).

The Meiji Restoration

Japan's second contact with the West had a very different outcome. By the midnineteenth century, western powers had colonized Africa, India, and much of Southeast Asia, forcing trade concessions upon China as well. Finally, in 1853, under Commodore Perry, the American Navy forced Japan to open its ports to American ships and sign a series of trade treaties. Fear of subjection to foreign powers brought on a national crisis in Japan. In 1868, rebel provincial rulers, backed by reform-minded middle- and low-ranking *samurai* (members of Japan's hereditary warrior caste) seized power from the shoguns. Their rule was called the *Meiji Restoration,* because they claimed to restore power to the emperor, the hereditary monarch. In fact, however, they ruled in his stead. The Meiji rulers successfully argued that the only way Japan could enjoy equality with western powers was to modernize and adopt western technology. This whole sequence of events was extraordinary. During the nineteenth century, western European empires were taking control all over the world, but nowhere outside Japan was western penetration so clearly recognized. Nowhere else was such radical defensive action even imagined. Yet Japan was able deliberately to bring about its own modernization.

The Meiji government in effect went shopping for new institutions, finding a model for its navy in Britain, its army in France, its universities in America, and its constitution in Germany (Tasker, p. 21). Meiji rulers created a new government bureaucracy, based on European models and staffed by a new university-educated civil service. They adopted a modern court system and public school system. Meiji Japan promoted economic modernization, making peasants owners of the land they farmed, and encouraging modern agriculture, based on American models. The government created western-style banks, railroads, and ports, and developed mining, steel, and weapons production, and silk manufacture. They sent students abroad to learn western skills and hired western experts to come to Japan. And all of this was done by the end of the nineteenth century!

Japan also emulated the imperial ambitions of western countries, both to demonstrate its military strength to the West and to build an empire of its own. In 1894–1895, Japan defeated China in a war for control of Korea, and in 1904–1905, it fought again for Korea, this time against Russia, gaining Korea and several other possessions in its victory. By World War I, Japan was a major colonial power, the equal of western powers. Militarism intensified in Japan during the difficult years of the 1920s and 1930s. Imperial ambitions once again led Japan into war with China, a war which dragged on and finally escalated into the Pacific theater of World War II. Japan's defeat opened a new chapter in its westernization and economic development.

The Occupation Reforms

Japan was utterly devastated by the war, and its people were demoralized and disillusioned with militarism. They were open to change and new ideas. And the American occupying forces, in their self-confident, well-meaning American way, were eager to make over Japanese society. General Douglas MacArthur, acting as supreme commander for the allied powers, dismantled Japan's military, reformed its government and constitution, broke up its industrial monopolies, and redistributed land ownership. MacArthur's reforms were radical, giving individuals rights beyond what is guaranteed in the U.S. Constitution, including equal rights for women, the right of labor to bargain collectively, and the right of all individuals to an equal education. The reforms, though not all effective, brought huge changes to postwar Japan and set the scene for Japan's postwar "economic miracle."

JAPANESE CULTURE

In its long history, Japan has three times adopted foreign institutions and practices. Today, Japan looks more and more like modern western industrial societies, with its sprawling cities, skyscrapers, traffic jams, global corporations, automated factories, and parliamentary government. Some American and European observers think that Japan is becoming completely westernized and indistinguishable from modern industrial societies in Europe and North America. The Japanese themselves say that isn't so: they say they adopted western technologies and institutions, but not western values and beliefs. In Japan, you can still hear an old slogan from the Meiji Era, *"wakon yosai"* (Japanese spirit and western knowledge), and Japanese people will tell you that the foreign models they adopt are transformed by the addition of a "Japanese heart" (Tasker, p. 21; Feiler, pp. 36–37).

You can understand *wakon yosai* better with the aid of sociology. Sociologists divide the culture of every society into two parts: **material** and **nonmaterial culture.** Material culture consists of things: houses, clothing, machines, art objects, tools, technologies, and so forth. Nonmaterial culture is abstract; it can't be touched. It includes values, beliefs, language, symbols, and norms and sanctions. Japan's material culture is indeed being rapidly westernized. Japanese people used to live in distinctive houses made of wood and paper, with *tatami* mat floors and special family altars; they wore *kimonos* and *obis* (wrapped robes tied with sashes), and slept on *futons* unrolled on the floor at night. Nowadays, most Japanese people live in western-style apartments in concrete apartment houses, filled with televisions, CD players, and video games, just like houses in New York, or Paris, or Berlin. They wear jeans and T-shirts, or suits and ties, like people anywhere in the western world.

But Japan's nonmaterial culture has changed much more slowly and remains much more distinctly Japanese. In fact, as a result, many important Japanese institutions, which are borrowed from the West, like parliamentary government and corporate business organization, actually function very differently in Japan than they do in the West. Japanese culture differs from western culture in many important ways. First of all, Japan has much less internal diversity than most western cultures. Distinctively Japanese values and norms, beliefs, and forms of symbolic expression are very widely shared in Japanese society.

Cultural Integration

Sociologists believe that one important way societies differ from each other is in their degree of **cultural integration.** Some societies have highly integrated cultures: norms and values are consistent throughout the society and the different elements of culture and social structure "fit together" well: institutions are organized in ways that seem to reflect the society's values, and living up to one norm seldom

It is Saturday night and the whole family is eating dinner together. Many Japanese fathers work late every weekday night and eat dinner with their families only on weekends. In this picture, the food and chopsticks are Japanese, but family members, like other Japanese people, are wearing western clothing. Japanese homes are small by western standards and this dining room is crowded with a large television, mementos, and furniture.

automatically puts a person in violation of another. Most highly integrated cultures are small, isolated, preindustrial societies like the ¡Kung Bushmen. It is rare that a large, modern, industrial society will exhibit a high degree of cultural integration. Most modern industrial societies are internally diverse: people in urban and rural areas have different lifestyles and interpret their cultures differently; various social classes, ethnic groups, and subcultures may subscribe to differing values and norms; and because of rapid social change, new norms and values may develop and clash with the old. For all these reasons, in most modern societies, culture is internally inconsistent and contradictory and people often disagree about the proper way to live one's life and behave toward others.

Japanese society is an extraordinary exception to this pattern. Despite its history of foreign borrowings, and despite an increasing rate of social change in the 1990s, Japan's culture is highly homogeneous; that is, the same culture prevails throughout the society. People tend to follow the same fashions in clothing, watch the same TV shows, buy the same new products, engage in the same hobbies and recreational activities, and follow the same religious practices, wherever they live and whatever their social position. Japanese people of all socioeconomic statuses even read the same newspapers and magazines. Children all over Japan learn the exact same curriculum (and probably read the same pages of their texts on the same days) and they likely eat the same sorts of foods, at the same mealtimes, listen to the same music, and have the same bedtimes and curfews.

Even more striking is the high level of agreement about norms and values in Japan, and the degree to which this agreement is explicit and conscious. Japanese people take pride in the cultural homogeneity of their society; it results, they will tell you, from the fact that the Japanese are "one people." As we will see, Japanese schools provide a great deal of very detailed instruction and drill in proper values and correct behavior. Such instruction is possible because parents and schools have no difficulty agreeing on the norms and values that should be taught. Moreover, the specialized structures of Japanese society—schools, universities, corporations, government bureaucracies—are set up in such a way that following the norms and values "pays off." Conformity in school, for example, is rewarded by success on exams and good jobs, and nonconformity quite reliably results in a life of marginal, low-paid work.

It would not be hard to imagine that Japanese society has been designed by a **functionalist** sociologist! Like functionalist theorists, the Japanese stress the importance of order and consensus in their society and they emphasize that individuals should subordinate their personal desires to common goals, so Japanese society can function smoothly. Looking at Japan, we see a highly integrated culture in which people agree on basic norms and values. Individuals and institutions work smoothly together toward shared goals, and the society is quite orderly and stable.

The Value of Harmony

Japan has a large population relative to its land mass, and most Japanese people live crowded together in an urban corridor squeezed along the eastern edge of the Japanese islands. The Japanese believe that crowding has taught them to place a very high value on public harmony and proper behavior. Every year on the first official day of spring (June 21), everyone in Japan puts away their winter clothes and wears summer clothes, no matter what the weather, and on the first day of fall, they change again. There is little crime, so you needn't lock your car or fear being mugged, and couples can safely walk in the park at midnight. The Japanese also believe that it is very important to avoid conflict in everyday life. You will never hear voices raised in public argument or see a fight outside a bar in Japan. But lest you get the idea that the Japanese just march in lockstep like robots, you should understand that people must work very hard to maintain public harmony and order. Japanese people get insulted or angry just like anyone else, but in their society values and norms forcefully promote self-control and the avoidance of direct personal confrontation.

The idea of two people openly expressing disagreement fills Japanese people with horror. In business or personal life, people avoid committing themselves to hard and fast positions; they try not to acknowledge or clarify their disagreements. Instead, Japanese people proceed by cautiously feeling each other out, making ambiguous statements, and using nonverbal clues to figure out what others prefer, aiming for compromise without revelation of conflict. Americans visiting Japan on business often complain that they cannot get Japanese executives to "talk straight" or to "level" with them (Reischauer, 1977, pp. 135–137).

Much has been written about "consensus decision making" in Japanese corporations. In fact, the head of a department in a corporation or bureaucracy has full formal power to make decisions and often exercises it, but rarely simply issues a command. In many cases consultation among the staff takes place through the circulation of memos, typically written by middle-ranking associates, and usually vaguely phrased. Each reader puts his seal on the document and may add comments to it. The memo is gradually revised as the members of the staff edge toward agreement. By the end, everyone is familiar with the problem under discussion, but no one stakes out a clear position from which they might have to retreat, and there are no clear winners and losers. The process is sometimes slow and inefficient, but there is no losing minority, licking its wounds and grudging support (Smith, pp. 54–55).

Another way the Japanese avoid conflict is by use of a "go-between," a neutral person who literally goes between two parties when there is some matter to be worked out. Go-betweens are frequently used in Japan in negotiating marriages. With a go-between, one need not turn down a potential bride or groom to her or his face, avoiding open disagreement and embarrassment.

The Value of Fitting In

Achieving smooth, harmonious relationships among group members may seem a very desirable goal, particularly to anyone who has endured a workplace or family filled with discord, or a city full of crime and conflict. But group harmony in Japan has its price: it is achieved by constant care and individual self-discipline. In Japanese society, the group comes first. Being alone, outside the web of group life, is unthinkable. In the Japanese view, it is only in groups that people can develop as individuals, experience the pleasures of human feeling, and enjoy a sense of secure interdependence with others.

Why do Japanese people consider group life so important? One significant reason is that the Japanese find their identities in groups. Self-expression, "being yourself," "doing your own thing" are all foreign to Japanese culture. The Japanese self is one that feels most at home in the company of others. One's self-esteem is fed by being selected to join a group, and, if asked to identify themselves, people offer their group affiliations. Thus, a Japanese man asked his profession is unlikely to answer, "I am a programmer." Rather, "I work for SONY" will be offered. Businessmen identify little with their particular jobs within the firm (they are likely to be rotated out of them anyway), and they tend not to see themselves as possessing particular skills they might take from employer to employer.

Each "salaryman" wears a little badge, identifying his company, and a stranger will often refer to him personally by his company name: "Toyota-san" (Mr. Toyota).[1]

---

[1]"Salaryman" is a Japanese word borrowed from English. It is used to describe managers who are, almost without exception, men. Women work in business as "office ladies"—secretaries. There is no gender-neutral language in Japan (like "businessperson") to describe employees, because men and women play sharply different workplace roles.

Women office workers are happy to put aside their own fashionable clothes and wear a demure company uniform; it is their "badge of belonging" (Tasker p. 94; Condon, p. 212). It goes along with this emphasis on the company that self-employment, even if highly successful, has less prestige in Japan than does working for a well-known corporation or government bureaucracy.

Maintaining Relationships

In Japanese society, people value being part of a group, and they work at getting along. But life in Japanese groups takes a great deal of time and work, because of the emphasis placed on avoidance of conflict. Self-assertion, overtly disagreeing with others, making demands, or even clearly stating one's wishes, all look like threats to group harmony and are out of the question. Such behavior is downright frightening to the Japanese. In relating to others, it is far preferable to express your feelings and wishes indirectly.

In Japan people try not to call attention to themselves. This *enryo* or "reserve" restrains people from giving opinions, expressing desires, or even making choices if they are offered. But how can a group function, if no one can express individual wishes? Because of *enryo,* it is of fundamental importance that people are highly sensitive to the unspoken wishes of others. The Japanese value *ninjo,* which means compassion, sympathy, rapport, or "fellow feeling." A good person strives to empathize—to understand the feelings of others and the situational difficulties others may be experiencing. Indeed, visitors to Japan are always impressed with the kindness of the Japanese. They never refuse help to a stranger, and go far out of their way to offer aid and make visitors feel at home. They seem to intuit when you are feeling bad and make you feel understood and cared for. In Japan, if something bad happens to you—if someone close to you dies, or your mate leaves you, or you fail your exams, your friends will rally round. They will keep you company and bring you food and try to distract you from your troubles. But they will never say "you must feel terrible about . . . " or even "do you want to talk about. . . ." That would seem terribly crude. In Japan, your friends support you by showing you they understand, but people don't believe that expressing feelings directly is especially useful or healing.

In ordinary Japanese life a good host knows a guest well enough to anticipate what food will be pleasing, and sets it before the guest so no choices are required. Good guests eat what they are given so as not to cause embarrassment by implying that the host has misunderstood their desires. If you make your wishes known, it is an insult to others: it implies that you believe the other person is too insensitive to perceive them. For example, the worst thing a husband can say about his wife is "I have to ask for what I want." Members of Japanese groups also expect other group members to anticipate their unexpressed desires (Smith, pp. 57–58).

How do the Japanese manage to do this? For one thing, spending a lot of time together helps. People who are in constant contact, in informal as well as formal situations, come to understand each other intuitively. Also, the Japanese place great emphasis on nonverbal communication. Because of *enryo,* people's words are not a good guide to their feelings. From childhood, people practice observing others' behavior for tiny hints in body language, tone of voice, the timing of silences. Just as children in many cultures can read their parents' disapproval in a glance or body posture, so members of Japanese groups come to read each other. In fact, a person who insists on explicit rational explanation is called a "reason freak" and is considered immature (Smith, p. 58).

The Value of Perseverance

Japanese contains many words, used constantly, that tell people to endure, or persevere, bear, accept, or accommodate. Children must endure after-school cram classes and long nights of study to pass their high school and college entrance exams. Principals tell their students that school is "life's first big battle," and they must put their all into it. Businessmen must endure after-hours parties with clients, even if they would rather be home sleeping or spending time with their families. Even a person lugging a heavy suitcase up a street in Japan can count on others to call out encouragingly, "go on, *gaman* (persevere), you can do it" (Feiler, pp. 60–61).

Perseverance is linked to another Japanese value, dedication or *seishin*. People judge others by how hard they try, how hard they work at whatever task or role is their lot. They are willing to make excuses for poor work, as long as great effort went into it, while good work produced without effort does not impress them. *Seishin* literally means "spirit"; it means the spiritual development that results from effort, discipline, and self-control. It doesn't matter what the task is: it can be studying for exams, paving a road, or learning the tea ceremony; if you persevere in working at it and try to do it perfectly, you will become a better person and people will respect you (Bayley, pp. 118–119).

Japanese Norms

Being Japanese requires self-control. Not only must you restrain the expression of your feelings, you must devote enormous effort to behaving properly in all situations. "Good form," compliance with very strict and specific norms of good conduct, matters greatly. Good intentions, or "having one's heart in the right place," don't count. Whether it is addressing an envelope or wrapping a gift, whether it is bowing to greet an individual or drinking at a party, there is only one correct way to behave in a particular situation. And there are very few all-purpose norms to rely on: Japanese norms tend to be **particularistic** (pertaining to a specific situation), rather than **universalistic** (good in all situations). This means there are no general norms—like "honesty is the best policy," or "just be yourself," to guide you in unfamiliar situations. Japanese people learn to be very tuned in to the behavior, dress, and language of others, so as to understand how they should behave. They find strange groups and new social situations anxiety-provoking, because the norms are unknown and one might unwittingly fail to conform. Westerners sometimes regard Japanese people as insincere, or even dishonest, because they see them behaving very differently in different social situations (for example, deferential and reserved in one situation, aggressive or joking in another). To a Japanese person, the western expectation of consistent individual behavior seems immature and foolish: the wise person matches his or her behavior to the requirements of the situation.

Situational Norms

In every society, norms are **situational:** they prescribe expected behavior in a particular situation. The Japanese are usually conscious of how norms vary depending on the social situation. They place special emphasis on the difference between two fundamentally different kinds of situations, *omote* and *ura. Omote* is the surface, or front of an object, the official, public face of a person, event, or social institution; *ura* is its back, its reverse or private side. In Japan, it is outward compliance to social norms that counts. People accept your conventionalized *omote* behavior at face value; they know your private feelings may not match it, and you can expect them to intuit your real feelings and have unspoken compassion for you. While standards for *omote* behavior are rigorous, and appearances are highly valued, they are not expected to correspond to realities (Tasker, pp. 67–71). Private feelings and behavior are never condemned as "bad," inappropriate, neurotic, and so on, as long as they remain in their place. Private feelings are accepted as only human, and outward behavior alone is judged.

Ura is the private side of life, the situations in which people are with close friends or family and can be relaxed, informal, and spontaneous and express their emotions. They will sit in the informal family room and loosen their clothing, drink from the old teapot and cups, and joke and gossip. Women friends or male coworkers spending the weekend together at an inn will put on *yukata,* the cotton robes the hotel supplies and drink and eat in a private room, after relaxing together in the hotel's hot tub. Children are controlled and orderly in the classroom, but are given frequent playground breaks when they are left to their own devices and play wildly and noisily. People are not "free" of norms in the world of ura, but the norms are different: they allow more spontaneous self-expression (Bachnik, p. 166).

It is difficult for westerners to accept that for the Japanese, *omote* and *ura* are equally rewarding social worlds. As sociologist Joseph Tobin explains,

> The word *omote* does not carry with it nearly as much of the negative connotations as does the English word "formal" of being constrained and pleasureless. Rather *omote* and *ura* refer to different kinds of pleasure and satisfactions and to different aspects of the self. To become a person in Japan is to learn to be comfortable in each of these worlds, to be able to receive and give satisfaction in each of these kinds of relationships. (Tobin, p. 36)

Reciprocal Norms

The Japanese view norms in an interactive way: behaving properly is something you owe the other people with whom you are interacting, in order to spare them discomfort or show them respect. In fact, Japanese people picture their society as a web of individuals linked together by ties of *giri:* duty or obligation. When another person does something for you, whether it is a small courtesy or a big favor, that creates a debt, it is your *giri* to pay it back. A person who doesn't live up to the reciprocal bonds of *giri* will be seen by others as without honor or integrity. The thought of being shamed in this way before one's family, neighbors, or colleagues, and perhaps even cast out of the group, is enough to ensure that most people take *giri* very seriously. At the same time, a person who overconforms, who is too fussy about duty, is seen as "hard." As sociologist David Bayley puts it, "a moral person embodies both giri and ninjo (compassion). Giri without ninjo lacks warmth; ninjo without giri lacks principle" (Bayley, p. 106).

Giri is felt as a burden by the Japanese, and it is acceptable to complain about the weight of one's obligations. In fact, there is admiration in Japan for a kind of noncomformist hero, or heroine, often appearing in popular novels, films, and plays, who is so sincere and strong-willed that he or she cannot resolve conflicts between *giri* and *ninjo* and make peace with the demands of society. But it is worth noting that these are invariably tragic figures, whose lives and careers are ruined by their conflicts, and whose stories end in suicide. When you grow up Japanese, you are taught that if your life is not to be a tragedy, you must learn to resolve conflicts between feelings and role demands. Human feelings must be kept in their place, and you must pay attention to norms, to the unspoken feelings of others, and to the obligations you incur or impose. The hardest thing for westerners to comprehend about Japanese society is that the Japanese do not see the constant effort to behave appropriately as a loss of individuality, but rather as the path to self-development. It takes self-knowledge and self-control to master one's impulses, and this is the true measure of character and maturity (Smith, pp. 96–101).

Religion and Japanese Culture

In some societies (like Egypt) religion is of major importance and norms and values are closely linked to religious belief. This is not the case in Japan. Very few Japanese people consider themselves religious believers and few are observant of religious practices. But, although formal religion has little influence, Japan has an interesting religious heritage which in a very general sense infuses its culture.

There are many religious traditions in Japan: Shinto, Buddhism, Confucianism, Taoism, and Christianity, as well as a number of more modern religious sects usually referred to as the New Religions. Except for a very small number of people (less than 2 percent) who are practicing Christians, most Japanese don't feel they must choose a single religious identity from this heritage. Instead, they practice a kind of folk religion, observing Shinto, Buddhist, and Christian holidays, having Buddhist funerals, and weddings that combine elements of Shinto and Christian rituals, and choosing lucky days by the Taoist calendar.

Shintoism is the most ancient Japanese religion; its tradition extends back to Japan's prehistoric past. Shinto reveres nature in the form of *kami,* deities that embody natural objects, like trees, mountains, the sun, and animals, and represent the life force. *Kami* are everywhere and they are worshiped at Shinto shrines where people ask for their blessings (Earhart, pp. 16–17). No one really takes the Shinto *kami* literally today, but Shinto is a lively part of Japanese folklore and shrines and shrine festivals figure in folk religion. Shinto does have one real influence on Japanese values: it survives in a love of nature, which is a deep current in Japanese culture and is expressed in poetry, landscape painting, and traditions of pottery, landscaping, and architecture that stress subtle, natural materials.

Buddhism, a religion that began in India, came to Japan by way of China in the sixth century A.D. In Japan it is both a monastic tradition and a family religion that honors family ancestors and offers the possibility of salvation and an afterlife in a

Buddhist paradise. For almost a thousand years, Buddhism was a very important part of Japanese culture and society, until, in the sixteenth century Japan's Tokugawa revolution attacked Buddhism as the religion of the old political system and substituted a new emphasis on Confucianism (Reischauer, 1988, pp. 206–207). Today Buddhism permeates Japanese values in a very subtle way: the Japanese belief in perfectionism, the idea of improving one's spirituality through dedication to any task, no matter how humble, is deeply Buddhist. It is notable that in Buddhism (and Shinto), it is the family, not the individual, that is the basic unit of religious participation. People participate in religious rites as family members and maintain family altars and objects of ancestor worship in the home. Traditional religions helped shape Japan's dominant group consciousness (Earhart, pp. 69–71).

Confucianism is not a religion in the same sense that Buddhism, Shinto, or Christianity are religions. It is a philosophical tradition, named for Confucius, its originator in China in the fifth century B.C. Confucianism became prominent in China in the twelfth century A.D., as a rational, ethical system with strict norms, stressing loyalty to the ruler, obedience toward one's father, and proper behavior. Confucianism has no priests, no temples, no religious rituals. From the sixteenth century to the late nineteenth century, Confucianism was very important in Japan, shaping values in a lasting way. You can see its influence today in the Japanese stress on loyalty and obedience, and in the importance of education, hard work, and doing one's duty to family, employers, and the nation (Reischauer, 1988, pp. 203–204).

Christianity came to Japan in the sixteenth century and it spread rapidly before being suppressed by the Tokugawa rulers. When Christianity was permitted again in the late nineteenth century, Protestant and Catholic missionaries entered Japan, but found only small numbers of converts. Today, however, Christian culture has come to Japan as part of a larger western influence, and most Japanese people celebrate Christmas, know Bible stories, and respect Christian values, though they are not themselves Christians (Reischauer, 1988, pp. 212–213).

Japanese people today who feel a strong need for religious faith generally turn to the New Religions, popular religious movements, the best-known of which are *Soka Gakkai,* and *Tenrikyo,* which combine ideas and rituals from Shinto, Buddhism, Taoism, and sometimes Christianity. The New Religions offer their members help in solving personal problems through faith and religious observance, and perhaps even more important, they offer close-knit communities, with festivities, rallies, study groups, and leadership hierarchies. *Aum Shinrikyo,* the group implicated in the 1995 poison gas attacks in Tokyo's subways, was completely atypical of the New Religions in its violence and doomsday predictions, but representative in its intense community life (Inoue, pp. 220–228).

SOCIAL STRUCTURE AND GROUP LIFE

In Japan, group life comes first. People think of themselves primarily as members of groups, and only secondarily as individuals. Japanese sociologists consider this **group consciousness** or **group identification** a traditional part of Japanese culture.[2] Over the course of the twentieth century, different groups have risen to preeminence in Japanese life, but group identification remains the basic pattern. In prewar Japan, when most people lived in rural villages, the *ie,* or household, was the primary social unit. The *ie* was a family—and more—a "house," with its property, perhaps its family business, and its good name, passed on down the generations. The *ie* was headed by its eldest male, who had authority over all the members of his household, and controlled their collective finances. Ideally, his household consisted of his wife and their eldest son and his wife, the eldest son of that marriage and his family, on down the family line. Younger sons formed multi-generational households of their own, regarded as branches of the ancestral *ie.*

The *ie* was an all-encompassing group affiliation: within it the Japanese raised their children, made a living, held religious worship, and satisfied their needs for companionship (Fukutake, pp. 25–28). The obligation of the individual to the *ie* was the basic fact of social life, and filial piety, or respect and obedience toward one's parents, was the ruling value. People's relationships with their parents were much more important than their relationships with their spouses.

Up to the start of World War II, people in Japan lived out their lives "embedded" in their *ie* and in their village or neighborhood (Fukutake, p. 214). Villages were small, consisting of not more than 100 *ie,* and they were closed, self-sufficient communities, within which most people spent their entire lives. Villages were self-governing units, responsible as a whole for collecting taxes imposed on the village, not its households. The households of a village worked together in the fields, or in maintaining the village irrigation system. They helped each other build and repair houses and hold weddings and funerals. Ties between superiors and subordinates were emphasized in the village as well as in the *ie,* since wealthier, landowning families and their tenants and laborers were in constant interaction (Fukutake, pp. 33–39).

Group Life in Modern Japan

The old-fashioned *ie* and village community are disappearing in Japan today. Since World War II, the size of Japanese households has gotten smaller and smaller. There are fewer three-generation households (although elderly Japanese are still more likely to live with their children—specifically their eldest sons—than alone), and there has been an increase in the number of single-person households (from 3.4 percent in 1955 to 21 percent in 1980). Nuclear families (those consisting only of a marital pair and their children) now comprise 60 percent of all households. (See Table 1.1).

The modern nuclear family is a much less dominating group than the traditional *ie.* Typically, the husband has less authority than the old head of household and he almost always works outside the home, often quite far away. Long commutes and many hours of work result in fathers seldom seeing their children. They return home after their children are asleep and leave home before the children awaken in the morning. Mothers and children are close, but children typically

[2]See, for example, Nakane, pp. 1–22; or for a recent discussion, Kuwayama, pp. 121–151.

TABLE 1.1. Household Size: In Japan, East Germany, and the United States many people live alone.

	Average Size of Household: Number of Persons	One-Person Households as a Percent of All Households
East Germany, 1981	2.5	26.5
West Germany	Not available	Not available
Japan, 1980	3.2	21.0
United States, 1980	2.7	22.6
Mexico, 1980	5.5	5.4
Egypt, 1976	5.2	6.0

Source: 1987 Demographic Yearbook, 39th ed. New York: Department for Economic and Social Information and Policy Analysis, United Nations, 1987.

spend long hours at school and after-school activities. Husbands and wives usually have different friends and don't socialize as a couple. Their leisure activities and even their vacations are spent separately (Fukutake, pp. 123–126).

Postwar industrialization has also broken up the village community. After the war, massive migration from the countryside to cities emptied the villages, as young Japanese searched for industrial jobs. Today, most Japanese, even those in rural areas, commute long distances to work, so few people both live and work in the same community. People are less involved in local community life, and less concerned about what their neighbors think of them, especially in big cities (Fukutake, pp. 134–136).

Many western sociologists expected Japan to follow a pattern observed in Europe and North America: when societies industrialize, people spend less time in **primary groups** (small, personal, face-to-face groups) like families and villages, and more time in **secondary groups** (large, relatively impersonal, goal-oriented organizations) like cities and corporations. Then, group membership becomes less important in people's lives and they begin to think of themselves as individuals and to value their liberty to make individual choices. This hasn't happened in Japan. When Japan became a modern, industrialized nation, the *ie* and the community became much less important. But individualism didn't take their place. Instead, Japan has been remarkably successful in creating new primary groups within the secondary groups of school and company, so much so that these new groups have become the focus of Japanese life.

Group Life in School

School dominates the lives of Japanese children. They have long school days and short summer vacations and they attend school on Saturday mornings. The authority of the school extends outward into the community and the home. Teachers make home visits, and each elementary school child has a little notebook in which the teacher writes notes to the child's mother and the mother replies. When police see children behaving improperly, they call their principal as well as their parents.

In elementary and junior high school, Japanese children are taught to see themselves first and foremost as members of their homeroom class, or *kumi.* (The word *kumi* is old: originally it meant a band of samurai warriors.) Starting in first grade, children spend nine years together in the same *kumi.* In elementary school, they stay with each teacher for two years. Each *kumi* of about forty to forty-five children is encouraged to think of its classroom as the children's own collective home. They arrange and rearrange its furniture, bring in plants and flowers from home, and each day the *kumi* and teacher completely clean the room—scrubbing the desks and floors, washing windows, cleaning blackboards and erasers. Each *kumi* also takes a turn cleaning the school halls and toilets, the teachers' room, and the street outside the school. The *kumi* eats lunch in its own room and even in junior high school, teachers for different subjects move from classroom to classroom, while the students stay in their own room. On the playground, members of a *kumi* play on the same team, competing with other *kumi* in their grade.

Teachers divide *kumi* into smaller groups, called *han,* which are like study or work groups, but they stay together for quite a long time. Each *han* elects a

It's lunchtime in Mitaka Middle School. Dressed in their informal exercise clothes, these students eat lunch in their classroom and good-naturedly clown for the camera. After lunch they will change back to formal uniforms and return to the restrained formal behavior expected for lessons.

leader or *han-cho,* whose job it is to lead the group into harmonious decision making, by patiently eliciting a consensus (Duke, pp. 25–29). Japanese schools do not practice ability grouping and, typically, children from both rich and poor families attend the same school. The emphasis is on keeping the whole class moving through the work at the same pace, with the more able students helping their slower *han*-mates.

> Keiko is nervous as she arrives in her fifth-grade classroom. Today her han must present its report on the Tokugawa Era. They've been working on it in school and for the past two days they have met after school at Yukichi's house to practice making the oral presentation. Keiko is afraid she will make a mistake and let her han down. She hardly hears the music over the loudspeaker that signals the official start of the school day, and she follows the kumi through the prescribed exercises without even noticing. But her teacher, walking up and down the rows, does notice. "Keiko seems distracted; not concentrating," she writes in her little notebook.
>
> After the presentation, Keiko is giddy with relief. They did well! "You are a credit to the second class of grade 5," the teacher says. Today Keiko's han has its turn to serve lunch and she gaily wraps herself in the white apron and puts on the surgical mask. She and her han-mates haul the heavy pots and bins of rice, stew, and salad up to the classroom from the school kitchen and dish them out. The whole kumi chants grace together, then breaks out in laughter and conversation while the students eat. Keiko is particularly animated. She has done her part in supporting her han.

Working and playing so closely together, members of a *kumi* come to know each other intimately and think of themselves as a group. Close friendships formed in the *kumi* often endure for life. Habits of group loyalty, a preference for uniformity, and the learned skill of building a group consensus through patient negotiation prepare children for the all-important work groups of Japanese adult life (Feiler, pp. 99–102; Leestma, p. 3).

But as much as group life in school illustrates the strength and importance of group life in Japan, it also illustrates its dark underside. It was American sociologist William Graham Sumner (1840–1910) who long ago articulated the principle that the more closely people identify as a group and the stronger their **in-group** feelings, the more hostility they direct toward **out-groups,** or people outside the group. We see this in Japanese schools in the practice if *ijime,* or bullying, usually after school or during free play, when children single out one child who is different in some way (perhaps Korean, or foreign-born, or poorer or richer than the others) and subject him (it is usually a boy) to ceaseless torment. They tease him, make fun of him, kick and punch, sometimes extort money or pressure him to commit petty theft. The Japanese are ashamed of *ijime,* and they are very disturbed that parents and schools seem unable to prevent it or even to acknowledge it, since often the victims tell no one of their experiences. Every year there are several reports of suicides of 12- or 13-year old children who are victims of *ijime.* It is a basic characteristic of Japanese social life that, just as people are exceptionally kind to the members of their group, they can be exceptionally cruel to people who are outsiders, or different (Pollack, Dec. 18, 1994, p. 20).

The Work Group

Following World War II, as Japanese industry expanded, and drew in an ever-larger workforce from the farms and villages, Japanese companies encouraged their workers to see the company as their family. They invented a new focus for group identity in modern Japanese life. Large corporations hired their employees right out of high school or college. Promised lifetime employment and guaranteed promotion, employees spent their whole working lives in one company, advancing in step with those hired in their year. Company housing, company sports teams and recreation complexes, cafeterias, health clinics, and company discount stores re-created the all-absorbing village within the company. Today, although no more than a third of Japan's labor force is employed by large corporations, their organization has set the tone for Japanese work life. Government employees, as well as employees in smaller companies look to work for a sense of community. They find it in the work group, or "section," of the office or factory.

> *When the bullet train suddenly slowed, Hiroshi glanced out the window and saw beside the track the village where he had been born. Staring, Hiroshi thought about how different his life was now from his village childhood. He spotted his family's old house—a large wooden structure with its own courtyard and small garden—where he had lived with his parents, brother and sisters, grandparents, and his uncle (his father's younger brother). Hiroshi looked down into the quiet streets of the town where he had spent his days at play, even as a 2-year-old, watched by his brother.*

> *Now Hiroshi lives in an apartment house outside Tokyo. He is home so little that he doesn't even know his neighbors and his children never play outside. They hurry from school to lessons to homework indoors. Really, his office is now the focus of his life. Hiroshi knows his family wants him at home, but he feels that he has to give his all to his job. His father, the potter, always said that you could tell from looking at the pot whether its maker had really concentrated and put his whole heart into the job. Hiroshi feels the same way about his work.*

> *Every morning the nine men of his section assemble, greet each other, and drink their first cups of tea together. Takeshi has become a close friend: he really knows what is in Hiroshi's heart. But all the men are important to him. That year when Hiroshi's mother was dying so painfully, they knew how he felt without his having to explain. Saying nothing, they took over most of his duties at work and took him out after work, making sure he ate and gently distracting him with stories and songs. Kenji-san had introduced Hiroshi's son to his niece, and they were soon to be married. Mr. Fuji, the department chief looked after them all, and was now arranging a marriage for Masao, the only unmarried man in the section. The "office ladies" don't stay long, but they take care of the men in their own way, preparing tea and cleaning their desks. When Hiroshi has to stay late to finish work, several of the other men usually stay to keep him company, and bring in beer and food for supper. After work, and before the long commute home, the section and its chief usually go out together to a local bar, to drink and chat more informally. Hiroshi enjoys the monthly evening parties paid for by the company, and the twice-yearly weekend retreats when the whole section goes away together to a country inn. His real home, he thinks, is at the office with his office "family."*

Status and Role in Japanese Groups

If you visit Japan, or even perhaps if you go to an authentic Japanese restaurant in a big city in Europe or America, you may well see a "section" like Hiroshi's out for dinner or drinks. Observe them unobtrusively so you will not be rude: the group will probably be all male, but they are of different ages and their clothing indicates varied statuses—the older, well-dressed section chief, his employees of various ages and statuses, and possibly even the limousine driver, more informally dressed or in uniform. Japanese people find it natural to belong to close-knit groups of people who are status unequals. Don't picture this unequal status as a hierarchy like the military, where orders flow down from a pinnacle at the top. There are, of course, institutional hierarchies in Japan, but more distinctively, Japanese hierarchy is personal: it pervades the relationships among individuals.

Japanese people are always keenly aware of their status relative to others. In a group of strangers they quickly assess relative status. The most obvious status difference is that of **gender.** Gender inequalities are of fundamental importance in Japan. Women are assumed to be of lower status then men. They defer to men and serve them. It is extremely rare to find a woman in a position in which she supervises and gives orders to men. In fact, the few Japanese women who are business owners tend to surround themselves with female employees.

In a group that is all men or all women, like a group of women at a food co-op meeting, people hasten to find out how old each member is, so that everyone will know where they are ranked by age. In big companies, male office workers are hired in age cohorts right after high school or college and they advance together as a group. Even an exceptionally talented worker will not be promoted ahead of his age cohort. It is only at the age of 55 or 60, when most of the cohort retires that some will be promoted into upper management. By this method companies ensure that older men need never take orders from younger men.

Judging relative status is further complicated by the importance of **job title.** A group of young businessmen, meeting for the first time, eagerly proffer their business cards to each other, almost before saying a word. They do this because Japanese cards contain vital information: more prominently than a person's name, they tell his title and what organization he works for. Once occupational statuses are clearly established, Japanese men feel more comfortable: they know how to treat each other as unequals.

To understand Japanese social structure it is important to grasp the difference between the concepts of **status** and **role.** You may occupy the status of man or woman, parent or child, assistant manager or a kindergarten teacher, but what role you will play depends on whom you are interacting with: a man or a woman, a coworker or customer, someone older or younger, a manager or clerk. In Japan, when you meet another person, you must be able to assess whether your status is higher or lower than theirs. Then you will be able to judge how low you should bow in greeting or taking leave of them, and what words you should use in addressing them. You must be able to switch smoothly from one role to another as you interact with people in different statuses. This social knowledge is explicitly recognized and taught to children in Japan. There is even a special word for it: *kejime,*

Businessmen meet and bow in a traditional greeting that is very much a part of Japanese life today. An employee of a small company will bow lower than one working for Toyota. A new employee at Toyota bows lower than the senior Toyota manager he meets. Who bows lowest when a senior official of a small firm meets a junior representative of Toyota? Everyday politeness in Japan requires that you solve such problems quickly.

the knowledge of what degree of *omote* or *ura,* self-restraint or self-expression, discipline or spontaneity is appropriate in your interaction with different people, or in different situations (Bachnik, pp. 155–199, 164).

Language and Status

Status hierarchy is structured into the Japanese language in such a way that you literally cannot speak to other people without knowing their status compared to yours. A very important part of Japanese is *keigo,* or "respect language." Japanese provides almost no vocabulary for use with a status equal. Every time you speak to another person, the language forces you to decide what level of formality to choose in your verbs and pronouns, depending on the status, age, gender, and intimacy of you, your listener, and anyone else you refer to. A question addressed to a woman, your younger brother, or your subordinate at work will be phrased in very different words then the same request to a man, your boss, or your father. Women always use the more polite speech forms, especially to men, but even to each other (Smith, pp. 74–77; Christopher, p. 40).

Japanese children learn early to sort out relative status, because *keigo* is employed even within the family. You cannot address any relative senior to you by either his or her personal name or a personal pronoun. So a child always addresses an elder sibling, parent, grandparent, and so forth, by a kin status name [for example, *onisan* ("elder brother")] and is, in turn, addressed by her or his personal name, even if there are only two children. A wife calls her husband by a kin name (typically, father or daddy), but her husband addresses her by her personal name. Outside the family, except when addressing children or people who have been friends since childhood, Japanese people call each other by status names. You call your neighbor *okusan* (Mrs. Lady of the Household), your teacher *sensei,* the government official *kyokucho-san* (Mr. Bureau Chief). Everyone of higher status than you is addressed with the suffix *san* added to her or his status name, or with great formality, *sama* (Hendry, p. 86; Reischauer, 1977, p. 163).

The most fascinating example of the problem of language and status in Japan occurs in television talk shows. All sorts of specialists—professors, authors, officials, and so on—speak on Japanese TV. Each speaker faces a heterogeneous audience; some viewers are of higher status than the speaker, and some lower. How are they to speak to this group, without giving offense or undercutting their own dignity? This dilemma is solved by the role of the *kikite,* "the listener," a young, clearly lower-status woman, to whom the speaker ostensibly addresses all remarks (Rudolph, p. 8).

Unequal Dependencies

People of unequal status address each other differently and they also expect different behavior from each other. Generally, lower-status people show deference, respect, and loyalty to higher-status people. Politeness is very important. In a group, older people walk first. In an office, or at formal meetings or parties, people are seated in order of status, and it is a common sight to find people jammed up at the door, deferring to each other and trying to sort out the correct seating. If people of higher status, or people you don't know well, come to your house, you will treat them with great deference, seating them in the best spot in the best room, and serving them special food and drink on the best dishes, and choosing topics of conversation they will enjoy. Your whole family will join in and cater to these important guests, and by self-restraint will coax their guests' self-expression to flower (Bachnik, pp. 160–162).

But those in higher statuses also owe much to the people below them. They are expected to act their age, or live up to their positions. Acting like "one of the boys" or "like a kid" is felt to be extremely unbecoming and embarrassing. Higher-status people are expected to treat those below them with parental kindness. A common relationship in Japan, particularly in business, is that of mentor and protégé, in which an older, higher-status man helps his younger protégé, not only in business, but in his personal life, advising him and commonly acting as his go-between in arranging a marriage. The protégé relies upon, and positively enjoys his dependence on his mentor.[3] Takeo Doi, 1977, provided the classic description of the pleasure the Japanese often take in relations of dependence.

---

[3] In the rare female-owned Japanese businesses, female executives play this mentor role in relation to their female employees.

SOCIALIZATION

Japan is a demanding society: it asks of individuals a high level of conformity with very detailed norms, and it demands self-discipline in subordinating individual needs to the requirements of the group. Most people do conform. The Japanese pride themselves on how orderly their society is. Most people embrace Japanese values, identify with their roles, and do what is expected of them. Foreigners often wonder how Japanese society achieves such a high level of conformity.

The Japanese believe that learning is the key to conformity. Japanese people learn the beliefs and role expectations of their culture and learn to play their roles properly through the process sociologists call **socialization.** While all societies and social groups socialize their members, in some cases the process is haphazard and disorganized and people may be largely unaware that socialization is taking place. In Japan, socialization is highly consistent, explicit, and carefully planned.

Studying Japan provides a wonderful opportunity to understand the process of socialization, how socialization actually takes place, because the Japanese carry out socialization so thoughtfully. First of all, Japanese groups give their members a tremendous amount of **explicit instruction.** Then they provide many opportunities to **practice** proper behavior, often through repeated drill. **Ceremonies** mark transitions to new roles and alert people to the need for changed behavior. **Role models** are often provided to help people learn roles. Finally, the Japanese are highly skilled in **framing** situations in such a way as to ease people into proper role performance. We can examine these processes of socialization in action in Japanese schools and businesses.

Socialization through Instruction

Since the beginning of the postwar Japanese economic boom, Japanese companies have treated worker socialization with extreme seriousness. Training courses for new workers often last for several weeks, and include socialization in the values and norms of company life as well as technical instruction. Many large companies maintain training centers in rural areas where new and old workers are brought periodically for intensive retreats, featuring motivational workshops and lectures on ethics. Large companies maintain an in-house staff of trainers, who create company slogans and chants, inspirational comic books and poems, and conduct training sessions (Chapman, pp. 132–134).

One of the most striking characteristics of socialization in Japanese society is that people in positions of authority don't hesitate to tell trainees exactly what is expected of them. They tell them formally, repeatedly, and in very great detail. Then they provide many opportunities for practice. In school and at work, people are constantly exhorted by signs, slogans, and maxims. Nursery school children are told that "the world is full of people just like them, who also have needs and desires, so they must learn to get along and cooperate and be considerate of others, to persevere in curbing their own wishes and feelings." A recent comic book distributed by The Fuji Bank, urges new employees to be like "Ultraman," the superhero who performs all his exploits in just three minutes; they are to get up three minutes earlier,

limit phone calls to three minutes, study new technology every day for three min- ⸀
utes, and so forth (Hendry, p. 64; Feiler, p. 40; Chapman, p. 133).

Socialization through Practice

It is the Japanese way to follow instruction with repeated drill, and no disapproval
or embarrassment is attached to making mistakes in practice. Perseverance and drill
are assumed to be necessary to learn anything properly. Japanese mothers teach little children "respect language" by repeating over and over again the proper forms
of address. Schoolchildren through junior high school are drilled in proper bowing,
formal greeting, sitting and standing (in unison), answering their teachers (immediately and loudly), and arranging their desktops for study (in a set format). A
teacher, preparing eighth graders for a class trip, arranges chairs on the floor of the
gym in the shape of a bus, and for hours students practice getting in and out of the
seats in orderly fashion (Hendry, p. 102; Feiler, p. 264; Leestma, p. 27).

When Mazda opened its first U.S. auto plant in 1985, employees were given a
training program lasting ten to twelve weeks, time the company considered necessary to communicate to American workers the values and expectations of a Japanese company. Training included a week of work on "interpersonal relations" using
group discussions with a trainer, videotapes of "correct" and "incorrect" ways to interact, workbooks and role-playing exercises. For example, in one workshop
trainees practiced the proper way to tell a coworker that his body odor was offensive. (Incidentally, some of the Americans hated the training and dropped out, but
many loved it. They said that the new techniques for relating to others transformed
their home lives). (See Fucini and Fucini, pp. 71–74.)

Ceremonies Support Socialization

Initiation ceremonies, marking the transition to new roles, are an effective part of
Japanese socialization. Ceremonies help people learn *kejime,* learn to recognize
that they are in a new stage of life, with new roles and norms. Carefully staged ceremonies are an important part of children's progress through school. Interestingly,
the Japanese place more emphasis on ceremonies that mark the beginning of different stages of education, than on graduation ceremonies. Corporations also often
provide elaborate welcome ceremonies for new recruits (described by one observer
as "a cross between a coming-of-age ceremony and initiation into an American fra-
ternity"). Starting in the 1950s, companies devised rituals in which cohorts of new
employees, and in some cases their parents too, were first greeted and lectured by
company officials in welcome ceremonies at the factory, then escorted on several
days of touring and partying (Chapman, p. 131).

Role Models Aid Socialization

The Japanese believe in providing role models to help people learn expected behavior. Mothers and teachers consciously "model" correct behavior for children.
Nursery school teachers wash their hands and brush their teeth alongside their

charges, and elementary school teachers eat lunch with their students and work alongside the students during the regular daily cleaning period. At home and at school older children are urged to set good examples for younger ones, and take pride in their roles as "elder brother" or "elder sister" (Hendry, p. 149). The elder child as role model is a recurrent pattern in Japanese society. Corporations appoint "elder brothers" to instruct new recruits in proper behavior; and in business, government, and even in organized crime, younger men seek out "mentors" to guide their progress.

Framing Opportunities for Socialization

Sociologist Erving Goffman used the term **framing** to convey the way people structure interaction symbolically, through gestures, the use of props, the physical arrangement of rooms, or spoken cues (see Turner, p. 70). If you are Japanese, from infancy through adulthood you find yourself in situations framed in such a way as to emphasize group consciousness and dependence on the group. This is actually a form of socialization, though it is much more indirect than instruction or drill.

Socialization to dependence on the group begins at birth, according to Takeo Doi, a famous Japanese psychiatrist. Care of infants is based on the assumption that babies should experience as little anxiety as possible. Caregivers try to anticipate the baby's needs and satisfy them before crying and fretfulness signal a problem. Cribs are placed beside adult beds, and children are never put in their cribs to fall asleep alone; they are sung to sleep before being laid down. Use of babysitters is highly unusual, and mothers and babies enjoy a constant physical closeness. The Japanese also avoid playpens, preferring instead that the child be protected by the constant close attention of an adult. Mothers' all-embracing, unconditional love and support results in bonds of tremendous emotional closeness with their children, argues Doi, and a taste for dependency that is expressed in adult group life. Children learn implicitly that if you conform, and do what others expect of you, then people will be kind and considerate, and they will gratify your wishes without your having to ask (Hendry, pp. 18–25, 97, 116; Christopher, pp. 68–70; Doi, p. 20).

Framing Interaction in School

Life in Japanese elementary schools is framed in such a way as to stress the similarity of all children, and the importance of the group. Teachers seldom address children individually, or overtly recognize differences in individual ability, and they minimize situations in which children compete individually with each other. Instead, each *han* is held responsible collectively for the progress of all its members. Also, teachers do not discipline individual students in Japanese schools. Rather, if a class or an individual is unruly, the teacher will turn to that day's assigned monitor and request him or her to restore order. The classroom situation is structured in such a way as to emphasize group participation, group loyalty, and the responsibility of the individual to the class. In this situation, students experience no conflict between loyalty to their friends and conformity with school norms (Feiler, pp. 30, 100–102; Leestma, pp. 3, 27).

Kiyoshi's high school baseball team was a world of its own. When he joined it as a freshman they practiced every day. The freshmen had to wear special headbands and chant while the senior team played. They had to come early to set up the field. One day Kiyoshi was late to practice. As soon as he saw Kiyoshi, the coach stopped all the playing and chanting. He called the freshmen out on the field and every man had to do 100 push-ups while the whole team watched. Kiyoshi was so ashamed! He apologized to each freshman teammate for putting him through so much pain and embarrassment. He never came late again. But there were times when other freshmen did something wrong, and then the whole freshman squad would do push-ups or sprints. Somehow, enduring this punishment together made them brothers.

Teachers are well aware of the importance of framing opportunities for socialization. For example, Bruce Feiler describes a seventh-grade class trip to Tokyo's Disneyland framed in such a way as to encourage students' dependency on their *han.* Students were required to stay with their han during the visit. In each han, one member was assigned to carry the money, one to wear the watch, one to take the photos, and one to take notes. "The management of this trip," Feiler explained, "revealed the skill with which Japanese schools transfer abstract goals into concrete educational practices" (Feiler, p. 266).

Schools also frame interaction with dress norms. As they move through their day, from formal classroom activities to informal recreation, lunch, and cleanup, elementary and junior high school children repeatedly change their clothes, from regular uniforms and slippers to warm-up suits and outdoor sneakers. Changes in clothing help children learn *kejime:* to distinguish between the private, relaxed parts of life and more public, formal settings.

Five-year-old Masako is learning kejime in preschool. Every day she feels like a big girl as she crosses the genkan (the entrance hall) of the school, where she slips out of her outdoor shoes and puts on her school slippers. School begins as Masako and her classmates chant a ritual good morning to their teacher. Masako is proud that she knows how to say it right and she enjoys the way it feels to shout in unison with her friends in the class. When the class goes every month to the local Buddhist temple, Masako knows just when to bow and how to remain silent with the rest of the class. She also enjoys the many play breaks every day, when she and her friends put on their sweatsuits and scream and run wildly around the playground. The teachers never tell them what to do during recess, even when the boys get into fights or say rude things.

Framing Interaction in the Office

When young people graduate from school and move on to the world of work, they again enter situations framed to encourage group identification. Japanese offices are physically arranged in such a way as to make it very difficult to behave individualistically, but easy to become part of the group. Offices are huge undivided areas, with the desks of each "section" grouped together. Within a section, desks are arranged in facing rows, all touching, so as to form one huge tabletop, with the section chief's desk perpendicular across the end. Among the eight or nine section members, every conversation is a group affair, every memo can be read by all. Even telephones are shared. Only one desk stands alone in a Japanese office: the director's (Feiler, pp. 19–20, 28).

A young "salaryman" poses before his place of work. In this office, coworkers can all see and hear one another, and it is easy for them to exchange information informally. Secretaries and managers work in the same room. Are offices in your society arranged like this, or are there separate rooms for managers and partitioned cubicles for other workers?

DEVIANCE IN A DEMANDING SOCIETY

Japan is a demanding society; there is strong pressure to conform to very detailed, explicit norms. Socialization is extensive. Families, schools, and businesses work hard to make sure their members learn their roles and play them properly. Under these circumstances, would you expect there to be very little, or a great deal of **deviant behavior** in Japan? Deviance is universal: every society establishes norms and in every society people defy socialization and group pressure; they violate norms, incurring disapproval and some sort of punishment. But in some societies there is a great deal more deviance than in others. In some societies crime rates are high, children cut school, teenagers dress in ways that upset their elders, and many people engage in sexual behavior or substance abuse that scandalizes others. This is not the case in Japan. Although it doesn't take much to violate social norms in Japan, there is, in fact, very little deviance. Even teenagers, rebellious in so many cultures, conform closely to normative expectations.

Low Levels of Deviance

Very strict standards for Japanese children begin with school uniforms and an extremely detailed school dress code, specifying, for example, the width of trouser legs and distance from the floor of cuffs and skirt hems. Teenagers do try to bend these rules, but they are given very little leeway. A daring act is to sew a red or purple satin lining to the inside of one's jacket pocket; but teachers and principals check uniforms for alterations, and there are sanctions, like confiscation and public display of offending jackets, for students who fail to conform. Teenage girls are expected to act innocent and cute, going about in giggling groups. In fact, two-thirds of the girls engage in sex by age 15, but they conform by hiding their sex life from public view (Feiler, p. 233; White, pp. 170, 189).

Crime rates are exceptionally low in Japan. With a population one-half the size of the United States, Japan has fewer robberies in a year than take place in two days in the United States; fewer rapes than in one week. In a recent year, thirty-eight people were killed by handguns in all of Japan, compared to more than 16,000 in the United States. Handguns are outlawed in Japan, except for sports use. There are only forty-nine legal handguns in the whole country and they are registered with the police and must be kept at the shooting range. There are about 425,000 rifles and air guns in Japan, held by people who have passed exams and rigorous licensing procedures, repeated every three years. (Compare this to the estimated 200 million guns owned by individuals in the United States.) More minor crimes are also uncommon. There is little drug use in Japan, and no graffiti or litter on the streets. Traffic laws are obeyed, and despite the importance of bars in Japanese culture, there is no drunk driving (Tasker, pp. 71, 73; Kristof, p. 8).

The Yakuza

There is some crime in Japan, but it is a particularly orderly sort of crime. Criminal activity is financed and organized by the *Yakuza,* Japan's organized crime syndicates. There really are no individual criminals. Approximately 90,000 Yakuza members are organized into three main syndicates and 3000 groups, running prostitution, pornography, gambling, drugs, extortion, and labor rackets, and taking in billions of dollars a year. The Yakuza also engage in violence on behalf of legitimate authorities who wish to avoid the use of violence themselves. They have broken strikes, silenced dissenters, evicted tenants from valuable real estate, and halted the work of lone criminals. The Yakuza have worked for corporations, the ruling Liberal Democratic Party, the American CIA, and the police.

But it is somewhat deceptive to speak of the Yakuza as "organized crime": they enjoy a legitimacy and acceptance in Japanese society very different from their American counterparts. The Yakuza is accepted as a public presence in Japan: their offices publicly display gang insignia on the door, like an insurance office or loan company. Members wear gang badges, like the company pins Japanese salarymen wear. People who join the Yakuza become part of a social group like others in Japan—one that stresses group identity and conformity to group norms (Wildeman, unpublished material; Tasker, p. 78; Sterngold, 1992, pp. A1, A6).

Public and Private Deviance

One reason why there is so little deviance in Japan is that a lot of behavior condemned as deviant in other societies is acceptable in Japan, as long as it remains private. In all societies deviance is situational: behavior forbidden in one situation may be quite acceptable in another. This is particularly true in Japan. It is characteristic of Japanese culture that no human behavior, and no person, is considered intrinsically bad, or sick, or evil: what matters is that you keep your behavior appropriate to the social situation.

For example, Japanese society is highly tolerant of male adultery, as long as it is kept secret. The whole family may really know about father's mistress, but as long as he never shames the family by being seen with her in public, everyone will tolerate his behavior. Similarly, the Japanese have never condemned homosexual sex or seen it as perverted or sinful. It would be highly deviant, shocking, and scandalous to "come out" as gay, but as long as you marry, and preserve a proper *omote* public image, what you do in private is not condemned. Similarly, it is common for the whole staff of a work section, including the boss (and sometimes the female workers), to go out drinking together after work. Drunk, the boss may make a fool of himself, singing and crying, but the next day in the office, when he is once again his proper, formal self, no one's respect for him will be in the least diminished. Employees, under cover of "drunkenness" may complain to the boss openly about their treatment, but the next day no one will "remember" that it happened.

Every Japanese city has its "red light district," a place for the nighttime entertainment of men. While traditional geisha houses are now disappearing, "hostesses" in the ubiquitous hostess bars will flatter and flirt with their all-male guests; "masseuses" in turkish baths offer an array of legal and illegal personal attentions, and sexually explicit stripper shows even feature (illegal) "open stage" events, in which a member of the audience joins the stripper in public sexual acts. Until they were closed down, "no-panties waitress" coffee shops, with glass or mirrored floors, offered the option of looking without touching (Condon, pp. 76, 82, 247; Bornoff, pp. 263–272, 295–296, 312–322). The women who work in such establishments may preserve an *omote* public life in distant apartments where they raise their children with propriety. Stories are often told of bored housewives who take up work as hostesses without their husbands ever knowing.

Japanese society is matter-of-fact about sex. It is commonplace for elderly women to work in sex-toy shops or sell condoms. Pornographic books and comics are sold in vending machines and porn videos are shown in bars. A magazine for teenage girls includes a pull-out sex manual with explicit instructions on sexual techniques and addresses and room rates of "love hotels"—hourly-rate hotels that are found everywhere in Japan and are much used (Tasker, pp. 69, 111, 113–114; White, pp. 180–182).

Japanese-Style Deviance: Making a Scene

By now you may be asking: isn't there any deviant behavior in Japan? There is some behavior, often tolerated in other societies, that is seen as major deviance in

Japan. One such behavior is deliberately creating conflict. People who create conflict—who oppose their opinions to those of others, who make demands, argue, or engage in public social protest—are seen as posing a shocking threat to unity and public order. Open social conflict is rare in Japan, but it has always occurred, from the peasant uprisings of the Tokugawa Era to student demonstrations in the 1960s and today's environmental and peace protests.

Susan Pharr, who studied social conflict in Japan, found a distinct repertoire of conflict-escalating actions, including failure to carry out expected role behavior (in one case, women in an office who were protesting their low status refused to pour tea); failure to behave respectfully to superiors, by bowing and using respect language, and so forth; sit-ins and hunger strikes; "denunciation sessions" in which an opponent is publicly confronted and accused of wrong actions. Confrontations that escalate to hostile behavior like stomping around, or slamming doors, or actual physical pushing and hitting, shock people profoundly. People who start a conflict in Japan have a certain advantage, because their opponents are likely to try to avoid conflict, even if it means making concessions. In the end, though, nobody wins, because all parties are seen as having brought shame to their group by allowing the social harmony to be shattered (Pharr, pp. 143–144).

Deviance and Stigma

Another kind of behavior strongly condemned as deviant in Japan is adopting a deviant identity. **Primary deviance,** that is, deviant acts, is much more readily forgiven than is **secondary deviance,** or the adoption of deviant statuses. When Japanese people adopt a deviant identity—one that proclaims their difference from other Japanese—they are strongly **stigmatized** or publicly labeled as different and deviant. For example, people who go to gay bars or bathhouses are tolerated, but people who announce that they are gay scandalize others and they bring shame on their family members who will experience difficulty getting jobs and finding spouses. Having AIDS is a matter of the deepest shame, and many AIDS sufferers move to Hawaii before their symptoms show so as to spare their families from ostracism. Even handicapped people occupy a deviant status in Japan. People in wheelchairs are almost never seen in public and, indeed, there are no wheelchair ramps or other accommodations for the handicapped (Sesser, pp. 62–63).

We can say that in a very real way being different is deviant in Japan. Even talking about people who are different is offensive. People use vague euphemisms to refer to the handicapped, to the *burakumin* (a hereditary low caste; see p. 40), or even to those who are left-handed. Japan's largest newspaper, the YOMURI SHIMBUN, has an actual list of 175 forbidden words and phrases, like "burakumin" or "blind" or even a common word for woman, *onna,* that implies a lower status. You might think that Japanese people are trying to avoid giving offense to others by their speech, but they are trying even more strongly to avoid any words that might call attention to the fact that Japan is not a completely homogeneous and harmonious society (Sterngold, Dec. 18, 1994, pp. E1, E6).

Effective Social Controls

Why is there so little truly deviant behavior in Japanese society? One explanation lies in the effectiveness of social controls. Thorough socialization to strict standards is followed by constant supervision and effective **social sanctions.** In every society sanctions are the muscle behind social control. Social sanctions reward those who conform and play their roles well, and punish those who fail to shape up. In Japanese society there are a variety of **positive sanctions** that are real incentives, coupled with **negative sanctions** that people very much wish to avoid. "The nail that sticks up, gets pounded down," say the Japanese, acknowledging the power of sanctions.

With great consistency and regularity, the reward for role conformity in Japanese society is inclusion in the warm and pleasant life of the group. Those who fail to play their roles correctly face exclusion: misbehaving children are excluded from family activities, or left standing alone outside the classroom or playground, ignored by teachers. A mother may say, "If you keep doing that, the garbage collectors will come and take you away," or she may punish extremely serious offenses by locking the child out of the house (Lebra, 1984, p. 149).

Ridicule is also a common sanction, and children are actually encouraged to make fun of a child who fails to conform. Mothers commonly censure misbehavior by telling children, "If you do that, people will laugh at you." Children come to fear ridicule, and this fear continues into adult life as an important social pressure to conform (Hendry, pp. 106–108, 114–115).

In Japanese corporations social sanctions back up all the slogans and chants and exhortations to work hard and be loyal to the company. Those who work for big companies are looked up to by others; their sons are sought out in marriage. They find it easier to get a home mortgage. Company expense accounts fund visits to bars and nightclubs and golf club memberships. Once past his twenties, a man who leaves his company pays a heavy price. Not only does he lose company benefits, but he loses his friends at work. If he finds a new job (and most companies won't hire a man they label as disloyal for leaving his company), he finds it hard to make new friends among men who have worked together for years. Positive and negative sanctions ensure that it pays for a corporate employee to act loyal, even if he or she doesn't feel loyal (Chapman, pp. 137–139).

Criminal sanctions in Japan are a serious matter. With crime rates so low, Japan actually has a very small prison population—only 37 people out of every 100,000 people are in prison, compared to 519 per 100,000 in the United States, and 80 per 100,000 in Germany. Jail sentences are relatively short, but harsh. Prisoners are often kept in isolation and not even allowed to talk to each other. There are no gangs in Japanese prisons, or any prison rapes or assaults. Also, Japanese people are ashamed to have relatives in jail. They seldom visit them and often refuse to accept them back home once they are released (Kristof, pp. 1, 8). (See Table 1.2.)

Surveillance

Japanese society is unusual in the sureness with which negative sanctions follow deviance. You can be certain that if you violate norms in Japan, someone will

TABLE 1.2. Homicides and Suicides, 1987–1991: Japan has moderate suicide rates, but very few murders.

	Deaths per 100,000 Population per Year	
	Murder	Suicide
East Germany	1.0	24.2
West Germany	1.0	15.8
Japan	0.6	16.0
United States	9.1	12.2
Mexico	16.8	2.2
Egypt	0.5	0.1

Source: 1992 Demographic Yearbook, 44th ed. New York: Department for Economic and Social Information and Policy Analysis, United Nations, 1994.

notice and will definitely take action, and you will surely pay a price. Strict norms are enforced through constant supervision. Teenagers actually have very little time when they are not at school, or school-sponsored activities, or at home. Some schools organize regular after-school patrols of the neighborhood by parents and teachers (to watch students, not to protect them from others, since all neighborhoods are quite safe). In many districts, even junior high school teachers make home visits once a term, writing reports afterward on each child's study habits and television watching and on the appearance of the children's rooms. Police will actually take a teenager into custody for smoking, an act considered seriously delinquent, then call both parents and the school guidance counselor to the police station (Feiler, p. 171; Leestma, p. 46).

Adults too find their behavior constantly scrutinized, with deviant acts reported to the higher-status members of their social groups. Bruce Feiler, an American who taught in Japan, has written of his surprise at the tightness of Japanese social controls. Feiler used a bicycle to travel around his town, and late at night when there was no other traffic he saw no need to stop for red lights. But someone observed him and called the board of education, which called his principal, and Feiler found himself rebuked by his supervisor (Feiler, p. 25). An adult man, arrested in a police sweep of an illegal stripper show or "massage parlor" can expect police to call both his wife and his boss. Publicly humiliated, his job lost and career ruined, such a man is a vivid lesson to all of the dangers of deviance.

Surveillance is constantly carried out by the police, organized in a national network of 15,000 police boxes, most manned twenty-four hours a day. Police take an active approach to surveillance, visiting each household in their district yearly, and discreetly keeping track of the private lives of all district residents (Tasker, p. 73). Police are given great leeway in searching and questioning people. They can hold suspects without a formal hearing for up to twenty-one days, and often subject them to long interrogations and pressure to confess. Evidence obtained illegally is admissible in court (Kristof, p. 8).

SOCIAL INEQUALITY IN JAPAN: CLASS, STATUS, AND POWER

Personal inequalities—relationships between unequals—play a key role in Japanese culture, and are the basis of everyday interaction. Let us now examine the social inequalities in Japanese society. Do different social groups or categories of people receive unequal amounts of society's rewards? This question doesn't have a simple answer; it depends on what aspects of inequality you are discussing. Max Weber's classic discussion of social stratification is useful for understanding social inequality in Japan. Weber said that there are three basic aspects of inequality: class, status, and power. **Class** has to do with the wealth and income people enjoy as the result of their property or job. **Status** refers to prestige. It is the cultural dimension of inequality, because it results from the way a culture views different groups of people—men and women, ethnic or racial groups, people in different occupations, people from particular families. Weber defined **power** as the ability to make people do what you want, even against their will. In every society, some individuals and groups have more power than others.

In Japan class inequalities make people uncomfortable. The Japanese don't want to have great inequalities of wealth or income in their society and they have made great efforts to minimize them. At the same time, Japanese people are undisturbed by sharp inequalities of status and power. Men and women occupy quite unequal statuses in Japanese society, and Japan also has several very small minority groups of quite low status. Power in Japan is closely held in the hands of a small elite of government bureaucrats and big business leaders.

A History of Change

For most of its history (up until the Meiji Restoration), Japan was a society of hereditary status rankings: it was a **caste society.** Everyone was born into their parents' caste, as aristocrat, samurai, commoner, or (those in the most menial occupations) outcaste. Caste was destiny: everyone had to live and marry within the caste, no matter what his or her talents might be, and there were rules regulating what members of different castes and subcastes were permitted to do and wear. Especially during the Tokugawa period (1635–1853), caste divisions were very carefully enforced (Reischauer, 1977, p. 158).

Meiji Inequality

Then, in one of Japan's most remarkable self-transformations, the Meiji government declared that "the four orders are equal" and legal distinctions between the castes were officially discarded (Fukutake, pp. 27–28). Remarkably, most caste distinctions faded from people's awareness after they were legally abolished. Although the descendants of samurai continued to be more likely than other Japanese to occupy elite positions into the 1960s, samurai ancestry came to hold little interest for Japanese people. Even noble ancestry is ignored in Japan today. The only exception is the descendants of the outcastes, the *burakumin:* those still identifiable face a persistent, though unacknowledged prejudice (Reischauer, 1977, pp. 159–160).

But inequality by no means disappeared from Meiji Japan, rather, it changed its character. In the early twentieth century, class inequalities grew as Japan industrialized. Rural land was concentrated in the hands of a wealthy landlord class, while the growing industrial economy quickly came to be dominated by the *zaibatsu*—the small number of vastly powerful, family-owned business conglomerates with close ties to government and the military (Chapman, p. 198).

Postwar Equality

But the story is far from over for, remarkably, World War II ushered in yet another era of Japanese social stratification. Defeat destroyed Japan's industry and left nearly everyone poor. Any remaining inequalities were leveled by the American Occupation reforms, which broke up the landlords' estates and distributed the land to the peasants, dismantled the great *zaibatsu* empires and purged their executives as war collaborators. Occupation authorities instituted progressive income taxes and (briefly) supported labor unions. The Americans, and radical Japanese, attracted to the Socialist and Communist parties, which flourished after the war, rebuilt Japan on egalitarian foundations (Chapman, p. 198).

Contracts between labor and management followed the principle of equal pay for equal work, regardless of the education, skill, or status of the employees. Unions aimed for a "livelihood wage" for all, and there was little difference in the pay received by blue- and white-collar employees. New schools, shaped by the Occupation authorities, and by teachers' socialist unions, tried to create equal opportunity through education. Teachers told their students that everyone had equal ability; hard work and perseverance were what counted for success. Schools did no IQ testing or ability grouping, so each class was a cross section of the community (Chapman, p. 199). Postwar egalitarianism drew on traditional values of simplicity and restraint, and a suspicion of wealth derived from trade that dated back before the Meiji Era. As a result, those in high positions tended to disguise their wealth. Executives avoided conspicuous luxury in dress or housing and took buses and trains like their employees.

Class Inequality in Japan Today

Much of the postwar egalitarianism has survived into the present. Class differences are weaker in Japan than in most advanced capitalist societies. Though there is certainly a range of incomes, the poorest and richest strata are relatively small in Japan. In fact, Japan ranks with Sweden and Australia as one of the three industrialized societies with the most equality in income distribution. Blue-collar employees are still paid only slightly less than white-collar workers. Only 1.2 percent of the Japanese population receive welfare payments (Fukutake, p. 158) and the number of people who are skid-row bums, petty criminals, able-bodied but permanently unemployed, or who are born to a life of welfare dependency is very tiny. In Japan, the richest fifth of the population receives only 4.3 times as much income as the poorest fifth. Compare this to Mexico where the richest fifth receives 13.5 times as much income as the poorest fifth, or the United States where the comparable figure is 9 times as much. (See Table 1.3.)

TABLE 1.3. Distribution of Income in Six Societies: Income is distributed more equally in Japan and Germany than in Mexico, Egypt, and the United States.

	Income Shares		
	Percent of Income Received by Poorest 20% of Households	Percent of Income Received by Richest 20% of Households	Ratio of Income Share of Richest 20% to Income Share of Poorest 20%
East Germany, 1985	12.2	29.8	2.5
West Germany, 1988	7.0	40.3	5.8
Japan, 1979	8.7	38.7	4.4
United States, 1985	4.7	41.9	8.9
Mexico, 1984	4.1	55.9	13.6
Egypt, 1974	5.8	49.3	8.5

Sources: World Bank. *World Development Report 1994: Infrastructure for Development,* New York: Oxford University Press, 1994; *World Development Report, 1988: Opportunities and Risks in Managing the World Economy.* The World Bank. New York: Oxford University Press, 1988.

Within Japanese corporations, there is also an unusual equality of incomes. The average corporate department head is paid approximately 3 times what the lowest-paid employee receives. Company presidents average 6 to 7 times the pay of newly hired recruits. (By contrast, in the United States and Europe, executive pay averages 30 to 40 times starting employee pay.) (See Chapman, p. 200.) In late 1988, Japanese company presidents averaged $240,000 per year in salary and bonuses, about 10 percent of average American CEO pay. Similar pay differentials prevail in Japanese government offices. Without high incomes, Japanese executives are unable to accumulate great wealth. High inheritance taxes and heavy taxes on high incomes also make it difficult to pass on any wealth amassed (Chapman, p. 200; Reischauer, 1977, p. 161).

Relative equality of income and wealth have gone hand in hand in Japan with a lack of social-class differentiation. People with unequal incomes and occupations mix socially. In city neighborhoods modern luxury towers have been built in the midst of old tumbledown houses, and since almost all residents send their children to neighborhood public schools, children from different class backgrounds become friends. Also, school uniforms mask class differences.

In addition, cultural differences among Japanese people of different social classes are minimal: there are no class accents, and style of dress, leisure pursuits, even the newspapers and magazines people read, vary very little along class lines. Japanese people spend a lot of time in association with those higher or lower in class position than themselves in the typical hierarchical relationships, and in the close group associations of school and office. They spend little time in groups which bring together those of one class or status. Even Japanese unions are distinctive in this respect, joining both blue- and white-collar workers of a particular enterprise. It is not surprising that feelings of class identity are undeveloped: 85 percent of Japanese people identify themselves as middle-class.

Social Mobility and Class Inequality

Because the Japanese are uncomfortable with class inequalities, they support an educational system that puts tremendous effort into making sure that children from all classes have a relatively equal chance to achieve success through education. All public schools in Japan are centrally controlled by the Ministry of Education, and it is ministry policy to make sure that all elementary and junior high schools are equal and uniform. There are no budget disparities between schools in rich and poor communities in Japan. All have the same facilities, and teachers are paid on the same scale in every school. Teachers are even rotated from school to school every five years to ensure that all children have the same quality of instruction. This system works to provide greater upward mobility for poor children than exists in most other industrialized nations. One in three children from the poorest 20 percent of Japanese families ends up attending a university, an unusually large percentage.

To a remarkable degree, Japanese society is a **meritocracy,** a social system in which one's place in the social stratification system is based solely on merit, or achievement, not on inherited advantage (or disadvantage). Education is the heart of Japan's meritocracy: academic excellence and high scores on achievement tests are the ticket to high-status jobs. A child's school performance, at an early age, has a lifelong impact, and there are very few second chances. As a result, competition is fierce and childhood is a serious time. From junior high school on, children are occupied with preparation for exams. They put in long hours of study and attend cram schools *(juku)* after school and on Saturdays. (It should be noted, however, that children don't compete directly against others in their *kumi.* They compete impersonally on national exams.)

Competition for Success

High school entrance exams are a conspicuous moment of truth in the lives of Japanese children. High schools are ranked in prestige, the higher-status schools serving as feeders for the most prestigious universities. Almost everyone goes to some high school, but only students with good school records are permitted even to take the tests for the most prestigious schools. At the end of high school they must again take very difficult, competitive exams for admission to college. But then those who excel can gain admission to prestigious "national" universities, practically guaranteeing access to higher-paid, high-status jobs. As many as three-quarters of the people hired for upper-level civil service jobs, and almost half the company presidents in Japan are graduates of prestigious Tokyo University. Many companies don't even bother to recruit employees outside a few select universities.

Whether they attend college or not, students' high school performance is crucial. For students who go into the labor market after high school, job placement depends on school performance: close coordination between employers and schools results in all hiring being done through the school. In fact, direct contact between employers and students is forbidden. Schools have a great deal of power to decide which student will get which job, with decisions based on grades, attendance, and behavior. Students who have failed to conform find themselves left with temporary, low-paid work (Leestma, p. 58).

Class Inequality Increases

Despite postwar egalitarian institutions and beliefs, inequalities of income, wealth, and opportunity, though still minimal, are increasing today in Japan. Economic conditions of the 1980s sharpened inequalities in Japan, as in many other industrialized nations. Land prices shot up to fantastic heights, particularly in downtown Tokyo, and the Japanese stock market soared, stock prices increasing by a factor of ten. Some quite modest families who happened to own or inherit downtown property found themselves millionaires overnight, and even greater fortunes were assembled by others through real estate or market speculation (Chapman, p. 202). Old values of frugality and restraint gave way to a burst of conspicuous consumption. Expensive western goods—designer-label clothes, foreign cars, and art works—became fashionable and credit cards were introduced. Corporate executives now lived lavishly at company expense, enjoying headquarters in palatial office towers, and sometimes even company apartments. Limousines took them to expensive restaurants, bars, and golf clubs, all paid for out of corporate expense accounts. The luxurious corporate lifestyle was emulated by the newly rich, and by young women and middle-aged couples who spent their earnings on consumer goods, rejecting traditional habits of saving (Chapman, pp. 174, 190–194).

Class Polarization

In the 1980s and 1990s, a minority of employees (less than a third of full-time workers) continued to enjoy lifetime security, high wages, and guaranteed promotions in their jobs with major corporations. An increasing percentage of workers, especially women, were much less well off: they worked full-time for smaller companies at lower wages; or they worked in the rapidly expanding force of part-time workers, often putting in as much as thirty-five to forty hours a week, but at low wages and without security, benefits, or union membership. Part-time workers are not even counted in unemployment statistics.

At the same time, Japan's thirty-year rise in real incomes and standards of living began to slow. In the 1980s, wages failed to rise as rapidly as productivity and profits. The cost of living rose, led especially by the price of housing, which for the first time began to put home ownership beyond the reach of middle-class families (Chapman, pp. 179–181). Japanese employees became aware that they lived poorly—squeezed into tiny apartments in concrete towers, often as far as two to three hours from work.

While many Japanese found themselves to be worse off, a new generation of wealthy Japanese inherited advantages from their wealthy parents. Doctors inherited their fathers' practices, and the children of politicians took over their fathers' seats in the Diet and their carefully nurtured political support groups (Chapman, p. 203). A new kind of private school, the "escalator school," attached to a prestigious university, enabled affluent families to advance their children from first grade to university without the stress of taking entrance exams (Condon, p. 128). In 1991, a scandal revealed corruption in the system of competitive exams for college entrance. Officials of Meiji University, a prestigious private school, secretly hired bright undergraduates to take exams for the sons of wealthy families, some of whom paid as much as $100,000 for the service (Sanger, 1991, p. 4). During the 1980s, increasing inequality of incomes, in lifestyles, and in taxation was widely noted and there was outspoken disapproval of the new trends, so contrary to the egalitarian values still inculcated in Japanese schools.

Status Inequality in Japan: Minority Groups

Japan is a very homogeneous society; it has few groups which differ racially, ethnically, or socially from the rest of the population, and the groups it does have are very small. At most, 4 to 5 million people out of the total population of 120 million could be classified as members of **minority groups,** groups which are seen as inferior and are treated unequally by the **majority** population. It may seem strange to you that even though Japanese minorities are very little different from other Japanese, they are nonetheless treated with distaste and face considerable discrimination (Reischauer, 1977, pp. 32–33; Tasker, pp. 23–24).

Sociologists note that societies treat their minority groups in a variety of ways, ranging from pluralism to genocide. A **pluralistic** society takes a positive view of group diversity and minorities are permitted, or even encouraged to keep their separate identities, languages, and customs. Pluralistic societies believe that people can be different without being unequal. Many societies reject pluralism and aim for **assimilation** of minorities, requiring that they adopt the values, language, and customs of the majority. If assimilation works, minorities join the majority culture and they are accepted and become equal. Japanese society officially promotes assimilation of minorities but, actually, minorities who may not be very different from majority Japanese are often excluded from mainstream society. They face **discrimination** in employment and marriage, and **segregation** in their place of residence. But Japan has never gone to the extreme of **genocide,** the physical extermination of minorities, which has happened in many other societies.

The Ainu

The oldest Japanese minority is descended from the Ainu, the ancient race that inhabited Japan before Asian settlers arrived more than a thousand years ago. The Asians pushed the Ainu north into the less desirable, wintry islands at the top of Japan. They also intermarried with the Ainu, so that today many of the Ainu have been absorbed into the majority population. About 20,000 Ainu still live as a distinct group. They are poorer than other Japanese and are looked down upon. Today, the Ainu are becoming more conscious of themselves as a minority group. They are writing down their aboriginal language before it disappears, and have come to identify themselves with the aboriginal peoples of Alaska and northern Canada with whom they believe they are racially linked, and whose experience with settlers they see as similar to their own (Reischauer, 1977, pp. 32–33; Tasker, pp. 23–24).

Ethnic Japanese

Only 900,000 foreigners live in Japan—less than 1 percent of the total population—and most of these are Koreans whose families migrated or were brought to Japan during the period when Japan annexed Korea in the aggression which led up to World War II. Even those Koreans who were born in Japan and speak only Japanese are not now granted citizenship and face discrimination by employers (Reischauer, 1977, pp. 32–35; Tasker, pp. 23–24).

A new minority in Japan is the growing community of approximately 150,000 people of Japanese descent who were born in Brazil and Peru. Faced with a shortage of unskilled workers, and fearful of illegal immigration from other Asian countries, the Japanese government decided to welcome Japanese of foreign descent whose ancestors had emigrated in the past. Japanese Brazilians and Peruvians, many of them skilled and educated, have come to Japan seeking escape from their countries' troubled economies. In Japan they take factory jobs, often living in company dormitories and working fourteen-hour days. These new immigrants are "racially" identical to the Japanese, but culturally they are different. They speak and laugh loudly and embrace in public, and hold street festivals with salsa and samba music. The Latin Americans face discrimination in Japan: they are treated fearfully in restaurants and stores and often exploited by labor contractors. "The Japanese treat us like some kind of inferior race," said one Brazilian immigrant (Weisman, p. 1).

The Burakumin

Not all Japanese minority groups are racial or ethnic minorities. The *burakumin* are Japanese, but they are rejected nonetheless. They are the descendants of Japan's ancient "outcastes," those who did dirty jobs (like butchering or leatherwork) considered offensive by others. The *burakumin* today are physically and culturally indistinguishable from other Japanese. Only their family names and sometimes the neighborhoods where they live mark them for discrimination and distaste. Estimates of the number of *burakumin* today range from 1.2 million to 3 million, no more than 2 percent of the population (Pharr, p. 76).

Burakumin faced the most intense discrimination during the Tokugawa period when they were required to live in separate villages, and to defer to majority Japanese in an exaggerated way, for example, by removing or prostrating themselves when they met a majority group member. They were forbidden to enter temples, shrines, and festivals. When the caste system was abolished during the Meiji period, *burakumin* became legally free of restrictions. But, in fact, discrimination continued. The Ministry of Justice itself referred to *burakumin* as "the lowliest of all people, almost like animals," and they continued to be excluded from temples and public baths (Pharr, pp. 76–77).

Today, *burakumin* face discrimination in employment and marriage. It is common practice in Japan for families to hire a "marriage detective" to research the background of a prospective spouse whose family is not known to them. Marriages are canceled when the family is traced to a *burakumin* village. The same thing happens when employers research the family background of new hires. "Buraku placename registers" are (illegally) sold in Japan. As a result of this discrimination, *burakumin* have lower incomes and less education than majority Japanese; they follow more insecure occupations, and have higher crime rates than other Japanese, and this feeds the contempt in which they are held, perpetuating their disadvantage (Pharr, pp. 77–79).

Since World War II there have been several active "*burakumin* liberation groups" with large memberships, which do research and carry out protest activities. In 1969 several major cities passed *burakumin* affirmative action policies, designed to improve the school performance of *burakumin* children, through remedial classes and counseling. These measures have often had the **unintended consequence** of calling attention to the children's *burakumin* background and low status, and exposing them to bullying. Other measures were devised to prevent majority Japanese from withdrawing their children from schools with a large *burakumin* population. *Burakumin* have been so excluded and isolated from majority society that it has been relatively easy for them to develop a strong sense of group identity and to organize protests (Pharr, pp. 85–88).

Status Inequality Based on Gender

The deepest inequality in Japanese society is also based on status. Gender inequality, the subordination of women to men, is built into Japanese institutions, shaping family life, education, and the economy. There is little public objection to gender inequality in Japan. Almost everyone assumes that the purpose of a woman's life is to serve others, especially her children and her husband.

Women in Japanese History

Centuries ago, early in Japanese history, women apparently held a higher status. After marriage, a man became part of his wife's family. The ancient Japanese religion worshiped a goddess, Amaterasu, from whom the royal family still claims descent. There were even a number of powerful empresses from the third through the eighth centuries A.D. (Condon, pp. 2–3).

Japanese society changed, however, between the sixth and eighth centuries when Chinese culture was so enthusiastically imported. Confucian belief in the inferiority of women was also adopted. Women were told it was their duty and their fate to be humble and self-sacrificing, to obey first their fathers, then their fathers-in-law and their husbands, then their sons. In public, they shuffled three steps behind their husbands. Especially during the conservative Tokugawa period (1635–1853), the subordination of women was strongly enforced. Women could own no property, and their husbands could divorce them readily for failure to produce sons, or even for quarreling with their mothers-in-law. Women who committed adultery could be punished by death (Condon, pp. 3, 20, 181).

The reforms of the Meiji Restoration gave a small boost to women's status. Girls were allowed an elementary education, and a few girls' high schools were established. Women were granted the right to divorce their husbands. This period also saw the first stirrings of feminism in Japan. But it was not until after World War II that any major changes in the status of women took place. Industrialization and urbanization liberated women from the *ie* and from the necessity of arranged marriage. With longer lives and fewer children, more women were drawn into the paid labor force. Immediately after the war, American Occupation authorities imposed legal reforms guaranteeing women new rights, including the right to vote, the right to attend universities, and the right to marry by "mutual consent." But while women were less oppressed after World War II than they had been before, they remained very much subordinated to men (Condon, pp. 23, 181).

Women's Status Today

Analysts disagree about the extent of women's subordination in Japan today. Some observers argue that Japanese women are still fundamentally unequal to men, in status, power, and wealth. Journalist Jane Condon contends that Japanese women now walk not three steps but "half a step behind" their men (p. 1). It is accepted by both sexes that women are fundamentally different from, and inferior to, men. Their role in life is seen as a supporting one, their duty to devote themselves to the care of children, old people, and husbands; to be patient and "endure" and put their own needs last.

Women defer to men; they giggle behind their hands, act shy, cute, and submissive, and lower their eyes. They are taught to listen and quietly observe men to interpret men's feelings and anticipate their needs. When women do speak, they are expected to have small, high voices and to use the forms of "respect speech" that express hesitation. At home and at work, women are the backup support, providing graceful personal service, but excluded from public life and institutional power. The feminist movement in Japan is tiny, and has little influence.

But many sociologists in the United States and Japan respond that the status of Japanese women is more complex. While women are certainly subordinate in the public realm of life, "offstage" at home they exercise considerable power. Japanese wives are in charge of family budgets and, with their husbands away at work so much, they are the emotional center of family life. Many psychologists and anthropologists claim that Japanese women manipulate their husbands and children by playing the role of the martyr. Feeling guilt for inflicting suffering on their wives and mothers, Japanese men and children spontaneously strive to please them. Other analysts depict Japanese men as dependent on their wives, both physically and psychologically. Anthropologist Takie Sugiyama Lebra describes the traditional wife as offering her husband so much "around the body care" that he cannot even find his socks without her. Women speak of their husbands as like another son, only older. Should we say that Japanese women occupy a powerful status in the Japanese family? Should we go as far as some analysts and call the Japanese family a "matriarchy"? Or are Japanese women exercising the kind of indirect, manipulative power which is the only resort of those who are dominated by others (Kato, pp. 184–185; Lebra, 1984, p. 133)?

> *Shoko Sato was born in 1947, part of the postwar baby boom generation. Her life experience as a woman has been somewhat different from her mother's, but there have also been strong continuities. Shoko began attending school at age 5 and she went to coed schools all through university. Like her mother, she married at age 24, but her mother's marriage was arranged through a go-between after only one meeting, while Shoko met her husband at the university and the young couple enjoyed spending time together and talking.*

Shoko worked in an office after graduating university (unlike her mother, who never worked outside her home). She enjoyed working very much. Her department chief was very kind to her and he allowed her an unusual amount of responsibility for organizing the legal work on contracts. Shoko wanted to continue working after she married, so she felt terribly frustrated and confused when her boss immediately began to talk about a party for her "retirement" when he learned of the engagement. It was too embarrassing to try to explain that she had imagined she could keep working, and she didn't want to suggest that he hadn't understood her. So Shoko went along. Anyway, her first child was born just a year after the marriage, and Shoko firmly believed that she should fully devote herself to her children.

While Shoko plunged into the world of babies and mothers, she was still in some ways disappointed in her marriage. The companionship she and her husband Hideo had enjoyed in college seemed to vanish in the face of his obligation to work long hours and travel frequently for his company. Shoko drove him to the station every morning at seven, and waited up for him at night until he returned at ten or eleven, since he didn't carry a key to the apartment. At any rate, she wanted to give him dinner and run his bath for him and lay out his clothes for the morning. Hideo turned his paycheck over to her and she arranged the family finances. They moved several times and each time Shoko searched for the new apartment and made the decision to buy it, since her husband was too busy at work to join her. Raising her children was a great joy to Shoko. At every milestone, like starting first grade, or graduating junior high school, she relived her own happy childhood and strove to make her children's as secure and loving as her own. Shoko became active in the PTA and found friends among the mothers of her children's classmates. Helping her son and daughter with their homework and driving them to lessons took a lot of her time. But when the children were sick, or when her son was difficult to manage, Shoko felt very much alone and anxious. As the children grew older, she missed taking care of them and life seemed somewhat empty. She took some adult-education classes with her friends in pottery and English. Her husband left her activities and the management of the household and children completely up to her (see Iwao, esp. pp. 31–51).

Gender Segregation

One thing is clear about Japanese adult men and women: their roles are highly segregated. They lead separate lives. The word "wife" in Japanese literally means "inside person" (Condon, p. 1). It is the wife's role to be in charge of the home and children. The husband is the "outside man," who goes out into the world, relieved of all worries at home. He is sometimes referred to as a "boarder," so uninvolved is he in household matters. In a real way, the primary ties in the family are those between mothers and children. Women are expected to live through their children, taking pride in their successes and blaming themselves for failures. A common figure of fun is the "education mama" who pressures and cajoles her child into excelling at school. She devotes her life to driving her children to extra classes, even taking notes during the lesson, the better to drill the child later on.

Women and Work

It is also clear that, economically, Japanese women are unequal to men. Their job opportunities are much more constricted and their earnings less. In Japanese society everyone is expected to marry, and almost everyone does. Adulthood doesn't really start until marriage, so single people in their late twenties or early thirties are considered peculiar. Age 25 for women and 27 for men are considered the cutoff points by which one should definitely find a mate. Between high school or university graduation and marriage, women are expected to work outside the home; but they are employed in ways that keep them dependent, separated from and subordinate to men.

Office Ladies. Young women find they have few job alternatives. They are excluded from the corporate system of lifetime employment with seniority pay, and are confined mostly to clerical jobs, with no prospect of promotion. Only a tiny percentage occupy managerial positions.[4] A job considered highly desirable for young women is "office lady" (called OL), especially with a prestigious company. OLs are selected for looks, since their duties are minimal: they do photocopying and filing, make tea, and tidy up. They are really a corporate status symbol, employed to be decorative and act as hostesses for business guests. Newly hired OLs are trained in bowing, greeting phone callers correctly, and offering tea. They are expected to live with their parents, and most companies will not hire girls who don't live at home, unless they live in the company dormitories provided for some female factory workers. Office ladies are expected and pressured to "retire" when they marry, and consequently companies often prefer to hire high school or junior college graduates who will have more years to work before marriage, rather than university graduates. Two-thirds of companies don't even accept applications from women university graduates (Tasker, pp. 102–103; Condon, p. 194). (See Table 4.1, p. 172.)

The most important economic role Japanese women are expected to play is not a paid job; it is their supporting role; because women take on all household responsibilities, men can devote themselves utterly to work, and can be available for transfer from one company location to another.

Changes in the Status of Women

Powerful forces are at work in Japan today, changing women's roles and values. But there are equally powerful counteracting forces, absorbing change and quieting protest. New demographic and economic trends have had the combined impact of drawing married women into the workforce. The average 40-year-old woman today in Japan has no small children at home, but has another forty years of life ahead of her. For women, middle age has become a period of crisis. Divorce rates are highest, and increasing most rapidly, among women in their forties and fifties. Many women tire, after a while, of filling their days by lunching with friends, taking classes at the local cultural center, or doing volunteer work. Often, they turn to paid work, both for meaningful occupation and to help pay rising family expenses.

Since 1977, more employed women have been married than single, and a full third of the workforce is female (Condon, pp. 219, 263). But married women work

---

[4]Condon (p. 276) reported in 1985 that top executives of the 27,000 companies listed on the Tokyo Stock Exchange included only twelve women, and ten of those headed family businesses.

on terms even more disadvantageous than do single women. Accommodating the needs of their families, most married women find unskilled work with flexible hours near home in supermarkets, fast-food shops, department stores, and small factories. One-fourth have been absorbed into the rapidly growing part-time work-force which is not unionized and receives no benefits (Condon, p. 194; Tasker, p. 103). More and more Japanese companies now hire a small core of men for full-time, lifetime security jobs, and then accommodate the ups and downs of the business cycle with part-timers, often women. (See Table 1.4.)

Young Women. Most young Japanese women embrace the roles for which they are raised, but some young women are orienting themselves to new goals and values. Many young women who attend four-year universities (and most do not, they go to junior colleges),[5] are no longer content with clerical work and are searching for managerial and professional, promotion-track jobs. Ambitious women often find such positions only with foreign companies (Condon, p. 194). (See Table 5.3, p. 247.)

Unmarried women are also taking new pleasure in their working years. Living at home, and relatively well-paid, they have money to spend on clothes and foreign travel, and they enjoy a freedom from obligation unequaled at any other point in their lives. There is a noticeable trend among such women to postpone marriage, ignoring the age 25 deadline, to the dismay of young men (Itoi and Powell, pp. 38–39).

Young women also want more companionate marriages. Many seek "love marriages," meeting their spouses through friends or at work, but 25 percent of all marriages are still arranged marriages in which the man and woman are formally introduced by a third party, who examines their family background and credentials. Though both men and women now say that spending time with family is important to them, the pressures of Japanese work life allow little more than a routine Sunday outing, and there is no sign that corporations are ready to decrease the demands

---

[5]Women are 90 percent of junior college students and only 23 percent of university students (Condon, p. 119).

TABLE 1.4. Working Women 1990–1992: Half of all Japanese women work, but they earn only half of what men earn.

	Percent of Women 15 and Older Who Work for Wages	Women's Wages as a Percentage of Men's
Germany	45	74
Japan	51	51
United States	56	70
Mexico	34	Not available
Egypt	30	80

Source: The World's Women 1995. Washington, DC: Population Reference Bureau, 1995.

they place on male workers. It will also be difficult for Japanese women to demand wider roles and greater social recognition, for to do so would run counter to all their training to duty and self-effacement in the service of social harmony.

Inequalities of Power in Japan Today

Formally and officially, Japan is a western-style parliamentary democracy. Democracy means rule by the people; it means power should be widely and equally distributed among all citizens. Democracy is the opposite of dictatorship or monarchy, in which a single person or a small group rules the people. After Japan's defeat in World War II, democracy was imposed by the American occupying forces, who saw Japan as a kind of test for democracy. If the Occupation could create the conditions for democracy in militaristic Japan, then, the Americans reasoned, democracy could work anywhere (Fukutake, pp. 78, 81–82). Occupation authorities created a legislature (the Diet) with an upper and a lower house, political parties, a prime minister, and a liberal constitution guaranteeing free speech, universal suffrage, labor's right to organize, and the rule of law. In theory, the people govern by electing representatives who make laws implemented by the bureaucracy. Japan's economy was also remade to resemble western ideals. The Occupation destroyed Japan's powerful family-owned conglomerates (the *zaibatsu*) hoping to encourage a free-enterprise economy in which economic power also would be widely and equally distributed among a great many small companies.

Government and Business: Western Structures, Japanese Spirit

Japanese society did not turn out the way Occupation forces intended. Though Japan today has a legislature, a prime minister, political parties, labor unions, interest groups, and stockholders, these western institutions function in a distinctly Japanese fashion. Parliamentary structures are actually the *omote* face of Japanese power. In reality, power is highly concentrated in the hands of a small elite. Japan is run by a partnership among government bureaucrats, legislators, and industrialists. Most powerholders are not elected, and power is exercised almost entirely behind the scenes.

In Japan's tripartite power structure, commonly called the "iron triangle," the government bureaucracy stands at the top, coordinating its power with that of business leaders and elected officials. The power of the bureaucracy in Japan is traditional; it goes back to the twelfth century. Through the centuries Japan's rulers developed a national administration, staffed by samurai (Ueda, pp. 131–133). In Meiji Japan it was this administration which acted to bring about modernization, subsidizing and nurturing new industries and building needed infrastructure. After a brief period in the 1920s when *zaibatsu* entrepreneurs, rather than government, dominated the economy, Japanese militarists reimposed state controls, beginning their war buildup. After Japan's defeat, General MacArthur removed the old *zaibatsu* chiefs, promoting middle-level managers in their stead, but left in position government bureaucrats who had wartime experience in economic coordination (Chapman, pp. 91–92, 97; van Wolferen, 1989, p. 7).

The Bureaucracy

Bureaucrats today, who work in the various government ministries like the famous MITI (the Ministry of International Trade and Industry), actually draft the legislation that is brought to the floor of the Diet. According to Atsushi Ueda, "we might go so far as to say that a Diet session is a kind of ceremonial performance, to give people inside and outside Japan the impression that decisions are being made democratically" (Ueda, p. 129). Then after passage, the bureaucracy implements laws and policies it has developed and sent to the legislature. But bureaucratic power extends further, because the bureaucracy doesn't simply mechanically apply the law; it exercises what is known as "administrative guidance," flexibility in enforcing regulations.

A major focus of bureaucratic efforts is economic development. For example, after World War II, MITI bureaucrats supplied investment capital to enterprises, choosing which companies and which industries to support; they selected foreign technology for import and decided where to send Japanese products for export and taught companies how to produce for export. In each important industry, they selected a few strong companies and encouraged them to compete with each other for market shares and profits, while sheltering them from foreign competition. MITI also helped companies unite in government-guided federations. As time went on, and private industry grew stronger and was able to raise more of its own capital, MITI relaxed its direct controls.

But even today, ministry officials guide, stimulate, and restrain the economy, using as tools their control of currency and exchange rates, direct government subsidies, tax breaks, grants for research and development, bank loans, import licenses for technology and raw materials, and permissions for joint ventures with foreign firms. Companies have learned to heed official "administrative guidance" because of the bite of bureaucratic sanctions (Chapman, pp. 103–107; van Wolferen, 1989, p. 33).

The Japanese accept bureaucratic power because it is traditional in their society and because they agree with the goals of bureaucracy. Japan's bureaucrats don't use their power for their own personal benefit. Instead, they use it to promote Japan's economic interests abroad and to limit competition and restrain the growth of inequality at home. According to Ueda, Japan's bureaucrats strive to improve the living standards of poor people, to help struggling new businesses, and to make sure that no business becomes so successful that it drives its competitors out of business (Ueda, pp. 130, 137).

Who are Japan's powerful bureaucrats? They are an elite group, but not a hereditary elite. Young people who attend Japan's top universities may enter the bureaucracy, and it is considered very prestigious, very respected work. There is no sense in Japan that bureaucrats are corrupt, or incompetent, or wasting the taxpayers' money. Because Japan's educational system provides opportunities for upward mobility to children of every class, the bureaucracy is open to talent. It is staffed by people from all class backgrounds, who have succeeded by excelling in school. People see bureaucrats as society's best and brightest. They see them as apolitical: bureaucrats are not allied to any political parties. They are pragmatic and solution-oriented. And the ministries are actually quite lively places, where officials in various departments and sections compete with each other to gather information, come up with new ideas, and solve problems. Japanese bureaucrats are flexible; they can shift policy readily when the situation demands it (Ueda, pp. 134–136).

Business

Bureaucrats are linked to business leaders in many ways. First of all, the corporations are the main source of the taxes which fund ministry operations, so it is in bureaucrats' self-interest to support business (Ueda, p. 137). In a way it is difficult to decide whether bureaucrats are the masters or the servants of business, since all their efforts are aimed at maximizing the long-run expansion of industry. Today, industry in Japan is far different from the thousands of competing small firms Occupation authorities envisioned. Japanese business is big business and it is highly organized to coordinate economic activity. Industries are organized by sector: auto manufacturers in one association, iron and steel companies in another, their industrywide organizations setting unwritten rules for business operations, and successfully pressuring members to comply. *Keidaran,* the federation of industrial organizations, brings together officials and chairmen of the boards of all the industrial associations.

But this is only the beginning of business organization. Most large corporations also belong to conglomerates: there are six giant ones which date to the early post-war years, and a number of newer, smaller ones. Conglomerates organize companies from many industries around a bank, also bringing in real estate, insurance, and trading firms. Conglomerates are united both by interlocking directorates and by joint stock ownership. It is customary for 60 to 70 percent of all shares in Japanese companies to be held by other companies in their conglomerate. These shares are never traded: held off the market they link the companies of a conglomerate together and make outsider takeovers of companies impossible. Organization goes further: each member of a conglomerate heads a *keiretsu,* a hierarchy of subsidiaries, suppliers, distributors, and subcontractors. Small enterprises produce for firms higher up in their *keiretsu,* both protected from the market and dependent on the larger companies (van Wolferen, 1989, pp. 34, 46–47). When bureaucrats use "administrative guidance" to direct the economy, they are dealing with organizations that collectively control fantastic amounts of capital, coordinate whole industries, and employ millions of Japanese.

The Elected Government

The official institutions of Japanese power: the legislature, the political parties, the prime minister, the cabinet, and the electorate, are probably the weakest partner in Japan's ruling triumvirate. This was especially true in the 1990s, after the first defeat of the Liberal Democratic Party (the LDP) inaugurated a period of weak, shifting party coalitions.

The LDP held power and dominated Japanese politics from 1955 until 1993, running what was essentially a single-party system. The LDP was a vote-getting machine: politicians treated politics as the business of getting elected; the legislature seldom legislated; the prime minister was often a relative unknown installed by behind-the-scenes kingmakers and had very limited power; and the cabinet served a merely ceremonial function, automatically approving policies developed by the bureaucrats. Over the decades, the party itself became divided into cliques, loyal to different leaders, but not distinguished by different ideologies or programs. The Socialist Party and a small Communist Party served as the perpetual opposition, but never had any chance of achieving power (van Wolferen, 1989, pp. 45, 110).

What then is the role of elected officials? What power do they have? Politicians play the role of go-between linking citizens with business and bureaucrats and helping all three groups informally trade favors and influence with each other. The politics of the construction industry illustrates this relationship. The Ministry of Construction controls licenses for the entire industry and it has a huge budget to spend on government construction. Politicians use their contacts in the ministry to get construction projects approved for their home districts. Then the communities that elected them benefit from jobs and local spending. Local construction companies are big contributors to political campaign funds, and they are rewarded with contracts. Then politicians reward retired construction ministry bureaucrats by helping them gain election to parliament, reinforcing the connections between politicians and the ministry (van Wolferen, 1989, pp. 114–120).

With regret, Seiichi Kawashima admits to himself that his graduation from the University of Tokyo is approaching. College has been fun; it has been the most relaxed period in Seiichi's life, but now the pressure is on again. His father had made it clear that he expects Seiichi to go on to the University of Tokyo law school in order to qualify for a job in one of the important government bureaucracies, like MITI. At 55, Seiichi's father is approaching retirement from his government job, but he has no intention of quitting work. He will become a director of one of the companies he has regulated all these years. Seiichi's maternal uncle retired two years ago and was elected as an LDP legislator.

Seiichi cannot help but be aware that he is the child of two of the oldest governing families in Japan. If nothing else, the busy matchmakers bring the point home to him. Though his father emphasizes that Seiichi may not even think of marriage until he is securely employed, Seiichi knows the matchmakers are already calling his father with the names of the daughters of important politicians, successful businessmen, and top bureaucrats. Seiichi would rather make his own choice. After all, he has certainly met enough of the same sort of suitable young women at the university and at summer resorts.

A Political Revolution? (Or Maybe Business As Usual)

Party financing, the most undemocratic part of the Japanese parliamentary system, has, in recent decades, given rise to a series of major scandals which culminated in the breakup of the long-ruling LDP. Everyone knows that politicians receive contributions from business in exchange for favors. As long as such exchanges don't emerge into the public, *omote* realm of politics, everyone looks the other way. But in recent years, influence peddling has become too obvious to ignore and several major scandals have broken out; the "Recruit scandal," the "Lockheed scandal" of the 1980s, and the 1992 scandal involving LDP leader Shin Kanemura and a Yakuza-owned company. The amounts of money involved in these scandals are huge ($4 million in the Kanemura scandal) (van Wolferen, 1989, pp. 29–32; Chapman, pp. 145–166).

The Kanemura scandal set off a major realignment in Japanese party politics. After thirty-eight years of political rule, the LDP split into seven reform parties and an LDP "rump." When the reformers (in alliance with the Socialists) elected a young, handsome prime minister, Morihiro Hosokawa, who promised to make politics a matter of issues, not influence, it seemed that a new era of politics had begun. Hosokawa offered an ambitious, detailed program for reform, unusual in a society where politicians seldom take any clear position on issues. He vowed to decrease government regulation of the economy, to tame the bureaucracy, and create a rule of law by elected officials. He promised to reapportion voting districts to put power in the hands of Japan's urban majority, and to stop political corruption by limiting business contributions to campaign funds.

But by 1994 political reform bogged down. Hosokawa's coalition did not have enough votes to pass strong reform legislation. While politicians negotiated, the bureaucracy moved in to fill a political vacuum, increasing its power. When Hosokawa was himself toppled from office by an influence-peddling scandal, Japanese politics began to return to business as usual. Hosokawa's government was followed by an even weaker reform coalition led by an old-fashioned politician who had only recently left the LDP and was part of Shin Kanemura's faction. This government lasted only two months and was followed by a strange new government: a coalition of the Socialist Party and the rump LDP, and headed by Socialist Prime Minister Tomiichi Murayama.

Now there are two broad political coalitions in Japan: a coalition of conservative "reformers," many of whom are old LDP politicians, and the Socialist/LDP coalition. There are few differences between the two coalitions, except that the reformers sound a bit more critical of bureaucrats than do their opponents. Perhaps Japan is headed for a new, competitive two-party system, but it is equally possible that party politics will continue to shift and splinter while the bureaucracy rules Japan.

SOCIAL CHANGE AND THE FUTURE

It is hard to assess just how much Japan is changing, culturally and socially. American journalists eagerly record every hint of American and European influence: when the Japanese play soccer, buy L. L. Bean clothes, or embrace Disneyworld, you will be sure to read about it in American newspapers. But Japanese culture is still tremendously durable. The Japanese still prize effort, self-discipline, education, conformity, and harmony. How much real change is taking place?

The Growth Consensus

Certainly there are some signs of change. For forty years after the Occupation, the Japanese were in agreement about their society's goals and the means to use to achieve their goals. Business, government, and the Japanese people agreed that industrial expansion was their nation's goal: everything was geared to it. Starting in the 1950s, companies competed fiercely, not for profits but for market shares.

Business executives took the long view, pouring revenues into capital reinvestment, always aiming for long-term growth, not short-term profits. The ministries used their power to lure business into growing sectors and advancing technologies and helped companies secure foreign markets.

Japanese workers and consumers supported this "growth consensus" because they benefited. Wages doubled and redoubled. Companies promised job security and rising wages in exchange for worker loyalty, and once-radical unions were de-clawed. The Japanese "embraced the drama of business growth," making business their national identity (Chapman, pp. 120–121). People looked up to big companies and business life became glamorous. The "salaryman" going to work became a kind of warrior, headed into battle, with the nation cheering him on. Today, how-ever, Japanese companies face stiff international competition. Real wages are no longer rising rapidly, fewer workers are hired with lifetime security, and Japanese employees no longer see their standards of living constantly improving. Can the "growth consensus" hold as the rewards from it diminish? Sociologists and jour-nalists see several sources of social change in Japan today.

Individualism

Japan's growth consensus depends on the willingness of the Japanese people to put the good of the group and the nation first in their lives. Japanese men work such long hours they have almost no time for family life or personal life. Children ded-icate themselves to study, sacrificing sleep, leisure, and time with their friends. Women become the devoted support staff for children and men, caring for their families alone or serving male employees in the office. If men or children or women rebel against these demanding roles, it will force change in Japanese society.

Since the early 1980s, Japanese opinion polls have tracked the growth of more individualistic attitudes, especially among the young. More and more Japanese say they value individual self-expression, independence, family, friends, and free time, over work and the company. The word *maihomu* (from the English "my home") has entered the Japanese language to denote the family as a private sort of refuge from the pressures of Japanese life. There is a new trend among younger families to spend Sundays together in family activities. But it is still too soon to tell whether these changes herald a broader shift in Japanese roles.

Women are one possible source of change. They are postponing marriage, but still marrying, leaving the workforce and having children. However, they are hav-ing fewer and fewer children, so that if they marry in their late twenties, by their late forties they are relatively free of child care responsibilities and increasingly ea-ger for some new outlet for their energies. Up to this time, Japanese society has not found any new rewarding role for the growing numbers of discontented middle-aged women.

Young people are also a potential source of change in Japanese society. In the last five years, thousands of young Japanese on student visas have settled in the East Village neighborhood of New York City, savoring the coolness and freedom of Vil-lage life. "In Japan people think too straight," said one Japanese store clerk. "Japan is a very conservative country," said another Village resident. "If people show their own personality or sexuality in public, people look down on them. Here it's like no-body cares" (Steinhauer, p. CY4). But in Japan, most young people are not rebels. They continue to work hard in school, devote themselves to their companies, and marry as expected. Perhaps the possibility of moving to New York is a kind of safety valve for discontent in Japanese society, allowing the most rebellious and nonconformist young people to leave.

Consumerism

With so much pressure to conform, it is not likely that any more than a small mi-nority of Japanese women or young people will rebel. Much clearer is a trend to in-creasing consumerism among Japanese of all ages, but especially the young. Japan-ese teenagers look upon shopping as recreation. They spend their money on brand-name clothing, "cute" novelty products, telephone party lines, karaoke boxes, and a tremendous amount of both information and entertainment media—magazines, comic books, CDs, music tapes, and the hardware to go with them (White, pp. 112–137).

With greater exposure to information about other countries, adult Japanese have come to realize that while their nation is rich, they themselves have a lower standard of living than their counterparts in other prosperous industrial countries. Because of protective tariffs, food and consumer goods cost more in Japan than in other industrial societies. Housing costs are very high, so most employees live in tiny apartments, a long, crowded train ride from work. They work long hours too, often six days a week, and take few vacations. Furthermore, the level of public amenities is low; there are few parks or libraries and half of all Japanese are not even connected to public sewer systems. In the past, the Japanese took for granted that the sacrifices they made were worthwhile; that they would gain as their nation prospered and that the company would take care of them in the meantime. But now, just as Japanese employees have begun to ask for an easier and more luxurious life, economic problems have made it difficult for companies to maintain even the past level of benefits.

Hosokawa, the first "reform" party prime minister promised to improve the quality of life for ordinary Japanese, by reducing prices on consumer goods and giving consumer needs priority over corporate expansion. Japan has been taking some tentative steps in this direction, by permitting discount stores, and by allow-ing the sale of (much cheaper) American rice. Some companies are campaigning to induce their employees to take all the vacation days due them, but without much success, since the pressures to demonstrate dedication to the work group are so strong. Japan's leaders have not yet addressed the problem of housing costs and long commutes. It will be interesting to see what solutions the bureaucracy can come up with when they do.

Citizenship

The third force for change in Japan today is the desire for a western-style democ-racy responsive to voter demands. Reformers have promised a multiparty or two-party system in which the parties represent clear political alternatives, and elected legislators, not appointed bureaucrats, make the decisions that shape the economy and society. The American press hailed the collapse of the LDP as a political revolution, ushering in an era of western-style voter activism. But, while politicians are addressing themselves more to consumers and voters, using TV for the first time to seek support, it is not at all clear that Japanese voters have really changed. Most remain apathetic and cynical about politics. According to Karel von Wolferen, there really is no such thing as public opinion in Japanese society. Newspapers present an *omote* face which never challenges the wisdom of the bureaucracy. Interest groups are narrow and national political action groups are lacking (van Wolferen, 1993, pp. 62–63). Most Japanese still seem to assume that for their country to prosper, direction must come from the top, from the highly educated and expert bureaucrats who are still enormously respected. The idea that sensible policy could emerge from public debate, political advertising, and voter opinion surveys is still totally foreign to Japan.

Predicting Change

Caution is in order when anticipating change in Japanese society. Japanese institutions of power are very flexible. So far, government and business have adapted readily to changing economic and social conditions, using the entry of women into the labor force to solve a potential shortage of workers, and finding ways to make environmental controls a source of profits. One must be cautious too in predicting major changes in Japanese values. While there are undoubtedly rebels and free-market advocates, it is not clear that they represent a direction in which most Japanese are headed.

Based on our understanding of Japanese society, we might predict that if major change does come to Japan, it will probably be concerted change, led by the bureaucracy, business, and the politicians, in order to respond to a perceived foreign threat. It probably will not be cultural change filtering up from the bottom.

Thinking Sociologically

1. When you read Chapter 1, were you ethnocentric in your reaction to the Japanese?
2. Using a highlighter pen, go through pages 7 to 15 of Chapter 1. Highlight descriptions of Japanese values in blue and descriptions of norms in yellow. Are you confident you understand the difference between values and norms?
3. When some large American luxury cars were recently put on display in Tokyo, many Japanese shoppers said they wouldn't want to purchase them. "I would get a lot of attention if I drove that car," one woman said. Using what you now know about Japanese society, decide what kinds of cars you would choose to export to Japan if you were making this decision for an American auto company.
4. What are some Japanese values that contrast sharply with values in your own society?
5. What social groups are most important in the lives of the Japanese? What groups are most important in *your* life, in your society?

6. How are offices in your society physically arranged? (Are the desks separated, or all touching, as in Japan? Are there cubicles? Separate offices with doors?) Are offices in your society similar to Japanese offices or different? What kinds of interaction and attitudes does office arrangement in your society encourage?
7. Turn to Table 1.2 (p. 33) and compare the homicide rates in Japan and in the United States. Thinking sociologically, can you explain what causes the tremendous difference in these rates?
8. Are there any similarities in the roles of women in Japanese society and in your society? What differences are there?

For Further Reading

BAYLEY, DAVID H., *Forces of Order: Policing Modern Japan.* Berkeley: University of California Press, 1991.

BUMILLER, ELIZABETH, *The Secrets of Mariko: A Year in the Life of a Japanese Woman and Her Family.* New York: Times Books, Random House, 1995.

FEILER, BRUCE S., *Learning to Bow: An American Teacher in a Japanese School.* New York: Ticknor & Fields, 1991.

FUCINI, JOSEPH J., and SUZY FUCINI, *Working for the Japanese: Inside Mazda's American Auto Plant.* New York: Macmillan, Free Press, 1990.

HENDRY, JOY, *Marriage in a Changing Japan: Community and Society.* New York: St. Martin's Press, 1981.

IWAO, SUMIKO, *The Japanese Woman: Traditional Image and Changing Reality.* New York: Free Press, 1993.

LO, JEANNIE, *Office Ladies, Factory Women: Life and Work at a Japanese Company.* Armonk, NY: M. E. Sharp, 1990.

PHARR, SUSAN J., *Losing Face: Status Politics in Japan.* University of California Press, 1990.

WHITE, MERRY, *The Material Child: Coming of Age in Japan and America.* New York: Free Press, 1993.

Bibliography

BACHNIK, JANE, *"Kejime,* Defining a Shifting Self in Multiple Organizational Modes," in Nancy R. Rosenberger, ed., *Japanese Sense of Self.* Cambridge: Cambridge University Press, 1994.

BAYLEY, DAVID H., "The Forces of Order in Japan and in the United States," in Gregg Lee Carter, ed., *Empirical Approaches to Sociology.* New York: Macmillan, 1994, pp. 101–119.

BENEDICT, RUTH, *The Chrysanthemum and the Sword.* Boston: Houghton Mifflin, 1946.

BORNOFF, NICHOLAS, *Pink Samurai: Love, Marriage and Sex in Contemporary Japan.* New York: Simon & Schuster Pocket Books, 1991.

BROOK, JAMES, "Jobs Lure Japanese-Brazilians to Old World," *The New York Times,* Aug. 13, 1992, p. A5.

BURUMA, IAN, *The Wages of Guilt: Memories of War in Germany and Japan.* New York: Farrar, Straus & Giroux, 1994.

CHAPMAN, WILLIAM, *Inventing Japan: The Making of a Postwar Civilization.* Englewood Cliffs, NJ: Prentice-Hall, 1991.

CHRISTOPHER, ROBERT C., *The Japanese Mind: The Goliath Explained.* New York: Simon & Schuster, 1983.

CONDON, JANE, *A Half Step Behind: Japanese Women of the Eighties.* New York: Dodd, Mead, 1985.

DOI, TAKEO, *The Anatomy of Dependence.* Tokyo: Kodansha, 1977.

DUKE, BENJAMIN, *The Japanese School.* New York: Praeger, 1986.

EARHART, H. BYRON, *Religions of Japan.* San Francisco: Harper & Row, 1984.

FEILER, BRUCE S., *Learning to Bow: An American Teacher in a Japanese School.* New York: Ticknor & Fields, 1991.

FUCINI, JOSEPH J., AND SUZY FUCINI, *Working for the Japanese: Inside Mazda's American Auto Plant.* New York: Macmillan, Free Press, 1990.

FUKUTAKE, TADASHI, *Japanese Society Today,* 2d ed. Tokyo: University of Tokyo Press, 1981.

HENDRY, JOY, *Marriage in a Changing Japan: Community and Society.* New York: St. Martin's Press, 1981.

INOUE, SHOICHI, "Religions Old and New," in Atsushi Ueda, ed., *The Electric Geisha: Exploring Japan's Popular Culture.* Tokyo: Kodansha International, 1994, pp. 220–228.

ISHIDA, HIROSHI, *Social Mobility in Contemporary Japan.* Stanford, CA: Stanford University Press, 1993.

ISHIDA, TAKESHI, *Japanese Political Culture: Change and Continuity.* New Brunswick, NJ: Transaction Books, 1983.

ITOI, KAY, and BILL POWELL, "Take a Hike Hiroshi, *Newsweek,* Aug. 10, 1992, pp. 38–39.

IWAO, SUMIKO, *The Japanese Woman: Traditional Image and Changing Reality.* New York: Free Press, 1993.

KATO, RYOKO, "Japanese Women: Subordination or Domination," in James Curtis and Lorne Tepperman, eds., *Haves and Have-Nots: An International Reader on Social Inequality.* Englewood Cliffs, NJ: Prentice-Hall, 1994.

KRISTOF, NICHOLAS D., "Japanese Say No to Crime: Tough Methods, at a Price," *The New York Times,* May 14, 1995, pp. 1, 8.

KUWAYAMA, TAKAMI, "The Reference Other Orientation," in Nancy L. Rosenberger, ed., *Japanese Sense of Self.* Cambridge: Cambridge University Press, 1994, pp. 121–151.

LEBRA, TAKIE SUGIYAMA, *Japanese Women: Constraint and Fulfillment.* Honolulu: University of Hawaii Press, 1984.

————, ed., *Japanese Social Organization.* Honolulu: University of Hawaii Press, 1992.

LEESTMA ROBERT, *Japanese Education Today.* U.S. Department of Education, Washington, DC: Government Printing Office, 1987.

LO, JEANNIE, *Office Ladies, Factory Women: Life and Work at a Japanese Company.* Armonk, NY: M. E. Sharpe, 1990.

MEYER, CAROLYN, *A Voice from Japan: An Outsider Looks In.* New York: Harcourt, Brace Jovanovich, 1988.

NAKANE, CHIE, *Japanese Society.* Berkeley: University of California Press, 1970.

The New York Times, "The Murayama Surprise," Oct. 23, 1994, p. E14.

PHARR, SUSAN J., *Losing Face: Status Politics in Japan.* Berkeley: University of California Press, 1990.

POLLACK, ANDREW, "Hosokawa's Failure Dashes the Hopes of Many," *The New York Times,* Apr. 17, 1994, p. 10.

———, "Suicides by Bullied Students Stir Japanese Furor," *The New York Times,* Dec. 18, 1994, p. 20.

REISCHAUER, EDWIN O., *The Japanese.* Cambridge, MA: Harvard University Press, 1977.

———, *The Japanese Today: Change and Continuity.* Cambridge, MA: Harvard University Press, 1988.

ROHLEN, THOMAS P., *Japan's High Schools.* Berkeley: University of California Press, 1983.

ROSENBERGER, NANCY R., ed., *Japanese Sense of Self.* Cambridge: Cambridge University Press, 1994.

RUDOLPH, ELLEN, "On Language," *The New York Times Magazine,* Sept. 1, 1992, p. 8.

SANGER, DAVID E., "Best College Money Can Buy" (Can It Be Bought?)," *The New York Times,* June 24, 1991, p. 4.

———, "In Japan's Astounding Future: Life with Father," *The New York Times,* Nov. 12, 1993, p. A4.

———, "The Outcome in Japan: Business Almost As Usual," *The New York Times,* Jan. 30, 1994, p. 3.

———, "Japan's Bureaucracy: No Sign It's Losing Any Power," *The New York Times,* Feb. 27, 1994, p. 3.

SESSER, STAN, "Hidden Death," *The New Yorker,* Nov. 14, 1994, pp. 62–89.

SMITH, ROBERT J., *Japanese Society: Tradition, Self and the Social Order.* Cambridge: Cambridge University Press, 1983.

STEINHAUER, JENNIFER, "Where Young Japanese Go to Get Away from It All," *The New York Times,* Dec. 4, 1994, p. CY4.

STERNGOLD, JAMES, "Mob and Politics Intersect, Fueling Cynicism in Japan," *The New York Times,* Oct. 21, 1992, pp. A1, A6.

———, "Life in a Box: Japanese Question Fruits of Success," *The New York Times,* Jan. 2, 1994, pp. 1, 6.

———, "Can Clamor for Change Be Stilled in Japan?," *The New York Times.* Jan. 24, 1994, p. A3.

———, "Japan Falls for Soccer, Leaving Baseball in Lurch," *The New York Times,* June 6, 1994, p. A6.

———, "Fear of Phrases," *The New York Times,* Dec. 18, 1994, pp. E1, E6.

TASKER, PETER, *The Japanese: Portrait of a Nation.* New York: Penguin Books, New American Library, 1987.

TOBIN, JOSEPH, "Japanese Preschools and the Pedagogy of Selfhood," in Nancy R. Rosenberger, ed., *Japanese Sense of Self.* Cambridge: Cambridge University Press, 1994.

TURNER, JONATHAN H., *Sociology: Concepts and Uses.* New York: McGraw-Hill, 1994.

UEDA, ATSUSHI, "How Bureaucrats Manage Society," in Atsushi Ueda, ed., *The Electric Geisha: Exploring Japan's Popular Culture.* Tokyo: Kodansha International, 1994, pp. 127–138.

UNITED NATIONS, DEPARTMENT OF INTERNATIONAL ECONOMIC AND SOCIAL AFFAIRS, "National Accounts Statistics: Compendium of Income Distribution Statistics," *Statistical Papers,* Series M, No. 79, 1985.

VAN WOLFEREN, KAREL, *The Enigma of Japanese Power: People and Politics in a Stateless Nation.* New York: Knopf, 1989.

———, "Japan's Non-Revolution," *Foreign Affairs,* Vol. 72, No. 4, Sept–Oct. 1993, pp. 54–65.

WEISMAN, STEVEN R., "In Japan, Bias Is an Obstacle Even for the Ethnic Japanese," *The New York Times,* Nov. 13, 1991, pp. A1, A10.

WHITE, MERRY, *The Material Child: Coming of Age in Japan and America.* New York: Free Press, 1993.

WILDEMAN, JOHN, "Crime and Crime Control in Modern Japan," unpublished material.

MEXICO

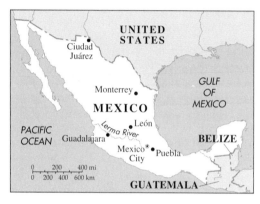 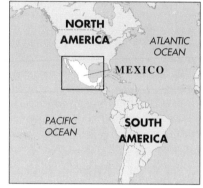

You can fly to Mexico from New York in five hours, from London in ten, or you can walk across a border bridge from Texas in five minutes. You will find yourself in a society created by the clash of Spanish and Native American peoples.

LOCATION: Mexico is just south of the American states of Texas, New Mexico, and Arizona. Mexico is bordered on the east by the Gulf of Mexico and on the west by the Pacific. To the south Mexico borders Guatemala and Belize.

AREA: One-fifth the size of the United States or Canada, Mexico (756,000 square miles or 2,128,600 square kilometers) is four times the size of Germany.

LAND: A rugged, mountainous country. Mexico City, the country's capital, is several thousand feet above sea level.

CLIMATE: Hot, humid, and tropical in the south, arid and desertlike in the north. Temperatures cool as one climbs higher. The year alternates between rainy and dry seasons.

POPULATION: 1995, 94 million people; in 2025 there will be 137 million Mexicans. A relatively young population, 36 percent of the people are under age 15.

CAPITAL: Mexico City: 21.6 million people.

INCOME: U.S. $3,750 per person per year.

POVERTY: 23 percent in absolute poverty.

EDUCATION: The average adult (25+) completes less than five years of school.

RELIGION: 93 percent Roman Catholic, 3 percent Protestant.

LANGUAGES: 91 percent speak Spanish, 8 percent also speak Indian languages such as Mayan, Nahuatl, Zapotec, and Mixtec.

CHAPTER 2

Mexico: Social Groups in a Diverse Society

INTRODUCTION

Visitors to Teotihuacán, the ancient Indo-American ruins 25 miles northeast of Mexico City, come upon richly carved walls, crammed with intricate patterns, picked out in sharp relief by the bright sunlight of the mountains. These stone carvings might well symbolize Mexico itself, a diverse society marked by strong social and cultural contrasts. There are really many Mexicos: urban and rural, rich and poor, European and Indo-American.

Mexico City is a twenty-first century megacity (Kandell, p. 8): it points the way to the problems of urbanization increasingly visible all over the world. Twenty million people live crowded into Mexico City's high, mountain-ringed valley: in apartment towers, leafy middle-class suburbs, and squatter shantytowns. They jam its highways, buses, subways, and markets, their cars spewing out a toxic haze of air pollution, their accumulating sewage and garbage a constant hazard. But in Mexico's rural hinterlands, village life proceeds at a very different pace. Though most villages now have electricity and roads, the modern world is distant. People grow the food they eat, often without machinery, and build their own houses; some wear traditional Indian dress. In the most remote villages, paths, not streets, link the houses; there are seldom any newspapers, and perhaps not even a telephone.

Even in Mexico City, the rich and the poor live so differently they might inhabit different societies. A rich teenager may drive an imported car, live in his family's air-conditioned house, wear European designer clothes, and dance at a club built to look as much as possible like one in New York or Los Angeles. The family's maid will probably travel four hours a day on packed buses and trains, returning at night to a one-room shanty with a bare light bulb (wired illegally to a city streetlight), a single mattress, and no refrigerator or running water.

Walk around Mexico City and you will see simultaneously the contrasting layers of Mexican history. At the famous Plaza of the Three Cultures, ancient Indian, colonial Spanish, and modern western cultures stand side by side. In this place where the Aztecs actually fought and lost their last battle against the Spanish, archeological excavation has uncovered ancient Aztec pyramids and carvings. Next to the ancient ruins you will see the sixteenth-century colonial church of Santiago Tlatelolco, built from the very stones of the defeated Aztec city. The plaza is

59

completed by the modern architecture of the Ministry of Foreign Affairs building (Nolen, p. xix; Kandell, p. 524).

For Mexicans, the Plaza of the Three Cultures represents their uneasy heritage of cultural diversity. The sixteenth-century Spanish *conquistadors* tried to obliterate Indian culture, but did not succeed. Through Mexico's tempestuous history, Indian and Spanish cultures became interwoven. Now a new element has been added to Mexico's diversity: the culture of the modern "global village," with its glass office towers, TV soap operas, and ubiquitous fast food.

Understanding Mexico: The Conflict Perspective

Just as Japanese society appears constructed to illustrate the structural-functionalist perspective in sociology, so Mexican society seems to call for analysis with the **conflict perspective.** When we examine Mexico we see all sorts of divisions and disagreements within the society. Diverse groups struggle for control of scarce resources and justify their claims with conflicting worldviews. Those who hold power use it to dominate others and to protect their own privileges. Disagreement about values is common. A conflict theorist, looking at Mexico's long history would contend that conflict and value **dissensus** (the opposite of consensus) are the normal condition of society, and any period of order is really a period of domination by one or another ruling group.

MEXICAN HISTORY

In order to better understand both the conflict perspective and Mexican society, you must first know something about Mexico's dramatic history. Mexicans themselves believe that their history holds the key to their character, and they relish its romance and extravagance. In every period in Mexican history, different groups struggled to control society so as to benefit themselves. Mexico's history is easy to understand, because it is divided by dramatic events into three clearly marked periods: the pre-Columbian, the colonial, and the modern.

The Pre-Columbian Period (c. 300 B.C.–A.D. 1519)

The earliest period of Mexican history was the longest: this was the pre-Columbian period (c. 300 B.C.–A.D. 1519) when the great Maya and Aztec and other Indo-American empires ruled Central America. By the first century B.C., there were great civilizations in Mexico, the equal of anything in Europe. The Indo-Americans built large cities, developed sophisticated systems of writing and mathematics, kept astronomy records, and built monumental works of architecture. These empires also fought frequent wars to subjugate neighboring peoples and make them pay **tribute** (goods which conquered people had to pay to their conquerors) and also to take captives who were made into slaves or sacrificed to the gods (Rudolph, pp. 5–8; Ruiz, pp. 18–20).

The Aztecs

The last Indo-American empire was that of the Aztecs, who rose to power in the fourteenth century. Dedicated to conquest, the Aztecs glorified fighting and bravery. Nobles ruled and merchants enjoyed a relatively high status, but commoners, conquered people, and slaves labored hard to build the gleaming pyramids, roads, and aqueducts of their capital, Tenochtitlán (site of today's Mexico City). The Aztecs exacted more and more tribute from subject peoples to make their gorgeous feathered cloaks and jewelry, and the resentment and hatred of the conquered peoples grew. The Aztecs' religion reflected their fascination with conquest and destruction. The sun and earth, they believed, were periodically destroyed and renewed. There had been four previous "suns" and their own epoch was the time of the "fifth sun," soon to be destroyed in its turn (Ruiz, p. 24; Rudolph, p. 14; Kandell, pp. 49–54).

The Conquest

The pre-Columbian period in Mexico ended in a new episode of struggle and domination in 1519, the year of the Spanish Conquest. Aztec religion predicted the next periodic destruction of the world in the year 1519. Legend held that at that time, the white-skinned Quetzalcóatl (god of the earlier Toltec people) would return from the sea and take back his empire from the Aztecs and their god, Huitzilopochtli. The prophecy proved uncannily accurate, since in 1519 Aztec society was indeed destroyed—but at the hands of the Spanish *conquistadors,* led by Hernán Cortés.

The Spaniards. At the time of the Conquest, Spanish society had much in common with Aztec society: both were shaped by war and religion. The most important force in Spain was the *Reconquista,* the politico-military "crusade" to recapture all of Spain from the Muslims or "Moors" who had ruled it for seven centuries. Under the leadership of Ferdinand and Isabella, Granada, the last bastion of the Moors, was reconquered in 1492. The crusader mentality glorified war and looked down upon agriculture and manufacture, which it associated with the Moors, and also looked down on finance, associated with the despised Jews (expelled from Spain in 1492). Spanish warriors found it proper to live off the labor of those they conquered, the crown rewarding them with land grants and "infidel" serfs.

Cortés and Moctezuma. Hernán Cortés was the very model of a conquistador, thirsting for adventure, greedy for gold, aggressive, brave, and ruthless. He was a brilliant strategist, able to switch gears instantly and turn misfortune to advantage. In 1519, at the age of 33, Cortés assembled 11 ships, 500 soldiers, 100 sailors, 200 Cuban Indians, weapons, and 16 horses and sailed from Cuba for the Yucatán (the southeastern coast of Mexico).

Once arrived in Mexico, Cortés quickly learned of the ruling power, the Aztecs and their current king Moctezuma in their capital, Technochtitlán. Chosen as king in 1503, Moctezuma was an unstable monarch, at times arrogant, but often paralyzed by depression and terror at the prophesied next destruction. The coincidence of Cortés's arrival from the sea in 1519 was extraordinary, and apparently unbalanced Moctezuma completely. Cortés's invading force was tiny, compared to the military might of the Aztecs. Three special weaknesses made the Conquest possible. First was the power of ideas: belief in the coming end of their world undercut Aztec resistance. Second, the Aztecs had made many, many enemies among neighboring peoples, who gladly joined Cortés, swelling his army from 500 to 10,000. It was not really Cortés who conquered the Aztecs, but the Aztecs' Indian enemies. Finally, if any European force really mattered, it was an army of European germs: smallpox—absent in the Americas—which arrived with the Spanish and ravaged Tenochtitlán.

The Colonial Period (1519–1810)

The Conquest ushered in 300 years of colonial rule in Mexico, now christened New Spain. Mexico's native peoples were inclined at first to see the Spanish as just the next in a long series of conquerors, but in many ways the Spanish empire was harsher and more destructive than any previous Indo-American rule.

The Spaniards wanted wealth from Mexico, gold or silver, ideally, but also sugar, indigo (a valuable dye), cattle, or wheat for export. They were not much interested in settling Mexico. The Spaniards in Mexico wanted to become rich and they wanted to do so by using Indian labor to extract the wealth of the land. The Spanish monarchy had similar ambitions: the king and queen hoped to tax Mexico's exports. The colonizers in Mexico had another goal too: they wanted to save souls and to convert the Indians to Catholicism and stamp out the worship of pagan gods.

A Genocidal Beginning

Spanish rule turned out to be much more disastrous for the native Mexicans than Cortés's Indian allies could ever have imagined. First of all, Spanish rule began with a tragedy—a "biological catastrophe"—a terrible plague of Old World diseases to which the Indo-Americans had no immunities. Measles and influenza, minor diseases in Europe, became killers in Mexico (as everywhere in the New World). Smallpox became epidemic. Demographers estimate a population of 25 million in central Mexico at the time of the Conquest; by 1650, only 1 million native Mexicans survived there (Kandell, p. 149; Wolf, p. 195). Disease wiped out families, villages, ruling classes, and whole cultures.

The Hacienda System

Without an abundant Indian labor force, Spanish colonizers' plans for wealth were frustrated. It took them until the seventeenth century to work out a sustainable system for colonizing Mexico: the *hacienda system*. The *hacienda* was an estate or plantation on which Indians were forced into a kind of slavery. Spanish colonizers helped themselves to the best land, and then offered to employ the now-landless Indians. They tricked the Indians into debt by giving them advances on their wages until they owed so much money they could never finish working off the debt. *Haciendas* were land-hungry: the more Indian land they could take, the more Indians they could force into dependence. They also imported some black slaves (Wolf, pp. 203–208; Ruiz, pp. 81, 102–103; Rudolph, p. 23).

The society the Spanish created in Mexico was highly race-conscious and racially stratified. Every person had an official racial classification: white, mixed blood, Indian, black, or one of the in-between statuses, and people had different rights based on their race. Having white skin conferred great privilege.

The Modern Period (1810–Present)

The modern period in Mexico began with the War of Independence, which freed Mexico from Spanish rule. Much of the modern period has been characterized by a high level of conflict between different groups. From 1810 until the early twentieth century, Mexico was in an almost constant state of upheaval as the different strata of Mexican society fought for justice, recognition, equality, or power. Every group had grievances: the wealthy colonists wanted more political independence; the middle class wanted greater economic opportunities, and the poor and the Indians wanted land, food, jobs, and an end to slavery and to tribute payments.

After declaring independence from Spain in 1824, rural guerrilla bands, royalists, and republicans fell to fighting each other. The next fifty years were marked by government instability and corruption and a succession of coups by generals. There were forty-two different governments between 1821 and 1855 (Kandell, p. 319). During this period of disintegration, Mexico lost Texas to the United States, lost the Mexican-American War, and suffered a French invasion and occupation. Finally, a new middle class emerged as the ruling elite. They looked toward Europe and sought to remake Mexico according to the ideals of the French and American Revolutions, as a capitalist republic. Mexico abolished slavery, established constitutional government on the American model, and guaranteed freedom of religion, but these paper reforms had little practical effect.

Order and Revolution

Order was finally imposed by a brilliant politician, Porfirio Díaz, whose eight terms of office as president, between 1876 and 1911 are known as the Porfiriate. Díaz advocated "order and progress" and threw all his tremendous power into modernizing the economy, securing international recognition, and attracting foreign investment. He built railroads and ports, extended electric and telephone service, modernized Mexico City, strengthened mining and agriculture, began oil exploration, and balanced the national budget. Díaz was ruthless in his exercise of power. He executed rival generals, massacred rebellious Indians, held fraudulent elections, and censored the press. The wealthy enjoyed a golden age during the Porfiriate, but the misery of the poor intensified, paving the way for Mexico's next great upheaval.

Mexico's revolution, begun in 1910, was one of the great early twentieth-century revolutions, like the Russian Revolution. The Mexican Revolution spoke for workers and peasants whose living and working conditions had steadily worsened in the late nineteenth century. The revolution rejected Europe as a model, asserted an Indian identity for Mexico, and committed the government to providing security for peasants and workers by redistributing land and income.

Middle-class liberals who wanted democracy started the revolution, but it blazed into violent struggle as it attracted those who had suffered most under the Porfiriate. Peasants and Indians, led by the famous Emiliano Zapata and by Pancho Villa, waged guerrilla struggles to take back land from the *haciendas*. Fighting continued for almost two decades, with every region convulsed by conflict between rival armies. A radical constitution promulgated in 1917 stipulated restoration of all Indian lands and national ownership of all natural resources, guaranteed free public education, an eight-hour workday, equal pay for equal work, and the right to organize and strike. Amid the prevailing disorder, most of these provisions were not put into practice for years, if ever.

Revolutionary Change

It was not until the 1930s, and the presidency of Lázaro Cárdenas that the government finally made good on its promises to retrieve for the Indians lands stolen by the *haciendas*. Cárdenas redistributed 46 million acres of land. Two-thirds of Mexican farmers received land, mostly through the creation of *ejidos*—landholdings given to villages to be held in common and assigned by the village for individual use—on the traditional Indian model. (Later, in the 1950s and 1960s, the government redistributed more land through *ejidos*.) Cárdenas also nationalized the whole oil industry (mostly foreign-owned), another enormously popular action.

Finally, poor rural Mexicans saw some improvements in their lives. Schools, roads, electricity, and hospitals began to reach the countryside. The number of people dependent on *haciendas* decreased. Now it became possible for the government to move from revolutionary change to the consolidation of power. Those who had benefited from reform were readily rallied as supporters of the government: *ejidos,* trade unions, and government workers were all organized into subsidiary units of the Institutional Revolutionary Party, the PRI. The party has dominated Mexican politics down to the present, making Mexican politics orderly, channeling benefits to organized peasants and workers, but also substituting one-party rule for democracy.

The Age of NAFTA

In the last decades of the twentieth century, Mexico has once again returned to the outlook of the middle-class modernizers like Porfirio Díaz. In the late 1980s and early 1990s, President Carlos Salinas de Gortari opened Mexico to free trade and foreign investment, assuring Mexicans that the best way to achieve a better life is to become part of the global capitalist economy. He signed the North American Free Trade Agreement (NAFTA), making Mexico, the United States, and Canada free-trade partners. But Mexicans are still very much divided in their views on development and westernization. Revolutionary peasants in the State of Chiapas demand a return to revolutionary values and land redistribution. In the more industrialized north, the business-oriented National Action Party (PAN) demands less government intervention and a more open economy.

MEXICAN CULTURE

Every era of Mexican history has left its own ambiguous cultural legacy. Spanish colonialism remade Mexico, but it didn't make it into a "New Spain." Nor did the revolution make Mexico an egalitarian democracy. A distinctive society developed, in which Indo-American, Spanish, western European, American, socialist, and Catholic influences were adapted and combined.

Mexicans debate the effects of Spanish colonialism on their society. In one view, Spanish and Indo-American cultures blended in Mexico. The Spanish colonizers tried their best to destroy Aztec civilization—its religion, cities, government, army, and system of social stratification—and to substitute their own church, Spanish law, and the *hacienda* system. They succeeded in eliminating Aztec institutions, but were less successful in destroying Indo-American culture. Instead, similarities between the two cultures facilitated blending: both cultures were warlike, hierarchical, and religious. Their family structures and norms were similar. Celia Falicov argues that "today the Spanish and Indian heritages are so fused that it is difficult to separate them" (Falicov, p. 135).

Some analysts (like Mexican writer Octavio Paz) have seen the colonial legacy as much more destructive. Paz argued that the experience of conquest and colonial domination caused lasting damage to the Mexican psyche. Mexicans, he contended, saw their origins in a historical act of violation and wished to deny both their Spanish and their Indian origins. Some contemporary socialists argue that today Mexico continues to be enmeshed in economic colonialism, distorting its development to serve the needs of multinational corporations, while unemployment, poverty, and undernourishment increase. In this view, relations of economic dependency are deeply embedded in Mexican society, shaping its political system as well as its economy (Paz, pp. 86–87; Barkin, pp. 11–22, 93–95).

Another view of Mexican society focuses on "cultures of resistance," rather than on a mentality of oppression. Advocates of this view point out that like conquered people everywhere, Indo-Americans adapted the culture of their oppressors to express their own values and goals. Struggling to survive the dehumanizing exploitation of colonialism, Indo-Americans were resourceful and creative, constructing new, adaptive institutions from whatever cultural materials were at hand. The legacies of colonial domination, of cultural blending, and of resistance to colonialism can all be seen in Mexico's religious heritage.

Catholicism in Mexican Culture

The most enduring legacy of the Conquest was Catholicism. Mexico became, and remains, a Catholic country. Colonial churches and images of Catholic saints are seen everywhere. Part of the legacy of Catholicism is the dualistic Mexican worldview, which sees life as divided into two realms: the "City of God"—the world of the sacred, of religion, home, and loyal friends—and its opposite—the "City of Man"—the public world of power struggles, appearances, and dishonesty (Goodwin, p. 6).

Catholicism arrived with the Conquest. Spanish friars immediately set about converting the conquered Indians. In Mexico City, one friar, Pedro de Gante, baptized Indians at the rate of 14,000 per day. Many writers have wondered why the work of conversion was so successful. In some measure, force was responsible: the Catholic Church drove out the old priests, destroyed the idols and temples, ended human sacrifice, and burned sacred books. Indians who refused to accept the new religion were sometimes tortured or whipped. But the Catholic clergy also offered genuine concern and care for the Indians and sometimes defended them against abusive colonial practices. Probably most important, the Church declared Indians to have immortal souls, to be human. In a dehumanizing colonialism, the Church offered Indians hope for justice.

In some ways too, Catholicism offered the Indians a way to continue their religious traditions after their own gods had failed. Colonial Mexico, like Aztec Mexico, was a society permeated by religious faith and ritual. There were similarities between Catholicism and Indo-American religions, so it was not difficult to join them. The Indians looked on the Catholic saints as an array of gods, similar to their own. They were familiar with rituals of baptism, confession, and communion, enacted in their own religion too. The cross was even familiar to the Maya, though their cross emerged from a base of carved snakes and represented the god of fertility (Brasch, p. 123).

In fact, the Indians adapted Catholicism to meet their own needs. Nowhere is this clearer than in the legend of the Virgin of Guadalupe, who became the patron saint of the Mexican Revolution. The story tells that in 1531, the Virgin Mary appeared before a humble Indian man at Tepeyac, just north of Mexico City, at the site of a temple to Tonantzin, the Aztec mother of gods. Miraculously her image appeared on his cloak, and lo! she was a dark-skinned Mary. Worship of the Virgin of Guadalupe spread rapidly in Mexico, and after initial opposition the friars accepted her (Wolf, pp. 165–175; Ruiz, pp. 66–70).

Catholicism in Mexico (as elsewhere in Latin America) absorbed and became joined to deep Indo-American religious feeling. As Carlos Fuentes, the famous Mexican novelist describes it, there is "a deep sense of the sacred and recognition that the world is holy." Shrines and altars, incense and flowers, religious ceremonies and processions make Catholicism in Mexico "a sensuous, tactile religion" (Fuentes, Mar. 30, 1992, p. 410).

Popular Religion

Everywhere that it has gone in the world, the Catholic Church has adapted to local practices of folk religion, and Mexico is no exception. Mexican Catholicism has absorbed local *fiestas* (festivals) and local Indo-American saints. All over Mexico, villages celebrate the saint's days of their patron saints with brass bands and processions, bright costumes, special masses, colorful decorations of the church and town, fireworks, bullfights, sports contests, food, drink, and dancing, and street sales of fruits, candy, and toys. Some *fiestas,* like Holy Week, Christmas, and the Festival of Our Lady of Guadalupe are national holidays.

El Día de Los Muertes. Probably the most famous of Mexico's fiestas is *El Día de Los Muertes* (The Day of the Dead). By an odd coincidence, both the

Dressed as the Virgin of Guadalupe, in her characteristic silver-starred cape and crown, a young woman walks at the front of a procession to celebrate the feast day of the Virgin, patron saint of this northern Mexican town.

Spanish and the Aztecs commemorated the dead on November 2, and this holiday fuses the two celebrations (as well as the Christian All Saints Day, November 1).

Weeks before November 2, candy vendors begin selling skulls of white sugar, decorated with sequins, ribbons, and foil, with first names on their foreheads. People buy skulls with the names of their dead relatives and set them on homemade altars, along with statues of saints, ears of corn, fruit, candy, foods the dead especially liked, soda, liquor and cigarettes, incense and candles. People give their friends gifts of cookies shaped like skeletons, or chocolate skulls, and engaged couples exchange sugar coffins with each others' names on them. Children are given macabre toys, like coffins from which skeletons jump (Braganti and Devine, p. 156; Nolen pp. 48–49). In towns and cities, there is a shopping rush to buy all these goodies.

Before midnight on November 1, Mexicans spread a path of flower petals from their doors to the altar, and settle down to await a visit from the dead. The next day, they jam the roads to the cemeteries, to bring flowers and candles and perhaps a toy for a dead child, and to clean up grave sites. There is a party atmosphere, as people picnic and chat with graveside neighbors. Afterward, at home, they feast on the food which the dead have enjoyed in spirit (Reavis, pp. 194–198).

Death. Death is not a taboo subject in Mexico. People like to remind themselves of the nearness of death. They treat death as an intimate, joking with it and cursing it. Many Mexicans find the lyrics of a recent popular song to be extremely funny:

Death you asshole, you basket of bones,
Quit kidding around!
Come take me to destiny!

People examine with interest the coffins displayed by undertakers in their shop windows, and they give thought to the nature of their own coming deaths, hoping to greet death calmly and scornfully.

It is hard to know whether the great emphasis Mexicans place on suffering is a legacy of Aztec culture, of Christianity, or of the experience of the Conquest. In any event, statues and pictures often show the Mexican Jesus bloody and exhausted, and Mexicans believe that suffering is an unavoidable part of life (Reavis, pp. 291–293).

The Saints. Every village in Mexico adopts a patron saint who watches over villagers. If you visit a village church, you will see a statue or doll representing the saint at a special altar. People pray to their patron saint and ask for miracles, often cures for illness, or good harvests. The saint of San Juan Jaltepac, for example, is a 3-foot-tall plaster statue of the Virgin of Candelaria. In Zapopan, the tiny doll-like Our Lady of Zapopan, covered in jewels, is said to protect against floods. The strangest saint, "Doctor Boy Jesus," saint of Tepeaca, is a doll dressed in medical whites, with an old-fashioned black leather doctor bag. "Doctor Boy" can heal the sick, and people keep pictures of him at home altars (Oster, p. 200; Reavis, pp. 200–203).

Doña Ana is a woman in her fifties who works as a maid for a middle-class family. Every night she takes the subway and two buses and returns to her family in Colonia Caultepac at the northern edge of Mexico City, where she lives with her husband, daughter, and granddaughter. When her granddaughter fell ill with hepatitis, the doctors at the clinic said they weren't sure they could save her. Doña Ana prayed to the Virgin of Candelaria. A special tiny room in her house contains an altar: a shelf covered with a lace tablecloth, with candles and a picture of the saint. Doña Ana burned candles to the Virgin and prayed every night. When her granddaughter recovered, Doña Ana cried with joy. She felt bad that she couldn't go to the Virgin's own church in San Juan Jaltepac to thank the saint. So Doña Ana saved her money and the next year, on the Virgin's own saint's day, she made the long trip to her village, bringing the saint flowers and candles. Doña Ana's foolish son José laughed at her, but she felt she did the right thing and that there could be no better use for her precious savings.

Religion and Politics

Despite the deep religious feeling of the Mexican people, organized religion in Mexico is treated with distrust, and associated with colonial oppression. Because Catholicism had been an essential part of Spanish colonialism, and because the Church was a huge and wealthy landowner, there was a great deal of anti-Church feeling in the War of Independence, and the new regimes that followed. The revolution was also intensely opposed to the Catholic Church. The Constitution of 1917 made the Church subject to civil authority and forbade clerics from running or teaching in primary schools, or even wearing their religious robes in public.

Today, paradoxically, Roman Catholic theologians are some of the most vocal and influential advocates of the values of the revolution. Clergy who believe in **liberation theology** argue that the church must take an active role in seeking justice and a better life for the poor. In 1991 Mexican bishops publicly condemned government corruption, torture of political prisoners, mistreatment of Indians, and election fraud. In 1994, church officials took an official role in negotiations between rebel Indian forces in the State of Chiapas and the Mexican government.

Dualities in Mexican Culture

The Catholic duality of the City of God versus the City of Man pervades Mexican society. Mexicans tend to see the world divided into opposites. One such fundamental divide is between the inner world of the home and family and the outer world of public life. Family and home represent loyalty, trust, and warmth to Mexicans. The family is "a fortress against the misery of the outside world" (Goodwin, p. 3). It is "the hearth, the sustaining warmth" (Fuentes, Mar. 30, 1992, p. 410). It could certainly be argued that Mexicans' colonial experience contributed to their dualistic view of the world. In colonial times, the public world was indeed a hostile, exploitative place for Indo-Americans. Developing a strong, protective family life was a healthy response.

Today, Mexicans who can afford it build high, solid walls around their homes, sometimes topped with broken glass. The mother is seen as the caring heart of the family, taking pleasure in serving her children and treasuring the loyalty they return. While respect for the father may keep him a somewhat remote figure, siblings are often very close, even in adulthood. For men, a small group of old friends may form another inner world of trust in which they freely let down their defenses and express their feelings, especially in the forgiving setting of a drinking party. In the popular mystery novels of Paco Taibo, for example, the hero is always rescued in a crisis by his drinking buddies or his sister and brother.

Negotiating the Public Realm

In contrast to the inner world of family and friends, the outer world is perceived as a dangerous, treacherous, corrupt place. Business, government, the police, unions, schools, towns, and neighbors are not to be trusted. Social relations in the public world require watchfulness. Outside the family, Mexicans hide their feelings and fears behind "masks of formality" (Riding, p. 10). Like actors, they practice what sociologist Erving Goffman called **role distance,** self-consciously playing a role fit for a situation, but not identifying with the role. Formal language, empty phrases, false promises, and even lies, allow Mexicans to meet role expectations without risking their real selves. Goffman would say that for Mexicans the world outside the family is a **front region** where people play their roles carefully and present a **managed impression** for public consumption, while at home in the **back region** they relax their guard.

Respect and Dignity

Mexicans attach great value to respect and dignity. *Respeto* in Spanish has a different meaning than does the corresponding word "respect" in English. In English, when one person "respects" another, it has a connotation of individuals acknowledging their essential equality. In Mexico, *respeto* is more like deference: it means that one person acknowledges the high status of another. Mexicans agree that people ought to be respected by others of lower status, by younger people and children, and that men ought to be respected by women.

Respect allows people to preserve their *dignidad.* Mexicans attach greater importance to honesty and the preservation of their dignity than they do to individual achievement. People will proudly depict themselves and their families as "poor but honest" (Falicov, p. 138). It is certainly possible to link these values to the colonial experience, when native Mexicans were so often humiliated by colonists, *hacienda* owners, and government officials. Under Spanish rule, it might have been impossible for an Indo-American to become a successful landowner, a wealthy man, or an official, but he could indeed be "poor but honest."

Norms of Public Formality

In the dangerous outer world, norms of public conduct help people show respect to one another and avoid unwanted provocation. Alan Riding points out that even in the dreadful Mexico City traffic jams, drivers are usually polite and rarely honk their horns. They are restrained by their distrust of potentially hostile strangers (Riding, p. 10). Mexicans also make heavy use of honorific titles to show respect. New acquaintances met at a party are addressed as *señor, señora,* and *señorita.* In business, people address managers with titles like director, doctor, *ingeniero* (engineer), or *licenciado* (someone who has a higher education degree).

Many Mexican folkways involve showing respect to another and allowing them to protect their dignity. Men reassure each other with rituals of physical contact. The *abrazo,* an embrace demonstrating friendship, always follows the same pattern: a handshake, a hug, two backslaps, another handshake, and a shoulder slap. Recoiling from the *abrazo* would be highly insulting, as would failing to say a formal goodbye when departing, or evidencing dislike for the food someone has served you. Showing respect is important in little gestures too. It is insulting to place money on the counter, rather than in the cashier's hand, and you would never toss a key to someone. If you bribe a policeman, or tip a maid, you tuck the money into their pocket or apron, so they needn't humble themselves by acknowledging it (Riding, p. 10; Braganti and Devine, pp. 139–155).

In the formal public world, appearances matter a great deal. Men try to impress each other with their importance. Being late to an appointment makes you appear a busy man; buying drinks a prosperous one. Poor neighborhoods bristle with TV antennas, though there may be no TVs inside the houses (Goodwin, p. 4).

Gender Dualities

One of the most important dualities in Mexican culture is the pair of strongly differentiated role ideals for men and women: the *macho* (more or less, "the real man") and the mother. Mexicans are fond of depicting these roles in film and fiction, self-consciously playing them in public, and also analyzing them in print. We must discuss Mexican gender roles carefully so as not to mistake a cultural stereotype for reality.

In Mexican culture, women and men are often depicted as deeply and tragically different from each other. Women, as mothers, belong to the City of God, set apart in the protected and protecting home. Motherhood is a sacred value in Mexico, and through motherhood, women become spiritual creatures, morally superior martyrs, long-suffering, patient, offering unconditional love and care to their families. Men, in contrast, are depicted as belonging to the City of Man. They live in the dangerous public world where they must guard their honor and battle for respect. Every man's life is an adventure story, a quest for recognition in a corrupt society. According to Celia Jaes Falicov,

> the ideal of "machismo" or "muy hombre" (manliness or virility) dictates that men be aggressive, sexually experienced, courageous and protective of their women (who include mothers, sisters and wives) and their children. The female counterpart of this ideal is a humble, submissive, and virtuous woman, devoted to her home and children. (p. 139)

Marianismo is the name given to the stereotyped martyred mother, who uses her self-sacrifice to inspire guilt in her children and manipulate the family (Falicov, p. 139).

It is important to realize that, as Falicov puts it, "cultural norms tend to refer to the public reality of how relationships or behavior 'ought' to be. These internalized behavioral prescriptions sometimes do not coincide with private realities, that is, how things 'really' are for each family" (Falicov, p. 137). In reality, some men are domineering, others have a more egalitarian relationship with their wives, and still others may be dependent on their wives' decision making.

The *macho* and the martyred mother are **stereotypes** as well as role ideals in Mexican culture. As stereotypes, people can "play" them; they can try to make others play them, and they can criticize and reject them. But stereotypes in any culture help "frame" interaction: they define alternatives and people respond to them as if they were real, even if they are too exaggerated to resemble any real individuals (Russell, p. 173). Some people do play the stereotypes, but they are more likely to be mocked than praised.

> *All his life, nothing had gone right for Wilfredo. He had been unable to make a living from the poor soil of his father's farm. Then, in Mexico City, the first house he built had been bulldozed in a government attack on the new squatter settlement it occupied. In the factory, he never seemed to get the promotions others received. But at least he was a man, a real man who protected his family, a man who could hold his own in any situation, hold his drink and give as good as he got in a fight. Wilfredo still bears a long, jagged scar from an encounter at work, when he confronted the man who was stealing finished work from his pile.*
>
> *But Wilfredo's wife Carmen sees it differently. Carmen says she still loves Wilfredo, but she wants him without his drinking. He gets insulted so easily; no wonder he can't get ahead at*

work. But what Carmen finds unforgivable is that he has driven away their oldest son, who moved in with his wife's family when they married. She can just see it coming: all their children will leave when they grow up and she'll be left, lonely and poor, still pacifying Wilfredo.

Now, Carmen thinks, Roberto, my brother, he's a different kind of man. I should have married someone like him. He doesn't drink or boast; he's always quiet and serious and dignified. Everyone trusts Roberto; his word is gold. Roberto never hits his children or threatens them. They respect him because he is a real man. (See Selby, p. 78 for a description of these two kinds of "macho.")

Just as people disagree about what it means to be a real *macho* man, so they debate about competing images of true womanhood. In traditional, dualistic Mexican culture there are two opposing images of the feminine: the sacred mother who submits and the aggressive, sexual woman who betrays. These are personified in two powerful symbols: the Virgin of Guadalupe, the miraculous Mexican Virgin Mary, the humble, long-suffering mother; and *La Malinche,* the dishonored other "mother" of the Mexican people. Octavio Paz, one of Mexico's most famous writers, helped shape his nation's image of *La Malinche* in his influential 1961 essay THE LABYRINTH OF SOLITUDE. As Paz told the well-known folktale, *La Malinche* was the Indian mistress of conquistador Hernán Cortés. Violated by Cortés, *La Malinche* betrayed her people and bore the first *mestizo* (mixed-blood) child. Mexicans proclaim their dishonored origins, Paz argued, by calling *La Malinche* *"La Chingada,"* rudely, "she who was raped," and themselves *hijos* (sons) *de la Chingada"* (Paz, pp. 74–87).

But some Mexicans now tell the story of *La Malinche* (or Malintzin, her real name) differently. Feminists see it as a "male myth" expressing distaste and fear of the female and portraying women as sexual pawns. They see Malintzin as the victim of two patriarchal societies (her own Indo-American society, since her parents sold her into slavery in order to increase her brother's inheritance, and Spanish colonial society into which she came as a slave) (Alarcón, pp. 183–185). Malintzin was a talented woman, who spoke many languages and was politically astute, and she struggled as best she could with oppression. She cannot fairly be blamed for causing the subjection of her Indian people. Blaming her simply distracts attention from the real roots of colonial exploitation (Madison, p. 11; Blea, p. 27).

Feminists today remind us that Mexican women have long been neither martyrs nor whores. They fought alongside men in the revolution, worked in factories, and participated in Mexican public life. Though they did not gain the right to vote in national elections until 1953, women have since become deputies and senators, occupied seats on the Supreme Court, and held high positions in the Institutional Revolutionary Party, the ruling party, known as the PRI. One woman ran for president as the candidate of a minor party and another served as secretary general of the PRI, the second-highest position in the party. In 1995, Rosario Green, from Mexico, is one of only six women who represent their countries at the United Nations, and she is the only woman who ranks as an assistant secretary general (Ruiz, pp. 425, 449; Riding, p. 249; Crossette, p. A14).

Individualism and Familism

Mexicans have been characterized both as individualistic and as **familistic** (that is, as putting the family before the individual). In the public world, Mexicans are individualistic: they see no reason to trust any institution that may demand their loyalty. They admire the matador or the boxer more than the team player in soccer or basketball. Mexicans personalize their history, telling it as a story about heroes and villains like Cortés, Zapata, Porfirio Díaz, and Lázaro Cárdenas. Successful politicians are never simply party functionaries; by force of personality they build a following of their own (Wolf, pp. 238–239; Riding, p. 5). Mexicans are clearly individualistic when compared with the Japanese or with Egyptians.

Mexican individualism makes sense as a legacy of colonialism. The Spanish conquerors purposely shattered Indo-American communities, evicting peasants from their land. During the colonial period a large population of displaced Mexicans roamed the country. They were landless Indians and people of mixed blood who had no official status and no legal rights. They traveled from place to place and job to job, living by their wits. Survival depended on adaptability, improvisation, and the ability to assume roles, and manipulate people, markets, and situations.

But Mexicans are also familistic: they are intensely loyal to their families and pride themselves on their willingness to put their families first. It is not uncommon for Mexicans to sacrifice opportunities for individual advance or enrichment in order to remain near their parents, or support their widowed sisters or other relatives. Mexicans see their status in society as an attribute of their families, not an individual quality.

In further contrast, those Mexicans who still live in traditional Indian communities are group-oriented, not individualistic or familistic. Anthropologist Eric Wolf makes a clear contrast: where the modern Mexican is rootless and individualistic, he says, Indians are rooted in their community. They cling to their group and their customs. Urban Mexicans value personal power and the ability to manipulate others, but Indians value collective control of land and avoid the accumulation of individual power (Wolf, pp. 238–240).

Cynicism and Fatalism

Mexicans don't believe they can control what happens in the future, so the idea of planning ahead seems foolish. Businesses aim for large, fast profits; government planning departments issue plans that no one believes will actually be acted upon; individuals save for a wedding or a fiesta, but not for retirement.

Also, Mexicans are cynical about the idea of "progress," about the value of modern science and technology. When things go wrong—when corrupt governments disregard the Constitution; when modern technology pollutes the countryside—Mexicans are cynically unsurprised. If the bus fails to arrive, if the store is out of what you need, people shrug and cynically say *"ni modo"* (literally "no way," but with the connotation, "that's life"). Fatalistically, they believe that people will always make mistakes; that life is mostly suffering and tragedy inevitable. They cite the old proverb "There is no evil that does not come from good."

Mexicans are cynical about personal accomplishments too, Dick Reavis explains. A Mexican who is ambitious says, *"tengo ilusiónes"* ("I have illusions"). He calls his ambition a weakness, and if you call him ambitious, it is a criticism. Mexicans have much more respect for qualities than accomplishments: a person is looked up to for strength, bravery, intelligence, or skill, rather than for particular achievements. People usually attribute a person's success to luck (Reavis, pp. 289–293). It is easy to attribute cynicism and fatalism to Mexico's tragic history of defeats and betrayals, but it is clear that fatalism was part of Indo-American culture long before the Conquest.

SOCIAL STRUCTURE AND GROUP LIFE

Sociologists often find it useful to distinguish between **culture** and **social structure.** So far, we have been discussing Mexican culture: Mexicans' distinctive norms and customs, their particular beliefs, attitudes, and values. When we are introduced to an unfamiliar society, we notice culture first. Sometimes it seems exotic: other peoples' religion, their holidays, food, art, and music may be noticeably different from our own. It takes longer to notice social structure, but it is equally important. Put most broadly, culture always involves meaning, while social structure describes how people organize their social lives. Every society is built out of **status positions,** like "student," "woman," or "employee," linked together in a **status system,** together with **roles** and **norms.** The resulting social structures may be small—like a nuclear family built of three statuses: mother, father, child—or they may be large and complex, like a corporation or university. Three distinctive types of social structures are found in all societies: **social networks, groups,** and **social institutions.**

Social Networks in Mexican Society

People in every society are members of networks. Networks are webs of relationships that connect each person to other people, and through them to yet others. People have family networks, and networks of friends, neighbors, coworkers, and so forth, and sometimes these networks interlock. You may find a job, or an apartment, or meet your spouse-to-be through your networks.

Networks are of enormous importance in Mexican society. Mexicans place great value on family loyalty, and as we have seen, they are distrustful of public institutions and nonrelatives. There is nothing in Mexican life equivalent, for example, to the importance of the company and the school in the lives of the Japanese. This leaves Mexicans with a problem: everyone needs relationships beyond the family, particularly in modern cities where one cannot count on being surrounded by relatives.

Compadrezgo and Personal Networks

Mexicans create relations of trust beyond the family by developing personal networks. One way they do this is by adapting the traditional Latin American practice of *compadrezgo* or godparenthood. It is customary for important occasions in a child's life, like baptism, confirmation, marriage, or even nonreligious events like graduation, or a first haircut, to be marked by the appointment of godparents, or "sponsors." A child then has many sets of godparents and the relationship between parents and their children's godparents is a special one. *Compadres,* as they are called, might be equals like neighbors, friends, or coworkers. Often people seek as *compadres* those of greater wealth or power, like bosses or local politicians. *Compadres* have a special relationship: they treat each other with formality and respect. The don't drink together or discuss personal matters. Because of this mutual respect, *compadres* can turn to each other for favors, like a loan of money. *Compadrezgo* creates personal networks, but not necessarily social groups, because each person's *compadres* are different, and one individual's *compadres* may not all know each other (Goodwin, pp. 8–9; Falicov, pp. 142–143).

Patronage

Mexicans also may construct networks by seeking out **patron-client relationships.** Traditionally, in rural villages, people sought out the local elite as *compadres,* to establish a kind of protected relationship with them. Nowadays, ordinary people are likely to become clients (or dependents) of patrons (or bosses) in other ways: by joining a political party, or community organization, or by becoming a follower of a local boss who controls access to stalls in a market or unionized jobs. Clients owe patrons loyalty, sometimes votes, and often payments of one kind or another. Patrons will often lend money in time of need, attend the client's saints' day celebrations, or even find ways to register a favored client in the national social security system (Selby, Murphy, and Lorenzen, p. 121).

Reciprocity Networks

Through kinship, friendship, *compadrezgo,* and patronage, ordinary Mexicans create what they call *redes de seguridad* (literally, "security networks"), or, as anthropologist Larissa Lomnitz terms them, **reciprocity networks.** Members of such networks are linked by exchange: they help each other find work; they lend each other food, money, pots and pans, even clothing. They visit back and forth and watch each other's children. They care for each other when ill, and in a crisis, they take in each other's children, for a day, or even for years. Economists used to talk of reciprocity as a mode of exchange found only in traditional societies (like the ¡Kung Bushmen) and absent in modern industrial societies, except for minor practices like Christmas gift giving. Lomnitz argues that reciprocity remains an important pattern in complex, modern societies, existing alongside exchange of goods for money: "the enduring importance of social connections and influence peddling in societies as different as Mexico, the United States and the Soviet Union attests to the fact that reciprocity as an economic force is today very much alive" (Lomnitz, p. 4).

A good example of a Mexican reciprocity network is a *tanda,* an informal, rotating credit arrangement. The members of a *tanda* are usually close relatives, neighbors, or coworkers who join together to help each other save and who must trust each other to continue contributing (Lomnitz, pp. 88–89).

Rosa, Carmen's daughter, is desperate to get married and leave home, but there is no money. She has only a slim hope. Next month is Rosa's turn for the tanda. She and Carmen and their two neighbors and two cousins each contribute 5 pesos weekly to the tanda, and then every month a different person gets to take the whole 120 pesos. When they began the tanda they drew lots to establish the order and now it is Rosa's turn. Her great plan is to use the money as a down payment on a sewing machine. With the machine, she figures that she and Héctor, her fiancé, will be able to afford to marry. They can live with Héctor's family, and she can sew piecework at home.

Social Groups in Mexican Society: The Household

Groups are more highly structured than networks. Group members occupy statuses, play roles that are special to the group, and have some kind of group culture: shared values and norms, perhaps group folkways, and even some special way of talking. Finally, group members interact regularly and they see themselves as a group, drawing a boundary between those who are members and those who are outsiders. Most people belong to many social groups: families, friendship groups, work groups, teams, clubs, and other organizations.

The social group of greatest importance to most Mexicans is the household, the group of people with whom they live. For poor urban Mexicans, it is household sharing and reciprocity that enables them to get along, to feed and clothe their families. In the majority of cases, the members of a household form one **nuclear family** (a family composed of two parents and their children), but it is considered desirable for households to shelter an **extended family** (several nuclear units linked by kinship), and, in fact, extended family households tend to be better off economically. Households may also include more distant relatives, godchildren, or even friends or neighbors.

Most urban Mexicans live in a detached house on a small plot of land (a *solar*). Ideally, they want a brick house with a wall to close the household off from the street. In this small domain, the household sets about *defendiendose*, or "looking after themselves" (Selby, Murphy, and Lorenzen, pp. 70, 89). Households are productive units, a functioning part of the economy. Households often raise animals for their own consumption or for sale; they sometimes open tiny workshops that produce textiles, carpentry, upholstery, or custom ironwork; or sidewalk businesses that do auto and truck repair or customize trucks. Sometimes household members take in washing or run sidewalk stands or rudimentary stores, selling fruit or milk, beer, crackers, and candy (Selby, Murphy, and Lorenzen, p. 71).

The Gómez household, consisting of fourteen people, lives in Ciudad Nezahuacóyotl, the huge working-class neighborhood east of Mexico City. Their solar contains a series of rooms grouped in a U-shape around a central patio. Here live three related nuclear families and two individuals, linked to the household by kinship. There is Don Ramón, the head of the household, his wife Consuela, their two teenage children, and a 5-year-old godchild, who all share the main room. Don Ramón's older son and his family live in another room, and a younger son and his family live in a third room. Both daughters-in-law have orphaned younger siblings living with them too. When each son married, the whole family worked together to build a new room. The children of all three families are raised by everybody in the household, and the women go out together to shop and visit church. They borrow food, money, and other items from each other.

Many facilities in the solar are shared by the whole household. There is a small pen for pigs, rabbits, and chickens, and a privy. Also, there is a woodstove, a barrel for water, which all share in refilling, and laundry tubs used by all. Consuela and her two daughters-in-law help support the household by taking in laundry. The two teenagers carry the laundry for Consuela when she collects and delivers it, and the two young mothers wash the clothes at home. The married sons work in the same factory and the older helped the younger get a job. Sometimes, when the factory is busy, they are able to get Don Ramón hired too. Each nuclear family keeps its separate finances, but the two married sons give their father a weekly allowance in exchange for the use of his solar. Don Ramón says that they all "stick up for themselves and keep going." (See Selby, Murphy, and Lorenzen, p. 70, and Lomnitz, pp. 112–114, for descriptions of similar households.)

SOCIAL INSTITUTIONS

The Gómez household is a social group, but it also illustrates a third aspect of social structure. It shows us some of the characteristics of the Mexican family, a major Mexican **social institution.** While social groups are concrete units of real people, social institutions are patterns of behavior. Sociologists use the term "social institution" when they need to discuss how clusters of social groups and organizations, statuses and roles, and associated norms and values operate to serve some important need in social life. In modern societies there are five major social institutions: the family, political institutions, the economy, educational institutions, and religious institutions, each performing functions that are vital to the continued existence of the society. Each of these institutions can be organized in a variety of ways, as you have seen in this book; but in each society, social institutions are long-lasting and widely accepted. Often, people don't even imagine different ways of organizing their society's institutions, and when institutions do change (see Chapter 5, Germany), they find it difficult to adjust.

Mexican Social Institutions: The Family

Families in all societies do similar things for society (that is, they perform basic functions), though they do them in different ways. Families regulate sexual activity, supervising their members to be sure they conform to sexual norms. Families are in charge of reproduction to keep the society going, and they socialize the children they produce. Also families provide physical care and protection for their members. They also provide emotional support and caring. When sociologists discuss "the family," they are talking about a cultural ideal: how families are supposed to work in a given society. The ideal may or may not coincide with what things are actually like in any given family group.

The Mexican family fulfills these universal functions in a distinctive way. The structures and the values, norms, beliefs, and attitudes that permeate family life are characteristically Mexican or Latin American. According to Selby, Murphy, and

Lorenzen, "it is difficult to overemphasize the importance of the nuclear family in Mexico, for it truly is the emotional center of the psychological and social life of all Mexicans" (p. 98). Ordinary Mexicans don't go downtown to shop, or eat out in restaurants, or go to clubs or concerts or sports events. Their lives revolve around home and work; family TV watching, family celebrations, visits among relatives and neighbors, and for men, going out drinking with close friends. Although Mexican families are typically large, only the well-to-do in Mexico live in houses with many bedrooms. Ordinary Mexicans will even rebuild the interiors of houses to make fewer bedrooms and more shared common space for family work and socializing (Selby, Murphy, and Lorenzen, pp. 22, 26, 98).

Practically everyone in Mexico lives in a family-based household, and almost all of these are headed by a man who is the principal wage earner. According to Selby, Murphy, and Lorenzen, no more than 7 percent of households are female-headed (compared to 27 percent for the United States in 1987). Divorce rates are low. Most married couples have children living in the house with them (Selby, Murphy, and Lorenzen, pp. 53, 99). Almost no one lives alone; indeed it is almost unthinkable to do so, and very inconvenient too, since Mexican society assumes the presence of children or servants in every household, to run errands, stand in line to pay bills (since the mails are so unreliable), or carry messages (since so many people lack telephones) (Selby, Murphy, and Lorenzen, p. 91). (See Table 2.1.)

Family Structure

In Mexico, the ideal nuclear family is part of an extended family network and the household willingly expands to include grandparents, uncles, aunts or cousins, related children who are orphans or children of divorced parents, or relatives who are single, widowed, or divorced. People feel close to their third and fourth cousins. Extended family members rely on each other to take care of children, help with money, or provide friendship and support. People live in families at every stage of their lives and families demand loyalty. "What you have to do," an informant told Selby, "is care for your family, so your family will care for you" (Falicov, p. 138; Selby, Murphy, and Lorenzen, p. 5).

TABLE 2.1. Marriage and Divorce 1990–1992: Mexican women marry relatively young and rarely divorce.

	Average Age of Women When First Married	Percent of Marriages That End in Divorce
Germany	25.6	33
Japan	25.8	22
United States	25.2	48
Mexico	20.6	6
Egypt	21.9	18

Source: United Nations Development Programme, *Human Development Report 1994.* New York: Oxford University Press, 1994.

Families are also hierarchical: the old have authority over the young, and men have authority over women, at every stage of the life cycle. People are expected to remain loyal to their family of origin throughout their lives. Indeed, ideally, married sons and their families will share households with their parents, and married daughters often do so as well. Married sons and daughters who live separately will try to live nearby and visit often, and sons will contribute money to their parents' household. According to Falicov, family values stress proximity, cohesiveness, respect for parental authority, and cooperation. Confrontation and competition are discouraged, and individual autonomy and individual achievement are not emphasized (Falicov, p. 138).

Roles in the Mexican Family

Role expectations for husbands and wives stress complementarity. Ideally, the husband is hard-working and continuously employed. He disciplines and controls the family. The husband hands over his wages to his wife, who manages the household. It is her task to maintain the home, physically and emotionally. She creates an emotional shelter, a refuge for her family, where they can recover from the stresses of life in the public world outside. Taking care of everyone is the mother's task: she sustains and nurtures and she also serves the men in the family.

The roles parents play in relation to their children are considered much more important than the roles they play toward each other as spouses. They don't expect much romantic intimacy or friendly companionship, but rather respect, consideration, and control of anger. As Falicov explains, "it is thought that *el amor de madre* (motherly love) is a much greater force than wifely love" and "a Mexican woman feels more challenged to perform as a mother than as a wife, companion or sexual partner" (Falicov, pp. 140, 149). In fact, since Mexican families are large, and adult children remain close, husbands and wives rarely live without children and are able to transfer their early involvement in raising their children to a lasting relationship with their grandchildren.

Children are expected to respect and obey their parents, but they wouldn't think of being friends with them. Ideally, children put the family's needs before their own. When they see their parents working so hard to maintain the family, they feel tremendous gratitude and a sense of protectiveness toward their mother. They are eager to help by working with their parents, or if they obtain paid work, by contributing their wages. Selby, Murphy and Lorenzen estimate that by the time working children are 20, they will have paid back their parents all the expenses entailed in raising them. When adult children live with their parents, or regularly give them money, parents soon realize a net gain in the financial calculus of childrearing (Selby, Murphy, and Lorenzen, p. 55).

Siblings are expected to have very close ties throughout their lives. Brothers and sisters and cousins are encouraged to play together, and it is not unusual for Mexican children to have few friends who are not relatives. Older siblings are usually given some authority over younger ones and these age hierarchies may continue into adult life. Adult brothers and sisters may quarrel and carry grudges, but they seldom break off relations with each other, because family celebrations or crises reunite them.

Built-in Strengths and Built-in Problems

The family offers Mexicans tremendous security in an insecure world. Most Mexicans have no pension plans or health insurance; they are not enrolled in social security and many lack steady jobs. The family is the safety net for Mexicans. In exchange for their loyalty and hard work, the family takes care of all its members. It cares for them in illness, supports them in unemployment and old age, and is flexible enough to take in any relatives left alone.

At the same time, certain kinds of conflicts and tensions are built into the way families are structured. Tensions between parents and their adult married children are common. Mothers-in-law feel that their daughters-in-law induce their sons to favor their own families at the expense of the extended family. When daughters and their husbands share a household with their parents, the older generation often feels that the sons-in-law don't contribute enough, while the sons-in-law feel the daughter's parents don't help her and her family enough (Selby, Murphy, and Lorenzen, p. 8).

The Mexican family system is hard on women and children. Increasingly, women work a "double day," working for wages all day outside their homes, but still carrying full responsibility for home and children. Children often are so intensely aware of their parents' burdens that it is difficult to persuade them not to drop out of school in order to supplement family income (Selby, Murphy, and Lorenzen, p. 108).

Mexican Political Institutions: The "Official" Party

Every society develops some means to maintain order, protect the members of the society from outside threats, control crime, and resolve conflicts among different groups. All modern societies have separate political institutions which exist to serve these functions: governments, political parties, the military, and legal institutions.

In Mexico, the political party overshadows all other political institutions in importance. The party is much more than a vote-getting organization that gears up at election time. It is a permanent institution that dominates the government and touches most peoples' lives on a daily basis. The Institutional Revolutionary Party (the PRI) is Mexico's "official" political party. It has ruled Mexico without interruption since 1929. Every president has come from its ranks and almost every governor and lesser official. It has dominated the Mexican parliament and the lives of ordinary Mexicans through its affiliated labor unions, peasant groups, student groups, and urban community organizations. For sixty-five years, participation in the PRI has been the only real route to political power and, in most cases, even economic advance. The distinction between party and government has been blurred in Mexico.

According to political scientists Wayne A. Cornelius and Ann L. Craig, Mexico has "a highly centralized political system," in which the president dominates the government. Mexico's political institutions are part free and part authoritarian. The government is not rigidly repressive, and it strives to include a broad range of interest groups, but political competition between opposing parties is very limited. The PRI government keeps benefits restricted to its own supporters, manipulates the mass media, and keeps decision making centralized in the federal government and in the hands of the president and his cabinet (Cornelius and Craig, pp. 23–31).

Teachers demonstrate in Mexico City. Demonstrations are very much a part of Mexican life. Political parades and rallies are held by those who oppose national government policies and by the PRI, the traditional governing party, to show its popular support. Women are frequently part of demonstrations. This reflects their long history of activity in Mexico's unions, political parties, and revolutionary movements.

Before the PRI

To understand the PRI you must know what came before it: the chaos and suffering of civil war. Although the Porfirio Díaz regime was officially overthrown in 1910, fighting raged all through the teens and 1920s. Historians estimate that $1\frac{1}{2}$ million Mexicans died in this long conflict and half a million fled across the border to the United States. For two decades, the regimes of rival generals were toppled in rapid succession; presidents and popular heroes were assassinated or exiled.

When the ruthless leader Plutarcho Elías Calles declared in 1928 that it was time to institutionalize the revolution, Mexicans hoped for an end to disorder and bloodshed. Calles created the forerunner of the PRI, the PNR (or National Revolutionary Party). The new official party, according to Alan Riding,

> incorporated assorted liberal, socialist and intellectual factions and it absorbed the bureaucracy and even the army. Everyone in and around the government— ministers, governors, congressmen, army officers, judges, civil servants—was simply pronounced a member, as were the rank and file of the 400 or so parties and movements that emerged from the Revolution. The PNR was born with perpetual power virtually guaranteed. It adopted the national colors and became instantly synonymous with the state. (Riding, pp. 51–52)

The PRI and Order

Under PRI rule, all the diverse groups: workers and businessmen, peasants and soldiers, rival politicians and their followers, that might have struggled for control of the state became organized factions under the umbrella of a single party. The party became the **patron** of them all, giving each something that it wanted, and in exchange, all the **clients** acknowledged the supremacy of the party and accepted its choice of president. Every president since 1929 has served out his term of office—an extraordinary record.

One reason why the PRI has been so successful is that it is firmly based in Mexican culture and social structure. The party is a hierarchical network of patron-client relationships, based on personal favors, gratitude, and personal loyalty. Sociologists and political scientists call this way of running a government **patronage politics.** Patronage politics is highly developed in Mexico, but it is found in many, many other societies too.

Don Miguel is a PRI jefe (or boss). He is the president of the Citizens Action Committee of Colonia "Lázaro Cárdenas," a newly settled colonia populare (or squatter neighborhood) on the outskirts of Oaxaca. Five years ago, Don Miguel got involved with his neighbors in order to build a much-needed school. To his own astonishment, he found he had a talent for organizing and leading people. With Don Miguel as president, the Citizens Action Committee collected signatures on petitions, visited the mayor's office, and searched for every possible personal connection to officials of the city government. Demonstrations in front of city hall finally culminated in a memorable visit by the mayor to the colonia, when he promised to provide sewer service.

By the time the bulldozers arrived, Don Miguel found he had a new profession. Residents of the colonia came to him with all sorts of problems: this one's brother needed a job; that one's son was brilliant, but needed a scholarship; that one's mother was senile and kept wandering off and getting lost. As he got to know the officials at city hall better, Don Miguel found he could get help for some of his neighbors. They looked up to him as a kind of protector, a patron, and they willingly gave 5 pesos a month per family to finance the Citizens Action Committee. In turn, Don Miguel felt grateful and loyal to the mayor and the other PRI officials for their help. When they asked him to bring his people to a campaign rally in Oaxaca to cheer the mayor and the PRI, he was glad to do it, and his neighbors were happy to come to show their gratitude and loyalty to him. The PRI even served them all a free lunch when they arrived.

Although the citizens of Lázaro Cárdenas know, in an abstract way, that the city is obliged to provide sewer service, they haven't demanded it with a feeling of entitlement. Rather, they believe that it is their personal relationship with a patron, Don Miguel, and his relationship with his patron, the mayor, which made the sewers possible.

A Successful Institution

The PRI has been extraordinarily successful in many ways. Not only has it maintained its monopoly on power, it has also kept Mexico politically stable through much of the twentieth century.

PRI success has been based on its ability to deliver real benefits to Mexican workers and peasants in exchange for their political loyalties. It was President Lázaro Cárdenas, remembered with gratitude to this day, who organized Mexican peasants into their own federations and actually put into practice the constitutional guarantee of land for any Mexican family that would farm it themselves. Between 1934 and 1940 Cárdenas redistributed 46 million acres of land, formerly held in large estates, creating more than 180,000 *ejidos* (tracts of land held communally by villages, which can be inherited but not sold), farmed by 750,000 families. Cárdenas formed confederations of peasants, workers, white-collar workers, and small businessmen, under the umbrella of the PRI. These groups made the PRI a powerful machine for gathering votes and channeling benefits (Riding, pp. 53–55).

Peasants received land and vital loans from state banks to buy seeds and equipment. Workers unionized by party affiliates received wage increases, some benefits, and also access to jobs in industries newly taken over by the state, like the railroads, the oil industry and, as time went by, thousands of smaller state companies as well. Public funds invested in rural development—road construction, power lines, health clinics, and schools—yielded benefits for peasants and also jobs for manual workers, teachers, health care workers, and government bureaucrats.

Social Mobility and the PRI. Ambitious Mexicans often thanked the PRI for providing them with opportunities for **upward social mobility** (that is, movement to a higher social rank or position). Like a good patron, the PRI "sponsored" the rise of politically talented individuals up the ladder of power. It was possible to become active in your local union or *ejido* or student group and then, supported by the power of the organization you controlled, to be tapped by the party for higher positions. Sociologists call this pattern of improving your social position **sponsored mobility.** In this way, some people who came from quite poor origins ended up in congress or in high government positions (Riding, p. 75). At the same time, the PRI created networks that linked together potentially opposed groups, granting benefits to each and absorbing into itself the natural leadership of each group.

What Price Stability?

If you are thinking that this political system sounds too good to be true, you are right. There is a substantial downside to a one-party patronage machine, a downside that worries more and more Mexicans. Because, for all practical purposes, the PRI and the Mexican government are identical, certain kinds of abuses of power are rather likely to occur.

Co-optation and Repression. Faced with any new organization, like a newly settled community, or a new union, the PRI/Mexican government has followed a consistent policy. When local authorities judge the new group and its leaders willing to play the game, the organization is **co-opted**—that is, it is given some benefits, allowed to achieve some of its goals in return for becoming a loyal part of the PRI. Leaders can be co-opted personally with recognition and paid positions. But organizations with interests and goals that conflict with those of the PRI, or organizations bent on achieving power independent of the PRI, are ruthlessly repressed. Because the PRI and the government are identical, it is an easy matter for the party to call out soldiers to bulldoze the too-independent shantytown, or police to crush the too-radical union.

Lack of Democracy. In theory, the PRI gives representation to all groups, through its subsidiary organizations. But in fact, this system is a far cry from representative democracy. Power is held by a hierarchy of bosses: union chiefs or local leaders who are appointed by those above. Election is a mere formality. Even the president is essentially appointed (by his outgoing predecessor); the election just legitimates his selection. Basically, Mexican elected officials are accountable to the patrons who appointed them, not the people they represent (Cornelius and Craig, p. 25).

Corruption. The practice of patronage, combined with the *sexenio,* the single six-year presidential term of office, has fostered corruption in Mexico. Every high-level politician has his following of loyal clients, who have helped him rise. When a politician is selected to be the next president, his patronage network has struck it rich. Every client can expect a government job, or perhaps a government contract, an import license, sewers and streetlights for the community, or other government funds, a portion of which will find their way into the private wealth of the client. But the largesse will last only six years, after which another politician and other clients will take over. The temptation to line one's pockets as fast as possible usually proves irresistible. Corruption filters down to lower civil servants, police, judges, businesspeople, and the media.

Police corruption is probably most notorious. To become a police officer in Mexico City, you don't take an exam or train at a police academy. You must know someone in the PRI and then you will have to buy your job with a payment to the bureaucrat in charge of hiring, or to someone to whom he owes a favor. The job itself is hardly worth having, since the pay is absurdly low. It is valuable only as an opportunity for corruption, for *la mordida* ("the little bite"), as police payoffs are called. In Mexico you can expect to be stopped for tiny, or imaginary infractions of the traffic laws, but the police officer will be happy to "pay your ticket for you" if you give him the fine. The police officer must pay a bigger bribe for a better corner, so he must also take more "little bites" from motorists. Police are also paid off by drug dealers and prostitution operators. They must be "tipped" before they will investigate a crime, and small criminals can buy their way out of charges. Like police officers, judges are poorly paid. Some simply give the decision to the party that makes the biggest payoff (Riding, p. 117).

In business it is difficult to accomplish anything without kickbacks and payoffs to suppliers, government bureaucrats, or union officials. Many union leaders use their power primarily to obtain the largest possible payoff in return for not striking. And union bosses often fill jobs by selling them to the highest bidder. Newspaper reporters, paid very low wages, make a living by accepting a monthly "retainer" from the government agency, industry, or criminal operation they are assigned to cover (Riding, pp. 123–124, 126).

For the past sixty-five years, the PRI has been a powerful force for the containment of conflict. But deep inequalities exist in Mexican society, and now, at the end of the twentieth century, Mexicans are fearful of inequality giving rise to intensified conflict, and are debating how best to respond.

SOCIAL INEQUALITY

What do sociologists mean when they say that a given society has deep inequalities, or that another is relatively egalitarian? How do we judge the extent of inequality in a society or compare the amount of inequality in different societies? In every society there are scarce resources that are distributed unequally: some people receive more and others less. Sociologists usually point to three categories of scarce goods: power, prestige, and wealth. Then, in examining any society, they ask who, which groups or categories of people have more or less power, prestige, or wealth.

In every society there is some degree of inequality between men and women. (We call this **gender inequality.**) We have seen how in Mexican society women are often economically dependent on men and defer to their husbands and fathers. In Mexican society (and in many other societies) there are also **racial inequalities** in which some races (or ethnic groups) enjoy higher status than others, more wealth, and more power over other races. Finally, in Mexico, as in many other societies, we can distinguish distinct groups or **strata** (layers) of the population whose access to power, prestige, and wealth differs because they start out with different economic resources. We call these groups **social classes** and this kind of inequality **class inequality.**

Class Inequality in Mexican Society

Is there a great deal of class inequality in Mexican society? Is there more or less than in other societies? In trying to answer these questions, we can start with two relatively simple comparisons. First, we can ask, do most people in this society make pretty much the same amount of money? Are there just a handful of rich people and a sprinkling of poor people, with everyone else clustered in the middle? Or are people spread out over the whole range of incomes? Second, we can ask, how big is that range from the richest to the poorest? Do the richest people receive double the share of total income that the poorest receive? Ten times as much? One hundred times as much? These are questions about **income distribution.**

According to these measures, Mexico is quite an unequal society: there are many poor people and they are very poor indeed, both **relatively,** compared to very rich Mexicans, and **absolutely,** in terms of the absolute minimum necessary for human survival.

Income Distribution

Sociologist James W. Russell calculates that Mexico's upper class is tiny—making up less than 1 percent of the population. The middle class, including well-off small business owners, privileged bureaucrats, managers, and well-paid professionals, is very small, encompassing only 16.5 percent of the workforce and their families. All other Mexicans, a group which includes farmers and farm workers, blue-collar workers, and most self-employed people, make up a huge 83 percent of the labor force and their families. Approximately half of this majority lives in poverty (Russell, p. 69).

We can learn a lot about the extent of inequality in a society by looking at income distribution by "income fifths," or **quintiles.** This calculation adds up all the income everyone receives—including wages and salaries, interest and dividends, rents and profits. Then we divide up all the households into five equal size groups: the 20 percent who are the top income earners, the 20 percent who are the bottom income earners, and the three-fifths in the middle.

In Mexico, in 1984, the richest income fifth received 55.9 percent of total income earned, and the poorest fifth received only 4.1 percent. That means the richest fifth received $13\frac{1}{2}$ times as much income as the poorest fifth. Compare this to Japan (in 1979) where the richest fifth received only 4 times as much of total income as the poorest fifth; West Germany where the richest fifth received less than 6 times as much; and the United States, where the richest fifth received 9 times as much (see Table 1.3, p. 36).

Social Classes and Standards of Living

Income distribution figures will make more sense if you know how much money rich people and poor people earn, or at least what their money will buy them. The official minimum wage in Mexico is $3.42 per day, or approximately $100 per month (and $1200 per year), a wage typical for unskilled workers in the city or countryside, but one that leaves them very, very poor. Earnings of approximately $800 a month (or $9600 a year) put you squarely in the middle class. Only 8 percent of Mexicans earn that much money. Rich Mexicans receive a great deal more income: Russell estimates that $60,000 a year puts you in the Mexican upper class, a level that fewer than 1 percent of Mexicans can attain (Russell, pp. 78–79). (See Table 5.1, p. 222.)

People with similar incomes and about the same amount of wealth often resemble each other in many aspects of their lives. Their income enables them to buy one or another standard of living, and they also develop shared values, norms, and customs. They live in the same neighborhoods, send their children to the same schools, and usually marry each other as well. We call these groups **social classes.** In Mexico, the various social classes live apart from each other and follow very different ways of life.

The Upper-Class Way of Life

Upper-class Mexicans have sufficient money to live like the wealthy of rich western societies, with cars, vacations abroad, designer clothes, and investments in foreign real estate. They think of themselves as an elite group, setting standards for their society (Rudolph, pp. 115–116).

Eduardo Sandoval's Lexus leaves the driveway of his home in the exclusive Polanco district of Mexico City, the gates closing behind him. While Eduardo argues over the telephone with his father, Geraldo, his driver pilots the car through traffic, the air conditioner blasting. Eduardo wants to accept a big partnership offer from a Japanese company. They want to contract with Eduardo's food processing company to produce frozen specialty vegetables for the American market. Eduardo likes the offer. He thinks they need to reposition the company in the new free-market NAFTA era. His father Juan, who started the business, and runs it together with Eduardo, is opposed. Juan says his company has always produced for the Mexican market and Mexicans have been good to the Sandoval family. Juan worries that competing in an unrestricted international market could hurt the company as easily as help it.

Eduardo's wife doesn't work. She is at home, completing preparations for next week's holiday trip. The Sandovals and their teenage daughter plan to fly to Vail, Colorado, to stay in the vacation home they own there. Their son, who is attending college at Stanford will fly in to join them so the whole family can ski together.

Traditionally, there are three somewhat overlapping sectors of the Mexican upper class, which are distinct, but linked through kinship and social interaction.

The Industrial Elite. Business fortunes in Mexico are often held by extended families, like the Garza Sada family fortune begun in the 1890s when the family founded Cervecería Cuautémoc, today Mexico's largest brewery. Descendants have invested in chemicals, oil, steel, banking, insurance, and finance. Families like the Garza Sadas intermarry with each other. They give relatives jobs in various family-controlled businesses, and form alliances with other family business groups (Rudolph, pp. 116–117).

The Landowning Elite. Another group of wealthy people in Mexico are rural large landowners. They are the owners of the (mostly northwestern) large estates of good, irrigated land used to grow winter vegetables for export to the United States. Large landowners make enough money to invest in the most modern farm technology: irrigation systems, farm machinery, fertilizers, herbicides, and pesticides. Many have also invested in commerce, industry, and banking, forming alliances with Mexico's industrial elite (Rudolph, pp. 117, 124–125).

The Political Elite. Politics is the most conspicuous route to wealth in Mexico. It is almost expected that elected officials and the networks of clients they bring with them into office will spend their six-year terms skimming government budgets and accumulating payoffs. As long ago as the 1960s, research revealed that the average senior official "finished his term with two or three houses, two or three automobiles, a ranch and the equivalent of U.S. $100,000 in cash." About twenty-five senior officials held posts worth fifty times that much to them (Rudolph, p. 118). In the oil-boom years Mexican presidents bought chateaux in France and built marble mansions for their families at home (Hellman, p. 3).

The Middle-Class Way of Life

Middle class in Mexico is an elusive term. Some people, like teachers, have professions usually considered middle-class, but in Mexico they are paid so little that in terms of their income they are poor. Other Mexicans own businesses, but their businesses are so small that they have no employees and their earnings don't keep them out of poverty. More than half the Mexican middle class earn less than $10,000 a year. At these wages it is hard to afford goods produced for the world market, like cars and TVs, which cost as much in Mexico as they do in the United States. But lower-middle-class families may still employ cheap household help. Often they are better off than their income indicates: many civil servants (and some unionized workers) enjoy government benefits like subsidized housing, pensions, free medical care, even coupons to exchange for food. Such families are part of the richest fifth: better off than the other 80 percent of all Mexicans.

Prosperous business owners, the top managers of Mexico's small number of big businesses, top bureaucrats, and well-off professionals make up the Mexican upper middle class. Though they earn less than $60,000 a year, they can afford a suburban middle-class life similar to that of their counterparts in the United States. Their children go to private schools and universities and are taught to be conscious of proper language and manners (Rudolph, p. 113).

Francesca Guzmán leaves the office early to take her two children to the dentist. She drives the family Ford up the hill to their home in a new suburb of Mérida. The house has four bedrooms and two baths, a modern kitchen, a stereo, and a two-car garage. When she thinks of how hard her mother worked in the fields all her life, she is very grateful for her luxurious life. But Francesca has one regret: she always wanted a big, noisy, lively family, like the one she grew up in. She could still have more children, but Francesca knows that in today's world, her children will need college education, even graduate school, and she and her husband Bernardo have decided to limit the size of their family so they can afford the best education for their children.

Also, Francesca recognizes that she is needed in the factory, where she runs the office. Bernardo and Francesca have built up the custom ironwork business, growing along with the city of Mérida. However, as Francesca would be the first to point out, they couldn't have done it without Bernardo's older brother, the accountant, who lent them the capital to get started and found them contacts through his business connections. Francesca and Bernardo are proud of what they have accomplished: they have a thriving business, a new home, with a maid and a cook; they take vacations at the beach, support Francesca's mother, and pay for her youngest sister's tuition at the university. They hope to send their own children to college in the United States.

The Lower-Class Way of Life

You have to admire the resourcefulness, tenacity, and hard work with which **lower- class** families struggle to put together sufficient income to survive. There is no "safety net" to fall back upon: no welfare, no unemployment insurance, no social security pensions. People can rely only upon their families and their networks of patrons and friends.

If a family has more than one adult wage earner, a favored strategy is for one person to find a job for wages—in a factory, as a bus driver, or even a teacher. Such jobs often pay no more than one minimum wage, but they are desirable if they carry health benefits, pension, and access to other government subsidies. Other family members look for work in the **informal sector,** where there is a chance of earning more, but no benefits. (See Hellman, especially pp. 220–221, for discussion of "survival strategies.")

The Informal Sector. One important difference between Mexico (and other "developing" nations) and the "developed" industrial nations is that many Mexicans lack "formal" paying jobs in business or government. They are "informally" self-employed in tiny businesses which usually have no employees or employ other family members working without wages. Russell estimates that more than a quarter of the Mexican labor force is self-employed in this way. Often people work for wages when they can, but if they are laid off they hustle work until they can find employment again. Many peddle goods or services from place to place (Russell, p. 59; Castells and Portes, pp. 11–37).

There are few chain stores or chain restaurants in Mexico, but lots of "Mom and Pop" groceries and cafés. Outdoor markets are crowded with stalls selling fruit and candy, cooked food, appliances, new and used clothing, and anything else you might want. In sidewalk workshops people make and sell shoes; they print stationery and business cards; they sew dresses. On a busy street or square you can buy a song from a mariachi band, have your shoes shined, hire a child to watch your car, or watch a sword swallower or fire-eater who hopes for your tip. In Mexico City, 2500 people work as garbage pickers, sorting through the city's huge garbage dump for recyclable materials to sell. (Incidentally, most of these "informal sector" occupations can't be adopted casually. The market or the street corner or the dump has its boss, and you must pay him or her for your spot. You will become his client and

This is "Colonia Emiliano Zapata," a new squatter settlement rising near an assembly plant (or *maquiladora*) along the border with the United States. The men you see are building their own houses out of material discarded by the factory. They are using abandoned pallets for the walls. There is no electricity, running water, or sewage system for these homes. Half of all Mexicans build their houses themselves.

he will try to provide you some protection from shakedowns by police and competition from other peddlers.) Struggling for a livelihood, poor Mexicans find every possible niche in the economy.

Absolute Poverty. The bottom line for Mexican families is that if they cannot somehow earn enough for necessities, they will simply have to do without. If they cannot afford rent, they will live in a shack in a squatter settlement, without electricity, running water, or sewage pipes. In 1989, 52 percent of Mexicans had no running water or toilets in their house. It is usual for the families of an apartment building or a squatter neighborhood to share a single water tap which runs continually. Often there is a rotating schedule for filling each family's containers at the tap: today your turn may come at 3 A.M. (Hellman, p. 15). Less money frequently means less food: 20 percent of Mexicans eat no eggs or meat; 40 percent never have milk. In the poorest Mexican states 80 to 90 percent of the population doesn't eat eggs, meat, or milk (Riding, p. 227, 1985 data). (See Table 2.2.)

The Way of Life of the Rural Poor

So far, we have been describing the lives of poor people in urban areas, but actually more than half of Mexico's poor families live in the countryside. A quarter of Mexicans who work, work in agriculture (compared to less than 3 percent in the United States). The southern agricultural states of Chiapas, Oaxaca, Campeche, Yucatán, and Quintana Roo are the poorest in the nation. (See Table 2.3.)

Félipe Vásquez is starting to feel desperate about his future. He is only 23, but he has already tried three different ways of earning a living. Félipe's parents in the tiny ejido of Santa Maria Tepayac in the State of Chiapas had been making a bare living raising coffee beans on their 5 acres, which they sell to the government warehouse in San Cristóbal de las Casas.

TABLE 2.2. Poverty, Hunger, and Disease, 1990–1991: The poverty of Mexicans and Egyptians is reflected in the many children who die before their first birthday or who are chronically malnourished.

	Poverty: Percent of People Who Don't Have Enough Money to Buy Food, Clothing, and Shelter	Malnourishment: Percent of Children 2–6 Years Old Who Are Chronically Malnourished	Infant Mortality: Number of Children in Every 1000 Who Die Before Their First Birthday
Germany	0	0	7
Japan	0	4	5
United States	0	2	9
Mexico	23	29	36
Egypt	21	32	59

Sources: World Bank, *World Development Report 1993: Investing in Health.* New York: Oxford University Press, 1993; United Nations Development Programme, *Human Development Report 1994.* New York: Oxford University Press, 1994.

TABLE 2.3. Percent of All Employed Working in Agriculture: Many Mexicans and Egyptians work in agriculture, but very few Germans and Japanese do.

	1960	1992
Germany*	18	3
Japan	33	7
United States	7	3
Mexico	55	23
Egypt	58	42

*Data are for West Germany only in 1960, Germany as a whole in 1992.
Sources: World Bank, *World Development Report 1993: Investing in Health.* New York: Oxford University Press, 1993; United Nations Development Programme, *Human Development Report 1994.* New York: Oxford University Press, 1994.

> *When he was younger, Félipe assumed he too would make a life working on the ejido. But then, in 1989, when the government turned the coffee business over to the private sector, coffee prices plummeted. The price they offered his parents for their coffee crop was laughable: their whole harvest brought in just $300, less than a dollar a day. Félipe went to stay with a cousin in San Cristóbal to look for paid work to help his parents, but all he could get was occasional day labor, at the minimum wage. At that rate, he could hardly help his parents, let alone marry his fiancée Juana.*
>
> *So when he was 20 Félipe went to the United States with his cousin who had been there before. He worked in California harvesting vegetables. He was actually able to save money to send home to his parents, but he hated the life. People treated the Mexican laborers like animals! And the wealth and luxury he saw around him electrified him. At home everyone was poor. He had no idea such wealth existed in the world. After three years he went back home, afraid Juana would tire of waiting and marry someone else. He found his village and the whole state in an uproar. Some of the men were calling themselves "Zapatistas." They had dug up their old rifles and forced out the Velasco de Leóns, the biggest landowners around, taking over their good, fertile land for the ejido. Félipe could scarcely restrain himself from joining them. That land once belonged to his people and the government had never acted on their claims. If they had the land back, he could marry Juana and they could live decently. But his father was furious and shouted at him that the rebels would bring death and destruction upon them all. (See DePalma, Feb. 2, 1994, p. 2, for discussion of coffee producers.)*

A third of the people living in poverty in rural areas work their own farms or *ejido* plots. They produce most of the food they consume: corn tortillas and beans and possibly eggs, chicken, and pork. Any surplus they sell for cash. A small percentage of households (3.2 percent) are really living outside the modern money economy: the value of what they grow for their own use exceeds their money income. Two-thirds of the rural poor have no land. They work for the large landowners, increasingly as seasonally employed migrants, moving around the country from harvest to harvest, living in shacks in the fields, and often paid less than the minimum wage (Russell, pp. 71, 79; Rudolph, pp. 125–126).

Historically, rural Mexicans have tried to improve their lives through political action, supporting the Mexican Revolution and then petitioning the government to create or expand *ejidos*. Though the government was obligated under Article 27 of the Constitution to redistribute land to any Mexican who would work it, after Lázaro Cárdenas, government enthusiasm for this commitment weakened greatly. *Ejidos* were created on the poorest land: steep, rocky, and dry. Although it was forbidden to sell *ejido* land, many peasants found their only alternative was to enter into arrangements with landowners in which they lost control of their land and had to work it as employees. Many found that as the fertility of their land decreased, and their families grew, they could no longer make a living off the land.

Migration and Emigration. Some peasants became agricultural laborers, but many more found greater opportunities in leaving the countryside. Since the 1940s, rural Mexicans have been flocking to the cities in search of work. Fifty years ago, 60 percent of Mexicans lived in rural areas and 40 percent in towns and cities. Today only 28 percent live in the countryside and 74 percent in towns and cities. Mexico City's population is now 20 times greater than it was in 1940; approximately 20 million people are living today in and around the capital. While urban population has increased at a staggering rate, rural population has grown also, though much more slowly, increasing by about 30 percent since 1940. (See Table 2.4.). But that is enough to ensure that without additional land and new technology, peasant farmers cannot grow sufficient food for their families. (See Table 4.2, p. 180.)[1]

Countless Mexicans from urban as well as rural areas make temporary visits to the United States as part of their survival strategies. No one really knows how many Mexicans work in the United States—estimates range from 1 million to 6 million (Riding, p. 332). It is difficult to count Mexican immigrants in the United States because they cross the border illegally, try to evade detection, and often stay for rela-

---

[1]Mexico's total population has grown from 19.7 million in 1940 to 88.3 million in 1990.

TABLE 2.4. Urban Population Growth, 1960–1992: Mexico and Japan are significantly more urban today than they were three decades ago.

	Percent of Total Population Living in Urban Areas, 1960	Percent of Total Population Living in Urban Areas, 1992	Increase in Percent of Total Population Living in Urban Areas from 1960 to 1992
Germany	76	86	13.2
Japan	63	77	22.2
United States	70	76	8.6
Mexico	51	74	31.5
Egypt	38	44	15.7

Source: United Nations Development Programme, *Human Development Report 1994.* New York: Oxford University Press, 1994.

tively short periods. Many cross repeatedly, sometimes emigrating every winter and returning in time for spring planting. Dick Reavis reports that in one Oaxacan village "virtually every male older than thirty has been to the United States, and most women beneath that age have gone too" (p. 239). Working at the most poorly paid jobs in the United States—as migrant farmworkers, in restaurant kitchens, or as maids, poor Mexicans can earn many times the Mexican minimum wage. The money they send home can buy seeds and fertilizer, a stock of goods to set up as a peddler, a sewing machine to start a business, or it can send a sibling to school. (See Table 4.4, p. 193.)

Racial Inequality in Mexican Society

Mexico is a racially diverse society, and it began as a **caste** society: one in which everyone was racially classified at birth and race determined people's rights and obligations. Modern Mexico has explicitly rejected caste structures. Race consciousness has been greatly reduced, but there are still racial inequalities.

Race and Class in Colonial Mexico

Colonial Mexico was a society of vast inequalities, in which a person's status was set mostly by race, but also by wealth. Most basically, there was a three-level pyramid, with whites at the top, followed by *castas* (mixed bloods) in the middle, and Indians at the bottom, with blacks (originally brought to Mexico as slaves) even below them.

Whites, while they dominated colonial society, were never more than a tiny minority of the Mexican population. In 1570, there were approximately 7000 Spaniards and 3½ million Indians. In fact, during the whole three centuries of colonial rule, no more than about 300,000 Spaniards ever came to Mexico. The *conquistadors* took Indian mistresses as soon as they arrived, fathering the growing *casta* population. By 1810, Indians were approximately 60 percent of the population, and people of mixed race nearly 40 percent (Ruiz, p. 85; Kandell, p. 213).

The colonial administration, highly race-conscious, tried to classify and regulate Mexico's varied people. A person born of Indian and white parents was a *mestizo;* someone of mixed black and white ancestry, a *mulato*. A person classified as Indian was entitled to a share in village communal lands, but couldn't own land as an individual. A person of African and Indian parents could not be enslaved, but had no rights to communal lands. Every racial category had a different legal standing.

But as time went on, *criollos* (whites born in Mexico) mixed with *mestizos,* with Indians who had left their communities, and with the descendants of African slaves. People came to call all poor urban dwellers *mestizos,* so the word became social, rather than racial in meaning. Today, a person stops being an Indian and becomes a *mestizo* through a social change of identity, by adopting the Spanish language and western dress.

The Revolution and Mexican Identity

After the 1910 revolution, Mexican intellectuals embarked on a period of intense soul-searching about their national identity. They rejected the idea that

Mexico should try to be like a European country, and began to find value in their Indian past. A very influential essay by José Vasconcelos (1882–1959), LA RAZA CÓSMICA (THE COSMIC RACE) praised Mexico's mixed-race character as a crowning achievement in world history, forging from the world's four races (whites, blacks, Asians, and Indians) a new "fifth race" (Russell, p. 172). The revolutionary murals of Diego Rivera depict Mexicans as proud brown-skinned people, and a plaque at Tlatelolco Plaza proclaims: "On August 13, 1521, heroically defended by Cuauhté-moc, Tlatelolco fell into the hands of Hernán Cortés. It was neither a triumph nor a defeat: it was the powerful birth of the mestizo nation that is Mexico today" (quoted in Riding, p. 3).

Race in Mexico Today

In Mexico today school textbooks and politicians proudly depict the *mestizo* as the ideal Mexican. Mexican society doesn't force people to choose between polar racial identities: anyone can adopt a *mestizo* identity. In its official census, the Mexican government does not ask people to classify themselves by race, a practice it considers racist. No data is collected on the percentages of Mexicans of different races and their residences, occupations, incomes, education, and so forth. Indians are recognized as a culturally distinctive group, but blacks, who are viewed as culturally identical to other Mexicans, are not recognized as a minority group (Russell, p. 95).[2] In general, in Mexico, as in other Latin American societies, skin color is viewed as an individual rather than a group attribute. Individuals may be lighter- or darker-skinned. Even within a family, one sister may be described as "white" and another as "black" without their feeling they belong to different racial groups.

But while government policies have minimized race consciousness in Mexico, racial inequalities persist. There is a strong association between skin color and status, and skin color and wealth. Whiteness is admired: *la guera* ("the blonde") is the ideal of feminine beauty, seen in advertisements, on television, and in the movies. Light skin and European features are associated with wealth and success; government officials and corporation executives look European. Dark skin is associated with Indians, with poverty, ignorance, and dirt. To call a person an *Indio* (Indian) is an insult. Cuauhtémoc Cárdenas, opposition candidate in the 1988 and 1994 presidential elections, was the first candidate to be seen in decades with dark skin and Indian features.

Indian Poverty. While Mexico collects no statistics about people who are racially Indian, data is available about people who speak Indian languages. Approximately 44 percent of such people live in Indian-majority counties *(municipios)* in eleven central and southern Mexican states. Indians are much more likely than non-Indians to live in rural areas, and they are more likely than other Mexicans to be self-employed peasant farmers. They are also much poorer than other Mexicans. Of Indians living in Indian counties 77 percent earn less than the

---

[2]Sociologists have had to estimate the percentage of Mexicans of different races. Russell suggests that Mexico's population is now 79 percent *mestizo,* 15 percent Indian, 5 percent white, and less than 1 percent black or Asian (p. 95).

minimum wage (compared to 27 percent of all Mexicans). Their median monthly income is only $30. Half live in houses without electricity, 90 percent have no indoor plumbing, and 45 percent are illiterate (Russell, pp. 125–128).

Rural Indians are much more likely than non-Indians to use their land for subsistence farming, growing their own food and minimizing their involvement in the modern money economy. While they would like to be better off economically, they greatly value their land, and their ability to maintain a traditional identity in an Indian community. They would be glad to have more land and better land, but they are reluctant to sell or leave their land for wages elsewhere (Russell, pp. 129–130).

SOCIAL CHANGE AND MEXICO'S FUTURE

Mexico is now in the midst of serious political and economic change. It is not clear what the outcome will be, either for the continued dominance of the PRI, or for the economy and the impoverished Mexican majority. Current changes have their roots in the crises of the 1970s and early 1980s. So to understand social change in Mexico today, you must know something about events of the past twenty years. Then you will see that political change and economic change have been closely linked in Mexico and that possibilities for the future are constrained by the world economy and by problems of poverty, population growth, and environmental destruction.

Protectionism and the Crisis of the 1980s

For forty years, starting in the 1940s, **protectionism** and the power of the PRI went hand in hand. Protectionism, or "import substitution," was a development strategy in which the Mexican government used high tariffs and import licenses to keep out foreign goods. This helped Mexican industries grow and sell their goods at home. The government gave new companies loans and tax exemptions and it restricted the number of companies competing in any one industry—all to help the domestic economy grow (Hellman, p. 8). The government itself became a major industrialist and employer, operating railroads, the oil industry, telephone service, and thousands of smaller companies. Business owners and employees who benefited from these policies, and all Mexicans who saw their standard of living rise in what was called the "Mexican miracle" of successful industrialization, felt grateful to the PRI.

Protectionist policies were very successful for thirty years, but they began to run up against their limits by the end of the 1960s. It was easy to produce simple goods, like beer or shoes, locally, at affordable prices, but substituting Mexican-made televisions or computers for imported ones was more difficult and expensive. So economic growth slowed down. It slowed for another reason too: lack of competition led to growing inefficiencies. Industries protected by tariffs, government regulations, or corruption were not driven by international competition to stay lean: they used old machinery, or old methods, or more workers than they needed, and the quality of their products deteriorated. People in other countries bought fewer Mexican products and by the mid-1970s, more money was leaving Mexico than was coming in from exports (Selby, Murphy, and Lorenzen, p. 65). As the economy slowed, the PRI found itself in a bind: government revenues decreased, so the PRI had less to spend on benefits (like roads, schools, hospitals, and other public works that created jobs) to be channeled down to party supporters. Just when economic slowdown made Mexicans demand more government help, the PRI could afford less!

The Oil Boom and Bust

But then a miraculous thing happened: vast new reserves of oil were discovered in Mexico. Gleefully the PRI and the Mexican people saw before them a bonanza, a resource that would bring in endless revenues from sales abroad. The government borrowed freely from foreign banks to set up the oil industry, and it borrowed more for other spending to keep Mexicans happy while the oil industry was starting up. In the early 1970s, oil poured revenues into government coffers, and government spending in every area soared.

Then, in 1982, oil prices plummeted worldwide and Mexico found itself in a debt crisis. There was insufficient revenue to pay the interest on loans. The International Monetary Fund required, as a condition of refinancing Mexico's foreign debt, that the government embark on an austerity program, cutting state spending in every area. Without loans and subsidies, companies collapsed and at least 800,000 jobs were lost, at the same time that government social spending was cut. Inflation rose and the standard of living of most Mexicans fell drastically, as real wages dropped 40 percent in just five years (Hellman, pp. 8–9). Now the PRI was in trouble again. People were suffering the worst economic crisis in many decades and the party could not increase government spending to help. To ordinary Mexicans it looked like the PRI wanted to keep them in line, without giving them any benefits. People became cynical about the PRI and its organizations, and about politics in general.

Alternative Parties and Faked Elections

Throughout the 1980s, Mexicans joined counter-PRI groups. Teachers, students, and manual workers, peasants and communities joined independent factions within their PRI unions, or organized independent groups that withstood PRI attacks and government violence. Two major opposition parties emerged: the PAN (National Action Party), a conservative, business-oriented party, centered in the more prosperous north, that attracts many Mexicans with its demands for an end to corruption; and the Party of the Democratic Revolution, created by Cuauhtémoc Cárdenas, the son of Lázaro Cárdenas, who left the PRI in 1988 and ran against Carlos Salinas de Gortari. Cárdenas advocated a return to his father's "populist" policies, putting the interests of workers and peasants before those of business.

The PRI, like other patronage machines, has always engaged in electoral fraud, calling out its clients en masse to vote for PRI candidates, offering payoffs, and tinkering with ballots. But as opposition grew, so did election fraud, culminating in the disputed 1988 election. Most people believed that Cuauhtémoc Cárdenas was the real winner of the 1988 presidential election, but the PRI "fixed" the vote by stuffing ballot boxes, changing regional vote totals, voting the dead, and all the usual means of electoral fraud. The party's reliance on fraud deepened Mexicans' cynicism and fueled opposition parties.

The New "Free-Market" Mexico

After 1982, continuation of the old protectionist economy was impossible. But the PRI needed to find a new way to rescue Mexico from economic crisis in order to remain in power. PRI leaders found their new strategy in the **neoconservative** policy of **free-market development.** This has meant opening the Mexican economy to the world market, getting rid of tariffs designed to protect Mexican manufacturers and price controls designed to prevent inflation, encouraging foreign investment, selling off government-owned companies to private investors, and reducing government involvement in both economic regulation and social welfare. Signing NAFTA (the North American Free Trade Agreement) in 1993 was part of this development strategy. Salinas and other "technocrats" were schooled in neoconservative economics in U.S. universities, but in any case this policy was the orthodoxy of the 1980s, triumphant as Soviet socialism collapsed. A free-market orientation would have been demanded by international banks and development agencies even if Mexico's leaders had not advocated it.

Salinas was Mexico's most dedicated modernizer since Porfirio Díaz. It is interesting that although Díaz has long been regarded as a villain in Mexican history, under Salinas, Mexican textbooks (which are government-controlled) were rewritten to treat him more sympathetically, while at the same time criticizing the revolutionary heroes Emiliano Zapata and Pancho Villa. A thirty-episode life of Díaz that stressed his positive accomplishments was shown on Mexican TV. Like Díaz, Salinas followed policies that made Mexico a more modern, industrialized society, but left peasants and workers worse off (DePalma, Aug. 30, 1993, p. 9; July 16, 1994, p. A4).

Salinas and other PRI advocates of neoconservatism were really a new generation of party leaders. One of the great strengths of the PRI political machine had always been its ability to recruit and absorb leaders from the bottom of Mexican society. By the 1970s, this ability began to break down. More and more, Mexican presidents and cabinet members were recruited from within the bureaucratic elite. A new patronage ladder of "technocrats," as they are known, was created that ran through the bureaucracies, not through the old PRI affiliates. Many were the sons of politicians. They came from wealthy families that educated their children at elite American or European universities. Mexican officials, trained at Harvard and Yale, learned to look at the world differently. They sought to make Mexico part of the modern global economy, and they grew impatient with protectionism, with unions and *ejidos,* with all the old-fashioned organizations which had formed the basis of PRI power. The technocrats began to create new "free-market" economic institutions for Mexico. They offered U.S. companies favorable conditions for locating factories in Mexico; they privatized Mexico's government-owned companies; and they ended the government's old commitment to protect peasant farmers.

Maquiladoras

Outside Mexico, *maquiladoras* are probably the best known aspect of the new economic institutions. *Maquiladoras* are foreign assembly plants. They are owned by U.S. multinational firms which send partly finished materials to Mexico for assembly into finished goods. Almost all *maquiladoras* are clustered near the

U.S./Mexico border so that the materials for clothes or electronics can be sent to Mexico one day and returned to the United States as finished goods on the next. *Maquiladoras* come to Mexico for cheap wages. The average daily wage of *maquiladora* workers (mostly women) in 1992 was $6.80 (Russell, p. 95). As an additional incentive to build assembly plants the Mexican government made the border a free-trade zone where foreign corporations can operate without taxation. The United States cooperates by charging customs duty only on the amount spent on wages in Mexico, not on the value added to the company's products at the *maquiladora*. Big companies like GE, Zenith, RCA, and General Motors, as well as many smaller businesses have set up *maquiladoras* in Mexico (Russell, p. 189). While the *maquiladora* program was first begun in the 1960s, its greatest growth has been in the 1980s and 1990s, when the number of assembly plants quadrupled (Russell, p. 195).

The importance of *maquiladoras* in the Mexican economy is probably over-rated outside Mexico. While they employ as many as 400,000 Mexicans, this is really a rather small percentage of the Mexican workforce, considering that every year more than 1 million new workers are looking for jobs (Barkin, p. 2). *Maquiladoras* exist because Mexicans are so desperate for jobs that they are willing to move to often-desolate border areas, accept low wages, long hours, and frequently unsafe working conditions, just to have a job. It remains to be seen whether the *maquiladora* industry will develop better-paid, more skilled jobs, but as long as Mexico has so many more workers than jobs, this seems unlikely.

Privatization

In the past ten years, the Mexican government has sold or closed down more than 80 percent of the 1155 businesses it once ran. Almost $21 billion from sales of government companies has gone into paying off the national debt, helping end the debt crisis, slowing inflation, and freeing up some government spending for new social welfare programs. Some of the businesses were old and inefficient; many employed more workers than necessary. Privatization was intended to make Mexican industry more efficient and productive. But as a result, 400,000 Mexicans who once thanked government-owned businesses for their jobs have been laid off since 1983. Also, many Mexicans believe that privatization has sharpened class inequalities. The number of Mexican billionaires has increased from two to twenty-four, at the same time that small and medium-size companies have found the going harder and harder (DePalma, Oct. 27, 1993, pp. A1, A8; Golden, Aug. 17, 1994, p. A3).

Free-Market Agriculture

President Carlos Salinas undertook the most radical changes in Mexican agriculture since the revolution. His purpose was modernization: to replace the inefficient subsistence farmer with modern "agribusiness"—big farm companies—often multinationals, that grow food for export to the world market.

The most radical of Salinas's reforms was the revocation of Article 27 of the Constitution, the article that had promised land to any Mexican who would work it himself, and had protected small farmers by prohibiting the sale of *ejidos*. (If *ejidos* were salable, the old reasoning went, then bad harvests or debt would force peasants to sell them.) The Mexican government had dragged its feet on creation of new *ejidos* for decades. But actually stating categorically that the old *ejido* policy was abolished was a revolutionary step. The *ejido* was a "sacred" symbol of Mexico's commitment to its Indian heritage and to peasants. Many Mexicans who would never benefit from its provisions felt attached to the revolutionary hopes embodied in Article 27.

There has been revolutionary change in Mexican agriculture in the past two decades. More food is being produced, much of it on large, modern farms, many owned by foreign companies. Mexican agriculture now produces more food for export and more grain to feed animals, but production of food for domestic consumption has fallen. Mexico is in the seemingly contradictory situation of no longer being self-sufficient in food, even while foodstuffs are a major export. Rural Mexicans especially (like many people in other third world countries that export food) are eating less and eating worse and experiencing more unemployment (Barkin, pp. 11, 16–22, 28–32). (See Table 4.7, p. 201).

Agricultural modernization has given rise to several practical problems. Agribusiness uses machines and chemicals; it needs far fewer workers than peasant subsistence agriculture. Where will displaced peasants go? Most peasants live in the impoverished south. Will they migrate all the way to the north and take jobs in *maquiladoras?* Will they cross the border, irritating the United States? Will they flock to other Mexican cities where people already lack jobs? Will they stay in the countryside and be content to live on whatever government welfare benefits are made available?

The Crisis of the 1990s

Advocates of free-market development have promised Mexicans that the new policies will make Mexico a "first world nation," like the United States, Japan, and the European industrial countries. This promise holds a powerful appeal for Mexicans who know how well people live in the United States, because they have been there or have seen it on TV. The problem is that while free-market modernization may benefit all Mexicans in the long run, in the short run it benefits only large businesses, many of them foreign, and reduces the standard of living of almost all Mexicans. Neoconservatives in the PRI have gambled: they have bet that they can make free-market economics produce benefits for many Mexicans before popular discontent overtakes them.

Population Growth and Living Standards

One major difficulty that makes it hard for neoconservatives to win their gamble is population growth. Stagnant for centuries, Mexican population growth took off after World War II. There were approximately 20 million Mexicans in 1940, 35 million in 1960, 70 million in 1980, and almost 90 million today. While the rate of growth has slowed somewhat, population continues to increase dramatically (Rudolph, p. 93). (See Table 2.5.)

Population growth is a very contradictory problem for Mexico. The nation attracts foreign investment because its labor is so cheap, and its labor is cheap

TABLE 2.5. Total Population Growth, 1960–1992: Mexico and Egypt more than doubled their population in three decades. Germany's population increased relatively slowly.

	1960 Population, Millions	1992 Population, Millions	Percent Increase 1960–1992
Germany	72.7	80.2	9.1
Japan	94.1	124.5	32.3
United States	180.7	255.2	41.2
Mexico	36.5	88.2	141.6
Egypt	25.9	54.9	119.7

Source: United Nations Development Programme, *Human Development Report 1994.* New York: Oxford University Press, 1994.

because population grows so fast that the economy cannot absorb all the people who enter the labor market. As long as population keeps growing rapidly, wages don't rise. That may be profitable for business, but it doesn't please ordinary Mexicans. Furthermore, it appears that when economic conditions worsen, and wages fall, Mexicans have larger, not smaller families, because they need more family members working in order to survive. This, of course, keeps wages down and the whole cycle repeats. Mexico's current leaders need to find a way to translate economic growth into higher wages and higher standards of living for ordinary Mexicans.

There is another problem: both poor peasants and rich industrialists create environmental damage. Peasants who lose their good land, or whose families are growing rapidly, must clear more and more of the infertile common lands, formerly considered unsuitable for farming. In poverty-stricken Chiapas, so much of the rain forest has been cleared that the border with forested Guatemala is visible from space. The soil in cleared rain forests or on mountainsides washes away, leaving barren land and even poorer peasants behind. Agribusiness also damages the land by pouring unregulated pesticides and other chemicals over it and by draining rivers and groundwater for irrigation. In the north, unregulated *maquiladoras* have polluted the land with industrial chemicals, while mushrooming cities pour untreated sewage into rivers.

The Political Crisis

In 1994, as the presidential election approached, it seemed entirely possible that the PRI could see its sixty-five-year rule ended. Just months before presidential elections, an unknown peasant revolutionary movement in the State of Chiapas (calling themselves the Zapatista National Liberation Army) took Mexico by surprise. They seized the state's major city, San Cristóbal de las Casas and several other villages and towns, before the Mexican army intervened. In the weeks that followed the initial armed attack, peasants in at least a dozen other towns seized their town halls and demanded the removal of local (PRI-selected) authorities. Sympathetic protesters held rallies in Mexico City and other cities to support the Zapatistas's demands for honest elections, redistribution of land, better treatment of Indians, and government development aid (Golden, Feb. 9, 1994, pp. A1, A9).

Tensions rose: the PRI's first choice of candidate was mysteriously assassinated and rumors of more armed rebellions swirled through Mexico. At one point, opinion polls showed both PAN leader Diego Fernández and opposition candidate Cuauhtémoc Cárdenas ahead of PRI candidate Ernesto Zedillo. Only 30 percent of Mexicans said they expected an honest election (Reding, p. A17). In the end, an unusually high percentage of Mexicans went to the polls (78 percent), and Zedillo won the election, but by the smallest percentage a PRI candidate had ever received, barely 50 percent.

PRI Strategy

In retrospect, it appears that the PRI changed just enough to win the election, without giving up any more power than necessary. The party made three changes: it adopted more modern vote-getting techniques; it built new networks to replace disillusioned groups of supporters; and when it was unavoidable, the PRI agreed to share power with PAN officials. The PRI also benefited from Mexicans' fear that a PRI loss would plunge the nation into disorder.

In 1994, the PRI developed a modern vote-getting apparatus that worked to reach people as individuals, rather than as members of PRI-affiliated organizations. The party spent millions on advertising and used its control of Mexican TV to flood the airwaves with pro-PRI publicity. It publicized new procedures designed to guarantee the honesty of elections and accepted opposition party poll watchers and foreign observers. On election day, almost 1 million "vote-promoters" canvased door-to-door getting out the PRI vote.

Also, recognizing that the old backbone of the PRI, labor and small farmers, had seen their standards of living fall in the past decade, the party moved away from relying on their support. As THE NEW YORK TIMES reported, PRI "loyalties shifted from labor and peasant groups that depended on government protection to middle-class people who relished cheaper imports and businessmen who bought up state companies" (Golden, Aug. 12, 1994, p. A8). Big business gave huge contributions to the PRI campaign fund in 1994.

Everyone recognized a split in the PRI between the old "dinosaurs," as they called them, the aging leaders of the traditional labor and peasant PRI affiliates, and the new "technocrats" led by Salinas and Zedillo. But the PRI couldn't afford to lose the votes of workers and peasants who are the majority of Mexicans. Instead the party built new networks to include poor Mexicans as members of their communities, not as workers or farmers. Rather than providing the poor with jobs or land, the PRI established a new government program, the National Solidarity Program, a $3.8 billion-per-year antipoverty initiative that provided water pipes, electricity, scholarships, and other benefits to poor communities, and organized many thousands of National Solidarity committees, tapping new leaders not previously involved in the PRI.

Political Reform

In its election campaign, the PRI also made a major new campaign pledge: it promised to share power with opposition parties. So far, it appears the PRI has followed through on this pledge to a remarkable degree. It allowed the election of PAN mayors and a governor in northern states, and of opposition legislators as well. Once in office, Zedillo continued to share power. He was the first president to invite opposition legislators to breakfast and lunch. He fired the entire PRI-appointed Supreme Court and replaced the justices with new, more independent judges. Zedillo appointed the first-ever attorney general from an opposition party. He gave the Mexican legislature more real power and allowed opposition legislators to head congressional committees. Zedillo even included opposition politicians in his cabinet. At the same time, he moved to suppress the Zapatista rebellion in Chiapas.

Finally, and most startlingly, Zedillo and his new attorney general aggressively advanced investigation into two shocking political assassinations that had marred the 1994 presidential campaign: the killing of José Ruiz Massieu, the secretary general of the PRI, and that of Luis Donaldo Colosio, the assassinated PRI presidential candidate whom Zedillo replaced. The Ruiz Massieu investigation led to the arrest of both Ruiz Massieu's own brother and the brother of Carlos Salinas de Gortari, the former president. There were accusations that the accused men and President Salinas himself had received millions of dollars in payoffs from big drug dealers. This investigation was unprecedented: never before had a PRI president allowed prosecution of PRI leaders, and especially not at such a high level. "This is a landmark in Mexican history. . . . The lid has been blown off the system," said one American expert, Professor Richard Craig of Kent State University (quoted in Sánchez, p. A12; Golden, Mar. 7, 1995, p. A3).

The Economic Crisis

No sooner did Zedillo begin his political revolution than he was blindsided by an unanticipated economic crisis. Less than three weeks into the new administration, a foreign-exchange crisis forced the government to devalue the peso. Salinas had encouraged foreign investment in Mexican businesses and government bonds, as part of his free-trade development program. The government had actually become increasingly dependent on foreign investments for dollars to balance Mexican imports. But then, in December 1994, foreign investors were suddenly panicked by rumors of renewed Zapatista activity. They sold their bonds and Mexico found itself with insufficient cash reserves of dollars. The government had to devalue the peso—to set a new, lower, value for pesos in exchange for dollars. The crisis was really financial, but it had far-reaching economic consequences.

Overnight, Mexicans found their wages worth less and the price of basic goods much higher. Gasoline prices increased by a third, electricity by 20 percent. The prices of milk and oil and eggs rose sharply. At least 500,000 people lost their jobs, as businesses, lacking customers, collapsed. The value of everyone's wages immediately fell by more than 30 percent. Inflation rose to 42 percent yearly. Even though Mexico's economy was actually much sounder than it had been in 1982, for ordinary people it was 1982 all over again. Mexicans' doubts about the new free-trade economy intensified. All over Mexico, people saw a potent symbol of current events in Popocatépetl, a long-dormant volcano south of Mexico City that suddenly rumbled into activity, spewing steam and ash, just as the peso crashed, the political scandals broke, and Zedillo began his term of office. Zapatista leader "Subcommandante Marcos" wrote a letter to Zedillo which began, "Welcome to the Nightmare" (DePalma, Dec. 29, 1994, p. A3).

The Future

Now, more than ever, Zedillo and the PRI and all Mexicans face a terrible dilemma. Will PRI officials be able to bring the promised benefits of a free-market economy to the majority of Mexicans? In the midst of the current financial crisis, their promise to make Mexico a "first-world nation" seems a bitter joke to poor Mexicans. Will the government be able to navigate the obstacles of increasing environmental pollution and growing population and unemployment? Will the PRI be able or willing to move from one-party patronage politics to multiparty democracy? Both the wealthy industrial nations of the world and the "developing" third world are watching to see if Mexico's new economic and political strategies will work.

Thinking Sociologically

1. Describe some norms that are important in Mexican culture.
2. Are there any similarities in the roles men are expected to play in Mexican society and in Japanese society? What differences are there?
3. Explain what is meant by the term "reciprocity network," using examples from Chapter 2. Do people in your society form reciprocity networks? Can you give an example of a reciprocity network from your own experience?
4. Compare the Gómez family household in Mexico (pp. 76–77) with the Sato family household in Japan (pp. 42–43). Which of these does your own household resemble more?
5. What are some of the reasons why Mexicans, even urban Mexicans, often have many children?
6. Are families in your society more like Mexican families in their structure, roles, and norms, or more like Japanese families?
7. Can you explain what political patronage is and how it works? Can you find an example of political patronage in your own society?
8. Look up the most recent data you can find on income distribution by quintiles in your society. Is your society more like Mexico or more like Japan in its degree of inequality?
9. Does the social category of "mixed race" exist in your society, as it does in Mexico, or does everyone have to be classified as belonging to one race or another? Which way of thinking about race would you prefer?
10. Refer to Table 2.1 (p. 78) and compare the rates of divorce in Mexico and in the United States. Use Chapter 2 and your introductory sociology textbook to help you explain why the divorce rate is so much higher in the United States than in Mexico.

For Further Reading

BARKIN, DAVID, *Distorted Development: Mexico and the World Economy.* Boulder, CO: Westview Press, 1990.

GUILLERMOPRIETO, ALMA, *The Heart That Bleeds: Latin America Now.* New York: Knopf, 1994.

HELLMAN, JUDITH ALDER, *Mexican Lives: Conversations on the Future of Mexico.* New York: New Press, 1994.

OSTER, PATRICK, *The Mexicans: A Personal Portrait of a People.* New York: Morrow, 1989.

REAVIS, DICK J., *Conversations with Moctezuma: The Soul of Modern Mexico.* New York: Quill, Morrow, 1990.

RUSSELL, JAMES W., *After the Fifth Sun: Class and Race in North America.* Englewood Cliffs, NJ: Prentice-Hall, 1994.

SELBY, HENRY A., ARTHUR D. MURPHY, AND STEPHEN A. LORENZEN, *The Mexican Urban Household: Organized for Self-Defense.* Austin: University of Texas Press, 1990.

Bibliography

ALARCÓN, NORMA, "Chicana Feminist Literature: A Re-Vision through Malintzin/ or Malintzin: Putting Flesh Back on the Object," in Cheríe Moraga and Gloria Anzaldua, eds., *This Bridge Called My Back: Writing by Radical Women of Color.* New York: Kitchen Table Press, 1983, pp. 182–189.

BARKIN, DAVID, *Distorted Development: Mexico and the World Economy.* Boulder, CO: Westview Press, 1990.

BERG, CHARLES RAMIREZ, *Cinema of Solitude: A Critical Study of Mexican Film, 1967–1983.* Austin: University of Texas Press, 1992.

BLEA, IRENE I., *La Chicana and the Intersection of Race, Class and Gender.* Westport, CT: Praeger, 1992.

BRAGANTI, NANCY, AND ELIZABETH DEVINE, *The Travelers' Guide to Latin American Customs and Manners.* New York: St. Martin's Press, 1989.

BRASCH, R., *Mexico: A Country of Contrasts.* New York: David McKay, 1967.

BRYDON, L., AND S. CHANT, *Women in the Third World: Gender Issues in Rural and Urban Areas.* New Brunswick, NJ: Rutgers University Press, 1989.

CASTANEDA, JORGE G., "Can NAFTA Change Mexico?," *Foreign Affairs,* Vol. 72, No. 4, Sept–Oct. 1993, pp. 67–80.

CASTELLS, MANUEL, AND ALEJANDRO PORTES, "World Underneath: The Origins, Dynamics, and Effects of the Informal Economy," in Alejandro Portes, Manual Castells, and Lauren A. Benton, eds., *The Informal Economy,* Baltimore: John Hopkins University Press, 1989, pp. 11–37.

CORNELIUS, WAYNE A., AND ANN L. CRAIG, *The Mexican Political System in Transition.* La Jolla, CA: Center for U.S.–Mexican Studies, University of California, San Diego, 1991.

CROSSETTE, BARBARA, "Albright Makes Her U.N. Post a Focal Point," *The New York Times,* Nov. 25, 1994, pp. A1, A14.

DEPALMA, ANTHONY, "New Battles Flare over Mexico's Past," *The New York Times,* Aug. 30, 1993, p. 9.

———, "Mexico Sells Off State Companies, Reaping Trouble as well as Profit," *The New York Times,* Oct. 27, 1993, pp. A1, A8.

———, "In Mexico's Poor South, Coffee Now Blights Lives," *The New York Times,* Feb. 2, 1994, p. 2.

————, "Rage Builds in Chiapas Village Where Land Is Life," *The New York Times,* Feb. 27, 1994, p. 10.

————, "Soap Opera from Past with Fears from Present," *The New York Times,* July 16, 1994, p. A4.

————, "A Year to Forget: 1994 Leaves Mexico Reeling," *The New York Times,* Dec. 29, 1994, p. A3.

————, "In Mexico, Hunger for Poor and Middle-Class Hardship," *The New York Times,* Jan. 15, 1995, pp. 1, 14.

————, "Mexicans Ask How Far Social Fabric Can Stretch," *The New York Times,* Mar. 12, 1995, pp. 1, 20.

————, "Mexico Lives by Virtual Law," *The New York Times,* Mar. 26, 1995, p. E3.

FALICOV, CELIA JAES, "Mexican Families," in Marian McGoldrick, John K. Pearce, and Joseph Giordano, eds., *Ethnicity and Family Therapy.* New York: Guildford Press, 1982, pp. 134–163.

FARRISS, NANCY M., *Maya Society under Colonial Rule: The Collective Enterprise of Survival.* Princeton, NJ: Princeton University Press, 1984.

FUENTES, CARLOS, *The Buried Mirror.* Boston: Houghton Mifflin, 1992.

————, "The Mirror of the Other," *The Nation,* Mar. 30, 1992, pp. 408–411.

GOLDEN, TIM, "'Awakened' Peasant Farmers Overrunning Mexican Towns," *The New York Times,* Feb. 9, 1994, pp. A1, A9.

————, "Mexican Conflict Heats Up, with Peasants Seizing Land," *The New York Times,* Mar. 14, 1994, p. 2.

————, "Torn by Change, Mexican Party Fights On," *The New York Times,* Aug. 12, 1994, pp. A1, A8.

————, "Big Business Puts Money on Mexican Status Quo," *The New York Times,* Aug. 17, 1994, p. A3.

————, "Mexican Is Charged with Cover-Up in Brother's Slaying," *The New York Times,* Mar. 7, 1995, p. A3.

GOODWIN, PAUL, ed., *Global Studies: Latin America.* Guilford, CT: Dushkin Publishing Group, 1991.

GUILLERMOPRIETO, ALMA, *The Heart That Bleeds: Latin America Now.* New York: Knopf, 1994.

HELLMAN, JUDITH ALDER, *Mexican Lives: Conversations on the Future of Mexico.* New York: New Press, 1994.

KANDELL, JONATHAN, *La Capital: The Biography of Mexico City.* New York: Random House, 1988.

LEWIS, OSCAR, *Five Families: Mexican Case Studies in the Culture of Poverty.* New York: Wiley, 1959.

————, *Tepoztlán, Village in Mexico.* New York: Holt, Rinehart & Winston, 1960.

LOMNITZ, LARISSA, *Networks and Marginality: Life in a Mexican Shantytown.* New York: Academic Press, 1977.

MADISON, D. SOYINI, *The Woman That I Am.* New York: St. Martin's Press, 1994.

MORRIS, STEPHEN D., *Corruption and Politics in Contemporary Mexico.* Tuscaloosa: University of Alabama Press, 1991.

MURPHY, ARTHUR D., AND ALEX STEPNICK, *Social Inequality in Oaxaca.* Philadelphia: Temple University Press, 1991.

NOLEN, BARBARA, ed., *Mexico Is People: Land of Three Cultures.* New York: Scribner's, 1973.

OSTER, PATRICK, *The Mexicans: A Personal Portrait of a People.* New York: Morrow, 1989.

PAZ, OCTAVIO, *The Labyrinth of Solitude: Life and Thought in Mexico,* New York: Grove Press, 1961.

RAMOS, SAMUEL, *Profile of Man and Culture in Mexico,* trans., Peter G. Earle. 1934. Reprint. Austin: University of Texas Press, 1972.

REAVIS, DICK J., *Conversations with Moctezuma: The Soul of Modern Mexico.* New York: Quill, Morrow, 1990.

REDING, ANDREW, "Mexico on the Edge," *The New York Times,* July 5, 1994, p. A17.

RIDING, ALAN, *Distant Neighbors: A Portrait of the Mexicans.* New York: Knopf, 1985.

RUDOLPH, JAMES A., ed., *Mexico: A Country Study* (Area Handbook Series). Washington, DC: U.S. Government Printing Office, 1985.

RUIZ, RAMON EDUARDO, *Triumphs and Tragedy: A History of the Mexican People.* New York: Norton, 1992.

RUSSELL, JAMES W., *After the Fifth Sun: Class and Race in North America.* Englewood Cliffs, NJ: Prentice-Hall, 1994.

SÁNCHEZ, RAY, "Drug Graft Seen in 'Old Mexico,'" *Newsday,* Mar. 13, 1995, pp. A7, A12.

SANDERSON, STEVEN, *The Transformation of Mexican Agriculture: International Structure and the Politics of Rural Change.* Princeton, NJ: Princeton University Press, 1986.

SELBY, HENRY A., ARTHUR D. MURPHY, AND STEPHEN A. LORENZEN, *The Mexican Urban Household: Organized for Self-Defense.* Austin: University of Texas Press, 1990.

WOLF, ERIC, *Sons of the Shaking Earth.* Chicago: University of Chicago Press, 1959.

WORLD BANK, *World Development Report, 1993: Investing in Health.* New York: Oxford University Press, 1993.

THE KALAHARI DESERT:
LAND OF THE ¡KUNG BUSHMEN

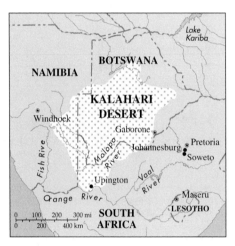

To get to the Kalahari Desert you would have to fly to the southern tip of Africa—a long day's flight from Toronto or Los Angeles. From one of South Africa's large, modern cities, a local airline would take you north to a remote airport at the edge of the desert. Then you would dip into your travel budget to hire a light plane to take you to the ¡Kung.

LOCATION: The Kalahari Desert stretches across much of Botswana. It dips south into South Africa and occupies a small area of Namibia on the west.

AREA: The size of New Jersey or Wales (8000 square miles; 23,200 square kilometers).

LAND: A dry, sandy plain 4000 feet high. Scattered trees, a few hills, and mostly dry riverbeds punctuate the rolling grassland.

CLIMATE: Temperatures go as high as 120°F in the summer and as low as 10°F in the winter. There is less than 10 inches of rain yearly in most areas.

PEOPLE: Most of the 45,000–60,000 Bushmen in Africa today live in Botswana and Namibia on the outer fringes of the Kalahari Desert.

CHAPTER 3

The ¡Kung: Bushmen of Southern Africa

INTRODUCTION

The ¡Kung Bushmen are a people sharply different from all the other groups in this book. For centuries, and probably for thousands of years, they have been a **hunting and gathering** (or **foraging**) people who live in small bands of ten to fifty people and gather wild plant foods and hunt game. Systematically moving among food and water sources, the ¡Kung are **nomadic:** they make no permanent homes, and carry with them their few possessions. They have no rulers, no schools, no money, no written language, no police, no hospitals, and no inequalities of wealth or privilege. The ¡Kung occupied the Kalahari Desert long before black people from southeastern Africa or whites from Europe arrived. Archeologists have found evidence of people like the ¡Kung living in this region as long ago as 11,000 years before the present and occupying the area without interruption ever since (Tobias, pp. 4, 30–31).

> *Bumping along sand tracks in the Kalahari Desert in dry season, you will not see the ¡Kung Bushman camp until your jeep is almost upon it: a circle of shelters roughly built of sticks and grasses, facing inward toward a cleared area, and almost invisible in the surrounding landscape of dry brush. The full band of perhaps twenty individuals gathers around their campfires. You see small people with yellowish-brown skins, partially clothed in animal hides, blending readily into their environment.*
>
> *It is dusk and they are blowing their fires into flames to cook the evening meal. Women are sorting through their day's collection of wild foods: nuts of the mongongo tree, tsama melons, water-bearing roots, perhaps birds' eggs or a snake, or in a wetter season, wild onions, leafy greens, tsin beans, or baobab fruit. The men have killed a small antelope and they are distributing the meat among their relatives. You may hear many voices: men tell the story of their hunt, women report on the tracks they have seen while out gathering; people gossip, tease, and joke. You hear the children's games, played to a rhythm of clapping and singing. The ¡Kung come forward to meet you, carefully leaving their weapons—their small bows with the lethal poison-coated arrows—behind. They will doubtless invite you to share their food and water, but they will expect you to return their hospitality.*

The ¡Kung Bushmen's Environment

The ¡Kung live in the Kalahari Desert of southwestern Africa, a harsh, semidesert environment. Their territory belongs to several African nations, chiefly

109

Botswana and Namibia. The Kalahari Desert is a vast basin of sand, occupying al-most a third of the African subcontinent. Much of the Kalahari is too dry to sustain human habitation, but in the more northerly parts, around places like Dobe and Nyae Nyae, where the ¡Kung live, there is enough rain to support drought-resistant plants, grasses, scattered trees, and the animals that feed upon them. There are many kinds of antelope, like eland, kudu, and gemsbok; there are warthogs, hares, and tortoises and also giraffe. (There are predators too, like lions and hyena, but the ¡Kung don't hunt these for food.) The rainy season leaves temporary pools of sur-face water and greens up the landscape so plants bear fruits, nuts, berries, and seeds. But rains are localized and unpredictable; while some areas receive abundant rainfall, others nearby may suffer drought. The whole region experiences drought approximately two years out of every five, with severe drought one year in four. There are dry riverbeds in the Kalahari, but they are rarely filled by runoff, perhaps only once in a decade. The ¡Kung are sustained during the dry season by a small number of permanent water holes, where underground water comes to the surface.

The Kalahari is "big sky country," flat and monotonous, with endless vistas of brush out to the horizon. Outsiders easily lose their way in the markerless land-scape. To this austere landscape is joined a harsh climate. During the hot, dry sea-son of September and October, temperatures reach 115°F in the shade, 126°F in the sun, and the temperature of the sand reaches 140°F. The Kalahari winter of May to August is cold and dry, with nighttime temperatures often below freezing (Marshall, pp. 62–71; Lee, 1979, pp. 87–88).

Who Are the ¡Kung Bushmen?

There are actually several distinct peoples in adjacent parts of Namibia and Botswana who are all considered ¡Kung, though they have different names for themselves. For example, the ¡Kung who live around Nyae Nyae, Namibia, call themselves *Ju /wasi* ("the real people"). All the ¡Kung peoples share a distinctive physical appearance and a common family of languages. The ¡Kung are quite small in stature (the men under 5 feet 3 inches, the women considerably under 5 feet) and they have light brown or "yellow" skin, small, heart-shaped faces with wide-apart eyes, eyefolds, and flat-bridged noses. Physically they are very different from the black Bantu-speaking people of Africa, who are tall and dark-skinned.

All the ¡Kung peoples speak one of three related "click languages," which will probably seem quite unusual to you. Click languages include a dozen or so click sounds, made by clicking the tongue against the teeth, the roof of the mouth, the cheek, and so on, as if you were going "tsk tsk" or signaling to a horse. The clicks usually function as consonants in forming words. The ¡Kung themselves have no written language so only anthropologists have attempted to write down these click sounds and they have developed a system of denoting the different clicks with sym-bols like these: ¡, /, //. The ¡ in ¡Kung is a click sound.

In southern Africa, the ¡Kung are also linked to other peoples who speak lan-guages unlike their own and who are also somewhat different from them in stature and skin color. These are the Nama-speaking peoples of the Kalahari region and the so-called Cape Bushmen of South Africa. All these peoples (and there are at least ten distinct groups in all) have been called Bushmen in southern Africa. The name seems to be derived from a Dutch term, *bossiesman,* which means "bandit," and it is an insulting term the early white settlers used to refer contemptuously to the native peoples they found in South Africa who hunted and gathered and who resisted when settlers took their land. Later, the Bushmen were called the *San,* a name used by Nama-speakers, and still later, in Botswana, they have been called *Basarwa,* a name meant to be more respectful. If you want to look up books about the iKung in a library catalog in the United States, you will need to look under "San Peoples of Southern Africa." We have chosen to call the iKung "Bushmen" in this chapter (despite the racist and sexist overtones of the name), because the iKung are now calling themselves Bushmen, emphasizing their ties to hunting and gathering peoples all over southern Africa (Gordon, pp. 4–8; Wood, personal communication).

Why Study the iKung Bushmen?

Now is the time to ask yourself: "Am I reacting to the iKung in an ethnocentric way?" Are you saying to yourself, "I have nothing to learn from these 'savages' who can't even read and write and go around in animal skins with bows and arrows"? We think you will find that the iKung have much to teach you: about human history, about living without war or inequality, and about living with nature without destroying it.

The Evolution of Human Societies

Using research by anthropologists, archeologists, and historians, sociologists have concluded that in all of human history there have been just four basic kinds of societies. The first human societies were **hunter-gatherer bands,** like the iKung Bushmen. Humans, and their prehuman ancestors before them lived like this for hundreds of thousands and perhaps millions of years. They lived in small nomadic bands, following game and harvesting wild foods. It was only about 10,000 years ago that humans learned to raise their own food. They settled down, often along rivers, and made gardens and raised tame animals. These people lived in **horticultural villages.** At about this same time, other peoples began to live as **pastoralists,** herding animals and often moving about with their herds. Approximately 6000 years ago what we think of as "civilization" began with the invention of agriculture. Agriculture applied new technologies (the plow) and new methods (fertilizing and rotating crops) so people could farm the same fields generation after generation. Farming raised more food and made it possible for some people to live on food others grew. They became artisans, priests, monks and nuns, kings and queens, professional soldiers, sailors, cathedral builders, artists, scientists and inventors, and all the other inhabitants of cities in **agricultural states.** Finally, the most recent type of society to develop (in the last 250 years) is that of **industrial nations,** in which farming has become so productive that most people can devote their lives to other work, producing goods in factories, building large cities, inventing new technologies, waging war, and so forth. All four types of societies still exist today, but there are fewer and fewer hunter-gatherer and horticultural societies.[1]

---

[1]Sociologists owe this commonly used classification scheme to Gerhard and Jean Lenski. See Lenski, Nolan, and Lenski, pp. 78-89.

The Importance of Hunter-Gatherers

Since the first humans were foragers, sociologists and anthropologists have long regarded hunter-gatherer bands as the cradles of human nature and culture. The first families must have been formed in hunter-gatherer bands, the first specialized roles and the first religions. It is easy to speculate (but difficult to prove) that early conditions of foraging bands fundamentally shaped human nature. Those who study hunter-gatherer societies have often asked whether widespread human characteristics—like competitiveness, or aggression—are a heritage from those first societies.

It is difficult to learn much about societies that existed 50,000 or 100,000 years ago, when all the world's peoples were hunter-gatherers. Archeologists dig up fossilized human and animal bones and the remains of hearths and sometimes huts, weapons, garbage heaps, and fossilized pollen, but these remains can tell us little about how people interacted in prehistoric times. To learn about humanity's ancient past, anthropologists and sociologists have turned to hunter-gatherer societies that still exist today. They have hoped that the study of the ¡Kung will open a window on the common ancestors of all humans—the ancient hunter-gatherer peoples.

Hunter-Gatherers and Human Nature

When you study the ¡Kung you must put away stereotyped images of "cavemen" fighting each other in a brutal competition for survival. The ¡Kung are a peaceful people and in this they are quite typical of hunter-gatherers. They avoid conflict and competition and share what they have so that everyone can survive. They have no formal leaders, no privileged class or deprived lower class. They don't hate or fight their neighbors. Though they live in a harsh environment, their lives are not brutal or debased. They value generosity and graciousness, joking and kidding around, and they find plenty of time for relaxation, playing music and singing, dressing up, and holding ceremonial dances, like parties that go on all night. If this is what our earliest ancestors were like, then we cannot blame our own greed and violence on our evolutionary heritage.

Living with Nature

The ¡Kung exemplify a kind of society we may well call the most successful human way of life of all times. The hunter-gatherer life sustained humanity for millions of years. Variations of foraging cultures allowed people to live in many different environments, gentle or harsh: by the shore, in forests, open grasslands, deserts, rain forests, and arctic tundra. Wherever they live, hunter-gatherers live close to nature: their food comes directly from nature, and everything they use—houses, tools, clothing, containers, jewelry, and weapons—is made by hand from natural materials. Hunter-gatherers use nature, but they don't use it up. They live in such a way that they don't kill off the animals they depend upon; they don't use up the water or pollute the land. They can go on living on the same land for thousands and thousands of years without harming it. Sociologists call this **sustainability.** In the last 10,000 years, since people learned to cultivate seeds and plants and domesticate animals, human impact on the environment has constantly increased.

Industrial society now pollutes the air and water and land. It pumps carbon dioxide into the atmosphere, creating a "greenhouse effect," and it alters ecosystems so many animal species become endangered or extinct. Many people are now asking: Is our industrial way of life sustainable? Perhaps we can learn from the iKung Bushmen about creating an environmentally sustainable society.

HISTORY OF THE BUSHMEN

We know very little about the history of the Bushmen for all the thousands of years before their contact with Europeans in the seventeenth century. There are some artifacts unearthed by archeologists and there are reports by early white settlers about meetings with Bushmen on their arrival in southern Africa, but evidence is very thin. The modern history of the Bushmen, recorded first by white settlers, then by colonial governments, and now by African governments, began in the seventeenth century. It is a tragic story of genocide and displacement.

Settlers and the Bushmen

In the seventeenth century, an estimated 200,000 Bushmen lived all over southern Africa—in the desert, in the mountains, on grasslands, and along the coasts. When the Dutch settled the Cape of Good Hope region at the southern tip of Africa in the 1650s, an indigenous (native) group of Bushmen, called the Khoi, were living there, fishing, hunting, gathering, and herding cattle and goats. Seizing their good land, the Dutch slaughtered the Khoi and drove them northward.

Other groups of Bushmen lived in more remote areas, in small bands and without domesticated animals. The Dutch were especially contemptuous of them and considered them "wild" people, little better than animals. In the eighteenth century, white settlers moved north and almost completely exterminated the Bushmen, killing the men and enslaving the women and children. Some Bushmen fought back, raiding settlers' farms and stealing cattle, and in remote areas they were able to hold off the whites for years. By the end of the nineteenth century, the Bushmen had been virtually wiped out in all of the country of South Africa. Further north, however, in the harsh lands of the Kalahari Desert, where no whites wished to settle, Bushmen continued to live as hunter-gatherers.

In the late nineteenth century, the Kalahari Desert Bushmen came into contact with another group of settlers: Bantu-speaking blacks from southeastern Africa. Relationships between the Bushmen and the Bantu peoples were not always harmonious. Both sides tell stories of armed conflict, cattle theft, and disputes over women, and the Bantu considered the Bushmen an inferior people. However, these forms of conflict have never become as extreme as the European genocide against the Bushmen, and in the twentieth century, trade and intermarriage between Bushmen and Bantu have peacefully developed. As a result of intermarriage, some Bushmen who live along the eastern edge of the Kalahari have come to resemble their Bantu neighbors physically. Two different Bantu cattle-herding peoples, the Tswana and the Herero, settled the margins of the Kalahari. iKung men worked for the Tswana as trackers and porters, and later as cattle herders, receiving tobacco and cow's milk in exchange for seasonal or temporary work. Many ǃKung, especially in Botswana, became attached to Herero farms, as unpaid dependents (Lee, 1979, pp. 32–33, 77–84; Lee, 1984, pp. 17–18; Lee, 1978, pp. 94–96; Silberbauer, p. 181).

The Fate of Hunter-Gatherers

As recently as 100 years ago, there were dozens of foraging peoples still living in isolation in the most remote corners of the globe—in the deserts of Africa and Australia, the rain forests of the Amazon, Africa, and New Guinea, and the arctic wastes of Canada. Today, the ǃKung are one of the last surviving foraging groups (along with some Eskimos and some Australian aborigines). Modern societies have not been kind to indigenous foraging peoples. Industrial societies have penetrated every corner of the earth, exploring, searching for precious metals or oil, for trees to log or land to clear for farming and ranching. Everywhere, they have dismissed indigenous hunter-gatherer peoples as subhuman savages. Settlers and explorers have not hesitated to kill indigenous peoples or take away their land, their means of survival. Western diseases spread through indigenous populations in devastating epidemics, and the bewildered survivors were converted by missionaries and enticed or forced into working for the outsiders. Under the assault of modern societies, indigenous cultures all over the world have disappeared. Surviving hunter-gatherers have been forced into the least desirable environments on earth. Even as you read this book, the last of the ǃKung may be abandoning the foraging life. Your children will grow up in a world in which hunters and gatherers are a lost part of history, not real peoples linking us to the human past.

Today, most ǃKung work on ranches and farms in Botswana and Namibia. They are the poorest, most despised people in those countries, often earning no wages at all for their work. The ǃKung have no government of their own, but they live, nevertheless, in a world of modern nations, and government action shapes their lives. For example, when a fence was erected along the border between Botswana and Namibia, customary ǃKung patterns of gathering and hunting were disrupted. After 1970, in Namibia, the ǃKung were caught between sides in the war of liberation from South African rule, and recruited by the South African forces as trackers and soldiers. Both Botswana and Namibia have also directly intervened in ǃKung affairs, taking some ǃKung lands away and designating special areas where they have encouraged Bushmen to live. In Botswana, the government put thousands of acres of ǃKung land into a game reserve where the ǃKung are permitted to live only by hunting and gathering, using traditional weapons. In Namibia, the government made a special "Bushmanland" reserve for the ǃKung. There the government has dug wells and built schools, encouraging the ǃKung to settle in one place and live partly as herders and partly as hunter-gatherers (Lee, 1979, pp. 424–431; 1984, pp. 147–150).

Anthropologists and the ǃKung Bushmen

The ǃKung are not only one of the last remaining foraging peoples, they have been studied with exceptional thoroughness. From the early 1950s, through the present, anthropologists, linguists, archeologists, musicologists, and ecologists have almost continuously lived with and observed one or another group of !Kung. These social scientists made a very detailed record of !Kung life in books and films, which we will draw on in this account.

The first major studies of the !Kung were done by Lorna and Laurence Marshall in the 1950s. The Marshalls made many trips to the Kalahari, accompanied by their daughter, Elizabeth Marshall Thomas, who wrote a famous book about the Bushman, THE HARMLESS PEOPLE, and their son, John Marshall, who filmed !Kung daily life. In the 1970s, anthropologist Richard B. Lee and his team studied several groups of !Kung, as reported in his books, THE !KUNG SAN and THE DOBE !KUNG. Today, a new generation of anthropologists has joined those studying the !Kung, including John Yellen, Susan Kent, James Denbow, Edwin Wilmsen, Robert Hitchcock, Robert Gordon, Megan Biesele, and Claire Ritchie. Their primary focus has been on how !Kung culture is now changing as the !Kung Bushmen settle in villages and adopt cattle herding.

Some present-day anthropologists (like Robert Gordon and Edwin Wilmsen) (Gordon, pp. 1–12, 64–129, Wilmsen, pp. 10–12, 15–32) have questioned the portrait of the !Kung Bushmen painted by earlier anthropologists. These scholars, they suggest, were too eager to discover in the !Kung an isolated living survival of Stone Age times. They caution that for a long time—perhaps as long as 2000 years— Bantu and Khoi herders lived nearby Bushmen, and well-used routes for trade in iron, glass beads, and shells passed through Bushman territory. Bushmen, they contend, have long herded animals and traded goods when they could.

This chapter first describes the !Kung who live as hunter-gatherers. You must keep in mind that relatively few !Kung still follow this way of life today—only a few thousand, at most. Even in the 1950s and 1960s, when there were many more people living the traditional foraging life, the !Kung were not fossils of the past. Prehistoric hunter-gatherers lived in a world of hunter-gatherers. Then, the whole world was wilderness; there were no towns, no stores, no roads, no lands cleared for farming. Small bands of people traveled about following game and harvesting wild plants, and meeting another band was a rare and important event. Nowadays, humans are so numerous they are crowding out other species, and the remaining wilderness shrinks year by year. It is difficult to picture a time when the total human population was small and its survival insecure. We can use our knowledge of present-day hunter-gatherers to help us picture the past, but we must remember that the ancient world of foragers is gone. Today, hunter-gatherer peoples are surrounded by more modern societies and often exploited by them.

!KUNG CULTURE: A DESIGN FOR LIVING

You can do a brief "thought experiment" to help you understand !Kung culture. Imagine yourself and your friends suddenly transported to the Kalahari Desert and abandoned there. Will you survive? Unlike the animals of the Kalahari, you will not know instinctively how to find water or food or shelter, or how to organize your group life. You will lack special physical adaptations to desert life. Your evolved human capacity to create culture will have to see you through.

The ¡Kung, like all human societies, have learned how to secure the necessities of life. They divide up their tasks efficiently. They have learned to keep order, resolve conflicts, and protect the group from outside threats. Their beliefs about the meaning of life sustain them. Even reproduction is not just left to nature; the ¡Kung make sure they have enough children, but not too many, and they teach their children how to live in their society and their difficult environment.

Sociology textbooks often adopt anthropologist Clyde Kluckhohn's definition of **culture** as "a design for living." Every human group must solve the basic problems of adapting to their environment: groups do so through **culture** and **social structure,** and if they are successful, the group survives. But there are many possible "designs for living."[2]

Foraging: A Successful Cultural Adaptation

Even in their harsh environment the ¡Kung have found a way to live that is environmentally sustainable, psychologically rewarding, and physically healthy. Four elements of ¡Kung culture make possible a more than adequate living in the Kalahari Desert. These are: the ¡Kung's comprehensive **knowledge** of their environment and its food sources; the custom of **nomadism,** or movement from one temporary encampment to another; customs of childbearing and childrearing that result in **population limitation;** and **values** that stress sharing, modesty, and cooperation.

Knowledge

Foremost in importance is the ¡Kung's detailed knowledge of their environment, itself a form of control over nature. Knowledge of plants, water sources, and animal habits enables the ¡Kung to use the desert as a larder, neither cultivating nor storing food, but rather turning systematically from one resource to another, each in its season. To some degree, knowledge is gender-based, since women gather plants and men hunt animals, but both women and men have some basic store of knowledge about animal tracks and plant properties.

¡Kung hunters are superb trackers. Not only can they identify animals from their tracks in the sand and their droppings, they are able to deduce detailed information from tracks. They can single out the tracks of a single animal (perhaps the one injured by an arrow) from those of a herd, tell if it is male or female, old or young, whether it is injured and how badly. Examining the freshness of tracks, ¡Kung men can deduce how long ago an animal passed, whether it was feeding, how fast it was going, whether it passed during the morning or afternoon (Did it seek the shade to the east or west of bushes and trees?) or at night. Both men and women can read human footprints in the sand, identifying the tracks of every individual.

Intimate knowledge of resources makes the foraging life possible. The ¡Kung know and name hundreds of plants, insects, animals, and birds. Tiny ¡Kung arrows

---

[2]See, for example, the chapters on culture in *Sociology* by Gelles and Levine, which begins with discussion of Kluckhohn's 1949 book, *Mirror for Man* (New York: McGraw-Hill, 1949) (Gelles and Levine, p. 80).

A ¡Kung hunter takes careful aim with his bow and arrow. His flimsy-looking arrow has a poison-coated tip and it is made to wound, not kill. Later, when the poison has done its work, weakening the quarry, the hunter will return and make his kill up close with a spear.

derive their lethal power from a poison coating made from the larvae and parasites of three different kinds of beetles.[3] In the dry season, when plants wither to near invisibility, ¡Kung women unerringly locate underground water-storing roots from the evidence of a few tiny leaves hidden in the dry grass. They know exactly when each plant resource will be ready to harvest, under various weather conditions. And they know how much water each permanent and temporary water hole can be expected to provide, so they are never caught short.

Nomadism

The ¡Kung adapt themselves to the desert by living in small **nomadic bands.** The ¡Kung have no permanent place of residence, but they cannot be said to wander either. They move about the desert in a planned, rational fashion, making temporary camps to exploit local resources of water and food, then move on when these

---

[3]The poison acts on the central nervous system, through the bloodstream, so animals killed by the poison can be safely eaten.

become scarce. In the dry season, they retreat to permanent water holes. In this way, the ¡Kung neither wear out nor pollute the desert; they distribute their impact over a wide area.

But nomadism means traveling light. When the ¡Kung move, they carry on their backs all their possessions, plus their young children. In fact, all of a person's belongings can fit into a leather bag the size of an overnight carrier that weighs no more than 12 to 15 pounds. Possessions include a woman's *kaross* (her leather all-purpose garment and blanket), her digging stick, items of personal adornment like beads and headbands, ostrich eggshell water holders, and, nowadays, an iron pot. A man carries his hunting kit—arrows, bow and quiver, and his fire-making kit; other possessions include musical instruments, toys, pipes, ceremonial rattles, tortoise shell bowls, nets, and leather bags. All ¡Kung possessions (except the pot) are handmade and can readily be made anew. Houses are built at each camp out of branches and grasses, and abandoned when the camp is moved. The ¡Kung possess little, but until they become involved in the modern cash economy, they desire no more, and feel no deprivation.

Population Control

Ultimately, the desert can support the ¡Kung because they keep their population proportionate to its resources. In the 1970s, in the central Kalahari, population density was no more than one person per each 4 to 6 square miles! (Silberbauer, p. 184). Significantly, it is a low birth rate, rather than an usually high death rate that keeps the ¡Kung population small. ¡Kung women reach puberty late, and generally don't have their first child until their late teens. Thereafter, children are widely spaced, without modern means of birth control, with an interval of approximately four years between babies. How this spacing is achieved has fascinated anthropologists. Richard B. Lee concludes that the nomadic foraging life and population control are closely linked. ¡Kung women nurse their children for as long as four years, and during that time they carry them everywhere, on daily foraging trips as well as on longer migrations, and they carry them in such a fashion that the child can nurse at will. Nursing is known to inhibit ovulation, but in most societies it is an ineffective means of birth control. Lee argues that ¡Kung babies nurse so frequently that ovulation is more effectively inhibited. ¡Kung women who settle on Bantu cattle ranches or farms carry their babies less and also give birth at more frequent intervals.

The ¡Kung understand the importance of spacing their children: it is very difficult for a mother to carry two children at once and, also, since young children live so entirely on their mother's milk, the ¡Kung believe that if a mother had two babies nursing, her milk would be insufficient and both would probably die. **Infanticide** (the killing of newborn infants) is infrequently practiced, but seen as a possible tragic necessity should a new sibling come too soon after the birth of a baby or in the rare case of twins. Infant and child mortality is high by modern western standards, but not compared to most poor agricultural societies. Close to 20 percent of ¡Kung children die before their first birthday, and only half of those born live long enough to marry (Shostak, p. 182).

The Value of Sharing

Critical to ¡Kung survival is the emphasis they place on sharing. The worst one can say of a person is that he or she is "far-hearted" or stingy. Generosity, graciousness, and modesty are highly valued. Indeed, it would be fair to say that sharing is a subject of constant discussion among the ¡Kung, with the question, "Who will give me food?" always on people's minds.

From the **functionalist perspective,** ¡Kung sharing makes sense; it helps the society to survive. You could say that sharing is the ¡Kung "social security system." They cannot store food for future use and they cannot buy food with money or any other goods, so when food is scarce, life is threatened. A man could be the ¡Kung's best hunter, but if he is injured or falls ill, there is no unemployment insurance or welfare, no savings account or pension plan. He must rely on the people in his family and band to feed him. Everyone needs to help others, so they can be helped in turn.

Sharing is not only a prime value in ¡Kung culture, it is a constant practice integral to their way of life. Sharing takes place on many levels. The plant foods women gather are cooked and shared with their immediate families. Big game is shared on a wider basis. The hunter to whom the meat belongs cuts it into large chunks and distributes these among his immediate relatives: his wife, in-laws, parents, and siblings. These recipients give some of their share to those who eat at their fire, but they also cut much of the meat into smaller pieces and make presents of these to their relatives, who pass it on in turn to theirs. In the end, everyone in a camp shares the meat, not in a wholesale distribution, but as a personal gift from some connection, and the meat is quickly consumed. The idea of a person hoarding meat is horrifying to the ¡Kung: it seems savage and uncivilized. "Lions might do that; people could not," they explain. Lorna Marshall noted that in one large dry-season encampment, the meat of a single eland (a large antelope) was ultimately distributed to sixty-three individuals (Marshall, p. 302).

But the ¡Kung struggle with sharing; it doesn't always come easily and sometimes hunger or possessiveness wins out over generosity. People grumble if someone keeps a particularly desirable ornament or tool, instead of passing it on as a gift. Disputes often arise over the sharing of food. ¡Kung customs facilitate sharing by blurring the ownership of meat. Meat belongs not to the man who brings it down, but to the owner of the arrow which first penetrates the quarry. And a hunter will usually carry arrows borrowed or received as gifts from many other individuals in addition to his own. Even a poor hunter may thus come to be the owner of meat, and people will not be put in the position of constantly receiving gifts of meat from the same superior hunter.

Sharing takes place on a wider basis too: between bands as well as within them. Kalahari resources are unevenly distributed, since localized drought may temporarily render one area barren while another is productive. At times like these, whole bands of individual families visit relatives in more fertile or better-watered areas. At another time, when conditions are different, they will reciprocate as hosts. Sharing evens out inequalities among the ¡Kung, between youthful and aging families, between talented and inept hunters, women and men, and people in different areas. Sharing constantly reinstates equality, ensuring that differences in individual ability or luck will not accumulate into institutionalized economic or status stratification.

An Integrated Culture

Knowledge, nomadism, low population growth, and sharing are critical elements of ¡Kung culture. Each supports the other, and all allow the ¡Kung to prosper in their harsh environment. We can say that ¡Kung Bushman society has a high degree of **cultural integration:** the different elements of the culture are consistent and fit together. For example, knowledge about resources, and norms and values concerning sharing make possible the nomadic way of life. Nomadism, in turn, holds down population growth, so the community does not outgrow its resources, or have too many babies to carry. Small, homogeneous, simple societies like the ¡Kung often have a high level of cultural integration.

Internal consistency like this is satisfying: people agree about most things; they share the same values and a single way of life. But integrated cultures are also fragile. Disruption of one of their elements may seriously damage or destroy the whole. For example, when the ¡Kung settle temporarily at Bantu cattle posts, women may have children so closely spaced as to prevent a return to the foraging life. Acquisition of cattle, goats, or chickens makes nomadism difficult too, but water and plant resources may be too scarce to permit settling in one place. Under pressures like these, ¡Kung society is now disintegrating.

How Hard Is the Foraging Life?

Until recently, life in hunter-gatherer societies was believed to be harsh and difficult, with constant labor the only shield against starvation, and population kept from outrunning resources only by famine, disease, and infanticide. In the last few decades, studies of the ¡Kung Bushmen and other foraging societies have resulted in a much rosier view of foraging societies and, by implication, of early human history. One of the most significant new insights is that foragers don't work very hard. In fact, they spend fewer hours working, and enjoy more hours of leisure, than people in agricultural and modern industrial societies. In a typical band observed by Lee, women went out gathering on an average of nine out of twenty-eight days. Counting all foraging, toolmaking and fixing, and housework, women put in an average workweek of forty hours. ¡Kung men spent more days in hunting, an average of twelve out of every twenty-eight days, and counting all hunting, gathering, toolmaking and fixing, and housework, their average workweek was forty-four and a half hours. Even at this low level of work, the ¡Kung are generally adequately nourished, and they have infant mortality rates and adult life expectancies somewhat better than those of most agricultural societies.[4]

---

[4]Richard B. Lee collected this data in 1964. See Lee, 1979, pp. 254–280. Lee notes that work in child care was not included in the calculations, but if it had been, the work totals for women would have been considerably higher, since they do 60 to 80 percent of all care of young children.

Work and Affluence

The ¡Kung Bushmen work little, but from our modern western point of view, they are poor and deprived. It is important to understand that ¡Kung living traditionally don't feel deprived. They don't crave permanent houses, running water, refrigerators, Jeeps, or diapers. They accept occasional hunger, secure in the knowledge that there will be food soon enough. In effect, the ¡Kung have made a trade-off—living at a low level of material affluence, they needn't work much, and can enjoy a great deal of leisure. And, in reality, since they live in a sparse environment, greater work would not necessarily produce greater abundance over the long run; it might instead disturb the ecological balance. For example, more intensive hunting might temporarily provide abundant meat, but it might also threaten the welfare of the wild herds and, therefore, ultimately the survival of the ¡Kung.

Leisure

The ¡Kung Bushmen devote their leisure to nurturing group life, cultivating relationships among individuals, and elaborating their culture. Perhaps it was the abundant leisure of foragers that allowed our ancestors to create human culture, incrementally freeing humanity from the bonds of instinct and biological necessity.

Those who study the ¡Kung all note that they are great talkers. They spend an enormous amount of time sitting around their campfires and talking, joking, arguing, exchanging news, telling stories, repeating the events of a hunt, planning tomorrow's hunting or gathering. There is a constant buzz of conversation in a ¡Kung camp, and uproarious laughter breaks out often. Women and girls sit close together at the campfire, their shoulders and knees touching, as do the men and boys. Members of a ¡Kung band truly seem to enjoy each others' company.

Playing Games. Unlike the children of farming and herding societies, ¡Kung children do not have to work. This is, in its way, a sign of affluence: you could say that the ¡Kung enjoy such abundance that they don't need the labor of their children (or of old people) to support the band. Since children don't go to school either, they are free to play all day long, until, in their teen years, girls and boys begin to accompany their elders in gathering and hunting. Adults also like to play games when they are at leisure in camp or in the evenings.

The games the ¡Kung play reveal much about their culture. There are no games in which people keep score or care greatly about winning or losing. Games are all played in groups, and in many, the players are bound together in rhythmic chorus and close physical contact. Typical is the ball game played by girls who stand in a line, singing and clapping. Each girl takes the ball in turn at the right point in the music, dances with it, then tosses it to the next in line (Marshall, pp. 313, 322, 332–336).

A Musical Culture. Music is not only a part of ¡Kung games, but a constant accompaniment to camp life. The ¡Kung have a rich musical culture in which everyone participates in some way. Their homemade instruments make subtle, vibrant sounds, and their compositions are always complex. The traditional *guashi* is a stringed instrument made from a hollowed-out log strung with animal sinew or

Surrounded by miles of open land, this band of ¡Kung, adults and children, men and women, cluster close together, talking, telling stories, joking and arguing in typical Bushman fashion.

hair. There is also a traditional one-string violin, and the more recently introduced drums (adapted from their Bantu neighbors) and the thumb piano, a handheld instrument made of wood and strips of tin. Women as well as men play the *guashi* and thumb piano. Talented men even produce music by plucking their upended bows. People carry instruments with them on trips, and traveling or in camp, they often sit listening to a musician, sometimes softly improvising a sung harmony interwoven with the intricate rhythm (Biesele, pp. 165–166; Thomas, pp. 223–225; Shostak, pp, 14, 310; Marshall, pp. 363–375).

Music is a means of individual self-expression for the ¡Kung. People who are troubled or sad or bothered by some trying incident may sit alone and compose "mood music"—songs with titles, but without words, that touchingly express emotions, often wistful or ironic. One song Elizabeth Marshall Thomas heard, called "Bitter Melons," expressed the musician's feelings when he returned to a remembered field of melons, but found them too bitter to eat. Another song expressed the composer's guilt and sorrow about an incident when his brother-in-law, lost in the bush near camp, had shouted to the band, and no one had bothered to answer him (Thomas, pp. 122–123). Some songs are mocking, and they are sung under cover of darkness, with words that reproach an individual for misbehavior.

There are also sacred songs, like the eland song, the gemsbok song, the giraffe song, and the sun song, which are part of the religious and ceremonial life of the group. These songs are sung at sacred trance dances, and some are also sung at important ceremonies, like the eland song sung by women at the ceremony for an adolescent's first menstruation.

Sacred Dances. In a small group, initiation ceremonies are infrequent, but trance dances are a regular feature of !Kung life, held on an average every ten days, with dances more frequent during dry season, when the nearness of several bands at a water hole makes social life more intense and exciting. Dances involve everyone in the band or bands, and last entire nights, with the women seated in a line or circle, shoulder to shoulder, singing the sacred songs and clapping complex rhythmic accompaniments. The men, their steps emphasized by the shaking of cocoon rattles tied around their legs, dance themselves into a trance in which they can converse with the spirits and heal the sick. Children excitedly dance and clap along, and then, as the night wears on, fall asleep in their mothers' laps.

Trance dances may begin spontaneously, as fun, often initiated by children, or they may be arranged in response to serious illness or misfortune. Trance medicine, *n/um*, is a kind of power, "owned" by the people who have learned how to achieve a trance state and use it to cure others. About half the adult men and a third of the women have achieved trance at some time. A smaller number are accomplished healers, the greatest of whom may travel from camp to camp when needed.

In trance, healers are able to draw illness out of the bodies of the sick and throw it away. The !Kung believe sickness (and misfortune and death) are caused by tiny invisible arrows shot into the sick person by the spirits of the dead. These spirits are not malevolent, but lonely, and wish the living to be with them. The spirits are especially likely to take away a person who is ill-treated by others. In trance, healers lay their hands on the afflicted persons and draw the arrows into their own bodies. Then, at a moment of crisis, healers violently shudder and shriek, hurling the arrows away again. It is believed that, in deep trance, healers' spirits can leave their bodies to meet and talk with the spirits of the dead, to find out why they want to take a sick person and try to persuade them to reconsider.

Though they may begin as social events, dances become serious ceremony when people enter trance, for it can be a frightening and exhausting experience. *N/um* is thought to be a substance in the dancer, which the music, the smoke and fire, and the strenuous dancing of the ceremony heat up. When *n/um* comes to a boil, it bursts into the brain and the dancer enters trance. The dancer trembles, sweats, and chokes for breath. The world spins and the dancer sees visions and can walk on coals without being burned. To learn how to enter and control trance, a person needs an experienced teacher, usually a relative of the same sex, who dances with the apprentice, massages tired limbs and offers reassuring restraint if the new dancer becomes wildly disoriented. Though not everyone chooses to become a healer, and some people's *n/um* is unusually strong, practically everyone who wants to achieve trance can do so; healing is not reserved for a privileged few (Biesele, pp. 167–168; Shostak, pp. 291–299; Lee, 1984, pp. 109–113).

Megan Biesele emphasizes that the dancers' *n/um* cannot be activated without the support of singers (or drummers for the women's drum dance). Singing actually protects the dancers as their spirits leave their bodies. The trance dance is thus "a concerted effort by the entire community to banish misfortune," and a central unifying force in ¡Kung life. As Emile Durkheim pointed out a century ago (in THE ELEMENTARY FORMS OF THE RELIGIOUS LIFE), dances like these are important shared experiences. Joining together in a sacred and risky ceremony intensifies group feeling, strengthening the bonds of group solidarity. While the ¡Kung may think of their dances as serving a practical-spiritual purpose—curing the sick—dances also fulfill a **latent function,** a secondary purpose of which the ¡Kung themselves are unaware, that of drawing the group closer together (Durkheim, p. 432).

As a student of sociology, you will recognize that trance dances are both religious and medical. There are no ¡Kung hospitals or doctors, though the role of "healer" is one of the few specialized roles in ¡Kung society. There are no ¡Kung priests or churches: everyone participates in sacred dances and many people learn to enter trance. But sacred dances are nevertheless part of religious life, as Durkheim recognized. Through the dances the ¡Kung enter the realm of the sacred and communicate with spirits. They seek otherworldly help for their misfortunes and affirm their beliefs.

Inventing Culture. In studying ¡Kung trance dances, we have a rare opportunity to see that culture is not simply learned and passed on, but is also constantly created and re-created, by real individuals. Traditionally, the gemsbok song was sung at trance dances, but within living memory, a new song, the giraffe song, was composed, by a woman, old Be, to whom the song came complete as a revelation from God. She taught it to her husband, who taught it to others, and this song became so popular that it largely replaced the gemsbok song. Also, while traditionally only men danced and entered trance, quite recently a women's trance dance, the drum dance, was invented, and it has swept ¡Kung society, with women in band after band learning from each other how to enter trance (Biesele, p. 162; Shostak, p. 297; Lee, 1984, pp. 113–115).

Gift Giving and Visiting. A great deal of the ¡Kung's abundant leisure is devoted to cultivating relationships—in talk and games, music making, and ceremony—that reinforce group solidarity. Leisure activities also link individuals with individuals in ties of friendship and reciprocal obligation. People all over the northern ¡Kung area are connected in face-to-face acquaintance through visiting. In rainy season, individuals, couples, and small family groups break off from their bands to visit relatives, especially people they like (Marshall, pp. 180–181; Lee, 1979, p. 72).

Visits are often occasions for gift giving, though gifts are also bestowed within the band, and exchanged by spouses. Gift giving is a constant preoccupation and a subject of talk second in prominence only to food. Interaction about gifts expresses feelings and carries weight in relationships. People talk about whom they plan to give gifts to; sometimes they complain about gifts they have received, or about people who take too long to reciprocate gifts. A person may ask someone for the gift of a particular object, as a way of inviting a closer relationship, or to cause discomfort because of jealousy or anger. It would be very rude to refuse a gift, and one must reciprocate, but not too soon, for owing a return gift links people together in friendship and is really the whole point of the exercise.

The objects given as gifts are really of secondary importance to the relationships created and sustained. Anyone can make any of the objects in daily use, or readily borrow them, and people tend to keep the gifts they receive for just a short while, before passing them on as gifts to someone else. People give objects in common use: ostrich shell bead headbands and necklaces, musical instruments, wooden bowls, arrows, pipes, dance rattles, or valued materials like eland fat (Marshall, pp. 303–305, 309–310).

SOCIAL STRUCTURE AND GROUP LIFE

One important lesson you can learn from studying the ¡Kung Bushmen is that people create social structure themselves, through interaction. When you live in a large, complex society, statuses and roles and institutions often seem like "givens." You are confronted with politicians or bosses, teachers or nurses, schools or courts, and you may feel you have had nothing to do with creating them. In ¡Kung society, it is clear that statuses and roles emerge as the result of repeated interaction between individuals. With the ¡Kung, we can see the building of social structure very clearly, because ¡Kung society is limited to the family and the band. The ¡Kung are distinctive (though typical of hunting and gathering societies) in that they have an extremely limited selection of statuses, roles, groups, and institutions. There are no chiefs or officials, no police officers, priests, managers, employees, teachers, doctors, servants, or generals, or any of a long list of specialized statuses and roles that may be found in your society. There are no committees, gangs, classes, clans, teams, parliaments, or clubs. Nor are there churches, courts, prisons, hospitals, schools, armies, governments, markets, or businesses. Because there is no central authority in ¡Kung society, ¡Kung Bushmen have a lot of individual freedom. They are not in the habit of taking orders from anyone, and if a person doesn't like what others are doing, their most usual response is to pick up and leave.

¡Kung society is a social system based on kinship: the band, the family, and kin statuses comprise all social structure and must serve all needs. It is most helpful to think of ¡Kung society not as socially impoverished by its lack of varied social structure, but as focused with extraordinary intensity on family relationships. Since social structure is created and maintained through interaction, it is easy to understand that the ¡Kung are constantly involved in forming and elaborating family relations.

The Family: Putting Flexibility First

The small **nuclear family** (the reproductive unit of parents and children) is the basic unit of ¡Kung society. ¡Kung families are "modular" and flexible. Nuclear family modules may link together to form larger **extended families,** and extended families may also break up into their constituent nuclear units. A series of nuclear and extended families link together to form a band, but bands are not necessarily permanent arrangements: some families may leave and others join, and sometimes a band will break up entirely. The modular structure of ¡Kung families and bands may readily be seen as a form of **cultural adaptation,** permitting flexible adjustment of group size to available resources.

Creating Nuclear Families

While a couple and their children form a long-lasting, firmly bonded group in ¡Kung society, nuclear families never live independently. (However, they may temporarily go off visiting on their own.) Nuclear families are small. In the 1950s, 1960s and 1970s, anthropologists found that the average ¡Kung woman gave birth to only four to five children altogether, and the average family comprised only two to three living children. Marriage creates nuclear families, and also links them in larger extended families and in an even broader kinship network.

When a couple marries, the ¡Kung expect the husband to move in with his new wife's family. Typically, they explain this custom in terms of food. The boy must feed his wife's parents, who are getting old, and he must feed his bride, they say, and prove he is capable and responsible (Marshall, p. 169). Members of the same band are not forbidden to marry, but such marriages are unusual. Consequently, marriages usually involve some reshuffling of band membership. This is especially so since the new husband may bring others with him to his wife's band. He remains responsible for his parents and dependents, and they may come with him. ¡Kung men are allowed to have more than one wife (**polygyny**), though this practice is rare, and in such a case, a man will bring his first wife, their children, and perhaps her relatives with him (in addition to his own), when he joins his new wife's family.

There is no set duration for this **bride service** with the wife's family (people say it should last long enough for three children to be born), but afterward a man has the right to return to his own people, taking his wife and dependents. He may or may not do this, depending on how well he gets along with his wife's band and what kinds of resources are available to each band. The couple and their dependents may in fact move back and forth between his relatives and hers (Marshall, p. 170). One way of understanding this is to say that ¡Kung society is **ambilocal:** people live with either the husband's or the wife's relatives. It is also **bilateral:** they reckon kinship on both their mother's and their father's sides.

The Band: Linking Families

There is no rigid pattern for band formation. Band members are always related to each other in some fashion (through ties of blood or marriage), but the actual linkages vary. The band grows like a chain, as in-marrying spouses bring their parents, siblings, and spouses, who in turn bring theirs. But band members are not mandated by kinship ties to remain together. People choose to stay in a band because they get along well living and working together. If they don't get along, families are free to leave the band, affiliating themselves with relatives in some other band. This is a real option, frequently exercised. Often families break off from their band to visit others—to exchange gifts, or news, or arrange a marriage, or attend a ceremony. Because bands are flexible, people can adjust the size of their group to environmental conditions and resources. Most people, Lorna Marshall found, have relatives who are parents, offspring, or siblings in five to thirteen other bands (Marshall, pp. 180–181, 195, 200). But everyone belongs to a family and a band; there are no un-attached people in ¡Kung society.

> *Dabe saw the straggling line first. A dozen people approached slowly through the bush. Dabe broke into a smile as he recognized his mother's favorite brother /Gao at the head of the line. /Gao had once lived for two years with Dabe's band and had taught Dabe to track and hunt. Dabe rushed to meet his uncle and shouted to attract his attention. /Gao embraced Dabe and croaked out a sad and weary tale. /Gao's band's water hole had run dry and they had walked north for six days, searching the area for Dabe's band. /Gao's infant daughter had died three days ago when her mother's milk dried up. As /Gao spoke, Dabe's mother Karu rushed for-ward and embraced her brother.*
>
> *Then /Gao's wife limped up, and her mother and brother and his family, and his wife's wid-owed sister and her sons. Karu brought water that had been stored in ostrich eggshells; soon the travelers had their first deep drink of good water in days. An hour later, Dabe's father Kwi and several other men of the band appeared, returning from a hunt. Kwi greeted his rel-atives warmly and invited them to make their camp next to his. Later, he gave them a share of the eland he had killed, but his heart was full of anxiety. There was not enough water here for even two small bands. How would they all survive?*
>
> *The next day it was decided: /Gao and his band would stay with Dabe and Karu and Kwi. They were too worn to go further. But the other people in Dabe's band decided to go to stay with their relatives at Nyae Nyae, where there was a permanent water hole and the rains usually began first.*

Kinship: Elaborating Connections

¡Kung kinship is rudimentary in some ways, extraordinarily complex in others. The ¡Kung are not much interested in keeping track of relatives more than two genera-tions back in time, or beyond second cousins. But they have developed several in-teresting devices for creating extra kinship bonds, weaving additional threads into the net of family that unites all the ¡Kung Bushmen.

The K'ausi and the N'ore

An important part of ¡Kung kinship has to do with the relationship of bands to their territories. Every band is attached to a territory—a water hole and the land and resources surrounding it, called a *n'ore*. It would be impossible for a band to exist without a *n'ore* (and since the number of water holes is limited, this serves to limit the number of bands). Each band is identified with a group of related older people, who have lived in the band a long time—usually siblings or cousins, who are con-sidered to be the "owners" or *k'ausi* of the *n'ore*. Visitors traveling through a terri-tory would ask the *k'ausi* for permission to gather plant foods and use the water hole.

The *k'ausi* are not formal leaders. They "own" the resources, but can't give them away or sell them; neither can they decide who joins the band, or tell people what to do. They may not necessarily be the informal leaders of the band either; they may be too old or lacking in the personal qualities needed for leadership.

Leadership is then likely to be exercised by someone else who has a strong personality (but is not arrogant or selfish) and who has qualities of wisdom and judgment (Lee, 1979, pp. 61–67; 1984, p. 88).

Generations and the Joking Relationship

Another kinship principle profoundly shapes life in ¡Kung society: the principle of alternating generations (Lee, 1984, pp. 63–66). ¡Kung kinship terms pair up alternating generations. You, your grandparents, and your grandchildren share a special kin relationship; so do your parents and your children. Special reciprocal kin terms are used by the alternating pairs.

Just to make all this more complicated, there is another principle related to alternating generations: the joking relationship. All of a ¡Kung person's kin are either people they joke with or people they avoid. The "joking relationship" is relaxed, affectionate, and familiar; the "avoidance relationship" is respectful and formal. Generally speaking, you joke with relatives in your generation, your grandparents' generation and your grandchildren's generation, and you avoid relatives in your parents' and your children's generations. An important rule is that you may never marry someone in the avoidance relationship.

At the end of the long dry season, when everyone was waiting impatiently for the rains to begin, five bands gathered at the large permanent water hole at Nyae Nyae. They had to—it was practically the only water left—but it was also a wonderful distraction from worries about the rain. Xama thought this was the best time of the year. She saw her married older brother, and her best friend who had gone to live with her husband's band. Almost every night there was a trance dance at one camp or another. Xama was 16 and knew she was ready now to get married.

At the water hole, Xama met her mother's uncle / 'Ase, who had long ago left Xama's band to do his bride service in his wife's band. "Come walk with me," he laughed, "I am so old that I need help from my grandchildren." Xama laughed also. In his mid-thirties, / 'Ase was muscular and smooth-faced. He stood half a head taller than Xama; he was known as "Tall / 'Ase." "Here is someone who makes me feel small," / 'Ase said, as a hazel-eyed young man walked into view. As tall as / 'Ase, Tu was in his early twenties and, in Xama's eyes, very handsome.

"This is Tu," / 'Ase introduced the young man, "he is your cousin's cousin." This made Tu a marriageable partner for Xama, and after a few comments, / 'Ase left the couple alone. In a few days Xama had decided that the future would offer few better opportunities than the tall young man with the hazel eyes. But there were problems. Xama's aunt confronted her and said, "You must not joke with Tu; people are talking. Tu is the brother of your uncle's second wife. You cannot marry him; he is of your parents' generation."

Xama was stunned and frightened, but Tu reassured her. "I am your cousin's cousin; that's what's most important. People will see that." Tu's father and brother argued openly with Xama's mother. "Tu and Xama," they said, "could marry." No one could agree and Tu and Xama were miserable. Tu's father said he would take them to his cousin's band. They wouldn't see any problem with the marriage. The young couple waited anxiously for the rains to come and make travel possible.

Fictive Kin: Making Kinship Really Complicated

Here is the tricky part: the ¡Kung Bushmen take the whole kinship structure—relationships by blood and marriage, alternating generations, joking and avoidance relationships—and apply it to fictive (imaginary) kin. The system is based on names. People who have your name address your kin as theirs—they call your wife "wife," your father "father," and so forth. And you can do the same: anyone with your mother's name you can address as "mother," anyone with your son's name you may call "son," and so on. Anyone with your sibling's name or your grandparent's name stands in a joking relationship to you. Those with your father's name or your child's, you treat with avoidance. Also, and very important, you may not marry anyone who shares the name of a relative you are forbidden to marry (your sibling, or parent, or child, or sibling's child).

Fictive kinship extends the benefits of kinship to everyone who bears a ¡Kung name. With it, no one among the whole people need be a stranger or an outsider. In the very few cases in which people have no blood relatives, they live in a band with fictive kin. It also makes kinship a complex intellectual challenge, since there are very few ¡Kung names (only about thirty-five first names for each sex, and no last names) (Lee, 1984, pp. 68–71).

Why do the ¡Kung bother to maintain such an elaborate kinship system? You may find the **functionalist perspective** very helpful in understanding ¡Kung kinship. In a society without specialized roles kinship finds places for all people. It helps the society function smoothly by ensuring that any two members of ¡Kung society will always know where they stand in relation to each other, and what roles they should play. Depending on their actual kinship, their ages, and their names, individuals will quickly establish kinship status and determine whether they have a joking or an avoidance relationship.

Roles: Focusing on Gender

In addition to kinship and age, the other fundamental basis of ¡Kung status and role is gender. More than anything else, who you are and what you do in life is determined by your gender. Male and female are the basic "specialties" in ¡Kung society; there are no other specialized occupations. One way of putting this is to say that the ¡Kung, like other hunting and gathering societies, have only the most basic **division of labor,** for there are only two jobs, two economic roles. And since these roles are gender roles, they are part of family life. In effect, there is no economy separate from the family and the band.

Is There a "Breadwinner" Role?

¡Kung women and men both "commute" to work (Fisher, p. 103). The work roles of men and women are different, but there is no sense in which women do "housework" and men "go to work."

> N¡uhka is hungry, but happy. Her brother found a field of tsin beans while hunting and she is off to harvest them. Tsin beans have been scarce, so many women are eager to come along.

Even Niuhka's mother, who is less active than she once was, wants to come. Gathering tsin beans is work, but it's also a social occasion, a break in routine. Twikwe, Niuhka's best friend plays a tune on her thumb piano as they walk along, and the women join in, singing a rhythmic chorus. Even though Niukha is burdened with her heavy toddler, whom she carries in her leather kaross, her step is light and her face is smiling.

Everyone seems lifted by the prospect of the beans. Even Dasina, whose running fight with her husband has made her sullen for weeks, is smiling and singing. Suddenly, as the women enter the bean field, a duiker, a tiny antelope, breaks from its hiding place and dashes away. The women take up the chase with enthusiastic shouts. Although the duiker can race faster than any iKung, it is young and confused and runs in circles. Niuhka and Twikwe pelt it with stones, knocking it over, but the duiker recovers and bounds off. All the women are disappointed. On other harvesting trips they have run down small game and feasted on the meat.

Soon the women turn to the work of harvesting beans and by afternoon have collected a huge pile, which they roll in their karosses. With her kaross tied around her waist, each woman will carry 15 to 30 pounds of beans, the babies perched on top. Weary and joking, the women return home, knowing they can rest in camp for three or four days without further gathering.

Women's Work

The food women collect constitutes about 75 percent of the iKung diet. Gathering is not random; the women have a plan and a clear objective. They know where fruits are ripe or roots and tubers may be found. When the band moves camp, women carry all their belongings and their young children. Lee estimates that each year the average iKung woman carries her child 1500 miles. Women also gather wood, tend fires, and cook vegetable foods. They build shelters and repair them and keep the family's living area clear of ash and grasses. They make household objects like ostrich eggshell water holders, tortoise shell bowls, and personal ornaments. Women don't use bows and arrows or spears to hunt, but they do kill snakes and tortoises and birds and, occasionally, even small animals (Marshall, pp. 92, 97, 102; Lee, 1979, pp. 310–312).

Men's Work

Hunting is the focus of male activity and talk. Men hunt small game with spears, clubs, or snares, and they hunt big game with bow and poisoned arrow. They hunt on an irregular basis, sometimes alone, but by preference in groups of two to four. They may stay around camp for weeks at a time, then hunt for several days in a row, but averaged out, they hunt around two or three days a week.

/Toma and Nieisi were very tired. They had followed kudu tracks all day, without sighting the animals. "Let's go back to camp," sighed /Toma; "I'm tired; my back hurts. Niai will rub my back." "Your wife will rub her belly in hunger if we return without meat," Nieisi protested. "Let's go on just a little longer." /Toma and Nieisi were lucky. They suddenly came upon the kudu in the slanting light of late afternoon, grazing as they settled for the night. Crawling to a clump of bushes only a few feet from the kudu, /Toma used his bow. The poisoned arrow hit a young male kudu in the flank and it fled. By morning, the poison would

These young women have walked out from camp for the day, to a place where they know grewia berries are ripe. Behind them stretches the Kalahari Desert: rolling grasslands, punctuated with clusters of trees and bushes.

weaken and then paralyze the 300-pound animal. /Toma and N¡eisi hurried back to the camp. The would need help to carry the meat.

The next morning they returned to the hunt with four more men from their band. They soon found the wounded kudu, but it was closely watched by a pair of lions. N¡eisi tried to chase the lions: "Go lions, this is our meat, not yours!" he commanded, tossing a clod of earth in the big cats' direction. The lions would not move and growled alarmingly as N¡eisi tossed another clod.

/Toma raised his bow, but only in frustration. The lions would devour the foolish hunters long before the weak ¡Kung poison could do its work. /Toma turned toward camp and shouted at N¡eisi: "Now we can all rub our bellies!" "There are other kudu to hunt," N¡eisi called out, but /Toma kept walking toward camp.

Game is used for many purposes besides food; almost nothing is wasted. Men make animal hides into clothing and bags; bone and horn are used for tools, sinews for bowstrings and nets. Men craft all their hunting gear—bows, arrows, quivers, spears, clubs, and implements for trapping. They collect the beetle larvae from which arrow poison is distilled and carefully prepare and spread the poison. Men also butcher and cook meat, especially the meat of large animals. They light fires, by twirling sticks, or in recent decades, by use of a flint and tinder. At a ¡Kung campground, both men and women are engaged in domestic tasks. Men know how to gather and sometimes do so—when they return empty-handed from a hunt, or when they go with women on overnight gathering trips (Lee, 1979, pp. 216–226; Marshall, pp. 124, 132–137).

SOCIAL INEQUALITY

Inequality in ǃKung Bushman society is notable mostly for its absence. There is very little inequality of any kind. As we have seen, there are no economic or **class** inequalities: sharing and gift giving ensure that food and material objects are distributed equally in families and bands. Visiting evens out resources between bands and *n'ore*. There are not inequalities of **power** either. The ǃKung have no chiefs and the position of the *k'ausi* is mostly ceremonial. Informal leaders do develop in bands, but they don't have the power to give orders or make people do things against their wills. They lead by example and by their interpersonal skills. The only kind of inequality discernable in ǃKung society is **status** inequality. Some people enjoy more prestige and respect than others, perhaps because of their skill as hunters or musicians or healers, or perhaps because of their pleasant personalities. But their prestigious characteristics don't result in increased wealth or power. Admired individuals don't eat better or have more possessions than others; they aren't given special titles or privileges. They may be sought out in marriages or as band members. But take note: these status inequalities are personal, not social; they result from individuals' personal traits, not from their membership in social groups, like classes or races. The only status inequality in ǃKung society that is social in nature is inequality between men and women. Gender inequality does exist, but it is minimal.

Gender Inequality

Women and men are not perfectly equal in ǃKung society, but they come pretty close. Women work longer hours than men, in gathering, child care, and household work, but their enormous contribution to subsistence is recognized, and the food they gather is considered theirs. Men don't scorn women's work, and they do sometimes go gathering. Women have a great deal of autonomy and power. They are not expected to obey men; the don't wait on men, and they don't eat inferior food or less than men. Women are seldom physically assaulted or coerced by men, and in fact, women hit men about as frequently as they are struck by them. Women have a voice in group discussions and a say in making arrangements. There are no formal statuses or laws that give power to men (Marshall, p. 177).

In marriage too, women are not disadvantaged. Mothers and fathers share authority over children, and divorces are as likely to be initiated by women as by men. Because of bride service, young women don't end up as powerless newcomers in their husbands' families. And finally, though there is polygny (multiple wives) and not polyandry (multiple husbands), its rarity seems to be the result of women's firm opposition.

Gender and Personality

In societies where men and women are very unequal, they are often socialized to develop personality traits that reinforce their inequality. In such societies, boys are taught to be aggressive and domineering and girls to be passive and dependent. Personality differences between ǃKung men and women are minimal. The ǃKung find conflict and violence abhorrent (as we shall soon see) and they disapprove of men who are aggressive, boastful, or dominating. It is no compliment to say that a man is a fighter, and in ¡Kung culture boys are never urged or taught to fight. Men who are easygoing and skillful and who help ease tensions in the group are preferred. Self-assertion, demandingness, and boldness are also discouraged in women, but perhaps slightly more so than in men. Women are expected to be gentle, modest, and gracious, and to comply with the wishes of others (Marshall, p. 176).

Gender Segregation

In many societies, women's lower status is reflected in their extensive segregation from men and from public life in general. Among the ¡Kung, women and men are segregated in some of their roles, but overall, the degree of segregation is not great. Most of the time, women and men work separately, each going into the bush with friends and relatives of their own gender. But this separation is not rigid. Parties of men and women do go gathering together, especially in major expeditions to the mongongo groves, or the tsin bean fields, and these are usually rather festive occasions. Women are sometimes part of the party that returns to track down and carry home big game fatally wounded in a hunt. Within the camp, men and women sit on opposite sides of the fire, but beyond this, there is a great deal of mixing of men and women, and boys and girls. Children of both sexes play together, and spouses are commonly real companions, sitting and talking by their fire and even arranging "getaways" to visit relatives or go gathering together in the bush.

The "Masters of Meat"

But overall, though women don't suffer subjection to men, they have less prestige. Everyone agrees that men are more influential. Fundamentally, the advantaged position of men results from the glamour of hunting. There is a disparity between men's and women's economic roles. As Lorna Marshall says, "There is no splendid excitement in returning home with vegetables." People crave meat and they call men the "masters of meat" and "the owners of hunting" (Marshall, p. 178). News of success in a hunt, particularly of big game, spreads rapidly even beyond the camp. Visitors arrive and everyone feasts and parties. Hunting confers not only prestige, however, but also concrete influence. Women distribute their plant food within their own families, but men distribute the enticing meat widely, and their gifts are a kind of investment, which gathers in honor and obligations, and grows into influence (Fisher, p. 215).

DEVIANCE AND SOCIAL CONTROL

Do you think that there is more deviance in your society or in ¡Kung Bushman society? If you think about this you will see that it is puzzling. The ¡Kung have no laws, or police or courts, no authority figures to make rules or mete out punishments. There are no **formal sanctions**—positive or negative—to make people conform: no diplomas to work for, no scholarships for merit, no promotions, no jobs to win or lose, no jail sentences, parole, or court martials. The ¡Kung rely entirely on the **informal sanctions** of small group life. Negative sanctions include the mocking song heard in the darkness, gossip and ridicule, teasing and avoidance. The ¡Kung fear having others laugh at them. Positive sanctions include group approval, loving attention, and companionship. Inclusion in group life is emotionally so essential that these informal sanctions are highly effective.

While there certainly is deviance in ¡Kung society, there are no **deviant roles** or **deviant careers.** There are no gang members, or burglars, no confidence men, no punk rockers, no cross-dressers who inhabit subcultures condemned as deviant by the rest of their society. Most of the time, members of ¡Kung society accept group norms and act and talk and think in ways that are expected of them. But they sometimes commit deviant acts, like failing to share food, or fighting, or boasting, or engaging in adultery, or even killing another person.

Deviance and Social Interaction

In the small ¡Kung bands, many norms concern how people are expected to interact with each other, and much of ¡Kung deviance involved disapproved modes of interaction. Sociologists distinguish four types of interaction, found in all societies: **social exchange, cooperation, competition,** and **conflict.** In every society, people value some of these forms of interaction and they disapprove of others. For the ¡Kung, exchange and cooperation are desired, competition and conflict feared and avoided.

Social Exchange and Cooperation

Many sociologists see exchange as a universally important interaction process, and the ¡Kung would agree. They tend to see the world in terms of exchanges (you give me a gift and then I'll give you one; you give me meat when you are successful hunting, and then I return the favor; you extend hospitality to my family or band when we are in your territory, and later we will do the same for you). In exchange, each person gives something in order to get something else—gifts, assistance, love, food, attention, companionship, and so forth. Like people in other societies, the ¡Kung are careful to reciprocate appropriately. Their society, like others, has many norms which sociologists call **norms of reciprocity.** These norms tell people what to exchange, how, with whom, and when. The ¡Kung worry about whether this relative or that deserves a shoulder of the antelope, or whether it would be better to give the hindquarter as well, and they think carefully about the timing of gifts as well as their nature—to reciprocate too quickly, or to wait too long could both be insulting.

People usually can find some way to reciprocate. Those who are too old or handicapped to hunt or gather can stay in camp with the children, or shell nuts or make music. People who fail to reciprocate are teased, reproached, or avoided. Some people work harder than others at reciprocal gift giving, spending many hours making ostrich shell beads and jewelry, for example. They are rewarded with an extensive network of social connections from whom they can expect gifts, perhaps help in matchmaking, or place they will be welcome to visit.

For the ¡Kung, exchange often takes the form of cooperation, when people pitch in and pool their resources to achieve a common goal. We see this in the dry-season sharing of permanent water holes, in the help ¡Kung give each other in carrying home large kills, or heavy mongongo nuts. Most games illustrate and teach cooperation, as the whole group works together to keep the ball aloft, or the rhythm going. In one popular game, girls make a circle, each girl crooking one leg around her neighbor's, then hop in unison. When one falls, the circle collapses and the game is over.

Competition

Like cooperation, competition requires agreed-upon social rules, but competition is repugnant to the ¡Kung, and they work constantly to squelch competitive tendencies in individuals and suppress arrogance in those more talented or successful. Acting competitive is a form of deviance for the ¡Kung.

¡Kung norms call for extreme modesty in presenting one's accomplishments. A man whose arrow badly wounds an antelope will return to his hearth silent and dejected. Asked about the hunt, he will doubtfully admit that he just might have grazed his quarry. Then the camp will celebrate, for they know this means the hunter has scored a certain hit and there will probably be meat tomorrow. As one Xai/Xai man, /Gaugo, explained to Richard Lee, when the carrying party finds the kill, they will loudly disparage the meat:

> You mean you have dragged us all the way out here to make us cart home your pile of bones? Oh, if I had known it was this thin, I wouldn't have come. (Lee, 1984, p. 49)

The ¡Kung call this "insulting the meat." Anyone who shows open pride is relentlessly teased, and the object of their pride disparaged. Tomazho, a famous healer, explained:

> When a young man kills much meat, he comes to think of himself as a chief or a big man, and he thinks of the rest of us as his servants or inferiors. We can't accept this. We refuse one who boasts, for someday his pride will make him kill somebody. So we always speak of his meat as worthless. In this way we cool his heart and make him gentle. (Lee, 1984, pp. 48–50)

Conflict

Conflict occurs when normative consensus breaks down, but actually, in most cases, the events of a conflict follow an accepted script, escalating through stages recognizable to all. In conflict, people try to meet their goals by destroying an opponent. The ¡Kung are horrified, and very much frightened by conflict, especially violent conflict, and make every effort to prevent disagreements from escalating into physical fighting. Much as they oppose conflict, the ¡Kung are only moderately successful in preventing it. In the worst case, arguments progress to insults and then into wrestling and hitting, followed by a general melee in which many people may be wounded or killed (Lee, 1984, pp. 93–95; 1979, pp. 396–399).

It seems like it has gone on all day. As Kushe sits shelling mongongo nuts, she carries on an endless shrill monologue, complaining about her husband. "He is so stingy; too stingy," goes the refrain. "He doesn't give me presents. He doesn't bring home enough meat." The whole band ignores her, and her husband's parents, who are visiting, tactfully disappear into the bush. By the time Ukwane and his brother-in-law return from hunting, the tension is so high you can practically see it. Ukwane begins to butcher the kudu and hands the first share to his mother. Kushe jumps between them, furious: "You're not going to give me any, are you?" she demands. Taken aback, Ukwane tries to deflect her with kidding: "No, of course not; I never give you anything." Kushe is beside herself. "That's right," she screams, "you don't; no food and no babies," as she hits and claws at him. Amazed by the suddenness of this emotional storm, Ukwane grabs Kushe and literally throws her out of his way. Kushe runs back and assaults him again. Ukwane's mother and Kushe's mother are now pushing and shouting at each other. Momentarily shocked, the rest of the group finds its feet and leaps into action, separating and holding the combatants. Everyone is talking and shouting and milling about.

Tempers have cooled by the following morning, but Ukwane wants no part of Kushe or her family. "They are like warthogs, not people!" Ukwane's mother spits out. "They all look like warthogs," grunts his father. Ukwane rises, declaring, "I want to go to hunt kudu, not to live among beasts!" Having said this in a voice loud enough to carry across the camp, Ukwane leads his parents off on the long trek to his brother's camp near the Herero village.

Managing Conflict. How do the ¡Kung ensure that most conflicts do not escalate to the point of violence? After all, they cannot call the police or campus security. While there are no separate political or legal institutions, the ¡Kung do have norms and procedures for handling conflict—within the band and the family.

One way the ¡Kung manage conflict is by providing plentiful opportunity for harmless venting of complaints. The ¡Kung are an exceptionally verbal people, and feelings like grief, envy, resentment, anger, or alarm are readily expressed in conversation. A great deal of the constant interchange in ¡Kung groups takes the form of semiserious argument, called "a talk," in which real discontents are jokingly aired. In such sessions, people complain about others' laziness or stinginess, about people who don't distribute meat properly, or don't reciprocate gifts generously. (Though complaints like these are common, the underlying problem in uncontrolled, fatal fights is usually adultery, or anger over a previous homicide.) "Talks" are potentially dangerous, but most of the time, the danger is defused by laughter.

A "Fight." If "talking" fails, then people lose their good nature and begin angry argument. When they begin to make sexual insults *(za)* against each other, then you know that anger will mount and actual physical violence is likely. Women are as likely as men to be involved in hand-to-hand violence, with men or with other women. In most cases, once people separate the combatants, they are usually able to use joking to calm everyone down.

Conflict Control. Separation in fact is one of the most effective means of limiting conflict available to the ¡Kung. It is relatively easy for one party or the other in a dispute to pick up and leave the group temporarily, and people often do so. Conflict avoidance and flexible group composition are closely intertwined, with conflict-induced separations keeping groups small, and flexible group composition making conflict avoidance possible.

The most extreme form of conflict management practiced by the iKung (and the one that comes closest to the exercise of political authority) is group execution. It is a last resort to even the score when people hold a grudge for a previous murder, or to put an end to fighting caused by a single, dangerously violent individual. Richard B. Lee has recorded several such cases, in one of which a whole community joined in shooting and stabbing a probably psychotic killer (Lee, 1984, p. 96; 1979, pp. 393–395).

Since the Tswana and the Herero have settled in the Kalahari, the iKung have been glad to make use of their legal institutions to manage conflict. As early as 1948, the Tswana appointed a iKung-speaking Tswana, Isak Utigile, as "headman" (really a kind of justice of the peace, or magistrate) of the iKung, and his "court" became very popular among the iKung as a place for mediation of disputes by a trusted authority (Lee, 1979, p. 396; 1984, pp. 96–97). Nowadays, as the iKung settle down in villages, people are less able to avoid conflict by leaving the group, so they are turning more and more frequently to Herero or Tswana headmen or to government officials to mediate disputes. Susan Kent describes a Bushman village in Botswana where villagers turned repeatedly to the game scout (the nearest government official) in cases of conflict (Kent, pp. 703–712).

SOCIALIZATION

One reason why there is relatively little deviance in iKung society is that socialization is quite successful. iKung Bushmen learn to play new roles all through life, as they move from childhood, through adulthood, to old age. These age-specific roles are in fact the major roles in iKung society since, besides the basic gender division, there are no other specialized roles. Like the rest of life, socialization takes place in the family and the band, and people are socialized by their friends and relatives. There is no formal socialization, since there are no schools or other formal institutions. However, there are formal ceremonies that mark important life transitions.

In the past, when the iKung Bushmen lived by traditional hunting and gathering, children could rely on their adult roles being just like their parents'. Adults had valuable knowledge and skills to transmit to children, and old people's long experience with the conditions of bush life made them respected advisers. Life was filled with difficulties, but had a reliable consistency from generation to generation. No iKung children needed to worry about what they would be when they grew up; but they didn't have very many choices either. Everyone had to accommodate his or her talents to the small number of gender and kinship roles that existed.

Today, the situation is changing, and as the iKung leave the hunting and gathering life, the experience of elders becomes less relevant to young people, and adolescents are faced with life choices never imagined by their parents. We will first examine socialization through the life cycle of the iKung in traditional hunter-gatherer bands, and then describe how the ¡Kung are responding to current conditions.

Childhood Socialization

The ¡Kung begin their lives with an immensely secure early childhood. Babies sleep beside their mothers at night and are carried all day in slings that permit constant skin-to-skin contact. They have free access to the breast, and nurse on demand, several times an hour. The ¡Kung believe babies need no training or discipline. Young children are carried and nursed up to the age of 3 or even 4, but once out of infancy, they spend more time out of their mothers' arms—in affectionate play with their fathers, held by the various aunts and uncles, grandparents, and cousins who surround them in the band, and often carried, like dolls, by the older siblings.

But then, when children are 3 or 4 years old, they are suddenly required to stop breast-feeding, relinquish the role of an infant, and adopt the much more independent role of a child. ¡Kung mothers bear children with an average birth interval of four years. Ideally, a new pregnancy occurs because the still-nursing toddler is self-weaning to solid food. Much of the time, however, the toddler is still emotionally wedded to nursing, and with the new pregnancy, mother and child enter a stressful period of angry conflict. The child feels rage and rejection, sometimes still unresolved by the time of the new birth. But the weaning crisis gradually abates as the 4-year-old tires of hanging around mother and infant and is drawn off into the more exciting life of the children's play group (Shostak, pp. 57–58).

There is no worry about whether children will succeed in learning new roles; no debate over proper methods of childrearing; no controversy about the contents of school curriculum. The ¡Kung assume that in the normal course of their lives, children will learn what they need to know and become prepared for adult life.

Children Socialize Each Other

Children from about ages 7 to 12 spend almost all their time in each others' company, playing in mixed-age and often mixed-sex groups. They play in the cleared central "plaza" of the camp or, even more often, in a nearby "children's village," out of sight, but not out of hearing of the adults. Children play traditional games, give their smaller siblings rides on an old *kaross*, or on their backs, and endlessly "play house." Girls build rough shelters and pair off with boys or with each other as "mommies and daddies." Children gather berries or roots in the nearby bush, snare small birds or collect caterpillars, or pretend to kill and butcher an animal. Girls and boys hold their own "pretend" trance dances. Away from disapproving parents, children also experiment with sex, imitating parents glimpsed in the dark, looking and touching, but not initiating actual intercourse (Lee, 1979, p. 236; Shostak, p. 83; Marshall, pp. 318–319). A great deal of children's play is obviously **anticipatory socialization,** in which they learn by observing and imitating the roles they will play as adults.

"We are masters of the meat," shouts 9-year-old Gai, as he leads two younger boys in a mock hunt through the tall grass. Gai and //Oma use their toy bows to shoot at the grasshoppers

they disturb as they run. Suddenly a shout from the youngest boy, Gwe, reveals a 3-foot-long grass snake. The three boys chase the snake, shooting at it, tossing rocks, and finally killing it with a branch used as a club. "We must cook our meat!" exclaims Gai, as they build a fire and roast the unfortunate snake.

Gai enjoys his new role as "hunter" and distributes meat to the younger boys. Four girls, including Karu, an 8-year-old who often plays "house" with Gai, look on hungrily, but no food comes their way. Finally Karu shouts, "Where is my food? I am your wife; you have to give me some!"

Gai's pals are beside themselves with laughter. Karu, nearly a head shorter than Gai, chases him around the clearing. What starts as a game soon becomes a tug of war, as Karu grabs the charred snake and Gai pulls back on the other end. The snake splits and the pair are dumped on the ground. Karu and Gai scream at each other until Karu's older sister arrives and shouts at both of them, "You're acting like a bunch of babies! Grown-ups share their food, especially husbands and wives!"

Actually, children learn a great deal from each other. Older children are patient with younger ones who try to join their games, and instruct them in the proper way to play. Older children act as peacemakers and mediators in the frequent minor conflicts of the informal play group. They often intervene when one child teases another, grabs someone's melon or toy, or when disagreements turn to physical fighting. They punish aggression—generally with ridicule—and give comfort to the victims. Also, they sometimes make fun of children who don't participate in games, or who play badly (Eibl-Eibesfeldt, p. 135). As children grow up, they gradually move from freely expressing aggression to controlling aggression in others, then to an adulthood in which suppressing their own aggressive, competitive impulses will be expected.

Adults Socialize Children

Children spend a great deal of time with adults of all ages, and learn from them by imitation and informal instruction. They learn to control their tempers and avoid offending others. When young children fight, mothers' most common response is to separate or distract them. Mothers may scold and compel the return of a grabbed object. Though threats of beatings are common, actual physical punishment is rare (Eibl-Eibesfeldt, pp. 132–133, 135).

Children also learn the many norms of daily life. They learn to receive food in outstretched hands, not to grab, to wait until asked to share food; to take a modest serving from a passed bowl, and to eat with restraint, not revealing eagerness. They are scolded for greed or stealing. Girls and boys also learn the norms of sexual modesty. They learn that adults do not hug or kiss each other in public. Girls learn to sit modestly, so their genitals are not visible. Both girls and boys learn that it is dangerous to sit where a person of the opposite sex has sat. The !Kung believe that if a man sits in a place touched by a woman's genitals, his ability to hunt will be impaired, and if a woman sits in a man's place, she will get an infection (Marshall, pp. 244, 249, 293–294, 311).

In adolescence, children begin to go gathering or hunting with adults, in order to learn these vital skills. Girls begin to gather in earnest as soon as they marry, which among some ¡Kung groups used to be as young as 10 or 12. (It is now closer to 16 for most ¡Kung.) But even then, the young wife gathers in the company of her mother, or perhaps her aunt or sisters. The transition to adult responsibilities is gradual. At about the age of 12, boys' fathers give them their first small bows and arrows and quivers, and they begin to hunt birds and rabbits. This is a time when they may also accompany an older man, perhaps a grandfather, in setting snares and tending a trapline. Finally comes the big step of going with their fathers, uncles, and older brothers on a hunt (Shostak, pp. 83–84).

Rites of Passage to Adulthood

In traditional ¡Kung society, major events mark the passage to adulthood: for boys, the first kill of a large animal, and *choma*, initiation into manhood; and for girls, first menstruation and marriage. All four of these events are marked by public ceremonies; they are the **rites of passage** that mark and celebrate a person's change in status before the whole community.

The First Buck Ceremony

A boy becomes a fully adult hunter when he kills his first big antelope with a poisoned arrow. This milestone event traditionally was achieved between the ages of 15 and 18, but nowadays, as young men spend more time working on Bantu cattle posts, it may occur much later. Killing the first big animal is the result of hard work on hunting, and this is recognized with two important ceremonies—for the first male and first female animals killed.

These ceremonies are male business, performed while the women are out of camp. The young man is given small cuts and tattoos on his chest, back, and arms; these mark him as a hunter in the eyes of the world. Further cuts are rituals to strengthen his vision, stamina, aim, and determination. Then the men gather to cook and eat some of the young hunter's meat. The ritual ends with the dramatic tale of a hunt (Lee, 1979, pp. 236–240). After killing his first buck, a young man is considered eligible for marriage.

Choma

Sometime between the ages of 15 and 20, boys participate in *choma*, a sacred six-week-long initiation rite. *Choma* is an elaborate rite, in which sacred male knowledge is passed on to a new generation. It is usually held every few years during the winter dry season when several bands gather at a permanent water hole, bringing together a large enough group of boys. *Choma* is a challenging experience of hunger, cold, and thirst. The boys sing the men's songs and dance to exhaustion. Like the first buck ceremony, *choma* is performed away from women (Lee, 1979, p. 365; Shostak, p. 239).

Marriage

Marriage and first menstruation are two important transitions in the life of a ¡Kung girl that are marked by formal ceremony. It will probably seem quite strange to you that of the two events, a traditional ¡Kung girl would be likely to experience marriage first. Neither event signals an abrupt transition to adulthood, and marriage especially should be thought of more as a process—beginning with marriage negotiations and ending with the birth of a child—than as sudden change of status.

Marriage is a stormy period in a ¡Kung girl's socialization. First marriages are usually arranged by parents or other close relatives (who will also arrange subsequent marriages if the spouses are still young). Arranging a marriage involves a lot of visiting, discussions, and gift giving, and it may actually be difficult to find a suitable mate within the restrictions of actual and fictive kinship. The marriage ceremony itself is an almost casual, hearthside occasion, attended mostly by children.

But learning to play the role of a wife is a very difficult, and often long transition for a ¡Kung girl. Girls typically resist marriage. They are usually preadolescent, and they are in no hurry to grow up. The disparity in ages and sexual maturity of the bride and groom is a source of real difficulties. The groom is sexually mature, but he is expected to marry a child and wait, often as long as five years, before he has sex with her. During that time he must sleep by her side, live with and help her family, and probably put up with her rejection, fear, and anger. Young men find this situation very frustrating, but they usually accept it, because marriageable girls are scarce. Polygyny, though uncommon, unbalances sex ratios, and young men know that if they reject a marriage, they may have to wait for another potential bride to grow up. Newly married girls are often frightened. Frequently an adult woman, usually a close relative, sleeps next to the bride on her wedding night, and longer, to reassure her, but nevertheless, a girl's introduction to adult sex is likely to be traumatic. Sexual relations may be postponed for years, but will be unavoidable as soon as she begins menstruation (at about 16) (Shostak, pp. 129–130, 148, 150).

> *When she wakes up, Kai doesn't see her daughter in her usual place, sleeping next to her fire. Could it be, she wonders happily, that Khoana has relented and agreed to sleep beside her new husband in their hut? But Khoana isn't in the hut and Kai's pleasure turns to panic. That girl has surely run away again! Hours later, they find her sleeping beneath a mongongo tree, hidden by sand dunes. "Are you crazy, girl," shouts Kai, "a lion could have eaten you!" Khoana bursts into tears and begins ripping the bracelets off her arms. "I won't go back to him. I'm afraid. I'm still a child; I'm not old enough yet for marriage."*

¡Kung society tolerates a girl's free expression of her objection to marriage. She may rage and storm and may even threaten or attempt suicide. Basically, if she insists, a girl can force an end to her marriage, either by driving her husband away with unpleasantness or by enrolling family members on her side. Divorce is very common in the early years of marriage, before children are born, and it is usually initiated by the wife. It is common for a girl to enter several such "trial marriages" before finally having children and settling down to a stable marriage (Shostak, pp. 130–131, 148).

First Menstruation

The onset of menstruation is celebrated in a more public, ceremonial manner than is marriage. The girl, elaborately ornamented, stays in a special hut, while the women of the band dance and sing in a sometimes suggestive fashion. Men must not see the girl, but they watch the dancing women from a distance, making bawdy comments. The rite marks sexual maturity, but not full adulthood. Girls are unlikely to conceive a baby for about two years after menstruation begins, and in this period, their relatives still help them with gathering, cooking, and other household tasks, while they continue to play with their friends (Shostak, p. 149).

After her first menstruation, a ¡Kung girl usually begins to settle down, with her original or a new husband. She may come to love her husband and enjoy a period of romance before the first child is born. The married couple grow into an easy, relatively equal relationship, in which they go about together, exchange opinions, and make decisions jointly. Fear of her husband usually eases into acceptance and even enjoyment of sex. Also, the girl may come to enjoy the status of married woman, the presents given her by her husband and his family, and the meat he brings to her fire (Shostak, p. 150).

With the birth of a first child, a woman becomes fully adult. She and her husband are now referred to as the parents of their children ("/Toma's father" or "Nisa's mother") rather than by their childhood names, and they settle down to their major life roles in rearing children and provisioning their household. The ¡Kung love and enjoy children and wish to have many, though not too closely spaced.

New Roles in Maturity

Growing into mature adulthood and then old age, ¡Kung adults must adjust to new roles. Both men and women in maturity find opportunities to express their talents, as hunters, storytellers, artisans, musicians, healers, and informal leaders. A few men will be able to enjoy the advantages of polygynous marriage. But because of relatively high death rates, almost every adult has experienced the death of at least one child, and many the death of a spouse. Family roles change as the result of deaths.

The ¡Kung are adequately nourished, in good physical condition, and suffer little from stress or diet-related diseases. But lacking modern antibiotics and other medicines, infectious and parasitic diseases like influenza, pneumonia, gastroenteritis, tuberculosis, and malaria take a high toll of children and adults. Close-knit nuclear and extended households are repeatedly disrupted by death. The ¡Kung support each other in deeply felt mourning. People travel to attend funerals; women publicly cry and wail, and men sometimes also cry. Family members struggle to understand the death of a child or sibling, asking why God would take a person so prematurely. But after a relatively short time, relatives and friends encourage the bereaved to stop mourning.

Death often causes the reorganization of families. After the death of the head of an extended family, the group may split up, with some of its constituent nuclear families leaving the band. There are many more widows than widowers, and they almost always marry again. Some remarriages also take place after divorce, which is relatively infrequent among adults, but readily accomplished by mutual consent, or as the result of one spouse leaving the other. No formal grounds for divorce are necessary, and there is no property to divide. Children remain with their mothers, except for teenage boys who may choose to stay with their fathers, or visit with both parents.

Polygyny

Adulthood is also the time when some ¡Kung men (approximately 5 percent at any time) are able to achieve their fantasy of having more than one wife. Polygyny has real advantages: a new sexual partner, more children, another person to gather food, and the forging of a whole new set of relationships with in-laws in another band, another *n'ore*. A second marriage may increase a man's status or political influence (Shostak, p. 169). But there are serious disadvantages too. A man must be a very good hunter to attempt polygyny, and he may even then regret his disruptive second marriage. The first wife will probably object, feel jealous and rejected; the two wives may fight so bitterly that the second one leaves. Polygynous marriages have the greatest chance of success when the second wife is the widowed sister, or the unmarried younger sister of the first (Shostak, pp. 170–171).

The Roles of the Old

Few of the ¡Kung live to old age: barely 20 percent of those born reach age 60, but those who do will, on the average, live another ten years. The old are relatively free of high blood pressure, heart disease, and deafness and many are still vigorous. Old widows (over 40 percent of the women over 60) may marry again, or live with children or grandchildren. Old people are treated with respect and often have an influential voice in the group. The older they are, the more likely they are to be the *k'ausi* of their band. Old people are consulted because their experience is valuable. They know how people are related, who married whom, and who is comparatively older or younger. They have seen so many seasons go by that they know where to find food under unusual conditions. They know the recent history of the people and the region and the folktales, songs, and legends. As long as the group continues to live the traditional hunting and gathering life, old people play an important role in the band.

Healthy old people continue to forage, but on a reduced scale. Old women may gather closer to home, old men may set snares and gather along with their wives. But most old people contribute little food; they are supported by sharing with their relatives. Old age may be a time of intense religious exploration, especially for women, who often wait until their children are grown before learning trance dancing and healing. For some people, spiritual powers strengthen with age; they achieve great control over their ability to enter trance and become valued healers and teach apprentices how to enter trance and cure.

For some people, old age is a satisfying time. If they are surrounded by children willing to provide for them, and grandchildren to be loved and cared for, they may enjoy inclusion in the life of the band: sharing the feasts and dances, telling and hearing the stories, sharing gossip, debating the merits of marriages. But for those who outlive their children and spouses (one-fifth of all women, but relatively few men) and become a burden on those with less affection for them, old age may be far less pleasant (Shostak, pp. 324–325).

SOCIAL CHANGE AND THE FUTURE

Tiikay grew up and lives today on a white-owned farm. His father had been "blackbirded" (abducted) from a hunting and gathering ¡Kung band by white settlers and forced to work herding cattle. Now Tiikay knows no other life. He lives with his wife and children and other relatives in the little ¡Kung encampment attached to the farm. Tiikay and his family live in a hut they built of scrap tin. They wear western clothes and a locked trunk holds their wealth: beads and extra clothing and blankets. They eat cornmeal given to them by the farmer and cooked in a bucket over the fire, supplemented by vegetables from their garden. The farmer also gives them milk and occasionally a cow or goat as a Christmas present. Tiikay has managed to build up his own herd of two cows and a bull which the farmer allows him to graze. Tiikay's problems start there. He would like to leave the farm and live independently as a herder, but he owns no land. His wages are so low that it is impossible for him to save up any money to buy land. If he leaves the farm he will have to sell or eat his cattle, for there will be nowhere to graze them. Tiikay feels he is stuck.

Niai was raised on a Herero cattle ranch, and after marriage she and her husband Bo worked for three years on another ranch. Then, however, bigger ranches began buying up the land and they could get no more work. Niai and Bo moved to Chumkwe (in Namibia) where the government was settling Bushmen, giving them food rations and land for gardens. Bo hated it there and he began drinking and getting into fights with other men. Niai left Bo and now supports their four children on government food relief, the charity of relatives, and occasional prostitution. Niai's situation is serious: she has gonorrhea and AIDS is inexorably making its way toward her remote region. Bo speaks despairingly, in a toneless, flat voice, of his inability to find work, and says that when he is not drunk he thinks more and more of suicide.

/Gau was raised in the bush, but after working for two years in a South African gold mine, he settled with his wife Niuhka at Chumkwe to be near the health clinic and the school for their two children. But /Gau and Niuhka would like to leave Chumkwe. A lively trade in home-brewed liquor has sprung up around the store, which sells sugar to women who make the brew and sell it by the glass. Behind the store, people drink all day and party and dance to radio music. They quarrel and fights break out. /Gau and Niuhka feel their children are becoming disrespectful and they fear the effects of the liquor trade on their growing boys. They have decided, together with Niuhka's parents, her sister and her sister's husband, and his older brother and his family, to return to living in the bush in Niuhka's family n'ore, now in Bushmanland. Niuhka and her mother have been able to sell enough handicrafts to the foundation to buy tools and seeds, and /Gau's brother has three cows and a bull. They plan to live in a village in the bush where the government has sunk a well. They will supplement cattle herding with hunting and gathering, skills still familiar to family members. They hope they can make a go of it.

These three families represent the three possible futures before the ¡Kung Bushmen. Which future lies ahead for most of the ¡Kung is unclear, but we can say with assurance that they will not be able to live as traditional foragers, isolated from outside influence. Expanding ranches, roads, planes, schools, stores, missionaries, and wars bring the outside to them and they must respond to changes not of their making.

The Forces of Change

¡Kung life has changed in a classic pattern, repeated all over the world now for four centuries. Starting in the nineteenth century, new peoples came to the Kalahari

Desert (the Tswana, the Herero, and the Europeans) and they introduced new technologies, new goods, and new ways of living. At first, the pace of change was slow, and ¡Kung culture was able to adapt and absorb the new elements.

First, the ¡Kung enthusiastically adopted the use of iron arrowheads and cooking pots, and the smoking of tobacco. They hammered arrowheads out of wire cut from the new fences (and later from extra wires cattle herders learned to leave next to their fences to protect them), but they could only get pots and tobacco by trade or in exchange for work. Young men became accustomed to working on Tswana and Herero cattle posts, as herders, hunters, or trackers, for a period of a few years before marriage or early in marriage. They earned little or no money, but were able to give their relatives gifts of milk and meat.

Some ¡Kung stayed permanently as farmhands among the Herero or Tswana. The children played together and learned each others' languages, and ¡Kung women married and had affairs with Herero and Tswana men. But ¡Kung men didn't marry black women, because the women's status was higher than theirs, though there were occasional affairs.

After 1950, ¡Kung men extended the pattern of early paid labor by traveling to the South African gold mines on months- or years-long work contracts. With their wages, they bought donkeys and saddles, and brought home blankets and clothes to give as gifts. They also brought gonorrhea, familiarity with money, and a taste for store-bought goods, radio music, and liquor.

Pushes and Pulls

Starting in the 1960s, money, modern goods, and deliberate government policy brought the ¡Kung to villages. They began to adopt patterns of village life—building more permanent Bantu-style huts, tending goats or cattle, fencing and planting gardens, selling crafts, and using the money to buy store goods: clothing and blankets, kerosene lamps, dishes and silverware, flashlights and radios.

At the same time, major new economic changes pushed the ¡Kung off their land. Tswana and Herero entrepreneurs started large-scale cattle ranching in the Kalahari. By the end of that decade, 460 ¡Kung Bushmen at Dobe were sharing their nine water holes with 350 Herero and Tswana who owned 4500 head of cattle and 1800 goats (Shostak, p. 347). Around the margins of the Kalahari, water holes became contaminated by animal droppings, new diseases spread, grazing cattle stripped bare the area around the water holes and encroached further and further into ¡Kung foraging territory, frightening away the game and trampling plant foods. Many ¡Kung in these areas could no longer live by hunting and gathering. Some became demoralized, finding only occasional work, and becoming increasingly dependent upon and looked down upon by their Bantu neighbors. Others stayed away from the villages as much as possible, coming to them only in the dry season, when they had to live near the water holes (Shostak, pp. 215–217; Silberbauer, pp. 181, 184).

Government Intervention

In many societies, all over the world, changes like these have destroyed native peoples, leaving them landless, demoralized, second-class citizens within modernizing countries. In both Botswana and Namibia new black governments, aware of the fate of indigenous peoples elsewhere in the world, have recognized the problem. Each government has followed a slightly different strategy to try to help the Bushmen achieve independence. In both countries, officials have decided that the ¡Kung can safeguard their land and livelihood only by leaving the hunting and gathering life for settled herding. Because Bantu herders dominate the culture, only people who live in villages and dig wells can file official claims to land, and people without herds are looked upon with contempt.

Rechristening the Bushmen the *Basarwa* (a respectful name), Botswana's leaders created the Office for Basarwa Development in 1974. This agency gathered data on the Bushmen, provided scholarships for children to attend elementary school, helped the Bushmen dig wells, tried to safeguard ¡Kung lands from takeovers by speculators, and provided seeds and agricultural advice. They also set up a craft-marketing program which paid ¡Kung craftspeople a fair price for ostrich eggshell bead necklaces, musical instruments, and other artifacts that it sold to tourists, a source of considerable cash income in ¡Kung communities. In Botswana today, the only place where a small number of ¡Kung live as traditional foragers is in the Central Kalahari Game Reserve.

In Namibia, the ¡Kung have experienced much more violent and uncontrolled change, as the result of the long war between the Southwest African People's Organization (SWAPO) and white South Africa for control of the country. The war raged through ¡Kung territory and many ¡Kung were hired by the South Africans as soldiers and trackers. After two decades of fighting, the war ended in 1990 with the withdrawal of white forces, and former ¡Kung soldiers, who had been paid as much as $200 a month, were left stranded. Many had never learned the traditional ¡Kung way of life, and they were fearful of the new Namibian society against which they had fought (Keller, p. A4; Lee, 1984, pp. 147–149).

Bushmen have been both helped and harmed by the Namibian government. In the 1970s, a group of white hunting enthusiasts proposed that the government make Bushman lands into a nature preserve, with one "authentic" Bushman village that tourists could be brought to see. The rest of the ¡Kung were to be resettled at Chumkwe. This plan was not adopted, but the ¡Kung were able to retain only part of their lands. A portion of the northernmost lands was made into a park and other large areas were given to Herero groups for settlement. Another area in the west was used to settle a group of Bushmen from Angola who are not ¡Kung but who had lived there while working as mercenaries on army bases. The government hired a group of missionaries to take care of these Bushmen. The eastern part of Bushmanland (about 150 square kilometers) became a protected area for the ¡Kung where 1200 to 1300 people have been settled in as many as thirty villages, with drilled wells, gardens, and cattle bought with money earned by selling crafts. The land is owned in common by all residents and cannot be sold by individuals. ¡Kung living in Bushmanland are allowed to hunt and gather, but they may use only traditional weapons and kill only their traditional prey (Wood, personal communication).

In both Botswana and Namibia anthropologists have played important roles in programs to settle the ¡Kung in villages. Westerners who have lived with the ¡Kung and studied them recognized that their presence helped introduce the ¡Kung to western goods, drawing them off the land and into towns. They wanted to help the

ǃKung find a way of life that would support them in the modern world. In Botswana, anthropologists created the Kalahari People's Fund, which works with the Botswana government on development projects, funding well digging, health clinics, and scholarships, and helping with the complicated legal work of registering land and securing water rights. In Namibia, John Marshall, who lived with and filmed the ǃKung during four decades, has played a major role. In the 1970s, he raised money and led a major political campaign to set aside land for Bushmen. Marshall helped establish a foundation which surveyed *n'ores* in Bushmanland and established ownership and he has promoted the policy of settling the ǃKung as cattle herders (Shostak, pp. 347–348; Lee, 1984, pp. 142–144; Wood, personal communication; Marshall and Ritchie, pp. vi, vii, 5–13, 153–157).

Consequences of the Settled Life

As the ǃKung have been drawn into modern society, their culture has changed dramatically. Sharing and cooperation among the members of each band has given way to a focus on individual families, who must act selfishly, for their own good only. Inequality has grown, and women and old people have become more isolated and less respected. Study of the ǃKung should teach us that where we see greed and

Bushman family seated proudly before their new home in Bushmanland. In the distance are the remains of some old-style, temporary houses built of bent branches and brush. This family has chosen to move to Bushmanland, Namibia, from Gobabis, further south, where they worked on a white-owned farm. Now they will live by herding their own cattle.

competitiveness and inequality, we cannot credit these characteristics to human nature.

The ¡Kung themselves recognize that as they make the switch to settled herding, they are both securing their independence and irretrievably changing their society. Richard Lee points out the important contrasts between foraging and herding and farming as ways of life. Foraging is based on sharing, and the ¡Kung created a whole social structure erected on the immediate distribution of food and widespread gift giving. But farmers must save: they cannot kill the cow to feed relatives, or eat up their harvest at once, so traditional ¡Kung norms and kinship patterns are unsuited for settled life. Those ¡Kung who wish to succeed as farmers must be willing to offend their relatives and cut themselves off from kinship webs so carefully cultivated in the foraging life (Lee, 1984, pp. 137–138).

Settling down usually proves to be an irrevocable choice. Once settled in a village, the ¡Kung are tied down by schooling and babies, and find it very difficult to leave again. As we have seen, living in a sedentary life, women have babies in rapid succession, making a return to foraging impossible. And if the ¡Kung are to defend their land and herds, it is very important for their children to go to school. Illiterate, they are at a tremendous disadvantage dealing with the government and the law.

Possessions and Social Change

Anthropologist John Yellen's detailed study of the Dobe ¡Kung has convinced him that accumulation of possessions is also a serious threat to traditional culture. Once craft sales made it possible for the ¡Kung to make money and buy possessions, they began hoarding, rather than depending on others to give them gifts. Ashamed of not sharing, they sought privacy, building their huts further apart and facing their doors away from each other. Heavy possessions tied down the Dobe ¡Kung. When serious conflicts developed between individuals, they could no longer resolve them in the usual way by traveling to join relatives elsewhere. As a result, the Dobe ¡Kung turned to Bantu chiefs for arbitration. They became more and more involved with the Bantus, more dependent on individual Bantus, and more likely to intermarry. Children of mixed marriages thought of themselves as Bantu (Yellen, pp. 96–105).

Growing Inequality

The herding and farming life has also dissolved the traditional equality between ¡Kung men and women, leaving women in a more dependent, subordinate position. As herders, men continue to go out into the bush, following their herds, but women become tied to the home by crops and an increased load of housework. They spend more time alone or with children, and less time on tasks performed in the company of other women. Tied down by babies, no longer the main providers of food, women become more dependent on men. Old people find village life physically easier than the old nomadic existence, but their traditional knowledge becomes superfluous. They know nothing of cows, wells, and arithmetic. Once the *k'ausi* of *n'ores,* they have no authority with government land boards.

It follows too, that once people cease to share everything, inequality immediately grows, for some are more successful than others. In Namibia, new differences in wealth have been particularly extreme, as certain individuals who allied themselves with the South African government during the war with SWAPO received large rewards (one woman worked making tourist films, a man became a cabinet minister in the regional white-dominated government, and others were well-paid as soldiers in the South African army). People who were able to establish claims to land and acquire cattle prospered, while their less lucky or less entrepreneurial relatives ended up landless and dependent (Lee, 1984, p. 148; Wilmsen, pp. 247–257).

Change and the Environment

We have seen that in the past, the traditional foraging ¡Kung Bushmen lived in harmony with their environment. Their numbers were small and their population grew slowly, if at all, and they did not exhaust the water or the animal and plant life of the desert. Today, the inhabitants of the Kalahari Desert are using its fragile environment in new, more destructive ways. Herding itself is not inherently damaging to the desert. Just as wild animals graze the Kalahari, so too can herds of goats and cattle. But the human and animal population of the Kalahari is increasing rapidly, placing unsustainable demands on the land and water. Commercial ranches cluster around the permanent water holes at the edges of the desert and large numbers of cattle pollute the water and strip away all plant life. Africans call this process **desertification,** since the denuded land becomes a real desert, in which the trees and grasses do not grow back and the wind erodes the soil. Ranchers must then move on to less desirable, drier land, which is all the sooner exhausted. As a growing human population tries to graze more and more cattle, the process of desertification accelerates. Population growth, displacement, and desertification feed each other in a destructive cycle.

Is a sustainable future possible for the ¡Kung? It all depends on finding a balance between people and the environment. It is possible that with government help in drilling wells, small groups of ¡Kung can establish herding and farming villages which raise their own food deep in the Kalahari, without overusing the land. But such villages will need to limit their population growth in some way, by either traditional or modern methods, so as not to outgrow their resources. They may still be threatened, however, by the growth of commercial cattle ranches and the influx of new people into the Kalahari region, who are themselves searching for survival on new land not already worn out by desertification.

Adaptation and Anomie

Studying the ¡Kung in changing circumstances, we see both flourishing cultural adaptations and disastrous losses. In many locations, nearby ¡Kung and Bantu villages share a permanent water hole, learn to live peacefully together, adopt each other's customs, and intermarry. Some elements of traditional ¡Kung life have been accommodated in the new settled life. For example, in many villages the ¡Kung use donkeys to travel to the mongongo nut groves and bring back sacks of this traditional wild food, still an important part of the ¡Kung diet. ¡Kung men maintain their tracking and hunting skills, now using rifles on horseback as paid huntsmen of the Herero and Tswana. The trance dance and the drum dance have endured and even grown in importance in villages where Tswana and Herero neighbors attend the popular dances along with the ¡Kung, and even send for ¡Kung healers in time of illness (Shostak, p. 219). Intermarrying ¡Kung and Bantu have invented the new status of *swara*—brothers-in-law by intermarriage—who are elaborately jovial and cordial with each other, avoiding potential anger at the "theft" of a sister, and disguising the real inequality in a situation where Bantus marry ¡Kung women, but ¡Kung men never marry Bantu women (Lee, 1984, p. 127).

But in other communities, ¡Kung culture has collapsed under the assault of expanding ranches, unemployment, dependency, drunkenness, violence, unrestricted population growth, prostitution, and disease. Without social moorings, caught between the values of a lost culture and those of another not yet their own, the ¡Kung suffer **anomie,** a state of normlessness, whose symptoms are depression, feelings of meaninglessness, aimlessness, and retreat into addiction.

The big question now is whether the great majority of the ¡Kung Bushmen will be able to stabilize their lives, creating a new way of life as settled herders, using parts of their old culture, and parts of Bantu and modern culture, or whether they will all in the end sink defeated into anomie and destruction.

Thinking Sociologically

1. Explain what the authors mean when they say that the ¡Kung "live close to nature."
2. Can you use the functionalist perspective to explain why the ¡Kung Bushmen emphasize sharing, why they are nomadic, and why they have small families?
3. What are the most important social groups in ¡Kung society?
4. Compare the status and roles of women in ¡Kung society and in Japanese society. Is the status of women in your society more similar to that of ¡Kung women or that of Japanese women?
5. Which of the four types of social interaction (social exchange, cooperation, competition, and conflict) predominate in ¡Kung society? How about in your own society?
6. What effects has the spread of large-scale commercial farming had in Mexico and in the Kalahari Desert?
7. When ¡Kung bands settle down in villages, how do their culture and social institutions change?

For Further Reading

LEE, RICHARD B., *The Dobe ¡Kung*. New York: Holt, 1984.
LEE, RICHARD, *The ¡Kung San*. Cambridge: Cambridge University Press, 1979.
SHOSTAK, MARJORIE, *Nisa*. Cambridge, MA: Harvard University Press, 1981.
THOMAS, ELIZABETH MARSHALL, *The Harmless People*. New York: Knopf, 1959.

Bibliography

BIESELE, MEGAN, "Religion and Folklore," in Phillip V. Tobias, ed., *The Bushmen: San Hunters and Herders of Southern Africa*. Cape Town: Human & Rousseau, 1978, pp. 162, 165–168.
DURKHEIM, EMILE, *The Elementary Forms of the Religious Life*. New York: Free Press,

1915, 1965.

EIBL-EIBESFELDT, IRENAUS, "Early Socialization in the ǃXo Bushmen," in Phillip V. Tobias, ed., *The Bushmen: San Hunters and Herders of Southern Africa.* Cape Town: Human & Rousseau, 1978, pp. 132–135.

FISHER, HELEN E., *The Anatomy of Love.* New York: W.W. Norton, 1992.

GELLES, RICHARD J., AND ANN LEVINE, *Sociology, An Introduction,* 5th ed. New York: McGraw-Hill, 1995.

GORDON, ROBERT J., *The Bushman Myth: The Making of a Namibian Underclass.* Boulder, CO: Westview Press, 1992.

HITCHCOCK, ROBERT, "Decentralization and Development among the Ju/wasi in Namibia," *Cultural Survival Quarterly,* Vol. 12, No. 3, 1988, pp. 31–33.

KELLER, BILL, "Misfits of Peace: Is This the End of the Bushmen?" *The New York Times,* May 10, 1993, p. A4.

KENT, SUSAN, "And Justice for All: The Development of Political Centralization among Newly Sedentary Foragers," *American Anthropologist,* Vol. 91, No. 3, Sept. 1989, pp. 703–712.

LEE, RICHARD B., "Ecology of a Contemporary San People," in Phillip V. Tobias, ed., *The Bushmen: San Hunters and Herders of Southern Africa.* Cape Town: Human & Rousseau, 1978, pp. 94–96.

———, *The ǃKung San.* Cambridge: Cambridge University Press, 1979.

———, *The Dobe ǃKung.* New York: Holt, 1984.

———, AND IRVEN DEVORE, eds., *Kalahari Hunter-Gatherers.* Cambridge, MA: Harvard University Press, 1976.

LENSKI, GERHARD, PATRICK NOLAN, AND JEAN LENSKI, *Human Societies: An Introduction to Macrosociology,* 6th ed. New York: McGraw-Hill, 1991.

MARSHALL, JOHN, AND CLAIRE RITCHIE, *Where Are the Ju/wasi of Nyae Nyae?* Cape Town: University of Cape Town African Studies Program, 1984.

MARSHALL, LORNA, *The ǃKung of Nyae Nyae.* Cambridge, MA: Harvard University Press, 1976.

SHOSTAK, MARJORIE, *Nisa.* Cambridge, MA: Harvard University Press, 1981.

SILBERBAUER, GEORGE B., "The Future of the Bushmen," in Phillip V. Tobias, ed., *The Bushmen: San Hunters and Herders of Southern Africa.* Cape Town: Human & Rousseau, 1978, p. 181.

THOMAS, ELIZABETH MARSHALL, *The Harmless People.* New York: Knopf, 1959.

TOBIAS, PHILLIP V., ed., *The Bushmen: San Hunters and Herders of Southern Africa.* Cape Town: Human & Rousseau, 1978.

WILMSEN, EDWIN N., *Land Filled with Flies: A Political Economy of the Kalahari.* Chicago: University of Chicago Press, 1989.

WOOD, ERIC, personal communication, 1995.

YELLEN, JOHN E., "The Transformation of the Kalahari ǃKung," *Scientific American,* Apr. 1990, pp. 96–105.

EGYPT

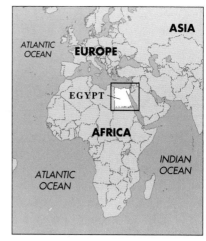

You can reach Cairo, Egypt's capital in a short flight from anywhere in the Middle East or the Mediterranean. Athens, Rome, Damascus, and Jerusalem are only hours (or minutes) away. You will set down in one of the oldest human civilizations. Thirty centuries before Christ there were cities, scholars, and kings in Egypt.

LOCATION: Egypt rests in Africa's northeast corner bordered by Israel and the Red Sea on the east, the Sudan on the south, Libya to the west, and the Mediterranean Sea to the north.

AREA: 384,000 square miles or 1,113,600 square kilometers. As large as Texas and New Mexico combined or about the size of Ontario.

LAND: Egypt is mostly desert. Population is concentrated in the Nile Valley and on the delta-one of the world's most densely settled areas.

CLIMATE: Hot and dry. The coast gets 8 inches of rain per year, while south of Cairo there is almost none. Egypt is hot from May to October (up to 107°F) and cooler from November to April (55° to 70°F).

POPULATION: In 1995 there were 62 million people; 40 percent were under the age of 15. By 2025 population is projected to reach 98 million.

ECONOMY: Egypt relies on agriculture, its millions of workers abroad, and tourism.

INCOME: U.S. $660 per person per year.

POVERTY: 21 percent of Egyptians live in absolute poverty.

RELIGION: 91 percent of Egyptians are Sunni Muslims, about 5 percent are Coptic Christians.

CHAPTER 4

Egypt: Faith, Gender, and Class

INTRODUCTION

It would be a good idea to start this chapter by thinking about what you already know about Egypt. When you think of Egypt do pyramids, palm trees, and mummies come to mind? Do you think of veiled women and Muslims kneeling in prayer? Does your mind turn to violence in the Middle East and militant Islamic fundamentalists? For many people, Egypt is a faraway place with an exotic past and a frightening present. Why should you learn more about it?

One good reason to study Egypt is that it is an Islamic society and today everyone needs to know something about Islam. Islam is one of the world's great religions, practiced by more than 900 million people worldwide. Followers of Islam are known as Muslims. The three nations with the largest Muslim populations are Indonesia, Pakistan, and Bangladesh, but there are millions of Muslims in other parts of the world too, including Egypt, Morocco, Algeria, and Nigeria in Africa; Saudi Arabia, Iran, Iraq, Jordan, and Syria in the Middle East (Lippman, 1990, pp. ix, x).

Another reason to learn more about Egypt is that it is an important third world nation, one of many former European colonies struggling with poverty, economic development, and rapid population growth. Like other societies in Africa, Asia, and Latin America, Egypt is also struggling to define its attitude toward the West in the post–Cold War world. Because of its sensitive geographic location—in the Arab oil-producing region, near Israel, in Africa, and not far from Europe, conflict in Egypt makes the news and reverberates around the world.

A final reason to study Egypt is that if you come from a western nation, you will find Egypt very different from your own society. You will learn a lot from contrasting the two. Three aspects of Egyptian society are absolutely central: faith, gender, and class. In Egypt, the Islamic faith imbues all aspects of life: people understand the values they cherish and the norms they follow in religious terms. They debate government and law and politics in the light of their religion.

Class contrasts are unavoidable in Egypt. There are sophisticated young men and women who live in luxury apartments in Cairo's modern high-rise apartment towers, who would not be out of place in New York, Paris, or London. Their clothing comes from Milan and Paris, their luxury cars from Germany, their electronics from Japan, and their income from high-level jobs in Egypt's banking and legal establishments. Not far from the apartments of such wealthy Egyptians, poor people fill the narrow alleys of Cairo's oldest quarters. Many are recent migrants from villages in southern Egypt, where electricity, doctors, and clean water have yet to make an appearance.

The aspect of Egyptian society that may make the greatest impression on you is the contrasting roles played by men and women. Egyptian men and women have different religious obligations, different family responsibilities, and different legal rights. In public and private, Egyptian men and women usually carry on their lives separately from each other. Let us introduce you to three Egyptians who illustrate these important aspects of their society.

Saad is tired. At 14, he rises very early each morning to study for his high school classes. His father is a small shopkeeper, but Saad badly wants to be a professional with a good salary and a house in a fashionable part of the city. He interrupts his studies only for a cup of tea, a roll, and morning prayers. As busy as he might be, Saad, like his father Ibrahim, prays 5 times a day. Ibrahim has a "raisin" on his forehead: a small dark bruise raised by touching his forehead to the ground thousands of times in a long lifetime of prayer. Although the future that Saad dreams of may be very different from his father's, Saad cannot imagine a life outside Islam. It is as much a part of him as his family, his friends, and his hopes. Every morning Saad spends the long walk to school listening to the Quran (the holy book of Islam) recited on his Walkman.

Fatima, 27, lives in the village of Bani Hasan in Upper, or southern, Egypt. Her husband Hussain is away in Saudi Arabia, working in construction. The money he sends home has paid for an extra room built onto the house, and an extra acre of land. Fatima and her children live with Hussain's parents, his two brothers, and his older brother's wife and three children. Fatima has never left her village; it is hard for her to imagine Hussain in a big city like Riyadh. Fatima stayed in school through fourth grade, so she can help her children a little with their homework and she can read the Quran. She worries about her husband, so far away, but life goes on much as usual, since she spends most of her time in the company of her mother-in-law and her sister-in-law. The three women work in the kitchen together and in the fields. At quiet moments in the late afternoon, they relax together chatting in the courtyard while the children play.

Anwar is a 31-year-old manager. Young, ambitious, self-confident, he hopes to rise in Egypt's business circles. He is a graduate of Cairo's American University and he holds a graduate degree in business from Michigan State. Employed by a large construction company, Anwar is already expanding his range of contacts. Not the least of these is Asya, his fiancé whose relatives hold important posts in business and government. Anwar is fluent in English and French and travels frequently to Europe and America. He met Asya, then a student in Paris, while consulting with a large French civil engineering company. In Cairo, Anwar lives with his parents and younger sisters in the affluent Garden City neighborhood. Cosmopolitan as he is, Anwar is devoted to his family, especially to his mother. He is concerned about his sister Mina, who wants to study literature in the United States. America is a fine place for a business degree, but is it any place for a carefully protected young woman? Anwar is a Muslim, but not a very active one. He rarely goes to the mosque, but he is careful not to offend his more religious coworkers.

To understand why Islam is fundamental to Egyptian culture, how class inequalities have come to divide Egyptian society so deeply, and why the position of women is the subject of such passionate debate in contemporary Egypt, you need information about Egypt's long and fascinating history.

EGYPT'S HISTORY

Because of its geographic location, Egypt has been a crossroads of cultures ever since the beginning of human civilization. In the past, Egyptians invented new technologies, arts, and sciences and many of these spread to other societies. But Egypt's location also made it vulnerable to invasion. Although it was one of the world's first nations, Egypt suffered conquest after conquest by other societies that successively imposed their cultures and social structures. Egypt embraced some of the invading societies and absorbed their cultures, but resisted others. Some of the most important periods in Egyptian history were the ancient pharaonic period (c. 3100 B.C.–671 B.C.), the age of Greek and Roman empires (333 B.C.–A.D. 641), the Arab-Islamic conquest of Egypt, and the long period of Islamic civilization (641–1798) which followed. In recent centuries, Egypt was conquered once again, this time by Europeans, and subjected to European colonialism (1798–1952). Then, in the mid-twentieth century, Egypt entered its present era of postcolonial independence (1952–present).

The Pharaonic Period

One of the world's first great civilizations developed in Egypt. Egyptians began farming as early as 9000 years ago, and by 4000 years ago they had built towns, and wealthy people lived in elaborate houses, adorned with gold and glass ornaments, musical instruments, pottery, and cloth. Merchants traveled and traded with other societies in Africa and the Middle East. By 3000 B.C., Upper and Lower Egypt were united and the reign of the pharaohs began, which lasted nearly 3000 years. Pharaonic Egypt created some of the first government bureaucracies, complete with record keepers and tax collectors. The power of the pharaohs and the energy and knowledge they commanded is still visible today in their surviving monuments: the pyramids, temples, deserted cities, and tombs of the Egyptian desert.

Greek and Roman Empires

Pharaonic Egypt lasted until 332 B.C., when Alexander the Great conquered Egypt—one step in a stunning series of victories over all of Greece and then over the armies of Asia and Africa. Alexander was the young ruler of Macedonia, a small, poor country in the Balkans, but he put together a historic empire. After Alexander's death, one of his generals, Ptolemy, took over rule of Egypt. Ptolemy and his successors drew Egypt into the Greek world. Greek began to replace Coptic, the ancient language of Egypt. Egyptian decorative arts began to follow Greek artistic ideas and depictions of Egyptian gods began to resemble Greek gods. Ptolemy and his successors built a new capital city, Alexandria, on the shore of the Mediterranean, facing toward Europe.

Greek conquest brought great changes to the lives of Egyptian men and especially Egyptian women. Women had been respected in pharaonic Egypt. There were important female deities and priestesses, and women and men were equal before the law. Women could own property and sue for divorce and they could socialize freely in public with men (Ahmed, pp. 31–33). All this changed with the Greek conquest. In Greek civilization, free women (as opposed to slaves) were **secluded** (that is, they were kept separate from men and out of public view). They could not be seen by any men except close relatives. Men engaged in public life—in the marketplace, the gymnasium, and the political assembly—while women stayed home in special rooms at the back of the house. Greek women were expected to be silent and submissive, and most important, to provide male heirs for a society that was focused on the male line. Women could not own property and anything they inherited was held in trust for them by male relatives (Ahmed, pp. 28–31).

The Roman Conquest and Christianity

Not long after Alexander's conquests, the city of Rome came to dominate much of Mediterranean Europe. Then, in the first century B.C., Rome defeated the Ptolemies and added Egypt to the expanding Roman Empire, which now ringed the Mediterranean Sea. International trade led to a burst of economic and intellectual productivity in Egypt. Egypt grew the wheat for Rome's bread, and Alexandria became the intellectual center of the entire Roman world.

In the years after Christ's birth, Christianity came to Alexandria and found a receptive audience. For several centuries, Christianity spread throughout Egypt, gradually replacing the worship of Amon and the other ancient gods of the Nile. Christian ideas about women were similar to Greek ideas. Early Christian women were frequently covered from head to toe in voluminous gowns and veils and they were strictly segregated in order to protect men from temptation. Saint Augustine, one of the most influential early Christian thinkers, said that women were biologically inferior to men, and he associated women with sex and shame (Ahmed, pp. 35–36).

But while Christianity blossomed in Egypt, the Roman Empire declined. The empire had grown so large, stretching from the Atlantic Ocean to the Red Sea, that Rome could not effectively rule it. In the fourth century A.D., Rome divided itself into an Eastern and a Western Empire. The Eastern Empire, which included Egypt, was to be ruled from the ancient city of Byzantium (today Istanbul, in Turkey). Byzantium proved to be a less friendly ruler than Rome. The Byzantine rulers objected to the way Egyptians practiced Christianity and persecuted Coptic (Egyptian) Christians. By the seventh century, Egyptians regarded the Byzantines less as brothers in Christ and more as hated tyrants.

The Arab/Islamic Conquest

When the seventh century began, Egypt was a Christian country; its language was Greek and it identified with the cultural traditions of Greece, Rome, and Jerusalem. All this was to change forever with the explosive growth of a new religion: Islam. Islam originated in the Arabian city of Mecca (now in Saudi Arabia), at that time a crossroads of trade between India and the Byzantine Empire. In the seventh century, Muhammad, a 42-year-old merchant, had a revelation from God and announced a new faith—Islam—that built upon Arab culture, Christianity, and Judaism. By 632, Muhammad's followers dominated Arabia. In 639 the militant followers of the new faith swept across the borders of the Byzantine Empire and rapidly conquered Egypt, Syria, and Palestine. In the decades that followed, they swept beyond Egypt, west through North Africa, and on to Spain and east to the borders of China.

Although the Arabs came as conquerors, they were not entirely unwelcome in Egypt. The bitterness that Egyptians felt toward the Byzantines led them to stand aside as the Arabs crushed the Byzantine forces. The Arabs, for their part, demanded much less than had the Byzantines: only obedience and taxes were required. Although the Arabs devoutly wished for converts to their new faith, they did not forcibly convert Egyptians—whether Christians or Jews or worshipers of the ancient gods.

Islam gradually transformed Egyptian society. Arabic became the common language of Egypt, replacing Coptic, the language of ancient Egypt, and the Greek of the Greco-Roman period. Cairo, a new Islamic city, replaced Alexandria in importance and became a world center of Islamic learning. Most Egyptians embraced Islam, and Islamic beliefs and practices became a fundamental part of Egyptian culture. (However, a minority remained Christians. About 6 percent of Egyptians today are Copts, Coptic Christians.) Arab literature, music, and the arts were absorbed into Egyptian culture.

Islam didn't much change the status of women in Egypt. It incorporated Christian gender norms and attitudes toward women. Islam did give Egyptian women limited rights to sue for divorce and a limited right to inherit, but it also introduced into Egypt the Arab practice of **polygamy** (which allowed men to marry more than one wife) (Ahmed, p. 33).

European Colonialism

For many centuries after the foundation of Islam, the Islamic world was a center of trade, knowledge, and wealth. At the same time Europe declined into its "Dark Ages," a period when government disintegrated, knowledge was lost, and trade withered. But by the fourteenth and fifteenth centuries, Europe began to develop and expand, gradually pushing aside the Islamic world. Europeans forced Arab rulers out of Spain in 1492. They took over trade with India in the sixteenth century, and in 1798, a French army, led by Napoleon, conquered Egypt itself. The French were soon expelled by the British and Turkish, with whom they were at war, but European political and economic domination of Egypt continued. England, in particular, believed it had a major interest in Egypt; it wanted Egyptian customers for its products and it wanted to control the Suez Canal, the most direct route to India, Great Britain's largest colony.

Some Egyptians prospered during this colonial period of European domination. An elite of landowners, government officials, and professionals, who cooperated with the Europeans, came under the influence of European culture and ideas. They adopted French (rather than Arabic) as their everyday language and sent their sons to schools where they were taught in French and read European books. They are European food, drank wine, and read European literature. Many thought and wrote about how a society could be at once modern and Islamic. Egypt's elite also absorbed European ideas about democracy, the right of nations to self-rule, and the need for equality between women and men. During the colonial period, some affluent Egyptian women publicly removed their veils and participated in the political struggle for independence. However, for most Egyptians life became much harder during the colonial period. Many peasants lost their land, artisans could not compete against imported European goods, and the growing ranks of industrial workers labored long hours for very low wages. Poor Egyptians had little contact with European culture: they spoke Arabic and took consolation in Islam. Both the economic and the cultural distance between rich and poor widened.

The European powers made increasingly restrictive demands on the Egyptian government, and in 1882 a revolt against these restrictions by the Egyptian army led to the occupation of Egypt by the British. From 1882 through 1954, the object of modern Egyptian politics was the end of the British occupation. Although a popular revolt in 1919 led the British to proclaim Egypt independent in 1921, the British army remained in occupation and the newly created king and parliament were dominated by the British ambassador. In 1952, following a humiliating defeat of the Egyptian army by the forces of Israel, the newly independent Jewish state, a group of junior officers deposed King Farouk and took control of the government. In 1954, these officers, led by Gamal Abdul Nasser, expelled the British army and created real independence for Egypt for the first time in 100 years.

An Independent Egypt

It is ironic that western ideas played so large a role in Egypt's revolt against European domination. Nasser, Egypt's greatest twentieth-century figure, transformed Egypt's government and economy and greatly improved the lives of the poorest Egyptians. While he respected Islam, Nasser looked to the West, to the United States, the Soviet Union, and Europe for political values and institutional models. Nasser moved his country in the direction of a **secular** (that is, not religious) authority: a system of business law separate from Islamic family law, a school system separate from religious education, and western-style parliamentary government separate from religious authority. Nasser established a public school system that was open to all but the poorest Egyptians, and open to women as well as men. He chose to build a **socialist** economy, in which most enterprises were government-owned and the government was the society's largest employer.

Nasser also challenged Egypt's deep economic inequalities, particularly in the countryside. His first target was the great landowning families who owned more than a third of Egypt's land. Nasser seized the land belonging to the royal family and required the other rich families to sell more than half their land. He redistributed this land to hundreds of thousands of poor peasant families. Many poor families received no land, and even those who did acquired only very small plots, but all felt grateful to Nasser; they felt released from oppressive landlords and they hoped to be given more land in the future (Hooglund, pp. 122–123; Mitchell, T., pp. 22–23).

Taha was a young man in his teens when Gamal Abdul Nasser deposed the king, but it is still a glowing day in his memory. Not only was the honor of the country restored, but the cruelty of the greedy landlords and their agents came to an end. As a young boy, Taha would rise to find a sickle before his family's home, a signal that a day's badly paid work was demanded by the landlord. Refusal to work was met with threats and beatings. Young Taha could feel the contempt of the landlords who drove out from Cairo in their luxurious automobiles. When Nasser made these fat Cairenes sell their land, they left Egypt. This made a good deal of sense to Taha; he thought of these rich people as foreigners. Nasser's revolt enabled Taha to buy 3 acres of fertile Delta soil. He married and raised three sons and a daughter in a freedom and prosperity he could never have imagined before Nasser: enough to eat, a radio, a television, and school for his children. At Nasser's death, Taha traveled to Cairo for the first time. Carrying a green palm frond, symbol of eternal life, Taha and hundreds of thousands of peasants followed Egypt's president to his grave. Gamal Abdul Nasser is dead more than twenty years, but for Taha, there is no one like him.

Egypt's peasants benefited in a limited way from Nasser's land reform. But Nasser's attack against the great landowners transformed the rural middle class. They bought much of the land the elite was forced to sell and turned themselves into prosperous commercial farmers (Vatikiotis, pp. 396–399).

Politics in Independent Egypt

Nasser won wide support from Egyptians because he helped many people become more prosperous and he succeeded in evicting the British. At the same time, however, he severely restricted democracy. The army crushed strikes and suppressed militant Islamic groups and jailed their leaders.

In 1956, the British, French, and Israeli armies once again invaded Egypt. Britain and France wanted to reassert their control over the region, and Israel wanted to end Nasser's support of the Palestinians who attacked Israel. Although Egypt's armies were defeated in the fighting with Israel, Nasser persuaded the United States and the Soviet Union to force the invaders to withdraw. Nasser emerged as the hero, not only of Egypt, but of the Arab world as a whole. Strengthened by political and economic support from the Soviet Union, Nasser led Egypt into a period of prosperity and international leadership. "Nonaligned" countries— those like India and Yugoslavia, that sought to avoid becoming a part of either the Soviet bloc or the U.S.-led western block—looked to Nasser for leadership.

But much of Egypt's progress was brought to a halt by the 1967 war with Israel. Israel defeated Egypt's armed forces so completely that it humiliated both the Egyptian leadership and many ordinary Egyptians. Many Egyptian soldiers were killed or injured and Egypt's economy was shattered by the closing of the Suez Canal, the capture of the country's developing oil fields in the Sinai Peninsula, and the wave of refugees that poured out of war-torn areas.

In the remaining years of his life, Nasser struggled to undo the damage of the war, but it remained for his successor, Anwar Sadat, to bring about the withdrawal of Israel's army from Egypt. In 1973, Egyptian forces crossed the canal and forced the Israeli army back into the Sinai Desert. Although Israel's forces later recrossed the canal, isolating the Egyptian army, and moved into Egypt's heartland, the initial defeats of the 1973 war forced Israel to negotiate a withdrawal from the Nile Valley.

Egypt Today

Although Egypt was politically victorious in 1973, and a 1979 peace treaty with Israel made it possible to reduce spending on defense, economic and social tensions increased. Egypt's economy failed to keep pace with the increasing size and expectations of its population. In 1947 there were 19 million Egyptians; by 1993 there were 56 million. In the 1950s, millions of Egyptians moved from the countryside to the city and found work and housing in an expanding economy. By the 1980s, there was neither work nor housing for poor Egyptians who continued to flock to Cairo, Alexandria, and other cities. Today, one Egyptian in five lives in or around Cairo. In recent decades, more than 2 million Egyptians have been forced to find work outside the country, mostly in the oil-rich nations of the Middle East and the Persian Gulf.

Anwar Sadat attempted to restore Egypt's economic health by fostering private investment in Egypt and encouraging private enterprise. In doing so, he reversed a long-standing policy of favoring state enterprises—such as the government oil companies—at the expense of privately owned businesses. Sadat's policy failed to bring substantial benefits to most Egyptians and many people came to believe that this policy of *infitah* (or "opening the door") created benefits only for a few rich business owners. Despite his foreign policy successes, Sadat faced growing hostility in the streets. In October 1981, during a celebration of the 1973 war against Israel, Anwar Sadat was assassinated by members of an elite military unit.

Today, many of the same dilemmas that faced Egypt under Sadat face his successor, Hosni Mubarak, an air force general, unknown to most Egyptians before Sadat's death. Yearly, Egypt's population rises and people's aspirations rise too, while economic growth lags behind. Increasingly, the promises of the largely secular state created by Nasser seem hollow and those who argue for an Islamic approach to building a modern nation are finding a more attentive audience. Whatever choices Egypt makes for its future will influence the course of regional and global history, because Egypt is the largest Arab state and one of the largest Islamic societies, an important actor in the theater of the twenty-first century.

EGYPTIAN CULTURE

Many Egyptians today believe their society must choose between a culture based on Islam and a secular culture imported from the modern West. Western culture is probably familiar to you, but Islamic culture is likely a subject you know little about. We can make good use of sociological concepts in exploring the character of Islamic culture.

Egyptians find it difficult to understand that for most people in Europe and America, religion is often irrelevant to daily life, engaging people only on certain occasions and in special places. In Europe and America, people are used to conflicts between science, philosophy, law, government, and religion. Sociologists call western societies **secular societies.** It is commonly said that Islam is a culture, a way of life, as well as a religion. In Egypt, even people who are not devout Muslims (and even those who are Christians) live in a world filled with Islamic values and norms.

We might say that Egypt is a **sacred society,** a society in which religious ideas and values are applied to every aspect of life.

Islamic Beliefs, Norms, and Values

Any Muslim will tell you that it is easy to get to know Islam; you need to begin with the five pillars of faith: declaring belief in God, prayer, charity, fasting during the holy month of Ramadan, and pilgrimage. Each of these fundamentals reveals important Islamic beliefs and each has major implications for the conduct of every-day life.

Declaring Belief

Five times a day, in the largest cities and the smallest villages, the voice of *muezzin* (the prayer caller) cries out from the *minaret* (the highest tower) of the mosque (the Islamic house of worship). Nowadays the voice is likely to be recorded and broadcast over a public address system.

> God is great (Allahu Akbar), God is great, God is great. I witness that there is no god but Allah. I witness that there is no God but Allah. I witness that Muhammad is his messenger. I witness that Muhammad is his messenger. Come to prayer, come to prayer. Come to prosperity, come to prosperity. God is great. God is great. There is no God but Allah. (Esposito, 1991*a*, p. 89)

The call is echoed by Muslims indoors and out, who all join in affirming their belief. They are thus daily and repeatedly declaring their faith: their faith in Allah, the God of Islam, and their belief in one single god ("there is no god but Allah"). You may take **monotheism** (the belief that there is only one god) for granted, but in the history of the world's religions, monotheism is relatively unusual. Most of the world's religions recognize many gods, major and minor. For example, when you read about Japan in Chapter 1, you learned that all the major religions of Asia—Buddhism, Hinduism, Taoism, and Shinto—honor multiple gods. Islam, Christianity, and Judaism all believe in a single god, and he is the same god, the god of Moses and Abraham. Islam recognizes Jesus as one of the four prophets—Moses, David, Jesus, and Muhammad—but Jesus is not believed to be the son of God.

All that is necessary to become a Muslim is to make the affirmation of faith: "There is no god but God (Allah), and Muhammad is the messenger of God" in the presence of other believers. But professing faith in God commits you to accepting the word of God, as transmitted through his messenger Muhammad and recorded literally in the *Quran,* the holy book. The word "Islam" actually means "submission" in Arabic, meaning submission to the will of God. "Muslim" means one who submits (Lippman, 1990, p. 1).

Values and Norms. Muslims believe in a Judgment Day on which each person will be sent by God either to paradise or to hell. Allah is a stern god, and on Judgment Day terrible agonies await the sinner, while paradise is filled with delights. Pious Muslims fear the wrath of God if they do not live by Islamic values and norms. For example, Islam values honesty, modesty and chastity, charity toward the less fortunate, and religious faith. To be virtuous and win paradise, the good man or woman must strive to submit to God, to make life a spiritual exercise so that in every situation he or she struggles to act virtuously, not for worldly benefit, but to honor God. It is important to follow detailed norms, but they must be obeyed in the spirit of faith.

The good Muslim does not drink, or profit from lending money, or gamble, gossip, or seek revenge. The good Muslim does not have sex outside marriage, gives to charity, helps orphans, and of course carries out the prescribed religious obligations of prayer, charity, fasting, and pilgrimage. Many of these norms are described in the Quran, which is so important that many Egyptian men and boys try to memorize it in its entirety. In Egypt the Quran is chanted continually on the radio, in the traditional schools that boys attend, and in public recitations held in auditoriums and stadiums. Other Islamic norms are recorded in the *hadith,* the collection of Muhammad's words as interpreted by religious scholars. Islam recognizes no distinction between religious law and secular law, or between religion and the state. *Sharia* is the name of the code of law based on Islam, which is interpreted by religious scholars, called *ulama,* who act as judges and have broad authority in regulating families and marriages (Rodenbeck, p. 105; Campo, p. 105; Lippman, 1990, pp. 30–32).

Prayer and the Social Construction of Time

Prayer is the second of the five pillars of faith. Muslims are required to pray 5 times a day: at sunrise, noon, midafternoon, sunset, and night, in response to the call to prayer. Daily prayers may be recited alone or in company, in a mosque or at one's place of work. In rural areas, men may keep clear a small spot in their fields for daily prayer. In busy cities, traffic may be blocked by rows of men kneeling for the noon prayer. According to Lippman, in Cairo you will see the policeman posted at the rear door of the Central Bank prostrate himself at the prayer call, leaving the door unguarded (Lippman, 1990, p. 12). Some people, who are not religious, or not Muslims, do not pray, but those who do are completely unself-conscious about it. Everyone takes for granted the brief interruptions in life's activity that punctuate the day.

Many norms prescribe the proper way to pray. People take off their shoes before entering a mosque and they ritually wash themselves before prayer, washing their faces, hands, and feet at a fountain, or perhaps just sprinkling a few drops of water if that is all that is possible. All believers face in the direction of Mecca (the city, today in Saudi Arabia, where Muhammad first heard the word of God) when they pray, so if there are many praying together, you will see them lined up in orderly rows. In daily prayer people recite standard texts; they don't make individual appeals to God. Recitation is accompanied by sequences of bows and prostrations, when people kneel, then lower their foreheads to the ground. Women generally pray separately from men, since the postures of prayer might prove immodest. In the street or the field, people avoid touching the dirty ground by praying on a small rug or even a piece of cardboard (Bassiouni, pp. 30–31). There is tension in Islam between the "official" religion of the mosque and the holy texts and the folk religion practiced by villagers and the urban poor. They often visit

On a busy Cairo street, outside a mosque, traffic comes to a halt for noontime prayers. Public space in Egyptian cities is "male" space and all those praying in the street are men. Since they face toward Mecca, they easily arrange themselves in neat rows. Not all Egyptians, not even all Muslims, pray regularly. Behind those at prayer we can see other people on errands and at work.

shrines and make personal appeals to popular saints. These practices are condemned by Muslim clergy.

Prayer Structures Time. How is time ordinarily divided in your society? Do you think in terms of the week and the weekend? The hours of classes? The time the coffee cart comes around in the office, lunchtime, and the end of the workday? In Muslim countries like Egypt, the hours of prayer divide the day, marking the passage of time as clearly as the clock. Businesses open after the morning prayer and the best bargains may be found before the call to noon prayer (Rodenbeck, p. 105).

In Egypt, Friday is the day of special religious observance. The week hurries toward Friday, when schools and government offices are closed. Women who work in private businesses, as typists or engineers, struggle to finish work early so they can go home and clean their houses by Friday afternoon, when the eye of God will be upon them. In towns and villages, the Friday market is the largest, since people flock into town for Friday prayers. People gather in the markets to shop for sugar, tea, or cassette tapes (Fakhouri, pp. 51–52; Campo, pp. 126–127).

On Fridays, Islamic tradition requires that Muslim men pray together in the mosque. Women may attend too, but it is not required. The prayer leader or *imam* leads Friday prayers and also delivers a sermon. He is not a priest, but rather an ordinary worshiper, normally someone with extra religious training. In a city, the *imam* is probably a person who has done a great deal of special study, but in a village he would likely be an artisan who has studied for a few years at a village religious school (Lippman, 1990, p. 14).

Finally, in Egypt, religious holidays punctuate the year. The most important of these is *Ramadan,* which lasts for a whole month. Because the Islamic calendar is a lunar calendar, Ramadan begins on a different date in each year and it is not associated with a particular season. Observance of Ramadan is so demanding that people must structure their year around it.

Ramadan and the Value of Community

Observance of Ramadan is another of the pillars of Islam. Ramadan is the Arabic name of the month in which God began to reveal the Quran to Muhammad and the month when Muhammad's small army won its first battle, at Badr in 624. During Ramadan all Muslim adults must fast from dawn until dark (neither eating nor drinking anything) unless they are pregnant, nursing, traveling, or ill, and refrain from smoking, alcohol, and sex. Fasting teaches self-restraint and also compassion for the poor and hungry. You can imagine how these obligations disrupt normal life during Ramadan. Especially when the fast occurs during hot weather, life slows to a crawl, with people working shorter hours and resting indoors as much as possible away from the desiccating sun. Families rise before dawn to eat the leftovers from the previous night's dinner and to take their last sips of water before the sun rises. Then, after dark, everyone celebrates, with a feast called the *iftar* ("breakfast"). Even the poorest Egyptians who rarely see meat on their tables, will scrimp and save to eat meat during Ramadan.

Like daily prayers, Ramadan vividly demonstrates the cultural and religious unity of Muslims. The rigors of fasting are shared and people feel linked in common endeavor with their community, their nation, and the worldwide community of Islam. In cities and towns all over the country, people who have fasted will sit before tables piled high with food and drink, waiting for the broadcast cannon shot with which Radio Cairo announces sunset prayers and the end of the fast. Radio and television, which often act as instruments of secularization, work in this case to reinforce the culture of a sacred society (Esposito, 1991*a,* pp. 91–92).

Charity and the Value of Equality

Charity (or *zakat*) is a major Islamic value and it is one of the five pillars of Islam. All Muslims are obliged, as an act of worship of God, to support Muslims in need and the Islamic faith. Some Muslims interpret *zakat* as requiring them to give a fixed percentage of their income and wealth to charity every year; or to leave money to charity in their wills. Others give money to help build mosques. People often distribute food to the poor at festivals and weddings and during religious holidays. They also give money to the homeless on the streets or outside mosques (Bassiouni, pp. 30–31; Lippman, 1990, p. 19; Campo, pp. 122–124).

Consideration for the needy is part of Islam's traditional emphasis on equality. In the mosque, all are equal; there are no preferred pews for the rich or influential—-all kneel together. Anyone can lead prayers and give the sermon; there is no church hierarchy, no official priests or sacraments, no recognized saints, no monks or nuns. Islam also requires that the rich respect the poor, even though they may be ragged and hungry. Kindness and compassion are the essence of what Egyptians refer to as *saddaqa.* The Quran warns, "A kind word with forgiveness is better than charity followed by insult" (Bassiouni, p. 30). Much of the moral energy and appeal of "fundamentalist" Islam comes from a sense that the rich and powerful have long since ceased to care about the needs of ordinary Muslims. Even when help does come from government agencies, it often comes with a kind of contempt that is especially resented because it violates the sacred norms of Islam. In the absence of government services some contemporary "fundamentalist" Muslims have organized clinics, built housing, and provided loans for the poor, and this dedication to charity earns them the respect of other Muslims (Campo, pp. 130–137; Lippman, 1990, pp. 78–90; Hedges, Oct. 4, 1993, p. A8).

Pilgrimage: A Culmination of Faith

The final pillar of faith and the last major obligation of all Muslims is to make the pilgrimage or *hajj* to Mecca at least once in their lifetime. Both personally and socially the pilgrimage sums up the meaning of Islamic faith. To make the journey to Mecca is certainly an affirmation of faith. In the past, when pilgrims journeyed overland, it was a grueling trip. Today, airplanes ease the journey, but it is still challenging, especially in summer. Also, for many Egyptians, the *hajj* represents an enormous expense, the fruit of many years' savings and perhaps a person's single trip ever away from his or her village. As prayer and holy days structure the Islamic day and year, planning and making the pilgrimage are key events in a lifetime. In many villages you will see "pilgrimage murals," painted on the outside walls of their houses by those who have made the *hajj.*

Finally, the pilgrimage expresses with special emphasis the Islamic values of community and equality. The pilgrimage is a yearly event, taking place only on specified days. During that short time, hundreds of thousands, even millions of pilgrims pour into Mecca from all over the world. In the huge crowds which walk through the required rites of the pilgrimage—trekking to the Sacred Mosque and back and forth to other holy places—you will see people of many races, speaking dozens of languages, visibly united by their Islamic faith. Symbolically, they all put on the special clothing of the pilgrimage, white wraps for the men and loose white dresses, without facial veils, for the women, reminding them that in Islam differences of race and class are surmounted (Lippman, 1990, pp. 22–27).

The Value of Community in Egyptian Culture

Islam gives Egyptians a tremendous sense of community with all Muslims. Perhaps this explains why they value group membership and group life so much. In every situation, Egyptians would rather be with others than alone. It is easy for them to establish a sense of community within a crowd of strangers. Sociologist Andrea Rugh describes how affluent Egyptians pitch their umbrellas close to one another on the beach, rather than seeking privacy. Expensive movie theaters and cheap buses fill up in the same way: people sit next to others already seated, rather than spreading out. Even in illness, Egyptians prefer company. A man who has a headache, or a fever, will be surrounded by a stream of friends and relatives who bring him soda, food, aspirin, and advice. Hospitals are crowded with residents and friends visiting patients (Rugh, 1984, pp. 37–38).

Even modern Cairo, despite its rapid growth and millions of residents, remains a place of intensely personal contacts (Abu-Lughod, L., p. 71). Egyptians are tied most closely to their families, their neighbors, and others with whom they have worked or gone to school. In the countryside, people live in a village, not spread out in farmsteads in the fields. Houses are tightly clustered, along narrow alleys, filled with children, water buffalo, and the bustle of everyday life. A village teacher asks children to find what's missing in a chalked outline of a peasant home, and their immediate reply is "the neighbors" (Ayrout, pp. 87–88; Fakhouri, pp. 17–21). According to a familiar Arabic saying, "the most important thing about a house is its neighbors" (Fluehr-Lobban, p. 58).

Egyptians also will make considerable sacrifices to live out their lives in the company of their families. Andrea Rugh describes a young city woman who refused a good job as a live-in companion to a wealthy widow. Despite the fact that her family was so poor they could hardly feed her, she regarded this well-paid job with horror, because she would have to sleep in a room alone, apart from her family (Rugh, 1984, p. 36).

Personal Ties

People in Egypt tend to place a low value on membership in large, impersonal organizations, like big businesses, labor unions, or political parties. Alternatively, people may make great efforts to turn impersonal groups into close-knit units. Men who own businesses, for example, will organize their enterprises around family connections even when this limits their expansion or economic flexibility. Egyptian businessmen like to think of themselves as "fathers" to their employees and often expect their employees to behave like children might: running employers' little personal errands and seeking their boss's advice on personal matters (Rugh, 1984, p. 43).

City neighborhoods may include people from all over Egypt: Saidis from the Upper Nile, as well as villagers from the Delta, Christians as well as Muslims. But residents emphasize their closeness, even to strangers, by addressing each other by kin terms. A younger woman calls an older, unrelated man "uncle." Women the same age call each other "sister." In this way, village patterns of relationship are extended to a more impersonal urban setting.

Egyptians treat their society as a collection of families and villages. Social life has a personal touch, and Egyptians' attitude toward each other is generally trusting, not fearful or suspicious. But Egyptians' reluctance to commit themselves to larger social structures sometimes frustrates the government's plans. Egypt's leaders have tried to develop large organizations for government, business, education, and health care, but their efforts have conflicted with family and personal loyalties (Springborg, p. 185).

The Value of Generosity in Egyptian Culture

Linked to Egyptians' broad sense of community is the value they place on generosity and hospitality. Anthropologist Carolyn Fluehr-Lobban traces Egyptian generosity to the influence of Arab culture, now absorbed into Islam. She describes the ancient nomadic desert life of the Arabs, when everyone might someday be a traveler, dependent on strangers for shelter, life-saving water, and food. Today, Fluehr-Lobban says, "generosity . . . is a core value in Arab society the importance of which has not diminished over the centuries or been fundamentally transformed by urban life and empire, by class division and social stratification." A generous person is a moral person, and everyone looks for generosity in friends, marriage partners, and politicians (p. 46). Thus, in Egypt today, shopkeepers offer their customers tea and a pleasant chat, motorists stop to offer help to a driver with a flat tire, bureaucrats offer coffee when you visit their office, and relatives and friends visit each other often, sitting down to tables piled with food and drink, as high as family finances afford. Visitors are urged to stay longer, eat more, and have another cup of tea.

Fluehr-Lobban also explains that in Egypt "sharing is so deeply engrained that to notice its expression is an oddity." It would be very impolite to refuse the offered cup of tea, and impolite as well to thank your host for it. Generosity is **normative:** it is expected and you don't have to thank people for their generosity. People in Egypt don't say thank you to the store clerk or the taxi driver or the waiter. On the other hand, if someone is generous to you, it would be polite to reciprocate at some later time. You should invite your host to your home, and you may bring fruit or candy to the family of the person who fixed your flat tire (p. 46).

The Value of Honor

Egyptians will tell you that their personal honor and the honor of their families is utterly precious to them. Carolyn Fluehr-Lobban defines honor as "the pride and dignity that a family possesses due to its longstanding good reputation in the community for producing upright men and women who behave themselves well, marry well, raise proper children, and above all adhere to the principles and practices of the religion of Islam" (p. 52). Dishonorable behavior brings shame upon a man or woman and their family. Use of foul language is shameful, so is losing one's temper, or gossiping in a way that harms others; failing to help a relative or neighbor when one could really do so is shameful, as is failing in one's obligation to support family members (Fluehr-Lobban, p. 53).

It is difficult to discuss honor without describing Egyptian gender roles, because maintaining honor places different obligations on men and women and much shameful behavior is sexual in nature. A man who is known to drink or to spend time with women of loose morals dishonors himself and his family. Men are expected to remain virgins until marriage and to dress modestly in loose pants and shirt or in traditional robes. But requirements for chastity and modest dress are more demanding of women than men and much smaller infractions of sexual norms endanger a woman's honor and bring shame on her family.

Honor and Women's Roles

A woman's honor is based on chastity and modesty. Virginity is a special treasure, which a girl and her family carefully preserve and guard until marriage. Lost virginity is a disaster for a young woman, for whom marriage will likely become impossible, and for her shamed family. Consider this incident: A 10-year-old daughter of an affluent family crashed her bicycle into a wall and tore her hymen. Her family rushed her to the doctor, who wrote an affidavit describing the injury. This document preserved the girl's marriageability. Girls who dress provocatively or who socialize in any way with unrelated men are assumed to be sexually promiscuous.

Egyptians' beliefs about sexuality underlie the importance they place on chastity and modesty. Egyptians look on sexual desire as something natural to men and women. They assume that men's desire for sex is easily aroused by the sight or company of nonkin women, and they believe that men cannot be expected to control themselves once aroused. That means women are a dangerous temptation to men. This way of thinking dates far back in Egyptian history, to the Greek and early Christian eras. If women are dangerously tempting to men, then they should act in such a way as to avoid attracting male desire and men should protect their female relatives from unrelated men. In Egypt, people think that women require *hudud,* "boundaries" in Arabic, like the walls of a house which form a protected space. In Arabic, both a house without secure outside walls, and a woman without a *hijab,* a covering veil, are described as *awra,* or naked (Mernissi, pp. 6–8).

Women should dress modestly, in a way that conceals their sexual attractiveness. The Quran, in a passage often cited as the source of modesty norms for women, required the wives of the prophets to cover themselves:

> And say to the believing women that they should lower their gaze and guard their modesty; that they should not display their beauty and charms except what (normally) appears of them; that they should draw their veils over their bosoms and display their beauty only to their husbands. (Quoted in Esposito, 1991*a,* p. 99)

In public, poor village women wear traditional long, loose cotton robes, often black, sometimes with a shawl thrown over their heads, but in cities there is great variety in styles of women's dress. Current fashion emphasizes "modest dress," and this may mean a western dress with its hem below the knee, a fitted waist, and long sleeves and perhaps a head scarf. Alternatively, it may mean one of the new "Islamic" styles—a loose-fitting gown, with no waist, a high neck and long sleeves, topped by some sort of *hijab* (usually translated as "veil," but actually a scarf or hood that fully covers the hair and neck). Women in poor urban neighborhoods may wear any of these styles. Often women wear cooler, less enveloping dresses inside their homes, but they cover them when they go outdoors. In the big western-style hotels and the fanciest restaurants you can still see women dressed in the latest western fashions, but their clothes are increasingly conservative. Ten years ago, you would have seen rich women at a wedding in strapless evening gowns. Today they wear the same gowns, but cover them with a gauzy, long-sleeved evening coat.

Purity. There is a traditional custom in Egypt, practiced today in rural areas and in some poor urban neighborhoods, which is loosely linked to norms about virginity and chastity. **Female circumcision** is an ancient North African custom that has nothing to do with Islam. In female circumcision, the clitoris is wholly or partially removed before puberty, a mutilation that is painful and frightening and which certainly reduces a woman's potential for sexual satisfaction. Female circumcision is called "purification" and it is believed to "purify" the girl of what would otherwise be a dangerous, growing masculinity. Folk beliefs hold that if a women is not circumcised, her clitoris will grow and grow and she will become wild and chase after men. Because of these beliefs, women may demand circumcision for their daughters even though they themselves have suffered from it. They see it simply as the counterpart of circumcision for men. Female circumcision is actually illegal in Egypt today and is opposed by Islamic scholars. Nevertheless, experts estimate that 50 percent of Egyptian women have been circumcised (Fakhouri, pp. 86–87; Atiya, pp. 11–13; Burstyn, pp. 30–33).

Seclusion. Separate social spaces for women and men also protect women from the attentions of men and protect men from sexual impulses. Traditionally, a woman's male relatives protected her by supporting her, so she had no need to go out into the world to make her way. A husband's wish to keep his wife hidden at home showed how much he loved and valued her. If a woman had to venture out in public, it was proper for her male relatives to accompany her.

Today, many Egyptian women will tell you that they appreciate the protection their male relatives give them. By protecting women, men guard their families' reputations, because sexual indiscretions are a stain on male honor: sexual indiscretions imply that the men of the family are too weak or careless to protect their women. In the conservative countryside, even today, a young woman who meets alone with an admirer, or a married woman seen with a man not her husband, commits a terrible violation of Egyptian **mores.** A woman seen with a man, or even merely seen alone outside her home, would be suspected of forbidden sexual activity. Her husband or brothers or father might well lock her inside the house, or even beat her. If the family agrees that adultery has taken place, custom allows her husband to kill her, to "wash away the shame with blood" and restore the family's honor (Fluehr-Lobban, p. 55).

You can see that a woman who dresses modestly and limits her public interaction is seen as honorable and brings honor to her family. Nowadays, many Egyptian women work outside their homes and attend school and college, but even so, men and women tend to gather separately. We call this **gender segregation.** The public realm clearly belongs to men. Even in the daytime, there are more men than women in the streets, and men gather in mosques and cafés. After dark almost everyone outside is male. Men stroll with friends, sit in restaurants, and go to the movies. In the daytime, women walk outside together, linked arm in arm. They may go with their children to the movies, and they gather in each other's homes. In poor neighborhoods, women move freely through the alleyways near their houses, fetching water or food from the market, or calling children in for meals, but not venturing far afield.

When women must travel to and from work or school this creates problems, because there are no clear norms specifying how men should treat unrelated women, particularly strangers, in public places. There is a traditional assumption that any woman away from the protection and seclusion of her family, especially at night, is sexually available, a prostitute. Even when it is clear that respectable women are on their way to work, they are often sexually harassed. As Arlene MacLeod describes it: "Men walking down the streets or sitting in the sidewalk coffee shops can compliment or comment. They attempt 'accidental' encounters; they touch and pinch. Women are consistently harassed in this manner as they walk the crowded sidewalks and are squeezed overenthusiastically on the overloaded trains and buses" (MacLeod, p. 63).

Sex. After all this discussion of sex and danger, it is important to stress that Egyptian culture is not opposed to sexual pleasure. Sex itself is not seen as sinful, and celibacy is not admired. (Islam has no celibate clergy, no monks or nuns.) It is sexual pleasure outside marriage that is condemned. Within marriage, sex for the sake of pleasure is accepted, even desired. When modern birth control technology was first introduced into Egypt, the religious *ulama* considered it and decided they had no objection—as long as it was used by married couples only. Today, the Egyptian government officially promotes the use of birth control. In a way, you could say that Egyptian culture isn't antisex, it is just very promarriage.

Honor and Men's Roles

While Egyptian men certainly enjoy wider rights and freedoms than women, the demands of honor set burdensome obligations on them too. A man's honor is not merely personal; it extends to his family, his property, and his clan. Just as a man who behaves shamefully dishonors his family and clan, so every man is obliged to defend his family against disrespect and insult. A man whose neighbor shouts insults at him in a drunken quarrel would be dishonored. So too would a man whose wife, gossip suggests, flirts with others. If one man steals crops from another man's field, it is an insult to the victim and his whole clan. Even an accidental death might still be seen as an assault on the honor of the victim's family.

In the traditional setting of a rural village, with strong family and clan ties, all these slights to honor must be erased; a man cannot ignore an insult or injury, even though Islam condemns revenge. If he does not respond to insult, a man will be seen as weak and unmanly. His family too will be obliged to back him or revenge him, and they may be drawn into disastrous and criminal violence. You might say that this is one reason why drinking alcohol and gossiping are both so much condemned in Islamic culture: they pave the way to conflict, insult, and destructive revenge.

Ibrahim and Ismail had quarreled for years over a piece of land that Ismail had inherited, but no one in El Mina thought this would lead to bloodshed. Both men were hot-tempered, but not foolish. Neither of them wanted to provoke a feud that might leave their sons and nephews dead. On a hot July day though the men parted after unusually bitter words. Driving off in his truck, shouting at Ismail, Ibrahim accidentally struck his rival's 11-year-old niece. The girl lapsed into a deep coma and died. Tension soared as everyone feared that Ismail and his brothers would strike at Ibrahim's family.

When the girl died, Ibrahim and his brothers left El Mina for their mother's village. There, his grandfather urged Ibrahim to find a way to end the dispute. Everyone talked about a feud thirty years earlier that had taken many lives.

Three days later, Ismail was approached by a man respected for his role in ending disputes. He asked Ismail's family to accept a traditional court which would set conditions for a peaceful resolution. Ismail and his kin agreed and all concerned met at the home of a man who was on good terms with both families. After long discussion, all agreed that while the girl's death had been an accident, her family should receive some compensation. They also agreed to resolve the dishonorable squabble that indirectly caused the accident. Ibrahim's family agreed to pay the substantial sum of 500 dollars to the girl's family and to give up their claims to the disputed land. In return Ismail's family agreed not to seek blood vengeance. Tension gradually eased and Ibrahim was relieved that he and his family could go about their lives without fear of sudden and deadly assault.

Given the importance of defending family honor, it is fortunate that Egyptian tradition provides peaceful ways of resolving affronts to honor. Tradition gives a victim's family only three days for violent revenge, and it permits the wrongdoer and his relatives to protect themselves by fleeing to their mother's kin. The institution of the traditional court allows older, often more powerful relatives, to mediate a settlement (Fakhouri, pp. 109–114; Ghosh, pp. 69–70, 135–137). It is a testament to the effectiveness of these customs that while norms call for men to defend their honor, the murder rate in Egypt is in fact very low (only 0.5 per 100,000 persons per year, as compared to 9.1 per 100,000 in the United States.) (See Table 1.2, p. 33.)

Honor and Role Conflict

In Egypt now, men's and women's roles are changing. More and more Egyptians are leaving the countryside for the cities, and more young people are attending high school and university. Urbanization and education offer new freedoms and pose new challenges for both men and women.

Changing Male Roles. In the city, men find themselves less burdened by the demands of clan loyalty and traditional notions of honor. On the other hand, they must confront a shortage of city jobs. Unemployment threatens not only family survival, but also male honor. A man without a job cannot marry, maintain his family, or protect his women. An unemployed man, whose wife or daughters work, may feel deeply humiliated and anxious. Unemployment is a particular threat for "over-educated" men whose high school or college degrees qualify them to do office work. They may feel entitled to government jobs, but find no jobs at all. Many men, suffering new status anxieties, turn to another role which confirms their masculinity and importance: the role of the observant Muslim. In Islamic societies, religion has an atmosphere of masculinity; the mosque is a male place and the history of Islam as a militant, fighting religion adds to its masculine tone. Attending mosque, praying, making the pilgrimage, demanding strict compliance with the laws of Islam are all activities which make a man more manly. Nowadays, many Egyptian men are attracted to Islamic fundamentalist groups, which stress the primacy of men and call for the withdrawal of women from the workplace and public life.

Changing Female Roles. Women have also experienced changes in roles and new anxieties. Nasser's reforms first opened jobs for thousands of women as schoolteachers and secretaries, doctors, lawyers, and engineers, and encouraged women's political participation (Ibrahim, B., pp. 294–295). Today approximately 30 percent of Egyptian women work for wages outside their homes—in offices, factories, stores, and on farms. Women have been elected to the parliament (the National Assembly) and the government supports working women by giving maternity leave to those who are government employees. It is mostly younger women who work; their mothers' generation was much less likely to venture away from home. That means working women can often rely on their mothers-in-law or other female relatives for help with child care. Nevertheless, working outside the home is fraught with conflicts and complications. (See Table 4.1.)

First of all, "housewife" is a highly respected, honorable role in Egypt. Especially among poor Egyptians, a woman who is a good housekeeper, who can always stretch the budget to feed the family, somehow find the money to pay the rent, arrange good marriages for her children, and solve their medical problems, is admired by all her neighbors and relatives. People recognize her wisdom and hard

TABLE 4.1. Working Women and Their Role in the Economy: Egyptian women are less likely to work than Japanese women, but more likely to be managers and professors than Japanese women.

	Percent of Women 15 and Older Who Work for Wages 1990–1992	Administrators and Managers, Percent Female, 1980–1989	National Legislature, Percent Female, 1994	College Professors, Percent Female, 1988
East Germany	83*	Not available	32*	28
West Germany	55*	Not available	21*	18
Japan	51	7	7	11
United States	56	38	10	24
Mexico	34	15	7	Not available
Egypt	30	14	2	33

*Data for 1985–1987.

Sources: Yanagishita, Machiko, and Nancy Yinger, *The World's Women 1995.* Washington DC: Population Reference Bureau, 1995; United Nations Development Programme, *Human Development Program Report 1994.* New York: Oxford University Press, 1994.

work and go to her for advice. The idea of a woman being "just a housewife" is foreign to Egyptian culture. Many poor women who must work outside their homes—in factories, as servants, as peddlers, or market women—would prefer not to. The role of housewife is much more rewarding than their menial, heavy, and poorly paid work. Educated, middle-class women are in a different situation. Many are clerical workers and secretaries, and their work is not particularly challenging or well-paid (they file papers and run copy machines and keep simple accounts). Government offices are very much overstaffed and everyone spends a lot of time drinking tea and chatting. Nevertheless, women employees greatly enjoy office life, with its bustle of visitors and links to a larger world. Many young, educated, middle-class women work before marriage and sometimes after it as well.

Role Conflicts. However desirable or undesirable it is, working creates many **role conflicts** for women, situations in which the expectations of one of their roles are incompatible with those of another. It is hard to be an honorable Muslim woman, and also go out in public and interact with unrelated men. The role conflicts of working women are intensified by the increasingly loud demands of the Islamic fundamentalists for a sexually resegregated public order (MacLeod, pp. 107–115).

> *Zaynab met her future husband, Kamal, an engineer, at the government office where she still works. Zaynab's father Mamduh, a mechanic for Egyptair, the national airline, was delighted. He had begun to despair that Zaynab, already 24, would ever marry, but now she would—and an engineer at that. What a catch for an uneducated man's daughter! Mamduh hoped Zaynab would leave her job and stay home where a wife and mother should be. When Mamduh was a boy in a tiny village in Upper Egypt, no woman left her home. But after the birth of her children, Zaynab returned to her office. "It's my life," she said, "my friends are there. Besides, no family can live on one income; Kamal, the children, and I would starve!"*

> *Mamduh was not entirely surprised. Zaynab had turned down a previous offer of marriage from a young man who had demanded that she leave her work. But Zaynab astonished her entire family in 1993 by announcing that from then on she would wear "Islamic dress," the concealing clothing of a devout Muslim woman. Zaynab, her parents, and her husband were not especially religious. Kamal thought it was ridiculous that the wife of an educated man should "cover herself," but Zaynab persisted. "Men do not respect a woman on Cairo's streets," she argued, "only a 'covered woman' will be left alone. Besides, even women at the university are 'covered'" (MacLeod, pp. 110–124; Ahmed, pp. 222–225; Mule and Barthel, pp. 328–331).*

Solving Role Conflicts with Islamic Dress. More and more working women and university women are wearing modern "Islamic dress," typically, a long, full, unfitted gown in a solid, light color, topped by a loose head covering that completely conceals the hair and neck. An outfit like this, usually made of polyester fabric, is a physical challenge in Egypt's hot climate. Even the alternative—a long dress with long sleeves and a high neck—is uncomfortable. Why would women give up fashionable lightweight western-style clothing for such a difficult mode of dress? Islamic dress solves problems for upwardly mobile working women. It declares that a woman respects Islamic values, even though she leaves her home. It declares that a woman is a bureaucrat or an engineer or other professional, not a sex object. Islamic dress also reduces sexual harassment in public places. Men who annoy a woman wearing western dress, break only a poorly defined secular norm, but men who harass a woman in Islamic dress profane Islam; they violate one of the sacred mores. Several sociologists have also argued that women in Islamic dress find it easier to interact with men, since their dress defines the situation as nonsexual, as this university student explained:

> Before I wore the veil, I always worried what people might think when they saw me speak to a man in the cafeteria or outside the class. I even wondered what the man himself thought of me. Since I wore the veil, I don't worry anymore. No one is going to accuse me of immorality. (Quoted in Mule and Barthel, p. 330)

Traditional Islam urges early marriage for women and sees an adult, unmarried woman as a sexual temptation and threat to public order. Islamic dress allows university women to put off marriage, while at the same time allaying public suspi-

Thuraya Al-Ghindi (right), chief music censor for the Egyptian government, works with two assistants. They are listening to a tape of the Cranberries to make sure it includes no sexually suggestive lyrics, before it is approved for sale in Egypt. All records, cassettes, and videotapes are censored. Mrs. Al-Ghindi wears modest western dress, her hair uncovered, while her two assistants wear the *hijab* over modern "Islamic dress"—full gowns with long sleeves and high necks.

cion. While wearing Islamic dress, young women can study with men, even walk with them to the station, without ruining their reputations, and thus are able to find their own husbands (Mule and Barthel, pp. 329–330; Ahmed, p. 224). For married working women, wearing Islamic dress reassures their husbands that they will not be treated as sexually available in the workplace or in public.

For university women, Islamic dress is a political statement as well as a practical solution to personal conflicts. It declares that they are proud to be Muslim women and even though they are attending university, they are not trying to be like European women. The new forms of "modest dress" were devised in the 1970s by politically active university women who used their dress as a form of political protest. Their clothing was a visible rejection of western influence—of the lure of western fashion and western-style advertising and marketing. It posed a visible alternative to the prowestern policies of the Sadat government. Today, some university women also seek an Islamic alternative to western feminism. They attend women's Quranic study groups in the mosque and reinterpret the Quran to stress passages which address men and women as spiritual equals. These women choose to seek legitimation for their changing roles within Islam, not outside it in western ideals (El-Gawhary, pp. 26–27).

SOCIAL STRUCTURE AND GROUP LIFE

All over Egypt, people strive to live in ways that express their values. They try to be good Muslims, honorable men and women, loyal members of their families. But everywhere, they are constrained by the social structures of their communities: by the availability of housing, the types of work they can get, the very physical layout of their surroundings, and the level of supervision of women and girls it permits. In both agricultural villages and in city neighborhoods, marriage, family, and community are the center of Egyptians' lives, but they take different forms. Also, in all settings, people center their lives around gender-segregated groups of friends, relatives, and neighbors, but these too vary in different social contexts.

Social Structure in the Countryside

Today, half of all Egyptians live in rural areas. Roads, buses, radio and television, schools, and health clinics link villages to modern cities, and villagers themselves move to the city or abroad to find work, but villages remain a distinctive social environment. Think for a moment of the geography of Egypt: life hugs the Nile. Green fields line its banks, interspersed with villages; but not far from the river, the barren sand begins. As a result, the countryside is crowded. People use as much of the good, irrigated land as possible for growing crops; they would never waste it on houses. Families never build houses in the midst of their farmland; they all live in houses clustered together in villages, along narrow, winding lanes. Men head out of the village each morning to work in their fields, which may be scattered in different locations. Poor families may have just a couple of rooms, built around a courtyard; rich families occupy a walled compound, with offices, storerooms, kitchen, and living quarters. In Egypt's heat, where rain may not fall for years at a time, much of daily life takes place out of doors in the courtyards where women prepare food and bake in outdoor ovens, on the rooftops, in the streets, and in the village center, where the mosque, the market, the coffeehouse, and the school are located (Fakhouri, pp. 119–123; Early, pp. 41–48; Rugh, 1984, pp. 1–4).

Egyptian peasants or *fellahin,* as they are called in Arabic, must cooperate with each other in order to prosper. Without rain, agriculture is entirely dependent on irrigation from the Nile's water. A village's land may be miles from the river and channels must be dug and maintained to sustain the flow of water to each field. *Fellahin* must work together to keep the irrigation system working and share the water. No single farmer and no single family could do it alone.

The Extended Family

The basic rural cooperative group is the extended family, an economic unit of production and consumption. A **nuclear family** composed of husband, wife, and children may live with the husband's parents and brothers, or in its own separate house. Either way, related nuclear families join together as an **extended family** operating as a single household. Such a family might include an older married couple, their two adult sons and their wives and children, and perhaps, if one of those children is old enough, a grandson and his wife and children. Extended family members carry out household tasks, work in the fields, and take care of the very young and the very old. When a father with married sons dies, the extended household formed by his sons' families dissolves. Each son then creates his own extended family including his sons, their wives, and children (Fakhouri, pp. 55–63).

The Clan

In villages, related extended families are linked together in clans, theoretically descended from a long-ago common male ancestor. In a village, the men of a clan, especially the elders, usually form a tight-knit social group. They are brothers, cousins, brothers-in-law, neighbors, and lifelong friends, who have played and gone to school together as children. They have spent their lives helping each other in the fields, sitting together in the coffeehouse, attending the same weddings and funerals. In practical terms, clans are political alliances of men. Village politics often consists of the maneuverings of rival clans (Fakhouri, pp. 56–57).

Family and clan membership are the most important source of identity in the village, far more important than an individual's wealth and possessions. *Fellahin* actually reject wealth as a genuine source of prestige. Prestige is instead a product of the collective prominence of one's clan and personal qualities such as generosity and courage. A man who openly sought recognition based on his wealth— his land or his car, television or other possessions—would be dismissed with such traditional retorts as "What makes you better than I am? We're from the same family." Clans actually try to moderate the economic inequalities among their members. Wealthy members of a clan are encouraged to pay for religious festivals and to distribute food to the poor in accordance with Islam and local custom (Fakhouri, p. 74).

Marriage

Marriage is a very important matter to rural extended families. Everyone is expected to marry and marriages are arranged by the parents or guardians of the bride and groom. Fluehr-Lobban says that "marriage is the single most important event in the life of a man or woman; the ties that are created through marriage are so important that traditionally, decisions regarding the choice of marriage partners were rarely, if ever, left to the future bride and groom alone" (p. 65).

Since a newly married couple becomes part of the husband's family, the bride and her relatives must be acceptable to the groom's whole family, and especially the most powerful elders. The bride's family, if they are wise, must concern themselves not only with the groom, but with the whole extended family with whom their daughter will live. Consequently, village marriages are a matter of careful negotiation between families. The wishes of the prospective bride and groom are secondary to the interests of their families, and may not even be consulted at all. Young women are especially powerless in this process. Even though Islamic law requires that they consent to their marriages, in practice they often are not asked. In the past, girls were given in marriage so young (as early as the age of 12 and sometimes before puberty) that they were not yet ready to form an attraction to any man. (Of course, this was the point of early marriage; it preserved the virginity and chastity of girls by ensuring they were already wed when their sexual interest awakened.) Nowadays, the average age at marriage for Egyptian women is still only 17, while the average age for men has risen to 25, because of the difficulty of finding good jobs (see Table 2.1, p. 78).

Egyptians do not date before marriage, not even in the city. A young man may ask his father to arrange a marriage for him with a woman who attracts him, but this will be possible only if his family considers the woman an appropriate choice—in terms of her age, her degree of religious piety, and her family's status. If the young man's family approves his choice they will negotiate with the prospective bride's family. Agreeing to a marriage is often a complex process, which includes settling the details of the wedding and the bride price to be paid by the groom's family to the bride's family. Families negotiate secretly to avoid shame if no agreement is reached. Because marriage is so important, Egyptians worry a lot about making the right choices for their children. A common theme of soap operas on Egyptian television (which often takes a rather modern, western point of view) portrays a dutiful daughter who has abandoned her true love to marry the man her father has chosen. Only too late does the father realize that he chose poorly and condemned himself, his family, and his daughter to unhappiness and misery (Rugh, 1984, pp. 249–254).

When a marriage is successfully negotiated, the prospective bride and groom sign a marriage contract. This is a detailed document that includes an agreement about how much money the groom and his family will give the bride at the wedding (the **dower**). The bride may require that the contract include a promise by her husband never to take any additional wives, or to permit her to work. While **polygyny** (the practice of a man marrying more than one wife) is legal in Egypt, as in most Islamic societies, it is actually quite rare. Definitive data are hard to find, but experts estimate that throughout the Middle East only 3 to 4 percent of women are wives in polygynous marriages (Omran and Roudi, p. 31). Few men can afford polygyny and few would attempt it against their wive's objections, so it is most common when a first marriage has produced no children.

The six months or a year between the signing of the marriage contract and the wedding is the closest Egyptians come to dating. Then the young man may visit his fiancée's house and get to know his future wife—in the company of her relatives—or the young couple may actually be permitted to go out together.

Weddings are joyous events in Egypt. They are one of the few occasions when young men and women can socialize together, perhaps even flirt with each other or see each other dance, albeit under the careful observation of their parents and relatives. Traditionally, weddings lasted for as long as a week of music, dancing, and feasting, culminating in a public procession of the groom and his friends and family to the house of the bride, where they picked up the bride and her entourage and accompanied her to the groom's house, to the music of a hired band. Today, in cities, weddings are one-evening events often held in big downtown hotels (Fluehr-Lobban, pp. 70–71; Fakhouri, pp. 63–70).

Divorce is permitted in Egypt, but divorce rates are rather low: 18 divorces per 100 marriages a year, compared to 49 per 100 in the United States (see Table 2.1, p. 78). In the twentieth century, new laws have restricted the traditional right of the husband in Islam to divorce his wife by proclamation. Now formal attempts at reconciliation must precede divorce. Women have gained additional rights to seek divorce themselves if their husbands desert them, or fail to support them and their children, or harm them physically or psychologically. The laws also guarantee divorced women custody of their minor children and a house, supplied by the divorced husband, in which to raise them. One interesting Egyptian custom—the **dower**—has helped to hold down divorce rates. The dower, the sum of money the groom customarily gives the bride at marriage, has grown to be very large, and it is usually divided into two parts: the "prompt" and the "deferred." The "deferred" part must be paid only at the time of a divorce, so it is kind of an insurance policy against divorce (Fluehr-Lobban, pp. 64, 69, 116–117, 124–130).

The Patriarchal Family

One important part of Egyptian marriage norms will probably puzzle you, until you understand more about Egyptian families. Both rural and urban Egyptians agree that the ideal marriage partner for a man is a paternal first cousin—a daughter of his father's brother. A more distant cousin on his father's side would also be preferable to a nonrelative. Marrying someone who is not kin is called "stranger marriage" (Fluehr-Lobban, pp. 65–67). The ideal cousin marriage is not often attainable in practice, however; only one marriage in five is actually between first cousins (Fakhouri, pp. 63–64).

Cousin marriage is preferred in Egypt because families are **patriarchal.** A patriarchy is a male-dominated social order, in which men enjoy more power, and greater rights, privileges, and prestige than women. In rural Egypt both men and women think that the family should be patriarchal. First of all, inheritance is **patrilineal,** that is, the family name and most of the land are inherited through the male line. People think of themselves as part of their father's family, not their mother's family. When the children of brothers marry, wealth and property can be kept within the extended family. Since the families know and trust each other, it is also easier to negotiate the marriage, and the bride's family can have confidence she will be well-treated by her in-laws, who are her own kin.

In fact, if two brothers marry their children to each other, the young bride may be able to remain in the same household as her mother. This is because rural marriages are **patrilocal,** that is, on marriage a bride moves to her husband's home and joins the household there, which includes his parents, his brothers, and their wives and children. As a result, except in cases of cousin marriage, women must leave their parental home, but relationships between fathers and sons and brothers are enduring; these relatives live and work together for their whole lives. The relationship between a father and son is very important in Egyptian culture: it is the ideal model for male interaction. A younger man respects and obeys an older man, particularly an older male relative (Fakhouri, pp. 61–63). Think about it: this means that if you are a young Egyptian man in a rural village, you will live with and obey your father until he dies.

Women are not without influence and respect in the patriarchal family, but their position is subordinate and their influence indirect. Traditionally, a married woman's allies are her sons, her father, and sometimes, her brothers. Sons and mothers are close in Egyptian society and adult sons, of course, continue to live in their mother's household. They are expected to take their mother's part in quarrels and to support and protect her (Early, p. 67). A mother of many adult sons is an influential person in an Egyptian village. Conversely, a married woman who has no sons has little influence in her household (Fakhouri, pp. 27–28, 61–63). Women are respected not only for their sons, but for their labor and knowledge. Men know that the family's prosperity depends as much upon the mother's household labor, management skills, and help in the fields as it does upon the men's work. Women often market a family's surplus produce or prepare cheeses to sell in the market. These cash sales are frequently a crucial part of the family's income and strengthen the woman's place in her husband's family. By virtue of her contact with the marketplace, her children's schools, and health clinics, a rural woman may also be more sophisticated than her husband, and the family may rely upon her knowledge. But there are strict limits to her assertion of influence. She may confront her husband in private, argue with him, or refuse him, but she will never do so in public.

Village Women and Group Life

Men dominate the public life of the village: you may see them in the coffeehouse, the mosque, and the marketplace, but women enjoy their own separate, more private group life. One of the greatest sources of satisfaction that countrywomen have is the community of women who share an extended household. These women share **primary** ties, bonds that are close, personal, and intimate (Sadat, pp. 181–190). Sisters-in-law and the unmarried daughters of their household work together to prepare food, store crops, make clothing, and do the housekeeping. Village festivals, weddings, and funerals bring together large groups of women. After a funeral, a bereaved woman's home fills with her female relatives and neighbors.

Day after day they bring cooked dishes and sit together crying and wailing and praising and telling stories about the deceased individual. Women visit each other on ordinary days too, and sit chatting over coffee and snacks, surrounded by their children. They exchange news of the village, analyze other people's problems and personalities, and give each other advice. The importance of the community of women in Egyptian life is marked by the many jokes men tell about the power of gossiping women.

Social Structure in the City

Egyptians have been city dwellers for thousands of years, so urban life is very much a part of Egyptian culture. In the past century, Egypt's urban population has expanded rapidly. Migrants from the countryside have poured into Cairo, Alexandria, and other cities, so that today nearly half of all Egyptians live in urban areas. Cairo is an exceptionally crowded city; it packs in almost 100,000 people per square mile. City dwellers live in a variety of distinctive environments. Some poor Egyptians live in the well-known, densely settled, and colorful old downtown slum districts, while others, likely newer arrivals, can find housing only in the bleak concrete towers of public housing projects far away on the outskirts of the city. Better-off urban Egyptians live in well-kept neighborhoods of gracious European-style apartment houses, and the richest people live in neighborhoods of private homes, shaded by trees and cooled by breezes along the river. (See Table 4.2.)

Poor city neighborhoods like Cairo's Bulaq have been slums for centuries and are well-known in Egyptian literature and folklore. The people of these neighborhoods are known as the *Ibn Al Balad* or *baladi*. The term literally means "sons of the place." Many *baladi* families are only recently arrived in the city from

TABLE 4.2. Urban Concentration and Density: The populations of Egypt, Mexico, and Japan are concentrated in the densely populated areas in and around their largest cities. People in Cairo are 10 times as closely packed as people in Berlin.

	Largest Urban Area in the Nation			
	City at Center of Urban Area	Population (Millions)	Percent of National Population	Density (Thousands of People per Square Mile)
Germany	Berlin	3.0	3.7	11.2
Japan	Tokyo	27.5	22.1	25.3
United States	New York	14.6	4.9	11.5
Mexico	Mexico City	21.6	22.7	41.4
Egypt	Cairo	10.4	18.9	99.7

Sources: U.S. Bureau of the Census, *Statistical Abstract of the United States 1994.* Washington, DC: U.S. Government Printing Office, 1994; World Bank, *World Development Report 1994: Infrastructure for Development.* New York: Oxford University Press, 1994.

the countryside, but others have lived in Bulaq or similar neighborhoods for generations. These urbanites resemble rural *fellahin* in their dress and their observance of tradition, but they contrast strongly with rural Egyptians in their cultural sophistication, their ability to do business, and their willingness to take their political grievances into the streets (Early, pp. 59–61).

In crowded poor neighborhoods old four and five story apartment buildings face each other across narrow, often unpaved alleys. Lines of laundry hang crisscross overhead, and in front of shops racks of merchandise encroach on the street. Coffeehouses place benches and tables out in front of the café. Peddlers sell clothing, sweets, vegetables, and prepared foods like beans in various sauces. The facades of old-fashioned buildings are decorated with carved wooden balconies from which women and children observe the street and reel in the laundry lines. Storefront workshops produce furniture, shoes, jewelry, and even industrial machinery, spilling some of their operations out into the alleys. Cars can pass through these crowded streets only with great difficulty; goats, sheep, and buffalos stand in muddy corners chewing grain, and donkey carts clog the intersections.

The Family in Poor Neighborhoods

In Cairo, as in Egypt's villages, people want to have close ties with their extended families, to live with them in the same buildings or at least in the same neighborhood. But the housing shortage makes this difficult. As adult children marry, they may be unable to find apartments near their parents, and so the extended family may be scattered, married siblings living in different neighborhoods, perhaps far from their parents. Family members may find it hard to get together regularly. In this situation, people have to make choices about which extended family members they remain close to. Sometimes two siblings will manage to buy apartments in the same building, so that they can share child care and home appliances and spend time together (MacLeod, p. 37). Interestingly, it is often sisters who make such arrangements, making female relatives the center of extended family life in a way that is impossible in villages.

As in the village, single young adults never live independently. They remain in their parents' home until they marry. The only exception is young men who migrate to other countries to find work. They disrupt traditional family patterns, both by leaving and by postponing marriage.

When the children of poor city families succeed in moving up in the world, they don't leave behind their family loyalties. Though they may seek western-style education and western consumer goods, middle-class Egyptians continue to put family first, socializing by preference with relatives, and seeking out traditional cross-cousin marriages. They take seriously their obligations to relatives: to be generous, to support the helpless, and to reciprocate favors.

Urban Reciprocity Networks and Social Groups

Many of the personal contacts that Egyptians rely on are with their families, but when they cannot make the crucial links they need to survive and prosper among their relatives, they look for others with whom they have developed personal relationships. If your family cannot find a house, a job, or a spouse for you, then they will their ask neighbors or friends. If they need a loan, someone to mind their children for an hour, or the use of a car for a day, they will turn again to those they know. A personal contact implies a commitment, even if the contact took place decades ago. Andrea Rugh describes a middle-aged, middle-class Egyptian woman in difficult economic circumstances who was sure that the president's wife, Mrs. Sadat, would help her. After all, they had gone to college together thirty years before (Rugh, 1984, p. 40)!

Patterns of reciprocity in *baladi* neighborhoods often revolve around the domestic roles of women. Women help each other by watching each other's sick children, plugging in a long extension cord for a neighbor without electricity, marketing for one another, exchanging small gifts, and raising each other's morale as the grind of daily life takes its toll. *Baladi* women find husbands and wives for each other's children and groups of neighboring women form loan cooperatives to raise money for weddings, and the purchase of sewing machines, televisions, and other expensive items. Women who work can extend their networks further: coworkers trade information about the best doctors, good tutors for their children, or the right bureaucrat to see for a visa. **Reciprocity networks** also extend beyond the urban neighborhood, to relatives in the villages of residents' birth, and to wealthier, more educated relatives in richer neighborhoods who may be called upon for help (Early, pp. 9–11, 75–80; Rugh, 1984, pp. 89–101).

While poor urban women spend less time with relatives than their village sisters, they still have a rich group life with other women. Loan cooperatives and reciprocity networks sometimes grow into quite ambitious women's projects. *Baladi* women form sewing cooperatives, with one skilled woman teaching others how to sew, so they can do piecework in their homes. Sewing cooperatives are often linked to informal schools in which illiterate women and their daughters learn to read and write and do arithmetic. Women with leadership abilities become an important neighborhood force in such quasi-political organizations. If they understand how government bureaucracies work—how to get a passport or a job, or how to get a place for a son or daughter in school—they become local power brokers, advocating for their neighbors and linking them to political representatives and parties.

In the city, the clan is no longer the center of men's social life. Instead, men look to social groups called *shilla*. These are small groups bound by friendship or family ties—friends from the village or from school, a group of brothers and their friends, and some of their friends' brothers. Often the members of a *shilla* have a regular table in the coffeehouse or a regular weekly get-together, and they are also mutual-aid networks. A group member who has prospered and moved high in the government bureaucracy will expect to help his friends and relatives. In some communities Islamic fundamental organizations have successfully adapted the structures of male group life. They call themselves a group of brothers, or a community of men, and offer men an active group life in religious study groups, political meetings, and community improvement associations, and the resources of the organization and its well-placed members. Fundamentalist "brotherhood" networks interweave, linking legal political and religious groups with illegal paramilitary and terrorist organizations.

Urban Male and Female Roles

Urban families, like their rural counterparts, are patriarchal, but the economic realities of city life have altered gender roles and given city women more independence and greater influence in the choice of their husbands. In rural Egypt, land is the foundation of life, and men control the land. Groups of men are tied together by common interests, cemented by kinship, and work together to cultivate, irrigate, and harvest the land. This unity of work and family gives men tremendous power. While peasant women often work in the fields, they have little opportunity to become economically independent. In the city, *baladi* men are not as united as rural men, nor do they have a monopoly on earning money. Women work in offices and factories; they sell produce or cooked foods in the streets, or even own and manage coffeehouses. They have much more opportunity to spend time away from their male relatives and the supervision of their families. As a result *baladi* women are more nearly equal to their spouses than are their country sisters (Early, pp. 41–45). In a culture which demands that women defer to men, *baladi* women are relatively assertive.

> *On Huda's fifteenth birthday she met her brother's friend Ali in the street as her brother walked her to work. Her 20-year-old brother amused her and guarded her reputation as they walked through the neighborhood. Huda decided that Ali was the most handsome young man in Cairo. She was delighted when her brother revealed that Ali returned her interest. Unfortunately, there was no easy way for the two to meet. They were not relatives and their mothers disliked one another. Worst of all, in her father's eyes, would be the fact that Ali was a Saidi, from a part of Egypt that had the reputation of breeding fools and hotheads. Huda's father was from the Delta and considered the people of the Delta sophisticated and clever, not clods like the Saidis.*
>
> *But Huda was not without resources. Some days later she and her friend Idil were walking home from work. They linked arms and chatted as they walked. Remarkably they encountered Ali and Huda's brother Ahmed. Ali and Ahmed strolled a few paces ahead of Huda and Idil. To any casual observer Ahmed and Ali ignored Huda and Idil, each couple taken up by their own conversations. But someone listening to what they said would see an interesting pattern. "I can't wait to see the Nights," said Huda Idil, referring to a popular TV soap opera. Ali then commented to Ahmed, "I watch the Nights whenever I can." In this way Huda and Ali exchanged the first of many conversations. Huda's aunt Fatima watched the four from her balcony and was not fooled for a minute. Fatima considered telling Huda's mother, her older sister, but she recalled that she too had once been young and in love with a handsome Saidi.*

SOCIAL INEQUALITY IN EGYPT

Egyptians have a lot in common with each other: their long shared history as a nation, the culture of Islam, a single language, similar family and community structures, a centralized government and school system. But at the same time, Egyptians are deeply divided by social inequalities. We have seen that because of gender inequality Egyptian men and women inhabit quite separate social worlds. Class inequality divides Egyptians as radically as does gender inequality.

Class Inequality

Sociologists use the term **class inequality** in discussing several related matters. They use it to talk about inequalities in the distribution of economic resources like income and wealth and to ask how broadly or narrowly these resources are spread through the society. They also use it to discuss **social classes,** groups of people whose economic resources and lifestyles are similar, and which may form real, self-identified social groups. Finally, sociologists use the term "class inequality" in discussing **social mobility,** the extent to which people in different social classes have a chance to move up or down in the social stratification system.

The class stratification system in Egypt is quite distinctive. It bears the imprint of Egypt's colonial past, when land and capital were owned by a tiny elite. It also shows the effects of Egypt's recent history as a socialist society, when the government took control of land and capital and strove to distribute resources more equally. Today, most Egyptians are quite poor. Per capita income is below $700 per year. Almost half of all Egyptians have incomes below their society's official poverty line, and one in every three Egyptians has an average monthly income of less than $25 (Schmidt, p. 10). At the very top of the stratification hierarchy there is a very small class of very wealthy Egyptians—probably no more than 1 percent of the population. A good way to understand Egyptian class inequality is to say that the top and the bottom of the Egyptian hierarchy are very far apart, but most people cluster near the bottom. As a result, if you examine distribution of income by quintiles (see Chapter 1, p. 36) for example, you will find that Egypt has a relatively equal distribution of incomes—about as equal as the United States; more equal than Mexico and less equal than Japan and Germany. There is little up-to-date information on Egyptian income distribution, but we can estimate that the richest income fifth receives about 9 times as much total income as the poorest fifth. (The poorest 20 percent of Egyptians receive 5.8 percent of all income and the richest 20 percent receive 49.3 percent.) (See Table 1.3.) Data on earnings by occupation reveal a similar level of inequality: skilled workers earn 6 times as much as unskilled workers, and supervisory and professional employees earn 12 times more than laborers (U.S. Department of Labor, p. 1).

Economic Resources and Social Class

For any society, knowing about income and wealth distribution gives us only half the picture of class inequality. We also want to know who these people are: Who are the Egyptians in the top income fifth? Who are the poorest Egyptians? Where do they live and what is the source of their earnings? The legacy of Egypt's socialist economy is quite clear. Even today, when it is official government policy to encourage private enterprise, very few Egyptians own or work for privately owned companies. Agriculture and government employment are the main sources of income. A very large number of Egyptians can get no regular employment at all; they make their way as best they can in the **informal sector** or else migrate abroad to find work.

Only 3 percent of Egyptian workers are employed in the private sector—in industry or manufacturing, retail sales, or services. One-third of all workers are government employees, working either in the government bureaucracy, the army, in the civil service (as postal clerks, teachers, bus drivers, mail carriers, etc.), or in government-owned companies like the Helwan Steelworks, the state-owned oil industry, or the Suez Canal Company. State-owned factories produce 70 percent of Egypt's industrial output—everything from steel to clothing (Hedges, July 17, 1994, p. A6). As a result, ownership of businesses, the "means of production" in Karl Marx's sense, isn't a very important source of income or class position in Egyptian society. Much more important is a person's **power,** or access to government-controlled resources. In Egypt, unequal access to government power results in unequal rewards. People who can get jobs as government employees (as skilled factory workers, clerical workers, or professionals) enjoy an enviable job security, even though their pay is usually low. They are likely to treat their jobs as a resource—a way to get medical insurance, or a way to find jobs, or contracts or connections for relatives and friends. They may supplement their wages by accepting bribes for ordinary services or by skimming government funds that come through their hands.

Even for those who are not government employees, access to government resources is critical to prosperity. Owners of private businesses operate in an economy which is largely government-owned. Banks are government-owned, as is transportation, and many industrial supplies must be purchased from government factories. Import and export licenses must be granted by the government and paperwork must find its way through the vast government bureaucracy. Business owners can't use their property profitability without government permission.

The same thing is true in agriculture. Ninety-five percent of Egyptian farms are tiny—below 5 acres. Many of these landowners have the government to thank for their holdings, having received them in the post-1952 land redistribution. But new landowners didn't receive outright ownership of their land. They were required to join farm cooperatives which decided what crops should be grown, supplied seeds and fertilizer, storage, transportation, and marketing. Farmers were given credit by government banks and sold their crops to the government at prices the government set. One problem small farmers experience is that what the government gives, the government apparently can take away. In the small village of Gharb al Banawaan, 70 miles north of Cairo, officials of the Ministry of Religious Endowment appeared in 1974 and announced that the redistributed land was now theirs and farmers would have to pay rent. Villagers fell more and more into debt to government banks in their efforts to pay rising rents, until finally, in 1994, police evicted them from their land, which the ministry is now selling for $9000 (U.S.) an acre, far beyond the means of farmers making only $700 (U.S.) a year (Hedges, Sept. 28, 1994, p. 4).

Egyptians look upon their ministry officials very differently than do the Japanese. In their eyes the bureaucracy certainly is not a rational, dispassionate agency committed to the public good. Ministries and bureaucrats operate in their own self-interest and they are open to influence and bribery. To get ahead, Egyptians need good connections, through family or *shilla* networks.

Social Classes in Rural Egypt

Four and a half million Egyptians, or about two-fifths of the labor force, work in agriculture and most of them are very poor. Many are landless agricultural workers, dependent for survival on employment on neighboring farms, seasonally or by the day. They are the lowest rung of the rural stratification system. Another 1 million Egyptians (occupying 62 percent of all farms) are sharecroppers, farming land for which they must pay rent in the form of a percentage of their crop. A smaller number of tenant farmers pay their rent in cash. The rest of the farmers own their own land, but almost all of them (95 percent) have very small farms—under 5 acres (Kurian, 1992, p. 568). They are better off than the landless, but are still poor and, as we have seen, dependent on the support and goodwill of the government. The size of their families makes a big difference in their degree of economic security too. A large family provides many working hands, but creates problems for the next generation. A farm of 2 or 3 acres can hardly be divided among two or three or four sons (see Table 2.3, p. 91).

Since such an overwhelming percentage of rural Egyptians are poor, it is easy to miss the rural elite. As a result of the land redistributions, there are relatively few large farms. Only 5 percent of farms are larger than 5 acres—but these farmers own 49 percent of the land! Landowners of middle-sized farms (owning between 5 and 20 acres) usually live locally and farm their land with hired labor. They are part of a rural upper class, together with village professionals like the town lawyer and doctor and perhaps a successful storekeeper. They live in comfortable houses, with gardens and shaded courtyards, and employ servants. Villagers look up to them and they are able to send their children to university in the city.

But while these landowners are the elite of village society, in national terms they are not part of the upper class. This distinction belongs only to the largest landowners—one-tenth of 1 percent of farmers who own more than 50 acres of land. These farmers don't live locally; they let their land out to tenant farmers, hire a manager, and live in the city. Many of them are actually foreign corporations from Saudi Arabia, Europe, or the United States that buy Egyptian land and employ landless laborers to produce crops like cotton and sugar for export.

Social Classes in Urban Egypt

Class differences are highly visible in Egyptian cities and city residents are aware of the hierarchy of classes and where they stand in it (MacLeod, p. 34). People of different classes live in distinctively different neighborhoods. The poorest live on the dusty fringes of the city in squatter settlements. Lower-middle-class people live in old crowded city neighborhoods or in the concrete high-rise towers of government-built "satellite cities" on the outskirts of town. More prosperous people live in spacious neighborhoods with solid apartment houses and paved streets. The wealthy elite are found in downtown luxury apartment towers or in gracious, tree-lined enclaves of private homes. Different social classes spend their leisure in different places too: the poor in the coffeehouses and on the rooftops of their quarter; the middle class in their homes and in the downtown coffeehouses, restaurants, and movie theaters; the rich in country clubs and modern western hotels. Only the rich own cars; everyone else must ride the slow, sputtering buses, jammed with people, or else walk. People of different classes dress differently too. Lower-class men are likely to wear the traditional *gallibiyya,* a long, loose cotton shirt, and lower-class women wear a loose black cotton overgown with a black head scarf when they are out in public. Middle-class Egyptian men generally wear western-style clothing and middle-class women wear some form of modern "modest dress," often home-sewn. The upper classes are easily identified by their fashionable clothes, imported from Europe (MacLeod, p. 34).

The Lower Class. About a quarter of urban Egyptians live in what is locally considered poverty. Here you must remember the sociological concept of **relative poverty.** Many Egyptians consider themselves middle class, even though their incomes are below the poverty line, because their family has two rooms to live in rather than one, and owns a radio, and can afford to let their children finish junior high or high school. In the same situation, you would consider yourself desperately poor. Standards of living for most Egyptians are so low that only the most destitute actually consider themselves poor. These families are usually dependent on one unskilled, illiterate breadwinner, who lacks a secure job. They live in shantytowns on the outskirts of the city, where the desert encroaches, in squatter neighborhoods without electricity, piped water, sewage systems, schools, health clinics, or markets. There is no safe drinking water and health problems are rampant. Poor families own only the most basic of household goods—beds, a table and chairs, pots and pans. As city population has grown, housing has become scarcer and scarcer. In Cairo, thousands of poor people have moved into the city's cemeteries, living in the small stone tombs in which well-off Egyptians inter family members' remains (see Table 2.2, p. 90) (Rodenbeck, p. 84; Abu-Lughod, J., p. 218).

Many of the poorest Egyptians find work only in the **informal sector** which employs 26 percent of all Egyptian workers. Informal sector is just a polite way of saying that people scrounge for work. Like poor people in other third world countries, Egyptians are enormously inventive in finding every market niche, every opportunity for work. Boys work as "tea boys," carrying trays of sweetened tea from tea shops to offices. They hope to get work when they are older as porters or doormen. Many young men work as laborers on construction sites. Others support themselves by peddling, selling sweets or fruit in the streets, peddling cassette tapes in the market, often switching strategies from week to week or seasonally. Thousands of people work the garbage dumps of big cities, picking through the trash for recyclable materials to sell. Others buy and sell old clothes from door to door, shine shoes, watch parked cars, hawk newspapers on the street. Some informal sector workers are educated, recent graduates unable to find work, or government workers who need second jobs. They make use of their literacy and bureaucratic know-how, by writing letters for illiterate Egyptians or taking sidewalk passport photos. Hundreds work as "facilitators," freelance guides to the bureaucracy, who for a fee will help people find their way through the bewildering corridors of Mugamma, Cairo's huge government building (Rodenbeck, p. 80; Hedges, June 7, 1994, p. A4).

The Middle Class. When thinking about Egyptian social class, you must remember what a relative matter poverty is. Any Egyptian above poverty level considers himself or herself middle class. About half of all Egyptians (and about three-quarters of urban Egyptians) identify with the middle class, but actually their circumstances vary greatly. Saad Edin Ibrahim divides the Cairo middle class into three **strata** (or layers); the lower middle stratum (including 26.5 percent of Cairenes), the middle stratum (36.1 percent), and the upper middle stratum (15.3 percent) (cited in MacLeod, pp. 34–35). The lower middle class includes manual workers who, in many other societies, would consider themselves "working class."

Egypt's industrial workforce is small, only about 10 percent of the whole labor force, mostly in government-owned enterprises. Relatively skilled industrial workers, who are literate and secure in their jobs tend to think of themselves as middle class, dress like middle-class people, and have middle-class aspirations for their children. They see themselves as socially equal to other government employees, like clerks or lower civil service workers, whose wages are indeed similar. In fact their wives and daughters very well may be clerical workers. The bottom of the lower middle class lives barely above the poverty line, with incomes running as low as $20 (U.S.) per month, and they live in the same neighborhoods as the poor.

Those who are better off may earn as much as $45 per month and have a larger apartment, with perhaps as many as four rooms, a TV, refrigerator, and maybe a few other appliances. In cases in which the husband has a skilled job in a private company the family will be better off, since pay is much higher in private companies

In Cairo's poorest squatter settlements carrying water is one of the daily tasks of women and children. Goats help keep the district clean by scavenging garbage, while cheese made from their milk provides essential nutrients in a monotonous diet of beans and grains.

than in the public sector, though jobs are less secure. Many lower-middle-class families would be poor were it not for income earned by the wife, who works in a regular job in the formal economy (MacLeod, p. 36). Women are rapidly entering the labor force today, with almost 50 percent of women aged 20 to 39 in paid work (U.S. Department of Labor, p. 6). Twelve percent of industrial workers are women (Hooglund, p. 130).

The middle stratum of the middle class has a more secure hold on its class position. They are university educated and many are young professionals or senior clerical workers in the government bureaucracy. They are self-employed workers in the skilled trades, like plumbers and electricians, or they are shopkeepers or small merchants. Many live in the *baladi* neighborhoods where their businesses are located, but they are actually quite prosperous (Barakat, pp. 89–90; Rodenbeck, p. 82). Middle-middle-class people live in much better apartments, usually of three or four rooms, and they have more elaborate home furnishings and appliances. They expect their children to go to university.

The upper middle class shades off into the upper class. These people are much more secure than the rest of the middle class. They are established professionals, government bureaucrats, army officers, the prosperous owners of private businesses. Upper-middle-class Egyptians live in air-conditioned modern apartment houses, or in large apartments in old-fashioned middle-class districts. Their homes may be lavishly furnished with inherited antiques or modern European furniture. They can afford servants and even perhaps to send their children to university abroad.

The Upper Class. The Egyptian upper class is very small. Ibrahim estimates the upper class in Cairo, the national center of business and government, as not more than 1 percent of the population. According to Hooglund, in 1990, only 2000 families in all of Egypt had incomes above $14,000 per year, so you can imagine how small the upper class is (Ibrahim, cited in MacLeod, p. 35; Hooglund, p. 114). Their occupations and the sources of their wealth are varied, but they are linked together by business ties, social relationships, and kinship. The upper class includes the elites of the government bureaucracy and the top managers of government-owned industries. It includes the most successful owners of private capital—entrepreneurs, big wholesale merchants who engage in international trade, and the owners of big construction firms favored by government contracts. The most successful professionals who work for the public and private elites are members of this class too. These people are dependent on each other to maintain their wealth. After all, exporters need government licenses and permissions; lawyers need clients, and bureaucrats, no matter how powerful, earn relatively low wages; they use their official positions and their contacts in the private sector in order to earn upper-class incomes, often through private commissions. For example, in recent years President Mubarak's sons have become very wealthy acting as business agents in the airline industry. They earned commissions from foreign airplane manufacturers when they negotiated contracts to supply planes to Egypt's government-owned airline.

Upper-class Egyptians form a small, self-conscious social group. They live in a few exclusive, guarded neighborhoods and their children attend private schools

Prosperous Egyptian men and women throng the Salam shopping center in the Heliopolis neighborhood of Cairo. The western practice of going shopping as a leisure activity is possible only for the affluent in Egypt.

together. In colonial times wealthy Egyptians adopted the English custom of join-ing a social club, a country club–like facility with a restaurant, bar, tennis courts, and golf course. The most westernized couples actually went out together to the club in the evenings. Today wealthy Cairenes still center their social lives on the club. Teenage girls are permitted to visit the club in the afternoons, where they meet their friends, drink cokes, and play tennis. Actually the club is one place, in addi-tion to school, where wealthy girls and boys may meet and talk together, safely sur-rounded by other young people and club employees. Wealthy Egyptians often send their sons (and sometimes their daughters) to university or graduate school abroad, in Europe or the United States, to acquire the knowledge, connections, and social fluency they need to compete in today's international economy.

Ahmad Moustafa looked out over the Nile from the balcony of his Zemalek apartment. At 64 he wished his country had done as well as he had in these turbulent times. A Mercedes, a luxury apartment in Cairo's most fashionable quarter, hand-tailored suits made in Italy, rich farmland in the Delta, and sons in business and the government—not bad! Even his grand-father, Abu Ali, a hard man, would have approved. Abu Ali looked out at him from a nineteenth-century photo, posed in front of the date palms and cotton fields of the family's estate; land the king himself had given Abu Ali.

When the monarchy ended in 1952 and the estates of large landowners were broken up, Ah-mad's father quietly left for Italy. But Ahmad remained to finish his engineering studies and his army service. He thought that while the rebels might not favor a rich man with ties to the royal family, they might look kindly on one who served them as an engineer and a sol-dier. Ahmad's service in the 1956 conflict with Israel brought him a reputation as a patriot and earned him a job with Egypt's state oil industry. To the amazement of his family, he left Cairo and found oil in Egypt's eastern desert, a place so desolate even Bedouin nomads shun it. Ahmad's success soon brought promotion. He returned to Cairo, married the sister of his former commanding officer, and started a family.

In the 1980s, Ahmad encouraged his eldest son Ali to work for an Italian oil company. When the Egyptian government sought foreign companies to develop natural gas resources, the Italian company received a profitable contract. The Italians demonstrated their gratitude and Ahmad bought a larger apartment and made numerous investments abroad. Ali secured his future with his useful "contacts" in the Egyptian government.

When Ahmad thought about his successful life, he realized that what gave him the greatest satisfaction of all was getting back his family's land. The courts returned part of the land, and the rest he bought back from poverty-stricken fellahin. Now there were some share-croppers working for him whose fathers had worked for his father.

Social Mobility in Egypt

All Egyptians today (except perhaps the tiny upper class) are threatened by their society's economic problems. Egypt's economy is in serious trouble and peo-ple find it hard to maintain their present standard of living. Opportunities for up-ward mobility are shrinking. This situation is particularly upsetting to Egyptians because their expectations were formed during several decades of rapid economic growth after the 1952 revolution, when living standards rose and opportunities for upward mobility expanded rapidly.

Closed and Open Systems. Sociologists make a theoretical distinction be-tween two kinds of societies: **closed stratification systems** and **open stratification systems.** In closed systems people must remain in the social class into which they were born and no amount of talent or effort can have any effect. In contrast, in open systems, parents are unable to pass any advantage on to their children. All children have an equal chance to prosper or fail, based only on their ability and hard work. In real life, no stratification system is completely closed or completely open, but it is useful to think about the two theoretical extremes in order to understand the situation in Egypt today. Before Nasser and the revolution of 1952, Egypt's stratification system was based primarily on inherited land and wealth. It was very difficult for people who didn't have these to acquire any. After 1952, Egypt changed from a rather closed system to a more open one, and opportunities for social mobility increased.

The Revolution and Social Mobility. Nasser created vastly more opportunities for Egyptians in two ways. First, he expelled the existing upper class, by ending colonialism and nationalizing almost all Egyptian businesses. European managers, Greek, Christian, and Jewish merchants, and even wealthy Muslim business owners fled the country. Their departure deprived Egypt of their skills, but created many new openings for those loyal to the revolution (Kurian, 1992, p. 550). A new class of Egyptian managers grew. Second, Nasser moved quickly to create a modern economy under state ownership. Economic expansion laid the foundation for a new middle class, and Nasser deliberately poured the nation's resources into training Egyptians for modern industrial jobs. He opened schools and universities and made education available to ordinary Egyptians. He created a modern health care system as well. Suddenly teachers, doctors, nurses, engineers, architects, accountants, managers, and industrial workers were required in great numbers. To encourage young people to go to school Nasser promised each college graduate a job in the bureaucracy or in government-owned industry. In Nasser's time, the sons of postal workers became doctors, and the sons of peasants became skilled workers (MacLeod, pp. 31–34; Fakhouri, pp. 40–45; Vatikiotis, pp. 390–396, 457–458). (See Table 4.3.)

Shrinking Opportunities Today. Today, opportunities for social mobility are shrinking as economic growth slows. People find it hard to keep their standard

TABLE 4.3. Increases in Secondary School Enrollment: Egypt and Mexico have rapidly expanded their secondary school enrollment in the last three decades.

	Percent of Persons 12–17 Enrolled in Secondary Education	
	1960	1991
East Germany	39	79*
West Germany	53	74*
Japan	74	98
United States	86	90
Mexico	11	55
Egypt	16	80

*Data for East and West Germany are for 1985.
Sources: World Bank, *World Development Report, 1994: Infrastructure for Development.* New York: Oxford University Press, 1994; World Bank, *World Development Report, 1988: Opportunities and Risks in Managing the World Economy.* New York: Oxford University Press, 1988.

of living from slipping and they fear their children will fall into a lower social class than their own. Every year 400,000 to 500,000 people enter the labor force for the first time and half of them cannot find jobs (Hedges, July 17, 1994, p. A6). The official unemployment rate stands at 10 percent, and that isn't counting the 3 million workers (one-quarter of the total labor force) who cannot find regular jobs, but work in the informal sector (U.S. Department of Labor, pp. 1, 4). It is two decades now since the government found it could no longer promise a job to every university graduate. However, Egyptians still look to education as the route out of poverty, and even quite modest jobs as clerks or semiskilled workers require a high school degree. Many educated young people find their expectations disappointed though. Nearly one-quarter of those unemployed in Cairo today hold university degrees (Rodenbeck, p, 82). Young people without jobs cannot marry, and until they marry they cannot leave their parents' homes. Intensified competition and unsatisfied aspirations fuel social unrest.

Migration. The most common response to shrinking opportunities is migration. About 2½ million Egyptian men—one in every seven people of working age—work outside Egypt today, mostly in the Persian Gulf states: Iraq, Saudi Arabia, Kuwait, Jordan, and Libya. Men don't take their families abroad with them and women never become migrant workers. Migrant work pays well: that is its great attraction. Those working abroad send home an average of $1600 apiece yearly (way above average earnings of $700). Don't think of migrant labor as something done only by the poor and unskilled. Men of every class work abroad, but especially the insecure children of the rural and urban middle classes—the sons of small landowners, shopkeepers, and government bureaucrats. They often work as engineers, teachers, and doctors. Egyptian universities graduate a great many students with degrees in education—more than 17,000 per year—but 80 percent of them go abroad to teach (Kurian, 1992, p. 569). (See Table 4.4.)

TABLE 4.4. Money Sent Home by Egyptians and Mexicans Working Abroad: Egypt depends increasingly on billions of dollars sent home by Egyptians working outside Egypt: Mexicans working abroad also send sizable amounts home.

| | *Money Sent Home by Workers Abroad* | | |
| | *1970* | *1992* | |
	Billions of Dollars	Billions of Dollars	As a Percent of the Gross National Product
Mexico	Not available	2068	0.74
Egypt	29	5430	18.10

Source: World Bank, *World Development Report 1994: Infrastructure for Development.* New York: Oxford University Press, 1994.

> Idris had always thought of himself as a man with a bright future. His parents had been born in the countryside, but in the flush times of the early sixties they came to Cairo. Idris was a bright child and did well in school, and his parents believed his intelligence and hard work would bring success. But this was not to be. By the time Idris left teachers' college in the early 1980s, there were no jobs for teachers in Egypt. For two miserable years he searched desperately for any job, but only found work tutoring neighborhood children to pass their exams.
>
> Idris was rescued by the offer of a job as a teacher's assistant in a private school in Kuwait. A college friend was teaching there and had some small influence. Idris was delighted, even though working in Kuwait meant leaving his family. He arrived in Kuwait penniless; the bribe he paid for his exit visa took the last of his cash.
>
> But then Idris hated Kuwait. Even though he was an educated man, an Arab and a Muslim, he was treated with contempt. And he thought Kuwait was a wasteland—no culture, no night life, no nothing. Idris lived with other Egyptians, rarely going out and sending most of his money home to his family. They needed it too. His father's wages as a factory worker failed to keep pace with rising prices.
>
> On one of his infrequent visits home, Idris married Aisha, whom he had known since childhood, and in the middle of the Kuwaiti school year he became the father of twins. He couldn't even return home for their birth; it was either a hospital room for Aisha or an airline ticket for him. What, thought Idris, had become of his life? What hope could there be for the future? Even in eight or ten years, when his name finally came up on the waiting list for a teaching job in Egypt, the salary would never be enough to support his wife and family and also help his parents.

Compared to the tremendous class and gender inequalities in Egyptian society, other status inequalities seem minor. There are racial and religious inequalities in Egypt, but they are of lesser importance.

Racial Inequality in Egypt

Egypt is a racially mixed society. Its people come from Africa, the Middle East, Central Asia, and Europe, but they have been mixing and intermarrying for thousands of years. As a result, Egyptians vary in their skin colors and facial features. There is no doubt that light skin is a source of prestige. Before the 1952 revolution, many families in the landowning elite were aristocrats descended from Egypt's earlier rulers (including Greeks, Turks, and Macedonians). They were conscious of their lighter skin and sought similar spouses for their children (Hooglund, p. 119). Today light skin is still associated with elite status, with wealth and power. Movie stars and women in advertisements tend to have light skin. On the other hand, skin color is only one of many sources of prestige in Egypt, including gender, education, occupation, family background, and city origins. Furthermore, while Egyptians are aware of skin color, they are not race-conscious. That is, they do not classify people by race: "she is black," or "he is white." They might note that among a family of siblings, some have lighter skin and other darker skin, but they would not feel a need to decide if the family was "white" or "black." Another way of putting this is to say that race is not a **master status** in Egypt. Skin tone does not determine a person's access to jobs, education, or choice of spouse in any major way.

Religious Inequality

More than 90 percent of all Egyptians are Muslims. Coptic Christians are a religious **minority group** in Egypt. Sociologically speaking, they are a minority not just in numbers (there are nearly 10 million Coptic Christians) but in terms of their lack of power. Arabic-speaking Muslims are the social **majority** in Egypt, and were so even when their numbers were small, because they controlled the military, the government, and the laws. At many points in Egyptian history, the Muslim majority permitted Copts to maintain their own communities and religious institutions, as long as they accepted their subordination to Muslim authority. At other times, Coptic institutions and property were attacked by the Muslim majority, despite their official protection under Islamic law. The situation was similar for the much smaller Jewish minority in Egypt (Nisan, pp. 115–121; Ibrahim, Y., Mar. 15, 1993, pp. A1, A8).

The Life of a Religious Minority

Egypt's Coptic community has traditionally been divided between those living in Cairo and Alexandria and those living in rural areas in Upper Egypt. Before the twentieth century, urban Copts often served as clerks and administrators for Egypt's Muslim rulers. Butros Butros Ghali, secretary general of the United Nations, is descended from a prominent Coptic family with a long tradition of government service. When Copts were forced out of government positions by the British colonial administration, they turned to the professionals and many became doctors and pharmacists (Nisan, pp. 122–127). Affluent, urban Copts have little informal social contact with their Muslim neighbors, except to some extent when they attend university. But the situation is far different for poor Copts in the countryside and the cities.

Poor Coptic Christians and Muslims are often neighbors and they come into close social contact as part of the same neighborhood social networks. Coptic and Muslim women shop for one another, watch each other's children, and lend each other money. Christian and Muslim neighbors attend each other's weddings and funerals and participate in the more social aspects of each other's religious celebrations. For example, it would not be unusual for Christian men to attend their town's annual festival at the Muslim shrine, nor would it be strange for a Muslim woman to go to Easter services with her Christian neighbor (Early, p. 73).

In some ways, Copts can be considered a highly **assimilated** minority, one which has taken on the culture of the dominant group. Copts cannot easily be distinguished from their Muslim neighbors. Centuries ago, Copts adopted Arabic as their daily language; the ancient Coptic language is rarely used. Copts wear the same clothing as other Egyptians and eat the same foods too. In daily life, only a visible cross or a Christian name (such as Butros) distinguishes Copt from Muslim (Hooglund, pp. 141–142).

Increasing Discrimination

Today, however, as economic conditions worsen in Egypt, and competition for scarce jobs and housing increases, Copts are experiencing more prejudice and discrimination. Militant Islamic groups have pressured the government to define Egypt as an Islamic state, ruled by Islamic laws. These groups frighten Copts and make them feel like outsiders in their own country. Terrorist fundamentalists have attacked and killed Copts and vandalized and burned churches. As many as 150 to 200 Copts have been killed and the government has been forced to station police guards outside churches. Coptic children are now shunned by their public school classmates, and women with the traditional tattooed cross are taunted and attacked in public. Copts say that despite its official opposition to terrorism, the government encourages attacks on them. Construction of new churches has not been allowed for thirty years and Copts have been barred from positions in the government, the army, the police force, and universities. In their efforts to appear pro-Islam, government officials sometimes make statements that reflect deep hostility toward the Coptic minority (Nisan, pp. 127–133, Ibrahim, Y., Mar. 15, 1993, pp. A1, A8).

SOCIAL CHANGE AND THE FUTURE

Egypt today is in a very unstable situation. The society is plagued by serious economic and social problems and life for most Egyptians has noticeably worsened over the past twenty-five years. Young people, especially educated young Egyptians, have high expectations for themselves and their country and find their actual situation very frustrating. They expect a lot from the government and are angry because it can't or won't help them.

Economic Stagnation and Social Problems

One of the most frustrating problems for Egyptians is lack of economic growth. Egypt's economy is growing very slowly or not at all. Few new jobs are created, total production has not increased much, and Egypt hasn't developed any new industries. Over the past twenty years there has been a growing split between older, middle-class Egyptians who have jobs, houses, and schools for their children, and younger Egyptians, even middle-class people, who can't find jobs, can't marry, and can't afford housing.

Nasser, when he was president, promised Egyptians economic prosperity and raised everyone's expectations. For a while it seemed that he could make good on his promises. He built new state-owned industries, greatly expanded education and medical care, and gave a job to every university graduate. Then came the 1967 war with Israel. Egypt's crushing defeat was very costly. Its army was destroyed, thousands of people were killed, and many of Egypt's cities and oil fields were occupied by the victorious Israelis. After the war, determined to wipe out its defeat, the Egyptian government poured all its resources into rebuilding the military. Little capital was left to rebuild and expand the economy.

Some responsibility for economic stagnation also lies with the peculiar nature of Egyptian socialism as it developed under Nasser. Government control of the economy left little opportunity for private enterprise to create businesses or jobs. And for the government bureaucracies that ran the economy, efficiency and productivity were not important goals. In order to provide work for all educated Egyptians, Nasser began overstaffing the bureaucracy even in his day, and this pattern has continued. Bureaucrats start work at nine and leave at two and spend much of the time in between drinking tea and chatting. They are poorly paid, so many treat their jobs as economic resources, opportunities to collect bribes or help relatives advance their fortunes (Vatikiotis, pp. 406–411).

> *Egyptians find this joke very funny; it rings true to them: "U.S. President Clinton visits Cairo and insists on jogging through the streets. He meets a poor man who pours out his heart and tells him about his sick wife and his son who can't afford to marry. Clinton is very moved and when he gets back to Washington he calls President Mubarak and tells him, 'I've sent you $5000. Please give it to Ibrahim Sayed of Bulak for me.' Mubarak calls in an aide. 'Here's $2500 from Bill Clinton. Find Ibrahim Sayed in Bulak and give it to him.' The aide calls his assistant. 'Go to Bulak and find Ibrahim Sayed and give him this $1000 from President Clinton.' The assistant calls his assistant. 'This $500 is from Bill Clinton. Find Ibrahim Sayed and give it to him.' The assistant calls his secretary. 'I want you to find Ibrahim Sayed and tell him Bill Clinton sends his regards.'"*

Egyptians today are very frustrated with corruption in government. They believe that corruption has grown so great that it is preventing growth, while government officials are too corrupt to really want to change things.

Economic Development and Government Policy

Since Nasser's time, both Egyptian presidents—Sadat and Mubarak—have promised to rebuild the Egyptian economy, but their efforts have not succeeded. Anwar Sadat, Nasser's successor, made peace with Israel and reduced military expenditures. He also distanced Egypt from the Soviet Union, reduced state control of the economy, and invited private enterprise, Egyptian and foreign, to invest in Egypt.

But Sadat's encouragement of private investment soon backfired. Investors built high-rise hotels and luxury apartments, but provided few jobs for ordinary people. Many traditional neighborhoods in Cairo were destroyed and replaced with expensive housing developments. At the same time, the World Bank persuaded Sadat to reduce Egypt's growing debt by cutting government spending. The government unwisely chose to cut the subsidies it provided for wheat, rice, and other basic foods. For ordinary Egyptians it was the last straw: luxuries for the rich and starvation for the poor! People in every sizable city and town took to the streets in protest. "Hero of the crossing," they shouted in reference to Sadat's victory over the Israelis, "where is our breakfast?" (See Vatikiotis, pp. 411–416, 421–430; Hooglund, pp. 118–120.)

Unhappiness spread not only in cities, but through the countryside. Land reform had never been completed and the government's focus on the war with Israel and restoring private enterprise allowed many individuals and foreign corporations to acquire significant amounts of land. Small farmers, heavily burdened with taxes, found it harder to survive, and many sold their land to richer men. Rural inequality increased and poor peasants left the land to try their luck in the cities (Mitchell, T., pp. 22–23, 26–27).

The government of Hosni Mubarak, an air force general who has ruled Egypt since Anwar Sadat's death in 1981, has generated enormous hostility by its inability to deal with Egypt's faltering economy and its ever-widening class divisions. Mubarak has substantially weakened the land reform laws instituted by Nasser and foreign business interests have bought up huge tracts of fertile land (Mitchell, T., pp. 22–23). In at least some instances, the government has taken away land that was distributed to peasants in the Nasser years. When peasants have protested these moves, heavily armed police have been used to enforce the government's orders (Hedges, Sept. 28, 1994, p. 4).

While Mubarak has attacked some aspects of Egyptian socialism, he has not succeeded in turning Egypt's huge, inefficient public enterprises over to private hands. Eighty percent of Egypt's economy is still owned and run by the government. Private business owners often complain that their efforts are blocked by the government. Mubarak's reluctance may, in part, be explained by his family's close ties to lucrative government-owned enterprises. For example, Mubarak's son runs Egyptair, the government-owned airline, and entrepreneurs trying to start private airlines have complained that government agencies have made it impossible for them to do business (Hedges, Nov. 12, 1994, p. 11).

All the time that Nassar, Sadat, and Mubarak were trying to promote economic growth in Egypt, population continued to grow rapidly, worsening Egypt's economic problems. Can you imagine a country that doubles its food production in thirty years, and in the same time period also doubles its population? Despite improved productivity, people will not be better off at all! The gap between increasing population and a stagnant economy is probably Egypt's most pressing political and social problem.

Population Problems

Egypt's population has indeed grown dramatically. In 1947 there were 19 million Egyptians, by 1976 there were nearly 37 million, and by 1993 there were 58 million. Although Egypt's population is not expected to increase as rapidly in the future, substantial growth is still expected. By some estimates, Egypt will have nearly 105 million people by 2025 (Omran and Roudi, p. 4).

The Demographic Transition

Why has Egypt's population grown so rapidly? Is growth likely to continue? Egypt's rapid growth is part of a process of **demographic transition,** which most of the world is experiencing. In a demographic transition, a society's population rapidly expands as a result of falling death rates. In 1950, twenty-four people out of every thousand Egyptians died every year; by 1990, only eight out of every thousand Egyptians died yearly. Sociologists and **demographers** (the scientists who study population) would say that the **crude death rate,** the number of deaths per thousand in a population, fell in Egypt, from twenty-four to eight (Hooglund, p. 124; Omran and Roudi, p. 4). A sharp decline in the number of people dying yearly leads to a rapid increase in the size of a population. The striking drop in Egypt's death rate coincides with efforts by the government to provide free or low-cost health care to all Egyptians. Between 1952 and 1976, government expenditures on public health increased 500 percent (Hooglund, pp. 148–152).

Death rates, however, are only part of the demographic transition; equally important are birth rates. In 1950, there were forty-eight births yearly for every thousand Egyptians. Sociologists call this the **crude birth rate. Natural increase,** the change in a population's size, is a product of the crude birth rate and the crude death rate. If the death rate drops rapidly, as it did in Egypt, then the size of the natural increase will depend on what happens to the birth rate. In Egypt, the birth rate dropped by 1990 to thirty-three per thousand yearly (Omran and Roudi, p. 4). The drop in the birth rate meant that Egypt's population increase, though astonishing, was not as large as it would have been if the birth rate had continued at its 1950 level. (See Table 4.5.)

Urbanization and Population Growth

Better health care brought down death rates. What changes made birth rates fall? One critical change has been the migration of people from the countryside to the cities and their involvement in an urban economy. In 1950, only one Egyptian in three lived in an urban area, but by 1990, half of all Egyptians lived in cities. In 1992, rural women had an average of five children each, but urban women had only three. In the cities, women in the paid labor force are likely to have fewer children. Also, city families see that educated children earn more than those who are barely literate. If a family thinks it likely that they will be able to send their children to school, then it pays to have fewer children so they will be able to afford to educate them. Conversely, a very poor family that knows education is out of the question,

TABLE 4.5. Birth, Death, and Natural Increase Rates: Birth and death rates have declined rapidly for Egypt and Mexico, but their rate of natural increase remains high. Germany's population, however, is actually declining.

	1960			1991		
	Birth Rate (Births per 1000)	Death Rate (Deaths per 1000)	Rate of Natural Increase†	Birth Rate (Births per 1000)	Death Rate (Deaths per 1000)	Rate of Natural Increase†
East Germany	17	14	0.3%	13*	13*	0.0%
West Germany	18	12	0.6%	10*	11*	−0.1%
Japan	17	8	0.9%	10	7	0.3%
United States	24	10	2.4%	16	9	0.7%
Mexico	45	12	3.3%	28	5	2.3%
Egypt	44	20	2.4%	32	9	2.1%

*Data for both Germanys are for 1988. The birth rate for the whole country in 1991 was 10, the death rate was 11.
†The rate of natural increase is the birth rate minus the death rate, indicating the annual rate of population increase without considering migration. The rate is expressed as a percentage of the entire population.
Sources: Haub, Carl, and Machiko Yanagishita, *1995 World Population Data Sheet.* Washington, DC: Population Reference Bureau, 1995; World Bank, *World Development Report 1988: Opportunities and Risks in Managing the World Economy.* New York: Oxford University Press, 1988.

will find it more rational to have many children, all of whom can work and bring in some income to help the family.

In the countryside fewer families can afford higher education. But also, having many children makes sense in an agricultural economy. Tenant farmers and small landowners find that the more hands there are to work, including children's, the greater the family income. Traditional Islamic values and norms in the countryside also encourage large families. The more children a woman has, especially sons, the more prestige and influence she gains.

It is puzzling though, that despite urbanization, Egypt's birth rate has declined more slowly than demographers expected. There are a variety of reasons for this, but one is apparently the influence of surrounding countries which are eager to increase, rather than reduce, their populations. Libya, Iraq, Kuwait, and other oil-rich states with relatively small populations have tried to encourage people to have large families. Youssef Courbage argues that the enormous numbers of young Egyptian men working in these countries have been very influenced by their values. At the same time that education and urbanization tend to reduce the number of children women desire, work abroad tends to reinforce male preferences for larger families (Courbage, pp. 19–22).

Population Policy

Since 1966 Egypt's government has encouraged family planning and the use of contraceptives to limit population increase. The government has created a national network of family planning clinics, conducted an extensive media campaign in favor of small families, and made contraceptives widely available. These efforts have not been as successful as the government hoped: Egyptians tend to distrust anything that their government promotes. Nevertheless, it is clear that programs to reduce family size have met with some success. In 1992, almost half of all married Egyptian women reported that they used a modern contraceptive method such as the diaphragm or the intrauterine device. The same survey also reported that 67 percent of married women wanted no more children (Omran and Roudi, p. 13). (See Table 4.6.)

But despite these very real successes, the number of Egyptians continues to rise. There are so many more families today that numbers escalate despite smaller family sizes. Demographers refer to the influence of increases in the childbearing population as the **momentum factor.** Each family is having fewer children, but there are so many more families that population growth continues at a rapid rate.

The Food Gap and Inequality

Today, Egypt suffers from a **food gap:** population is growing faster than food production. Money that might be spent on schools, housing, and health care is used to import food. While few would dispute that Egypt's growing population poses serious problems, some authorities have argued that inequality as well as population growth accounts for Egypt's food gap. Even while malnourishment increases, a smaller number of Egyptians are increasingly affluent and well-fed. Affluent Egyptians in the government and the private sector can afford to pay for a western-style diet that is rich in meat, while poor Egyptians rarely eat meat. Timothy Mitchell

TABLE 4.6. Use of Contraception and Number of Children: Increasing contraceptive use has reduced Egyptian family size, but the typical Egyptian family still has four children.

	1970		1993	
	Total Fertility Rate (Average Number of Children a Woman Has in Her Lifetime)	Percent of Married Women Using Contraceptives	Total Fertility Rate (Average Number of Children a Woman Has in Her Lifetime)	Percent of Married Women Using Contraceptives
West Germany	2.1	Not available	1.3	75*
Japan	2.1	56	1.5	64
United States	2.5	65	2.0	71
Mexico	6.5	39	3.1	65
Egypt	5.9	24†	3.9	47

*Data for 1993 are for Germany as a whole.
†Data are for 1981.
Sources: Haub, Carl, and Machiko Yanagishita, *1995 World Population Data Sheet.* Washington, DC: Population Reference Bureau, 1995; World Bank, *World Development Report 1993: Investing in Health.* New York: Oxford University Press, 1993.

argues that farmers find it more profitable to raise beef for the rich than wheat or corn for sale to the poor. Egyptian farmers plant twice as many acres of clover for cattle feed as they use to grow wheat. Mitchell argues that if this imbalance were corrected, Egyptians would not have to import grain to feed themselves. Imported grain is, of course, very expensive and this adds to Egypt's economic burden. In addition, the government has allowed American and other foreign investors to buy thousands of acres to raise cotton and sugar for export. Obviously, this also reduces domestic food production in Egypt (Metz, p. 358; Mitchell, T., p. 21). (See Table 4.7.)

TABLE 4.7. Dependence on Food Imports and Food Aid: Mexico and Egypt increasingly depend on food imports and food aid to feed their people.

	Food Imports as a Percent of Total Food Supply		Increase in Food Imports, 1969–1990	Food Aid in Millions of Dollars, 1988–1990
	1969–1971	1988–1990		
Mexico	3.2	24.8	675%	31.7
Egypt	19.8	42.6	115%	410.0

Source: United Nations Development Programme, *Human Development Program Report 1994,* New York: Oxford University Press, 1994.

Environmental Damage: The Unintended Consequences of Economic Growth

In the 1950s, Gamal Abdul Nasser attempted to increase Egypt's productivity in two ways: by farming more land and by developing heavy industry. His approach to development was heavily influenced by American and European ideas about irrigation and industrialization. These policies had serious unintended consequences when applied to Egypt. Americans and Europeans now know that industrialization and irrigation projects can damage even hardy environments. In a fragile environment such as Egypt's, development has produced as much damage in a decade as it did in a century or more in the United States.

The Aswan Dam was the most important element in Nasser's plan to increase agricultural production. In the short run, the dam was a great success: it controlled the destructiveness of the Nile's annual flood, it permitted more effective allocation of irrigation water, and new land was brought under cultivation. A lake, Lake Nasser, formed behind the Aswan Dam. As time went on, however, the Aswan Dam produced more and more negative effects. The absence of the annual flood severely reduced agricultural productivity. In the past, the flood brought soil from central Africa to the banks of the Nile. This new soil gave the Nile Valley its remarkable fertility. The land is now less productive and more reliant on expensive fertilizers. The reduced flow of the Nile has also increased the salinity of the water at the northern edge of the Delta where the Nile meets the sea. Eventually, this could make the land too salty for farming. The absence of the annual flood has also facilitated the spread of parasitic diseases. The parasites flourish in still waters and perish in turbulent ones (Hooglund, pp. 100, 150). Concern over the negative effects of damming the Nile has been so great that Egyptians are now turning to alternative farming methods that work without massive irrigation, often methods developed by their former enemies, the Israelis. The Aswan Dam, once Egypt's proudest hope, has become another of its problems (Hedges, Dec. 18, 1993, p. A5).

Industrial Pollution

In the 1950s and the 1960s, influenced by ideas shared by virtually all economists at the time, Nasser worked to introduce heavy industry to Egypt. One of the centerpieces of this effort was the mammoth steelworks of the Helwan industrial complex. This project transformed the countryside and the lives of the people. Villages that existed on the fringes of the modern world gained electricity, paved roads, schools, radio and television, modern consumer products, and the wages that permitted people to buy them. But now, several decades later, these same villages are paying an environmental toll for industrial development: water and air are polluted, the land has lost some of its fertility, and agricultural produce is contaminated by industrial wastes (Hedges, Nov. 26, 1993). Industrial pollution from petrochemical plants has begun to wear away Egypt's most famous tourist attraction, the pyramids. The survival of these ancient monuments is also threatened by an eight-lane highway and its fumes and pollution (Hedges, Dec. 10, 1994, p. 4). Not only pyramids, but people are endangered by Egypt's burgeoning auto traffic. Cairo's air is dangerously polluted with lead (Ethelson, pp. 4–5).

The Islamic Alternative

If you were a young Egyptian, what would you think about the future? Nasser's socialism had failed and so had the private enterprise efforts of Sadat! What direction could the country take? Since colonial times, some Egyptians had been arguing that Egypt was following too slavisly the path laid down by the West. In doing so, it was abandoning its Islamic heritage. The only way Egypt could rebuild, they argued, was to find Islamic models for a modern society. Nasser repressed these fundamentalists, but Sadat permitted them to speak freely, hoping to use them against his socialist opponents.

In 1981, Anwar Sadat was gunned down at a military parade by members of an elite military unit who belonged to Al Jihad, a militant Islamic movement. Although not all Islamic movements are secret, armed, or prepared to do violence, those that are constitute a real challenge to Egypt's secular government and culture. Movements such as Al Jihad are best understood as **revolutionary terrorist organizations,** groups that use violence against individuals in order to change their societies. Islamic terrorist groups have attacked writers, teachers, members of the Christian minority, and European tourists as well as police and political figures (Abu-Lughod, L., p. 25). Terrorists attacked one of Egypt's most respected writers, Naguib Mafouz, a Nobel Prize winner, because they charged his novels slandered Islam (Esposito, 1992, pp. 120–140).

Although terrorist movements like Al Jihad may grab headlines, they are only a tiny fraction of a much larger social movement. Egypt's Islamic movement includes groups like the Muslim Brotherhood, which the government sometimes permits to function openly as a nonviolent political party, contesting elections and sending representatives to Egypt's parliament. The movement also includes professional associations of doctors, lawyers, and others dominated by officers elected on "Islamic" slates. Beyond this, there are many Egyptians who belong to no "Islamic" organizations, but who sympathize with many of the values and goals of these organizations.

Ever since he was a small boy, Nabeel had loved cars, trucks, tanks, planes—things that moved. His parents despaired when he failed the high school entrance examination, but he thrived in the local technical and vocational school, learning to be a mechanic. On graduation, Nabeel looked for a job in Asyut, the city in Upper Egypt where he was raised, but there was little work to be found, only unskilled and poorly paid labor. Unhappy, but resigned to the need, Nabeel left to join one of his uncles in Cairo who promised to help him find work. Nabeel's uncle found a job for him repairing postal vans, but the pay was low and he had to make a large payment to the garage manager "for his help." After three years, Nabeel, now 22, owned only his clothes and a few books. His wages fed him, but let him save little. When his mother was ill, Nabeel sent most of his small savings to pay for doctors and medicines.

Cairo was not the bright promise it had once seemed. He was poor, had no future, and every day rich men and women drove past him in expensive cars and foreign clothes. Nabeel was shocked by the women in Cairo; they walked the street uncovered and immodest. Bared bosoms were displayed on every movie poster! It was all part of the influence of the afrangi— the westernized Egyptians who thought and acted as foreigners, not Egyptians, and not Muslims.

Later that year, Nabeel's mother came to visit him in Cairo and he took her to a free health clinic run by the Muslim Brotherhood. There were dedicated young doctors there who took their work seriously. The doctor really listened to Nabeel's mother and she was able to diagnose her breathing problems and get the asthma under control. Nabeel was overjoyed, but he was also furious at the government clinics that had made his mother wait and wait, then hadn't helped her. Nabeel listened to sermons by imams who sympathized with the Muslim Brotherhood. They called for an Islamic Egypt where the government would care about ordinary Egyptians and there would be jobs and decent wages for all. "Perhaps," thought Nabeel, "this is the path we need to follow."

Unable to follow Muslim norms that call for men to marry and support their families, young men like Nabeel turn against the government and its social and economic policies with tremendous anger. Educated, but unemployed, barred from marriage by poverty, disgusted by violations of Islamic mores, their very identity is challenged (Rugh, 1984, pp. 205–234; Esposito, 1992, pp. 93–100, 120–140). Even Egyptians who reject fundamentalist goals are frequently sympathetic to Islamic groups because they help poor and middle-class Egyptians. In addition to health clinics, fundamentalists provide free day-care centers for women who must work, and free books and tutors for poor schoolchildren. Fundamentalist leaders are well-educated young people who have attended elite universities, often to study medicine or engineering. They understand the plight of Egypt's professionals, who cannot afford to go into private practice and don't want to work for the government. The fundamentalists help young professionals by giving them loans to set up clinics and offices and by underwriting health and life insurance policies. Islamic militants today are seen as earnest and dedicated and, above all, as honest, especially in contrast to Egypt's corrupt government (Hasan, pp. 60–63).

At the same time, Egyptians understand that the Islamic fundamentalists want Egypt to follow a much stricter interpretation of Islamic norms and laws. They want to place men clearly before women and they want to see the community of Islam placed before the interests of any individual. They want to make Islamic religious law, *sharia,* the law of the land, instead of secular law. Such changes would remove many of the protections Egyptian women have been given against the exercise of arbitrary male rights to divorce their wives, take a second wife, and take custody of the children in a divorce.

The response of the Mubarak government to the militants has left Egyptians with a difficult choice. Mubarak has proved unable to remedy Egypt's economic problems or to help young Egyptians. What he has done is to use government security forces to crush all opposition to his government—Islamic opposition and any other opposition as well, however peaceful or legal it may be. The government has persecuted Christians, feminists, and westernized intellectuals, as well as fundamentalists. Security forces have imprisoned as many as 20,000 Egyptians for opposition activities and they have used torture and forced confessions. Every terrorist act has been followed by immediate arrests, summary convictions, and executions. Government control of the press has increased (Hasan, pp. 60–63). Mubarak has certainly succeeded in making things hard for the fundamentalists and preventing them from coming to power in legitimate elections. But repression alone, without reform of corrupt government and without economic growth, is bound to make Egyptians still more frustrated.

It is certainly possible that an Islamic government will someday take power in Egypt. If this happens, however, the new government will face many dilemmas: How will Egypt's failing economy be restored to health? Can effective limits be placed on the country's growing population? Can the severe environmental damage of the past few decades be undone? Islamic movements in Egypt have had little to say about how they would address such problems. But problems of inequality, environment, and population will be the issues that confront any future government of Egypt.

Thinking Sociologically

1. Explain why sociologists consider Egypt a sacred society and Japan a secular society.
2. How do Islamic norms shape daily life in Egypt?
3. What are the norms for "modest dress" in your society?
4. How has modernization changed the roles Egyptian women play? Has it changed the roles of ¡Kung women in the same way?
5. Is it ethnocentric to condemn female circumcision?
6. What role conflicts do women in your society experience? What strategies do women pursue to resolve them?
7. In what ways are rural Egyptian families patriarchal? Are ¡Kung families patriarchal? How about families in your society?
8. Discuss the importance of work in the informal sector and work abroad for Egyptians and Mexicans. Is there an informal sector in your society? Who works in it?
9. Is the social stratification system in Egypt becoming more open or more closed? How about the stratification system in your society?
10. Based on what you have read in this chapter, do you think the Islamic fundamental movement in Egypt will become stronger or weaker in the next few years?
11. In Table 4.5 (p. 199), which societies appear to have reached stage 3 of the demographic transition? Explain your reasons for your answer.

For Further Reading

AHMED, LILA, *Women and Gender in Islam.* New Haven, CT: Yale University Press, 1992.

ATIYA, NAYARA, *Khul-Khaal: Five Egyptian Women Tell Their Stories.* Syracuse, NY: Syracuse University Press, 1982.

FERNEA, ELIZABETH, ed., *Women and Family in the Middle East: New Voices of Change.* Austin: University of Texas Press, 1985.

FLUEHR-LOBBAN, CAROLYN, *Islamic Society in Practice.* Gainesville: University Press of Florida, 1994.

LIPPMAN, THOMAS, *Understanding Islam: An Introduction to the Muslim World.* New York: Penguin, 1990.

MACLEOD, ARLENE, *Accommodating Protest: Working Women, The New Veiling and Change in Cairo.* New York: Columbia University Press, 1993.

RODENBECK, JOHN, ed., *Cairo.* Singapore: APA Publications, 1992.

Rugh, Andrea, *Family in Contemporary Egypt.* Syracuse, NY: Syracuse University Press, 1984.

Springborg, Robert, *Mubarak's Egypt: Fragmentation of the Political Order.* Boulder, CO: Westview Press, 1989.

Bibliography

Abu-Lughod, Janet L., *Changing Cities.* New York: HarperCollins, 1991.

Abu-Lughod, Lila, "Islam and Public Culture: The Politics of Egyptian Television Serials," *Middle East Report,* Vol. 23, No. 1, Jan.–Feb. 1993, pp. 25–30.

Ahmed, Lila, *Women and Gender in Islam.* New Haven, CT: Yale University Press, 1992.

Aldred, Cyril, *The Egyptians,* revised and enlarged edition. London: Thames and Hudson, 1984.

Ammar, Hamad, *Growing Up in an Egyptian Village.* New York: Octagon Books, 1966.

Atiya, Nayara, *Khul-Khaal: Five Egyptian Women Tell Their Stories.* Syracuse, NY: Syracuse University Press, 1982.

Ayrout, Henry, *The Egyptian Peasant.* Boston: Beacon Press, 1963.

Badran, Margot, "Dual Liberation: Feminism and Nationalism in Egypt, 1870s–1925," *Feminist Issues,* Vol. 8, No. 1, Spring 1988, pp. 17–34.

Barakat, Halim, *The Arab World: Society: Culture and State.* Berkeley: University of California Press, 1993.

Bassiouni, M. Cherif, *An Introduction to Islam.* Chicago: Rand McNally, 1989.

Binder, Leonard, *In a Moment of Enthusiasm: Political Power and the Second Stratum in Egypt.* Chicago: University of Chicago Press, 1978.

Burstyn, Linda, "Female Circumcision Comes to America," *Atlantic,* Oct. 1995, pp 28–35.

Campo, Juan Eduardo, *The Other Side of Paradise: Explorations into the Religious Meanings of Domestic Space in Islam.* Columbia: University of South Carolina Press, 1991.

Clarke, Lynda, "Suicide," in John Esposito, ed., *The Oxford Encyclopedia of the Modern Islamic World,* Vol. 4. New York: Oxford University Press, 1995, pp. 133–135.

Courbage, Youssef, "Demographic Change in the Arab World: The Impact of Migration, Education and Taxes in Egypt and Morocco," *Middle East Report,* Vol. 24, No. 5, Sept.–Oct. 1994, pp. 19–22.

Department of Economic and Social Information and Policy Analysis, Statistical Division, *Statistical Yearbook,* 38th ed. New York: United Nations, 1993.

Early, Evelyn, *Baladi Women of Cairo: Playing with an Egg and a Stone.* Boulder, CO: Lynne Rienner, 1993.

El-Gawhary, Karim, "An Interview with Heba Ra'uf Ezzat," *Middle East Report,* Vol. 24, No. 6, Nov.–Dec. 1994, pp. 26–27.

El-Messiri, Sawsan, "Traditional Urban Women in Cairo," in Lois Beck and Nikki Keddie, eds., *Women in the Muslim World.* Cambridge, MA: Harvard University Press, 1978.

Elmusa, Sharif, "The Economy," in Helen Chapin Metz, ed., *Egypt: A Country Study,* 5th ed. Washington, DC: Federal Research Division, Library of Congress, 1991.

ESPOSITO, JOHN, *Islam: The Straight Path.* New York: Oxford University Press, 1991*a*.

———, *Islam and Politics.* Syracuse, NY: Syracuse University Press, 1991*b*.

———, *The Islamic Threat.* New York: Oxford University Press, 1992.

ETHELSON, SALLY, "Gender, Population, Environment," *Middle East Report,* Vol. 24, No. 5, Sept.–Oct. 1994, pp. 2–5.

FAKHOURI, HANI, *Kafr El-Elow: An Egyptian Village in Transition.* New York: Holt, 1972.

FAY, MARY ANN, "Historical Setting," in Helen Chapin Metz, ed., *Egypt: A Country Study,* 5th ed. Washington, DC: Federal Research Division, Library of Congress, 1991.

FLUEHR-LOBBAN, CAROLYN, *Islamic Society in Practice.* Gainsville: University Press of Florida 1994.

FRIEDMAN, THOMAS, "Almost Egypt," *The New York Times,* Oct. 25, 1995, p. A21.

GHOSH, AMITAV, *In an Antique Land.* New York: Knopf, 1993.

HASAN, SANA, "My Lost Egypt," *The New York Times Magazine,* Oct. 25, 1995, pp. 60–63.

HEDGES, CHRIS, "As Egypt Votes on Mubarak, He Faces Rising Peril," *The New York Times,* Oct. 4, 1993, p. A8.

———, "Industrious Egypt Is Choking Its People to Death," *The New York Times,* Nov. 26, 1993, p. A4.

———, "Bananas Become Fruit of Egypt-Israel Friendship," *The New York Times,* Dec. 18, 1993, p. A5.

———, "In Bureaucrats' Castle, Everyone Else Is a Beggar," *The New York Times,* June 7, 1994, p. A4.

———, "Domestic Problems Hurt Rising Stature of Egypt," *The New York Times,* July 17, 1994, p. A6.

———, "Peasants See the Promised Land Snatched Away," *The New York Times,* Sept. 28, 1994, p. 4.

———, "An Airline Fears Cairo Will Kill It with Rules," *The New York Times,* Nov. 12, 1994, p. 11.

———, "Novelist's Unwitting Role: Sword against Militants," *The New York Times,* Nov. 15, 1994, p. 4.

———, "Now Even the Sphinx Might Protest," *The New York Times,* Dec. 10, 1994, p. 4.

HOOGLUND, ERIC, "The Society and Its Environment," in Helen Chapin Metz, ed., *Egypt: A Country Study,* 5th ed. Washington, DC: Federal Research Division, Library of Congress, 1991.

HUBELL, STEPHEN, "Cairo's People," in John Rodenbeck, ed., *Cairo.* Singapore: APA Publications, 1992.

HUFF, TOBY, "Rethinking Islam and Fundamentalism," *Sociological Forum,* Vol. 10, No. 3, Sept. 1995, pp. 501–518.

IBRAHIM, BARBARA, "Cairo's Factory Women," in Elizabeth Fernea, ed., *Women and the Family in the Middle East: New Voices of Change.* Austin: University of Texas Press, 1985.

IBRAHIM, YOUSSEF, "With Islam in Vogue, Egypt Follows in Its Fashion," *The New York Times,* Feb. 3, 1993, p. A6.

———, "Muslims' Fury Falls on Egypt's Christians," *The New York Times,* Mar. 15, 1993, pp. A1, A8.

Kurian, George, *The New Book of World Rankings,* 3d ed. New York: Facts on File, 1991.

———, ed., *Encyclopedia of the Third World,* Vol. 1. New York: Facts on File, 1992.

Lacoutre, Jean, *Nasser: A Biography.* New York: Knopf, 1973.

Lewis, Paul, "U.N. Lists Four Nations at Risk Because of Wide Income Gaps," *The New York Times,* June 2, 1994, p. A6.

Lippman, Thomas, *Egypt after Nasser.* New York: Paragon House, 1989.

———, *Understanding Islam: An Introduction to the Muslim World.* New York: Penguin, 1990.

Lufti, Hudda, "Manners and Customs of Fourteenth Century Cairene Women," in Nikki Keddi and Beth Baron, eds., *Women in Middle Eastern History.* New Haven, CT: Yale University Press, 1991.

MacLeod, Arlene, *Accommodating Protest: Working Women, The New Veiling and Change in Cairo.* New York: Columbia University Press, 1993.

Mernissi, Fatima, *Islam and Democracy.* Reading, MA: Addison-Wesley, 1992.

Metz, Helen Chapin, *Egypt: A Country Study,* 5th ed. Washington, DC: Federal Research Division, Library of Congress, 1991.

Mitchell, Richard, *The Society of the Muslim Brothers.* London: Oxford University Press, 1969.

Mitchell, Timothy, "America's Egypt: Discourse of the Development Industry," *Middle East Report,* Mar.–Apr. 1991, pp. 18–34.

Mule, Pat, and Diane Barthel, "The Return to the Veil: Individual Autonomy versus Social Esteem," *Sociological Forum,"* Vol. 7, No. 2, 1992, pp. 323–332.

Nisan, Mordechai, *Minorities in the Middle East.* London: McFarland, 1991.

O'Connor, David, *A Short History of Ancient Egypt.* Pittsburgh: Carnegie Museum of Natural History, 1990.

Omran, Abdel R., and Farzanneh Roudi, "The Middle East Population Puzzle," *Population Bulletin,* Vol. 48, No. 1, July 1993, pp. 1–39.

Robinson, Francis, *Atlas of the Islamic World.* New York: Facts on File, 1982.

Rodenbeck, Max, "Religion," in John Rodenbeck, ed., *Cairo.* Singapore: APA Publications, 1992.

Rugh, Andrea, *Family in Contemporary Egypt.* Syracuse, NY: Syracuse University Press, 1984.

———, *Reveal and Conceal: Dress in Contemporary Egypt.* Syracuse, NY: Syracuse University Press, 1986.

Sadat, Jehan, *A Woman of Egypt.* New York: Simon & Schuster, 1987.

Schmidt, William E., "A Deluge of Foreign Assistance Fails to Revive Egypt's Stricken Economy," *The New York Times,* Oct. 10, 1993, p. 10.

Springborg, Robert, *Mubarak's Egypt: Fragmentation of the Political Order.* Boulder, CO: Westview Press, 1989.

Stowasser, Barbara, "Women's Issues in Modern Islamic Thought," in Judith Tucker, ed., *Arab Women: Old Boundaries, New Frontiers.* Bloomington: Indiana University Press, 1993.

United States Department of Labor, Bureau of International Labor Affairs, *Foreign*

Labor Trends: Egypt, 1992.

VATIKIOTIS, PETER J., *The History of Egypt,* 3d ed. Baltimore: Johns Hopkins University Press, 1991.

WATERBURY, JOHN, *The Egypt of Sadat and Nasser: The Political Economy of Two Regimes.* Princeton, NJ: Princeton University Press, 1983.

WOLF, MARGERY, "Uterine Families and the Women's Community," in James Spradley and David McCurdy, eds. *Conformity and Conflict: Readings in Cultural Anthropology,* 8th ed. New York: HarperCollins, 1994.

GERMANY

Five hours east of Montreal and New York by air, less than an hour from London and Paris lies Berlin, the capital of a reunited Germany, one of the most prosperous countries on earth and the birthplace of Albert Einstein, Ludwig van Beethoven, and other figures who shaped western civilization.

LOCATION: In the center of Europe. France, Belgium, and the Netherlands border Germany to the west; Denmark and the North Sea to the north; Poland and the Czech Republic to the east; and Austria and Switzerland to the south.

AREA: 135,000 square miles or 391,500 square kilometers; the size of California or Japan.

LAND: Lowlands in the north, highlands in the center, and a mountainous region in the south bordering the Alps.

CLIMATE: Temperate, similar to the northeastern United States, Canada, or Japan.

POPULATION: 81.7 million in 1995, expected to decline to 76 million in 2025. An older population, 15 percent are 65 or over.

ECONOMY: An industrial society producing automobiles such as the Mercedes Benz, Germany also has a productive agriculture.

INCOME: $23,560 per capita.

EDUCATION: The average adult (25+) completes almost twelve years.

RELIGION: Protestant 42 percent, Catholic 35 percent.

ETHNIC MINORITIES: Turkish immigrants, about 2 percent of the population.

CHAPTER 5

Germany: Social Institutions and Social Change in a Modern Western Society

INTRODUCTION

"Periods of bliss are history's blank pages." Does this quotation from Georg Wilhelm Friedrich Hegel, Germany's most famous nineteenth-century philosopher, make sense to you? Hegel means that people are most likely to find private happiness in uneventful times. Historians write books about history's interesting periods—times of war, revolution, and social transformation—but for most people, these are very painful periods to live through.

If Hegel is right, modern Germans surely have been the most unhappy people. In the past century, Germans have lived through many successive social transformations. Germany was agricultural and then rapidly became industrialized at the end of the nineteenth century. Germans experienced humiliating defeat and devastation in two world wars and they lived under the greatest variety of political systems: a monarchy, a republic, a fascist state, an authoritarian Soviet satellite state, and a democracy. After World War II, East Germans and West Germans experienced two different economic systems: socialism and capitalism. Finally, East Germans today are finding their lives transformed as their society is absorbed into West Germany.

It will be helpful for you to learn about German society for several reasons. First of all, you will become acquainted with all the varieties of political and economic institutions that are found in modern western societies. For example, Germans practice their own national variety of capitalism. If you live in a capitalist society, you will see that German capitalism is different from your nation's capitalism. Also, by studying Germany you will learn how changing social institutions shape people's lives. Sociologists, because they deal with real-life societies, cannot conduct experiments in the same way that physicists or even biologists can. But in the past forty-five years, Germany has been a kind of natural experiment in the consequences of adopting two different sets of political and economic institutions. You can see how different institutions in East and West Germany shaped contrasting values and norms and interpersonal relationships.

Finally, it is important to study German society because so many important sociologists were German. They used their experiences with dictatorship and democracy, with bureaucracy and social inequality, in creating some of sociology's most important concepts and theories. To really understand Karl Marx's theories or Max Weber's works, you need to know about German society.

Social Change Today: Reunification

One of the most fascinating things about Germany is that dramatic social change is going on today. Reunification is an experiment in deliberately remaking social institutions that is happening before our eyes. Germany was originally divided into two separate states in the wake of its defeat in World War II. The eastern part of Germany, occupied by the Soviet Union, became East Germany (the German Democratic Republic, or GDR), a Soviet satellite state with a socialist economy, an authoritarian government, and sealed borders—symbolized by the famous Berlin Wall. The western part of Germany, occupied by Britain, France, and the United States, became West Germany (the Federal Republic of Germany, the FRG, or the Federal Republic, as Germans called it); a close ally of its former enemies in their fight against communism. West Germany became a western-style parliamentary democracy and one of the world's richest, most powerful capitalist economies. It was twice the size of East Germany and had a population 4 times larger (62.6 million, versus 16.4 million in the GDR in 1990) (Heilig, Buttner, and Lutz, p. 4).

Until Gorbachev came to power in the Soviet Union and loosened the Soviet hold on eastern Europe, no society had ever before abandoned socialism and adopted capitalism. Now, since 1988, East Germany, like Poland, Hungary, the Czech Republic, and many other former Soviet-bloc nations, is engaged in adopting some form of democratic political institutions and capitalist economic institutions. In East Germany, the transformation has taken the particular form of reunification with West Germany, or, in reality, absorption into West Germany. West German institutions have remained essentially unchanged, while the former GDR (East Germany) has changed its government and economy, values and norms, and social group life. Acknowledging this political reality, this chapter will refer to West Germany in the present tense, even though it no longer exists as a separate nation, but it will refer to East Germany in the past tense.

Since the Wende (literally, the "turning," as in "a turning of the road," the term Germans use for the fall of the East German regime and reunification), life in Leipzig (in the former GDR) has changed more than Inge Reuter ever imagined. This New Year's Eve, for the first time, Inge and her husband went out to a restaurant—alone. In the old days there were no restaurants worth going to, and no one had any money anyhow. They spent all their New Year's eves (and most other weekend nights as well) gathered around someone's kitchen table, eating bread and cheese, and drinking beer, laughing and singing and enjoying the company of family and friends. That was all they had: friends and plenty of time to enjoy them. No one worked very hard, because working hard didn't get you more pay, and even if it did, there was nothing to buy.

Now Inge finds herself a successful businesswoman, and nostalgic for the old days. When the western companies began to build all the new shopping malls outside Leipzig, she started a cleaning company. She is busy all the time, hiring and training employees, supervising, getting new contracts, and doing her accounts far into the night. There are no more kitchen-table parties. It's not just time either: the old crowd has split up. Some, like Inge, have prospered, but others are still unemployed. They are no longer all in the same boat, and tensions have sprung up among them. Everyone is out for themselves now; working hard to earn money and busy spending it. It seems like things have become more important than friendship.

In West Germany no area has been more affected by reunification than West Berlin. Geographically, West Berlin was an isolated outpost of the Federal Republic, stranded hundreds of miles within East German territory and reachable only by plane or through a fenced auto corridor. West Berlin was half a city, sliced down the middle by the Berlin Wall, dividing it from East Berlin. But in the days of the Cold War, West Berlin was an exciting place, full of artists and hippies and new trends. West Berliners felt a sense of camaraderie derived from danger. Government employees earned extra "hardship pay" for working in Berlin.

Joachim Hasselblad is the 58-year-old owner of a tobacco shop in what was formerly West Berlin. He says he was happy in the old days before reunification, but now much that was certain in his life is changing very rapidly. Joachim had gotten used to West Berlin; he hardly noticed the Wall.

Now, suddenly, the Wall is gone and Berlin is twice as big, twice as populous, open to the outside world, and utterly strange. It is soon to be the capital of Germany again—and it lies at the heart of post-Soviet Europe. Berlin is now full of big corporations and real estate developers buying up land; rents are going up all over. And it is full of "Ossis" (East Germans) in jeans made of spotty Soviet denim, demanding help, using embarrassing words like "führer," never used in the West. Joachim has to pay an extra 7½ percent "solidarity tax," and all those Poles and Russians and Slovaks in the "Polish Market" are selling black market cigarettes and undercutting Joachim's prices. "I want to be a good German," Joachim says, "and help out our brothers in the East, but they're not like us anymore and I'm afraid the cost will ruin me."

Inge and Joachim come from two different societies: East Germany and West Germany, but they are both Germans, and as Germans they do still have much in common. Forty-five years of division into two societies did not erase all their common heritage. First of all, their societies have a history that was shared up until 1946 and it has left preoccupations and scars common to both societies. Also division did not entirely alter the German culture common to both East and West. Let us begin by examining the two Germanys' common history and culture.

GERMAN HISTORY: CENTRAL THEMES

First of all, Germany's national history is briefer than that of Egypt or Japan. Germany didn't even exist as a separate nation until modern times. Nevertheless, Germany's history has been very eventful. It is studded with wars, treaties, monarchs, changes of borders, and successive governments and policies. We cannot begin to tell you the whole involved story in a sociology text. Instead we will describe a few key issues that Germans have repeatedly fought over. The first is: Should Germany have a single government with centralized power or should it be a collection of small states with most power held on the local level? Over the centuries Germans have fought about this and they have also fought about whether Germany should be an authoritarian nation, with unrestricted power in the hands of its rulers, or whether it should be a democracy, with a constitution, a bill of rights, and a parliamentary system to give its citizens political say and protection from rulers' power. Finally, Germans have struggled about what protection the government owes its citizens against the impersonal destructiveness of market forces in an industrial society. In this battle, a system of social welfare protections has been the alternative to government control of the economy.

Centralized Power versus Local Power

Germany was not fully unified as a nation-state until 1871. Before that, Germany experienced many centuries when periods of national unification alternated with fragmentation into small kingdoms. In the first and second centuries B.C., Germanic tribes settled the area that is now modern Germany, battling the Romans, and after the collapse of the Roman Empire they spread over northern Italy, Britain, and France. In early medieval times (A.D. 800) Charlemagne unified these peoples in an empire known in Germany as the First *Reich* (or empire) and elsewhere as the Holy Roman Empire. After Charlemagne's death, his empire broke up into hundreds of small kingdoms. Through the centuries they sometimes formed local unions, then broke up again. In modern times, centralization gained. Prussia was first united after the Thirty Years' War ended in 1648. In 1815, after Napoleon's defeat, the Congress of Vienna established a German Confederation of thirty-nine monarchies, headed by Austria under Prince Metternich as chancellor. After the Franco-Prussian War, in 1871, German states voluntarily joined Prussia in a Second Reich, a new imperial Germany, led by the Prussian King Wilhelm I and his prime minister Otto von Bismarck. This time the Reich took the form of a federal union, with all the small monarchies represented in a Federal Council.

Imperial ambitions for military might and global political power led Germany into World War I, a war the nation expected to win within months. When, after four grueling years of trench warfare, Germany finally conceded defeat, it lost some territory and was forced to disarm, but it remained one state through the Weimar Republic and Hitler's Third Reich. Only after World War II did Germany once again suffer division—into two separate states. But as we shall see, West Germany, the FRG, mindful of the harm done by Germany's past imperial ambitions, established itself as a federation of states, carefully balancing centralized power with the rights of separate state governments.

Authoritarianism versus Democracy

Germany has a long tradition of authoritarian rule and a much newer commitment to democracy. Monarchs with absolute power ruled Germany at least from the time of Charlemagne, and the most successful joined absolutism with empire, a strong military, and especially in the modern period, an efficient bureaucracy, which the monarch tried to keep subordinate. But in the nineteenth century, absolutism came under attack in Germany, from liberals influenced first by the French Revolution and later by German socialism.

During the time of the German Confederation some aristocrats, influenced by liberal thought, joined with officials of the bureaucracy to press Metternich for reforms like a constitution, parliamentary government, guarantees of civil liberties, and market freedoms. The French Revolution of 1830 inspired further efforts, and liberals, allied with artisans and peasants actually seized power briefly in the German Revolution of 1848. They succeeded in establishing a constitutional monarchy in the form of a federation of states. But the alliance among middle-class liberals and artisans and peasants soon broke down, because the latter two groups wanted more radical reform. Then conservatives seized their chance to restore monarchical absolutism.

It was Bismarck who healed the split between liberals and monarchists by dividing power between the king and parliament in such a way as finally to favor the king. His strategy of attracting the support of liberals through a policy of militarism and imperialism was to prove surprisingly durable, from the 1870s, straight up to World War I, and then, of course, in Hitler's Germany as well. Germans were continually attracted to the idea of military strength used to conquer an empire under the leadership of a heroic, absolute ruler.

One interlude in German history built democratic institutions. Germany's military defeat in World War I was accompanied by workers' revolts all over the country which deposed monarchies and replaced them with revolutionary councils. In Berlin, the Social Democratic Party in the Reichstag proclaimed a federal republic, instituted a parliament, drafted a constitution with universal suffrage, and elected a president. The new republic was the Weimar Republic, named in reference to the birthplace of Germany's beloved poet Goethe, who symbolized German humanism, in contrast to Prussian despotism and militarism. But despite its democratic values, the Weimar Republic left the door open to authoritarianism. Bowing to German tradition, the republic created a strong president, elected for seven years with extensive powers. When communists put down an antidemocratic coup, Social Democrats allied themselves with the military to suppress the Communists. This opened the way to extremism on both right and left and prepared the way for Hitler's rise in the desperate times of the depression of 1929–1933.

Once in power, Hitler established an extreme authoritarian dictatorship, arresting liberal, socialist, and communist critics, and putting all independent institutions under Nazi control. The secret police, special courts, and concentration camps were used to crush all opposition. State governments were replaced by appointed governors, trade unions were abolished, and other political parties were disbanded. Hitler appointed himself *führer* of the Third Reich. Nazi propaganda glorified the authoritarian state, the heroic leader and military power. Military might was used for conquest, adding *lebensraum* (living space) to the new German empire, and for a racist genocide against the Jews, at least 6 million of whom were slaughtered in the Nazi holocaust.

After the Nazi defeat, the Federal Republic was founded as a democracy, consciously building on the legacy of Weimar democracy. East Germany, while formally adopting democratic institutions, actually became another authoritarian regime.

Welfare Capitalism versus Socialism

Germany experienced a late and rapid industrialization during the final quarter of the nineteenth century. Primarily agricultural in 1875, by 1900 Germany employed more people in industry and mining than in farming. It became the biggest industrial power in Europe. Germans flocked to industrial cities and towns and population grew by 50 percent. Germany specialized in heavy industry: coal mining, iron production, and manufacture of chemicals and electrical equipment. Laboring under the oppressive conditions of early capitalism, industrial workers were attracted to Germany's tradition of Marxist socialism.

Marx wrote the COMMUNIST MANIFESTO in time for the Revolution of 1848. Characteristically, for Germany, it fused a demand for popular democracy with the call for socialism. In authoritarian Germany, these two goals were joined: working people wanted the right to form trade unions, the right to political representation, and the power to control industry themselves. When the 1848 revolution was crushed, more than a million German republicans left their country for the United States. Others remained to form many democratic and socialist opposition parties, including the forerunner of today's Social Democratic Party.

Fear of socialism motivated every German government of the late nineteenth and early twentieth centuries. Bismarck, always the clever politician, succeeded both in repressing socialism and in co-opting it: he outlawed all Social Democratic organizations and trade unions, while at the same time attracting Social Democratic support by instituting comprehensive social insurance to protect workers against the cost of illness, accident, old age, and disability.

Later governments were more obvious in their opposition to socialism. After Bismarck the German monarchy pursued militaristic nationalism and overseas colonies to distract the public from social reform. Even the Weimar government, though founded with the help of revolutionaries and Social Democrats, became so fearful of Socialists and Communists that its president Hindenburg appointed Hitler chancellor rather than seek Social Democratic support. After World War II, Germany faced the future with a strong socialist tradition, an equally enduring history of opposition to socialism, and a culture that, since Bismarck, had assumed social welfare to be the government's business.

East and West Germans are united by their common history. They all understand Germany's historic conflicts over centralism, authoritarianism, and socialism. Germans are also united by a common culture inherited from their shared past.

GERMAN CULTURE: CONTINUITY AND CHANGE

Because Germany was for so long divided into separate monarchies, there are still regional variations in customs and identity. The cultures of Prussia (in the north) and Bavaria (in the south) are distinct. Nevertheless, we can easily single out certain enduring values and norms in German culture. Germans have long been known for their love of order, their respect for authority, their seriousness, hard work, and social responsibility. These values still animate Germans today in both the former GDR and the FRG.

Order

Germans prefer order in all aspects of their lives. Norms require promptness, tidiness and cleanliness, careful conformity to the law, and a proper formality in relating to others. West German managers keep to careful schedules and they prefer to do only one thing at a time. If you have a business appointment with a German executive you must get right down to business, because when your time is up, the manager will become impatient and soon send you on your way (Hall and Hall, pp. 35, 53, 83–84). Social small talk will not be appreciated. If you are late to a job interview, there is no way you can get the job, and if you are late to dinner, your hosts will be insulted and annoyed. Stores close at 6:30 on weekdays and at noon on Saturdays (and are closed all day Sunday) so people are expected to be very well organized to get their shopping done in time. You can't run over and borrow a cup of sugar or a snow shovel from your neighbors either, because it would be shameful to admit to running out of anything (Hall and Hall, p. 39).

Germans also carefully order the space around them. Spending the day at the beach, West German families pile up sand as high as 4 feet in a wall around their blankets, defining their own private territories (Gannon, p. 75). In a business, the offices of different departments are separated by closed doors and the department chief carefully closes the door of his private office. It would be very rude to pick up or move a chair in someone's home or office in order to make yourself more comfortable (Hall and Hall, pp. 40–41). In a German hotel, the maid arranges a foreigner's jumbled shoes in a neat row and lines up the toothbrushes.

Obedience

Germans have long seen it as their duty to obey the law and to submit to the authorities—government officials, bureaucrats, police officers, and judges who make and enforce the laws. The famous German philosopher Immanuel Kant (1724–1804) once wrote, "The characteristics of a child must include, above all, obedience. This obedience may be obtained by force—then it is absolute; or by confidence—then it is voluntary. The latter is important, but the former is an absolute necessity because it prepares the child for adherence to the laws he will have to obey as a future citizen, whether he likes them or not" (quoted in Ardagh, pp. 518–519).

Ordinary Germans believe it is their duty to correct anyone they see disobeying the law. They don't hesitate to reproach strangers. On West German buses, people deposit their fares in a box on the "honor system" and an unknowing stranger who fails to put in the money will be hissed by all the passengers on the bus. Neighborhoods have informal rules about when and where you can wash your car, or hang out the laundry, or put out the trash, and people will reproach a neighbor whose windows are unwashed or whose lawn grows too high (Hall and Hall, p. 47).

Germans cross only when the light is green and let their dogs off the leash only in specially marked areas. In East Germany people also corrected each other's behavior. Factories had special workers' committees that acted like courts. They could find their coworkers or make then apologize in cases of fights or petty theft or damage to factory property. Unions also disciplined their members. A worker who failed to show up on a weekend to clean up the union vacation camp would find a reproachful letter posted on the lounge bulletin board Monday morning.

While many other cultures rely on informal understandings, Germans like to make all the rules explicit. It is typically German to make thousands of detailed laws and regulations which people carefully obey to the letter. In each German state detailed laws specify how schools should operate: from the marking system to the types of punishments permitted. Businesses must conform with endless and growing legal regulations: health and safety laws, laws regulating competition, and laws specifying the structure of corporate boards and their membership.

Ulrich and Helga, after living together for a year, have decided to marry. Tonight they are sitting over glasses of wine with their friend Otto, a lawyer, to draw up a prenuptial agreement. "We agree to share domestic tasks equally," the document reads. "We will take turns in cooking, cleaning, and dishwashing, laundry, grocery shopping, and bill paying. We each agree to contribute 10 percent of our salaries monthly toward a fund for buying a house, to retain 10 percent for private use, and to place the rest in a joint bank account. We agree that each of us shall have the right to go out alone with male or female friends, but we pledge ourselves to sexual fidelity. We agree that if we have a child, Helga will stay at home for six years and, during that time, Ulrich will support her and the child." Ulrich, Helga, and Otto see nothing unusual about this document. All their married friends have done something similar and they believe it is good to discuss all these matters explicitly and reach a formal agreement.

The Authoritarian Personality

Why are Germans so obedient and respectful of authority? One German sociologist who addressed this question was Theodor Adorno, whose famous book, THE AUTHORITARIAN PERSONALITY (Adorno et al., 1950) was based on research done in the United States in the 1940s after he fled Nazi Germany. Adorno later returned to Germany where he became one of the founders of the famous "Frankfurt School" of sociology.

Adorno used survey research to question subjects about their attitudes toward Jews and other minority groups, authoritarian government, and cultures different from their own. His findings showed that people who were anti-Semitic tended to be prejudiced toward other minorities as well; they tended to approve of authoritarian leadership and to display ethnocentrism toward other cultures. They were rigid conformists to social norms, were anti-intellectual and antiscientific and were disturbed by religious, moral, or sexual ambiguity. Adorna said that these traits formed a personality type he called **the authoritarian personality,** and he suggested that it resulted from childhood socialization by parents who were rigid disciplinarians and openly showed little love. This sort of upbringing produced anxious, angry adults who looked for scapegoats for their hostility. Adorno's work inspired thousands of subsequent works of research and critique and influenced the way sociologists think about authoritarian societies and social movements—in Germany and elsewhere.

Questioning Authority

Since World War II, Germans have worried about the dangers in their traditional respect for authority. In Hitler's time, people treated Nazi troops with respect, as they paraded and drilled in their smart uniforms. After World War II, many Germans said that they had been "just obeying orders" when they massacred civilians and sent Jews off to concentration camps. If that was the result of obedience, West Germans reasoned, they were going to have to educate their children to resist authority and make their own moral choices. Nowadays, German school exams ask questions like "Discuss the problem of how an individual is to behave in a state based on false norms" (Buruma, pp. 183–184). Germans of the postwar generations have indeed shown less deference to state authority. Students of the rebel "Generation of '68" challenged the state with demonstrations, acts of terrorism, and the creation of a hippie counterculture which has thrived ever since in West Berlin. Today's young people in both West and East are attracted to Germany's active peace movements and to the environmental movement and its political party, the "Greens."

The German culture of obedience also supported the Soviet-installed regime in East Germany. People certainly didn't welcome the Communist government, but with rare exceptions (like the rebellion of 1953) they passively went along. As the years went by, however, the irrationalities of the East German economy made unquestioning obedience impossible. People had to "work the system" in order to get by. For example, if you ordered parts to fix your car in the proper way, you could wait years for them, but West German money earned illegally and spent on the black market could get what you needed right away. East Germans were schooled in petty disobedience to authority and in contempt for authority. One cynical saying went, "We pretend to work and they (the government) pretend to pay us."

Seriousness

Germans take life seriously. They are very concerned with ideas and principles and they insist on things being done right. Many observers have characterized German culture as "intellectual." West German TV features many earnest discussion programs in which people sit at round tables and solemnly debate current issues. The TV audience sits before them at smaller tables, sipping drinks and listening attentively (Buruma, p. 23). Germans are idealistic. They want to find the right principles and follow them, no matter what.

In the nineteenth century, Germany was a breeding ground for trade unionism and socialism, developing a tradition of working-class organization and an analysis of class conflict expressed most influentially by Karl Marx. German dedication to improving the condition of working people influenced societies all over the world, and particularly the United States, where many German immigrants became involved in the antislavery movement, and the trade union and socialist movements. As immigrants in America, they fought successfully for higher wages, shorter hours, limits on child labor, safer working conditions, and recognition of contracts with labor unions.

Dedication to principle has had some admirable results, but some ghastly ones too. German fascination with absolute principles facilitated Nazism. People were willing to accept a simple principle—"Aryan supremacy"—that explained everything in life and told them what to do, and they closed their eyes to its immoral consequences. But you mustn't forget that German conscientiousness also underlay resistance to Hitler by some German aristocrats, Catholics, and Communists.

> *Hermann Schnabel is a seventeen-year veteran of the Hamburg police force, recently promoted to detective. He has been assigned to track down foreigners who have overstayed their visas and are now in Germany illegally. One day Hermann is called by an angry landlord to a shabby walk-up apartment building on the industrial outskirts of the city. "That woman up there never pays her rent on time, and she looks so foreign and her apartment smells funny; I want you to investigate," the landlord demands. Climbing up to the top floor, Hermann finds a terrified woman who falls weeping at his feet. "Please don't arrest me," she pleads, "it's not for me, but for my daughter. If you send us home my relatives will circumcize her. Do you know what that means? I can't let her be mutilated like that." Hermann does know what it means. He has heard this story before. And this is on top of yesterday's encounter with an Algerian journalist who wrote an exposé of a fundamentalist militia. If he is sent home, the militia will hunt him down and kill him. Mumbling with embarrassment, Hermann takes a 20-mark bill out of his wallet and gives it to the woman, then flees.*
>
> *Trudging back to the station house, Hermann feels anguished and torn. "It's my assignment," says one side of his mind; "it's my duty." "I can't do this," says another side. "I can hear my history teacher telling us, 'Germans must never simply acquiesce in persecution again.'" "How can I send foreigners home to be killed or mutilated?" Back at the station house, Hermann drags himself into his captain's office. "I can't do this," he says. "I want to resign from the illegal alien detail. Please, can you transfer me to another duty?" "Well Hermann, I'm not surprised," says the captain. "You're the third officer in the last four months to ask for transfer off this duty. Maybe I'll ask for a transfer too."*

Taking Responsibility

In the aftermath of World War II, Germans hastened to forget the horrors of Nazism. But in the late 1960s, a new generation of young West Germans insisted on confronting the public with the truth about Nazi crimes. Germans began a serious national self-examination of their guilt, a process of *Trauerarbeit,* as they call it (the work of mourning) that continues to this day (Buruma, p. 21). Schools made study of the Holocaust a required part of the curriculum. In West Berlin in recent years, it has been fashionable for young German couples to give their children conspicuously Jewish names like Sarah and Abraham, and the only Jewish day school is oversubscribed with applicants—all non-Jews!

Government policy reflects Germans' fear of repeating the past. The West German constitution grants draftees the right to refuse to fight on grounds of conscience (Buruma, pp. 24–25). West Germany has also made it state policy to welcome refugees from political persecution, despite Germans' discomfort with foreigners. And West Germany has maintained a careful tolerance of free speech, despite distaste for nonconformists. Many analysts see West Germans as very torn in their response to today's neo-Nazis, their wish to squelch all stirrings of Nazism warring with their commitment to free speech.

In East Germany, the 1960s self-examination of war guilt never happened. After the war, the East German regime removed former Nazis from all levels of government and industry (much more thoroughly than this was done in the West). More than 90 percent of all schoolteachers were fired and most former Nazis in high places were removed from power. Thousands were tried and jailed and 500 executed. Then the government declared, all the guilty have been punished and East Germans no longer have to bear a burden of guilt for the war. Furthermore, East Germans were told Nazism had been an inevitable outgrowth of capitalism. The Socialists and Communists now in power had been steadfast opponents of Nazism, so the East German regime was innocent of responsibility for the past. East German children, it was said, were all "children of the resistance." But different as they were in their response to Nazism, West Germans and East Germans were similar in their earnest, conscientious belief in guilt on the one hand and in innocence and the superiority of socialism on the other (Buruma, pp. 156, 178, 181).

Though they differed in their response to the Nazi past, East and West Germany shared a common belief about social responsibility in the present: both believed that societies have an obligation to protect their members who are weak or sick or disadvantaged or dependent. Both East and West Germany continued the German **welfare state** begun by Chancellor Otto von Bismarck in the 1880s, providing free medical care, old-age pensions, unemployment and welfare benefits, child care, company-subsidized vacations, and so forth. West Germans today will tell you that social welfare benefits support the social peace and relieve class tensions. Though their taxes are high, they believe the benefits are worth it.

Working Carefully

Dedication to work is another aspect of German seriousness. Germans are renowned for their hard work and efficiency and their "insistence on precision." Germany has long excelled in industries that produce quality goods to exacting standards, like machine tools, cars, cameras, arms, and small appliances. Cars like Mercedes Benz are built to be driven for hours on the German *autobahnnen* (highways) at speeds over 100 miles an hour. German businesses, even retail stores, don't employ casual workers or part-time workers. They want only employees who are thoroughly trained, usually in two- to three-year apprenticeships that teach every detail of the business and stress the importance of "precision, cleanliness, and order." Business managers are slow to reach decisions, because they require a great deal of very detailed technical information. Slide presentations, reams of data, long histories of background events, are all carefully attended to and digested (Lewis, p. 375; Hamilton, p. 58).

The Protestant Ethic

In his 1904 work, THE PROTESTANT ETHIC AND THE SPIRIT OF CAPITALISM, Max Weber addressed the question of why Germans are so serious and hard-working. Weber was actually working on an even more difficult question: how beliefs and values can shape social institutions and social change. He argued that the beliefs of German Protestantism, specifically Calvinism, influenced adherents' behavior and supported the development of capitalism. Calvinist norms and values, which Weber called "the Protestant ethic" required steady, conscientious work and frugality. Calvinists believed in "predestination," the idea that before birth each person was already destined for heaven or hell and their fate could not be changed. On earth, all they could do was work for God's glory. But these beliefs caused great anxiety and Calvinists began to search for signs of salvation. They began to take success in this world as a sign of salvation in the next, so they were motivated to work very hard and to save and reinvest their profits, avoiding indulgence in sinful pleasure.

Divergent Values in East and West

Though East and West Germany had much in common, during the forty-five years of their separation their cultures diverged. After all, the two societies were completely isolated from each other, divided by an armed border. East Germans were not allowed to cross the border, and West Germans could do so only with difficulty. For several decades even phone calls across the border were blocked. In the West, German culture was shaped by consumer capitalism and in the East it was changed by socialism.

West German Consumerism

West Germany became one of the world's most affluent societies. Yearly per person income was $23,030 in 1992, putting the West Germans behind only Japan, Sweden, and the United States in international income comparisons. In West Germany smooth, carefully engineered highways are filled with Mercedes Benzes, BMWs, Audis, and Porsches, zooming along at 100 miles per hour. Modern high-speed trains connect cities filled with upscale shopping districts and malls, sleek apartment towers, and new housing estates. Landmark buildings destroyed in World War II have been perfectly rebuilt or restored. Few neighborhoods in West German cities are old or crumbling, dirty or neglected. If you go to West Germany you cannot help but notice that this is a rich society. (See Table 5.1.)

TABLE 5.1. Measures of Affluence: In rich societies like Germany and Japan, people have higher incomes and own more cars and TVs than in poor societies like Mexico and Egypt.

	Gross National Product per Capita (Income per Person in U.S. $), 1992	Television Sets per 100 People, 1990	Passenger Cars and Other Motor Vehicles per 100 People, 1991
Germany	23,030	57*	41
Japan	28,190	62	45
United States	23,240	81	74
Mexico	3,470	15	11
Egypt	640	11	3

*Data are for West Germany only.

Sources: World Bank, *World Development Report 1994: Infrastructure for Development.* New York: Oxford University Press, 1994.

Helmut Schmidt, leader of the Social Democratic Party, is pictured in this publicity photo as a typical middle-class west German, enjoying a private lunch with his family in his very carefully tended garden behind his substantial stone house.

The Value of Possessions. In West Germany, people are busy making money and spending it. They have many labor-saving devices but are always in a hurry. Meetings with friends are carefully scheduled on busy calendars. In many regions, the simplest single-family house costs $300,000 and people spend heavily on luxury furnishings: leather couches, oriental rugs, and original paintings. Designer clothes and upscale cars and trendy sports equipment are the means to declaring one's status and expressing an individual identity. *Luxus* (luxury) and leisure are key words in West Germany today (Rademaekers, pp. 9–10). West Germans invest a great deal of money and time in their homes and they enjoy their possessions in privacy.

The Value of Leisure. In recent decades, West Germans have moved away from the traditional German dedication to work. They have devoted themselves less to duty and more to pleasure. West Germans now have the highest wages, the shortest work week, and the most holidays of any industrialized nation. They work an average of thirty-seven hours per week, compared to forty-one in the United States, and over sixty in Japan. Plus, they get six weeks of paid vacation, with an extra month's pay at vacation time, a Christmas bonus, and noncash benefits equal in value to 80 percent of their take-home pay (Glouchevitch, pp. 112–113). Employers complain that workers are so focused on their weekend plans that no real work is done after noon on Fridays. On their long vacations, West Germans are dedicated travelers, filling the beaches of the Greek islands, Miami, and Cuba during the winter months and seeking the latest tropical resorts on remote Asian islands. Travel agents do a booming business in tour packages.

The Value of Individualism. West Germany is an **individualistic** society: people see themselves as individuals, autonomous actors, free to join groups or remain separate. They value their privacy and their right to speak as individuals. Businesses and politicians address citizens through advertising and the mass media, but people are expected to make individual decisions and act on the basis of their own needs and judgments. In West Germany it is not unusual or deviant behavior to belong to no group beyond the family, friendship circles, and a rather formal work group membership. Few West Germans do volunteer work with the elderly or any other needy group.

John Ardagh vividly describes West Germans' sense of their separateness as individuals and their distance from the rest of society. For example, at a West German health club an elderly person needing help or a mother who needs someone to watch her child for a moment would not turn to other club members. If asked, their response would be "That's not my business—the officials (staff) are paid for that." The West German welfare state provides generous support for people who are handicapped, disabled, addicted, or ex-prisoners. This is perhaps fortunate, since individual West Germans try to avoid such people and feel no obligation to help them. No one describes West German individualism more clearly than an old East Berlin couple, interviewed by THE NEW YORK TIMES after reunification: "In the old East Germany people were closer. . . . We helped each other," they said, "In the west, people say this is my space, it is separate from you, and do not disturb my space" (Ardagh, pp. 526, 527–528; Cohen, p. D3).

East German Socialism

In the East consumer goods were drab and sometimes in short supply. Housing was cheaply built and often in disrepair. People had to take their vacation in East Germany or in nearby Soviet-bloc nations. Life moved slowly; people spent hours waiting in line in stores and for buses, but everyone seemed to have lots of time; time to go visiting, take coffee breaks, chat with a neighbor, or cheer up people at the old-age home (Darnton, pp. 297–309).

When Peter Marcuse visited the two Germanys in 1989, just before the Wall came down, he called the two countries, "the society of the elbows" and "the society of the coffee breaks." In West Germany he thought that people were always elbowing each other out of the way in their hurry to get to the cashier or on the plane. In East Germany he was amazed to find that all work at his office stopped every day at 10 A.M. sharp. The secretaries cleared off a table, laid a cloth and dishes, and put up the kettle, and everyone in the office came in and had coffee and cake and chatted together. No one answered the phones and appointments waited (Marcuse, p. 43). East German customs reflected distinctive values, different from those in the West.

The Value of Labor. Socialist theory holds that workers are the most important part of any economy, because their labor produces the goods on which wealth is based. Capitalists are really parasites who feed on workers, because they take their profits out of what workers produce. In East Germany there were no capitalists—no businesspeople, no entrepreneurs. To make a profit, or charge interest was seen as profoundly immoral. Socialist East Germany taught respect for labor. Each elementary school class was paired with a factory unit where they visited and helped out and got to know individual workers. Classes planted gardens and learned to use machinery. The East German government tried to give heroic workers as much publicity as entrepreneurs like Donald Trump received in the United States. The only problem was that people were aware that workers in East Germany didn't live as well as workers in capitalist West Germany.

Because they valued labor so highly, East Germans believed that people's jobs should be productive and satisfying, not mindless or debasing the way labor so often was in capitalist societies. This ideal came from the writing of Karl Marx. But East Germans frequently complained about their society for its failure to provide satisfying work. Shortages of supplies, or mixups in deliveries often shut down production, and because materials were of poor quality the goods produced were often shoddy. Everyone was employed, but there really wasn't enough work for everyone, so many people were working way below their capacities. These problems bothered people, because they really believed in the value of work.

The Value of Equality. Egalitarianism was a very strong value in East Germany. If ordinary working people are the real source of wealth, then it makes sense for everyone to be paid what workers are paid; no one deserves any more. East German society was strongly committed to providing necessities for all. Everyone had a job; there was no unemployment. Housing was very cheap, though its quality was poor. There was no homelessness. Basic foods like bread and cheese and beer were cheap. Health care was free, education was free, old people received pensions, and preschool day care was available to all. But luxuries were distrusted. The only car for sale was the sputtering, smelly Trabant; clothing was all cheap and styleless. **Conspicuous consumption,** acquiring possessions as signs of wealth and status, was condemned. In fact, a key event in undermining the East German regime after the fall of the Soviet Union was a series of revelations about the privileges of the ruling Communist Party elite. When East Germans learned that the party chief's wife traveled to Paris every month to get her hair cut, and that the party leadership lived in luxury homes in guarded compounds and drove Mercedes Benz cars, they were furious.

The Value of Collectivism. An important part of socialist culture in East Germany was belief in the virtues of group participation and distrust of individualism. People were expected to involve themselves in **collectives** (organized groups): to join youth organizations, women's organizations, the Communist Party; to attend meetings at their office or factory. Individualism was suppressed. If you avoided joining group life, and insisted on setting yourself apart, that was seen as "antisocial" and it was actually a legal offense.

East German **collectivism** was at one and the same time resented and absorbed. The coffee break Peter Marcuse observed was a benign aspect of East German collectivism. People did really become very involved with their coworkers socially and emotionally. They depended on friends and workmates for mutual aid, much more so than in the West. Friends helped each other find scarce goods and cope with bureaucracy. Typical friendship groups of perhaps two dozen people often linked individuals with very varied occupations, from doctors to auto mechanics, who all had contacts or skills to share with the group. But oddly enough, these warm, close-knit groups which exemplified the value of collectivism were in their own way a form of retreat from the demands of official socialism. East Germans called it "niche society" *(Nischengesellschaft)* and it was seen as a passive protest against the regime. Friendship groups were a substitute for official party organizations like the youth and women's groups that the government insisted people join. These groups were disliked and they disappeared immediately after reunification.

SOCIAL INSTITUTIONS OF THE TWO GERMANYS

In some ways the two Germanys were very similar: both were modern industrial societies with specialized social institutions. If you were a ¡Kung Bushman visiting Germany, you would probably notice little difference between the East and the West; the contrast with your own small-scale hunting and gathering society would be overwhelming. In both Germanys large-scale formal organizations—businesses, collective farms, parliaments, political parties, trade unions, management boards, planning boards, universities, armies, government ministries, and so forth—were critical to the functioning of society.

Bureaucracy

Max Weber, the most famous German sociologist of the early twentieth century, saw **bureaucracy** as the defining feature of modern industrial societies. As a person living in a modern society, you certainly have a feeling for what bureaucracy is. Weber saw bureaucracy as the essence of the **rationalization** of society that comes with modernization, when formal rules and procedures for attaining specific goals are substituted for traditional or spontaneous forms of social relations.

In addition to formal rules, Weber saw some other special features in bureaucracies: people perform specialized jobs, and they are ranked in a hierarchy, so they take orders from superiors. Employees can make a career of work in a bureaucracy, climbing the levels of the hierarchy. Bureaucracies are also impersonal. They treat people as cases, not individuals, and they place great emphasis on careful record keeping. Weber argued that though it has definite drawbacks, bureaucracy is the most effective way to organize large numbers of people to serve practical, well-defined goals. He expected that whatever its political and economic system, any modern society would require bureaucracy (Gerth and Mills, pp. 196–216). Like Weber, we can certainly see bureaucracy well-illustrated in Germany. It is clear that German culture, with its stress on obeying authority and following the rules, is quite supportive of bureaucratic organizations. German bureaucrats take their jobs seriously and people trust them not be capricious.

Katerina Wolf is a certified social worker in the office of Immigration Services in Berlin. Her department handles the cases of Ausseidler (ethnic German "resettlers") from lands that were once German, but were taken by the Soviet Union after Germany's defeat in World War II. Germany has a policy of accepting as a citizen anyone who is of German ancestry. Since the fall of the Soviet Union, three-quarters of a million Soviet Germans have applied.

Today, Stefan Z., an ethnic German who comes from East Prussia, has come to consult about his case. Katerina is looking down, studying his file while he sits down. When she looks up, she is stunned. He is the most handsome young man she has ever seen. Despite his accent, he has a beautiful voice and a winning smile; she can hardly focus on what he is saying. When she finally concentrates she understands two things: he is asking her out to coffee and he is asking her to speed up the process of getting state aid for an apartment. "But you're not even close to the top of the list," she exclaims in surprise; "there are many people before you." "Please, it's not for me," he begs, "my parents—they are old, sick—we have only a tiny room; it's not well-heated—they suffered for many years." "Just look at their papers," he pleads, un-folding a worn packet of letters from dissidents in the Soviet Union, Lutheran ministers, and even a TV personality. Folded between the pages is a 100-mark note. Katerina gasps. Forcing herself to respond, she shoves the papers toward Stefan and in a voice choked with anger she says, "You cannot do this—others are in need also. You are a German now; you must follow the rules—everyone does. This is not the East; not Russia!" Astonished at his rebuff, Stefan rises in awkward silence and moves toward the door. Katerina's eyes follow him; then she stares dumbly at the door until her supervisor approaches with a questioning look.

The Capitalist Economy in West Germany

In 1945, Germany lay in ruins after its surrender. The people were starving, the cities were smoldering rubbish heaps, about half the factories were destroyed, and roads and railroads were torn up by the bombing. Inflation made the German currency worthless, so people who had food or anything else of value refused to sell it. Germans call this time *die Stunde Null,* zero hour, the lowest point, which had to be a new beginning. But in capitalist West Germany, once rebuilding began, production grew with astonishing rapidity. They called it "the German economic miracle." People once again had enough food and clothing and shoes. Millions of houses were built and cities were reconstructed. By the 1950s, West Germany had achieved full employment and it exported more goods than any other country except the United States (Turner, pp. 59–62). By the 1980s, West Germany had become one of the world's richest countries, in the same league with the United States and Japan. You can learn about the basic features of capitalism—private property, competition for profits, and market forces—by studying West Germany.

Private Ownership

In Germany, businesses are almost all privately owned and they compete in their efforts to make profits. This makes the economy very dynamic. You may be surprised to learn that Karl Marx was one of the first to recognize the productivity of capitalism. In his 1848 COMMUNIST MANIFESTO Marx wrote: "The bourgeoisie (that is, the class of capitalists) during its rule of scarce one hundred years, has created more massive and more colossal productive forces than have all preceding generations together" (Marx, pp. 13–14).

Many West German businesses are corporations. They have no single owner; rather, shareholders have the right to vote on company decisions and the company is legally headed by boards of directors and run by managers appointed by the boards. German manufacturing companies are famous all over the world and some of their names may be familiar to you. Cars are produced by Daimler-Benz, BMW, Volkswagen, and Porsche. There are major chemical companies like Bayer, and electrical manufacturing companies like Siemens. Big banks like Deutsche Bank are also privately owned.

West Germany also has an unusually large number of middle-sized businesses (called the *Mittelstand*) which often are owned and managed by single individuals or families. These companies account for half of all West German production, employ two-thirds of all workers, and produce two-thirds of all exports. Many produce precision parts, like machine tools, parts for cars, and laser cutters. Farms are also privately owned. Most are very small (averaging about 35 acres) and they are owned by the families that work them. Less than 1 percent of the farms are larger than 120 acres (Glouchevitch, pp. 57, 63; Nyrop, pp. 182–184).

The Profit Motive and Competition

Like other capitalists, the owners and managers of West German firms are in business to make money. They try their best to maximize the profits of their enterprises in order to increase their own wealth and prestige. In search of profits, they try to produce and sell more, to produce more cheaply, to develop new products that customers will want to buy, and to find new customers for their products. In an economy based on the **profit motive,** businesses find themselves in **competition** with each other, for customers, and for the best workers and suppliers.

For example, in the 1960s, Volkswagen did fabulously well selling budget-model VW "Beetles" to buyers all over Europe and America. But as buyers became more affluent they abandoned the Beetle for more luxurious cars, made by other German and non-German manufacturers. VW profits fell and the company might even have gone out of business had it not designed several new, fancier cars and vans. Today, German makers of luxury cars like Mercedes Benz and BMW build cars with such precision that they can be driven at speeds exceeding 200 miles per hour. Buyers seem to want their cars to have that capability, and German companies are successful in international competition because they can deliver it.

German firms also compete for capable workers, and workers compete for the best jobs. The most profitable companies are able to provide very fine apprenticeship programs that lead to well-paid jobs and opportunities for promotion. Many German high school students choose apprenticeship rather than university, and the programs run by big companies are considered very desirable. Students must compete for admission and companies have their pick of students with the best grades and recommendations, and the best presentation at interviews.

Market Forces

Capitalist economies are sometimes called **free-market systems** because, in theory at least, the interaction of supply and demand determines how much is produced, and by whom, and at what price it is sold. Adam Smith, the first theoretician of capitalist economies said that the market acts like an "invisible hand," directing workers to this firm, or capital investments to that firm. Smith was amazed at how smoothly the market worked, weeding out the inefficient and the overpriced, encouraging innovation, and giving the buyers what they demanded.

German-Style Capitalism

West Germany built one of the world's most successful capitalist economies, but it built in characteristically German style. German capitalism is different from Japanese capitalism and different from American capitalism. The particular nature of German capitalism is consistent with German culture and values.

When West Germany was established in 1949, the British and American forces wanted it to become like Adam Smith's ideal capitalist society: an economy of many small producers, all competing feverishly, and all subject to the operation of market forces, without government interference. Today this ideal is often called **laissez-faire capitalism.** But as soon as the West Germans began running their own government they set about controlling and limiting the operation of free-market forces. For competition among thousands of tiny firms, they have substituted government regulation, **oligopoly,** and labor-management cooperation.

Valuing order and social responsibility, Germans find the workings of free-market forces unacceptably cruel and disorderly. In unregulated competition, some companies become so successful that they drive out all others, becoming monopolies and destroying competition itself. Also, unregulated market economies often exhibit strong **business cycles,** periods of boom when profits rise, businesses grow, and more workers are hired, followed by terrible depressions when companies go bankrupt and many workers are unemployed. Workers may be forced to accept very low wages and bad working conditions, just to have a job. Even business owners in Germany want the government to step in to control free-market competition. For example, the head of the 100,000 member German Retail Trade Association recently explained why business owners are pleased with government restriction of business hours: "Germans need rules and regulations, and want a well-ordered, harmonious society, not the law of the jungle" (Whitney, Jan. 16, 1995, p. A6).

Government Regulation

Germans agree that it is right for the government to set the rules for business and use its power to make sure the economy works well. Complex laws regulate business practices, the use and disposal of toxic materials, the kinds of packages permitted on products, work conditions in factories and offices, how businesses should bargain with unions, and how corporate management should be structured. While Germans sometimes complain about the difficulty of complying with so many regulations, they think that their society is better off because of the role government plays in the economy.

The West German government also uses its resources to steer the economy. The government makes plans for economic development (sometimes in coordination with industrial associations) and it gets business to do what it wants by using incentives. Tax breaks spur capital investment and are used to target investment in vital industries. Subsidies and tariffs protect small farmers against competition from large commercial farms (Nyrop, pp. 218–220). The most important way the West German government intervenes in the economy is by providing benefits to workers to guarantee their security (see p. 243, The Welfare State).

Another form of government intervention in a capitalist economy is government ownership of enterprises. There is some government-owned business in Germany—about the same amount as in Sweden or pre-Thatcher Britain—most notably monopolies over telephones, railroads, airlines, and the post office. Germans believe that government ownership of such essential industries works in the public interest, for example, by allowing the government to subsidize rail fares so rural communities are not cut off from transportation (Dalton, pp. 326–328).

Oligopoly

West Germany allows a good deal of **oligopoly** (situations in which a few very large firms dominate an industry), again for the purpose of making its capitalist economy more orderly and controlled. The firms in oligopolies can get together to control market forces instead of being at their mercy. Soon after the end of the war, the coal mines of the Ruhr region, backbone of German industry, reorganized into a single corporation. Later, thirty-one steel companies formed four **cartels,** organizations whose members agree on a single set of prices, eliminating competition which might drive down prices and cut into profits (Nyrop, pp. 203–204). The same thing happened in the electrical industry and in banking.

Today, Germany's biggest businesses and banks have **interlocking directorates.** They hold shares of each other's stock and bank representatives and directors of large companies sit on each other's supervisory boards. Through these connections they are able to cooperate with each other instead of competing. German companies also form industrial associations, in which the biggest companies lead others in planning investment and research for a whole industry.

Labor-Management Cooperation

German capitalism is distinctive in the emphasis it places on workers' security. In Germany, businesses must be profitable, but maintaining the social peace by recognizing the rights of labor is an equally important value. This is apparent in the organization of firms and in management goals.

Approximately one-third of German workers are union members and almost all of their unions belong to a powerful central federation, the German Trade Union Federation (DBG). Employers and unions run big businesses together in a unique system known as **codetermination.** By law, all big companies have two boards of directors, a management board and a supervisory board. Union representatives must make up half the members on the supervisory boards. The idea that workers should have a say in running the businesses where they are employed goes all the way back to nineteenth-century Marxism. German workers first demanded it in the revolution of 1848, and workers' councils were enacted into law for the first time in 1920 (Glouchevitch, pp. 134–142; Nyrop, pp. 232, 234). You can see that Marx's ideas have had a big influence on West German society as well as on East German society.

Working together, unions and management have become allies in Germany. They join together to advocate increased capital investment by companies, which produces growth and more jobs, and they oppose investors' efforts to pay out company income in profits (Glouchevitch, pp. 106–107, 114). They advocate investment in industries that require skilled, well-paid workers and they avoid creating unskilled, low-wage jobs.

The Socialist Economy in East Germany

Socialism existed as an ideal before any society actually adopted a socialist economy. It was meant to be a new form of modern industrial society that would correct the defects and abuses of industrial capitalism. Now that you know something about capitalism, the logic of socialism will be easier to understand.

In the nineteenth century, Karl Marx was the social thinker most influential in describing and criticizing capitalism and calling for a socialist alternative. Marx was German, but he fled Germany and lived in France and finally England. The capitalism he saw in Europe was a harsh system. Factory workers toiled long hours in unsafe conditions for very low pay. Even young children were employed in factories. Every decade or so there was a financial crisis and a huge economic depression, and millions of workers found themselves without any means of support. The market economy, Marx said, far from being a miraculous system that automatically works for the public good, as Adam Smith claimed, is actually an irrational, ruinous system, in which successful business owners (**capitalists**) get richer and richer by **exploiting** their workers (that is, paying them less than the value of the products of their work). Marx also condemned the **irrationality** of capitalism, which he said produces what is profitable, not what the public needs. Marx expected that once workers knew about socialism, they would revolt against the capitalist system, seize control of their governments, and create worker-states, where working people would run the economy to benefit the public. Marx considered collective ownership, planning, and cooperation the essence of socialism.

The first socialist economy was created in the Soviet Union after the 1917 Bolshevik Revolution. Following World War II, variations of Soviet-style socialism were established in all the Soviet-bloc countries of eastern Europe: East Germany, Poland, Czechoslovakia, Hungary, Yugoslavia, Bulgaria, Romania, and Albania, and in other socialist countries like Cuba and Mozambique. In Asia, China adopted its own socialist system after Mao Zedong's revolutionary forces triumphed in 1949.

Collective Ownership

East Germany's postwar administration established socialism while the country was still occupied by the Soviet army. The first step was **collectivization,** when privately owned farms and businesses were turned into public property. In East Germany, collectivization began with the estates of great landowners (who owned approximately half the farmland). About two-thirds of this land was distributed to small farmers and the rest was organized into large collective farms. The businesses of active Nazis were seized and also certain types of enterprises considered essential, like banks and power utilities. These became "peoples' plants" operated at first by the administration of the Soviet Zone and later by the GDR. Later, many more firms were harassed out of business by taxation and difficulties with government supplies or price controls. By 1952 over three-quarters of industrial workers were employed in state-owned enterprises. Small farmers were also pressured to join collectives (Turner, p. 109). Collectivization continued until, by 1985, 95 percent of agricultural land was farmed by collectives and 98 percent of the labor force was employed in collectivized enterprises, which earned 96 percent of total national income (Burant, pp. 121–122; Ardagh, p. 373).

A Planned Economy

The East German economy was a **planned economy.** Economic decisions were not left to market forces; rather, various planning boards set economic goals and decided what would be produced, and by whom, and how resources would be used and at what prices products would be sold. The government not only planned the economy, it also commanded: it told the various economic institutions and actors what to do. For this reason, some sociologists call socialist economies **command economies.** Ideally, a planned economy would extend political democracy to the economy, because important economic decisions would be made by the people or their representatives, not by the tiny class of capitalists. A planned economy would work for the public good by producing what people really need and deliberately distributing it equally, so everyone would have at least the minimum to live in health and dignity. Congresses of the ruling Communist Party (called the SED) passed successive two-year and then five-year economic plans that decided what the society should invest in, where resources should go, and what trade should be permitted. At first, all efforts were aimed at developing heavy industry, which East Germany had lacked before the war (Turner, pp. 111, 112).

Cooperation, Not Profit Seeking

Socialists in East Germany expected that once collective ownership and a planned economy were created, new relationships among people would develop too. Socialist society would be humane: competition would be replaced by cooperation, individual greed by a spirit of comradeship. People would no longer try to make profits by selling things or by exploiting others; instead they would do work that benefited everyone.

In fact, over the forty years of socialism in East Germany, people did stop thinking in terms of profit. They thought of providing basic goods for everyone, and the idea of persuading people that they needed more and more so that you could sell more and make more money, became foreign to them. When Peter Marcuse visited East Germany in 1989–1990 he talked with a hotel manager about the new private bicycle store down the road. The manager was puzzled: "When everyone has a bike, they won't be able to sell any more," he explained. The capitalist idea of inventing racing bikes, then mountain bikes, then dual-use bikes, and convincing people they needed them was totally beyond him (Marcuse, pp. 263–264).

German-Style Socialism

East German socialism had a lot in common with the socialist systems of other eastern European Soviet satellite states. In large measure this was so because Soviet domination set limits to what institutional variation was allowed. The socialist economy in East Germany was distinctive in that it was heavily industrial, it was run by a huge bureaucracy which was not corrupt, and it was quite productive. Serious, skilled East German workers turned out relatively high-quality goods in great demand throughout the socialist world. The GDR economy was also quite effective in raising the living standards of the poorest East Germans and making all citizens more equal, but this was a socialist goal as well as a German goal.

Productivity

The East German system never aspired to produce luxuries for anyone. Its goals were to achieve material comfort and security for everyone, equally shared, and to build an economy collectively and democratically run by the people. An idealistic East German socialist told John Ardagh that "this society may be far from perfect, but at least we have eliminated real poverty, and that's more than you have done in the West." In terms of output, East Germany's socialist economy made great progress in the early postwar years, rapidly restoring production to prewar levels. This was quite a feat, considering that the East received no aid from the United States and instead had to pay reparations to the Soviet Union. The U.S.S.R. dismantled and took away factories producing 40 percent of East Germany's industrial goods; this was twice the damage done by the war. Also, the Soviets took 25 percent of East Germany's output, without compensation (Ardagh, pp. 371, 373; Turner, pp. 110–111).

Between 1963 and 1973, GDR national income grew at an annual rate of 5 percent and East Germany became the strongest Soviet-bloc economy. Consumer goods like cars, refrigerators, washing machines, and TVs became widely available. Much more housing was built. According to the World Bank, in 1974, per capita income was higher in the GDR than in Britain. But this was the high point of East German production. Thereafter, the oil crisis of the 1970s made it difficult for the GDR to sustain capital investment and production of consumer goods at the same time. Growth and improvement in living standards slowed (Turner, p. 139; Ardagh, p. 372; Steele, p. 7).

Collective Ownership

In East Germany, people took the idea of collective ownership very seriously. But large numbers of people rejected it. Their problems with collective membership revolved around a central issue: when enterprises are "collectively" owned, who really owns and controls them? The people who work in them? All the people? The government? In East Germany, "collective ownership" was really **state ownership** and control. In effect the state owned the means of production in the name of the people and it acted, so it said, in their interests. The East German government really tried to make people feel like members of collectives. In every workplace there were dozens of committees and hundreds of meetings about the "plan," and employees made thousands of suggestions; but in actuality, the "plan" was made at the top levels of the party and orders came down from the top through all the levels of the party, down to each factory department, and everyone knew it.

East Germans themselves had never demanded collective ownership; they never made a socialist revolution. Collectivization was imposed by the Soviet Union, and many people didn't want it. The most common form of opposition was flight to the West by small farmers, small businesspeople, and workers too. By 1961, when the Berlin Wall was built, 2.5 million East Germans (from a total of 19 million in 1948) had fled their country. Many people defied collective ownership in a smaller, less risky way—they worked privately in addition to their regular jobs, doing house building, babysitting, car repair, dressmaking, and so on. This hidden private economy was probably quite large (Ardagh, pp. 390–391). Some East Germans believe their experience demonstrates that socialism is a hopeless failure, impossible to achieve. Others belive a truly democratic socialism might be possible, but that the Soviet Union never permitted East Germany to try it.

Planning and Bureaucracy

East Germany's experience is very interesting, because it shows something about the strengths and weaknesses of bureaucracy. A huge state-planning bureaucracy developed in East Germany. There were factory committees, regional and state planning boards, *Kombinaten,* the huge combines of factories, with their production quotas, joint prices, and distribution outlets. German-style, bureaucrats took their jobs relatively seriously. They were not open to bribery and they didn't use their power to favor their relatives. They behaved like good bureaucrats, systematically and rationally advancing the goals of their organization.

Nevertheless, Marx would have been greatly disappointed in the East German government bureaucracy. Marx had predicted that under socialism the state would need to rule for the proletariat at first; but eventually, as collective institutions developed, the state would "wither away" and the people would run their economy and society directly. This ideal future state would be **communism.** Neither East Germany nor any other socialist society has even come close. In all socialist societies, collective ownership has meant increased centralization of power in the hands of a ruling party and a swollen government bureaucracy.

Weber always said that Marx was wrong on this score. He believed no industrial society—capitalist or socialist—could do without bureaucracy. While aware of the advantages of bureaucracy for rationally coordinating large organizations, Weber would not have been surprised to hear about its limitations.

Planning in East Germany turned out to be clumsy and inefficient. You could say that it was like having the Department of Motor Vehicles run the whole economy. Once a plan had been made, it was very difficult to change it, even if it didn't seem to be working. Information from the factory moved very slowly up the layers of party bureaucracy. For example, if a condom factory had been sent too little latex, it would take a long time for word to get back to the planning boards and a long time for them to respond. Perhaps a girdle factory had received too much latex, but they just hid it away to compensate for future shortages. Factories often came to a stop when some vital material was lacking, or else everything waited while the factory manager made an informal arrangement trading some parts he had stockpiled for the missing material stockpiled in some other factory.

> A lion in a GDR zoo complains to the zookeeper that he's being discriminated against. "All I ever get to eat is bananas and every now and then an apple, but the lion in the next cage gets meat all the time."
>
> "But there's a good reason for that," says the warden. "The lion next to you is in a cage planned for a lion, but you're in a cage planned for a monkey." (Marcuse, p. 127)

Recently economists have argued that defects in planning are an intrinsic, fateful flaw of socialism. Robert Heilbroner contends that it is impossible, in principle, for a large modern economy to be run by central planning. No one could ever build a computer with sufficient capacity to keep track of all the supplies, products, prices, and exchanges. Blind as it is, market allocation of production avoids this colossal bookkeeping task.

It seems clear that while the East German government was committed to raising standards of living, reliance on centralized planning caused many unforeseen problems. For example, it took the East German government until the 1970s to decide that building housing had to be a priority, and then the plan poured resources into housing. Investment was diverted away from factories, which kept on producing with old, outdated machinery. As a result, the quality of East German products declined, and it became harder to export them to countries outside the Soviet bloc. Also, aging factories and power plants spewed more and more pollution into the air and water and land. But since the plan called for increasing production of housing and consumer goods, this problem was ignored. This is one of the saddest defects of socialism: it proved to be no better, and perhaps worse, than capitalism at controlling environmental pollution (DeBardeleben, pp. 144–164).

Because planning was so clumsy and imprecise, it could deal best with highly standardized goods. Newly built housing endlessly repeated the same modular concrete apartment blocks; clothing was offered in only a couple of basic designs; even cars came in only one model. State-owned stores were identified only by number: "Women's Clothing Store #32," "Butcher Shop #1658." Such standardization, combined with the poor quality of much consumer goods, made East Germany a kind of "grey society," lacking color and variety, in sharp contrast to the bright lights, vivid advertising, and glittering shopping districts found in the West.

Economic Inequality in East and West

Despite the differences in their economic systems, the societies of East and West Germany shared a common commitment to reducing economic inequality. Both societies were relatively successful in limiting inequalities of income, and the welfare state further equalized families' resources. West Germany showed a moderate degree of income inequality. In the mid-1980s, the poorest quintile of West Germans received 7.0 percent of total income, while the richest fifth received 40.3 percent or 5.8 times as much (World Bank, 1993).[1]

Data on East German income distribution show that income was more equally distributed in the East than the West. In 1980, the poorest fifth of East German households received 12.2 percent of total income, and the richest fifth received 29.8 percent, approximately 2.5 times as much (United Nations, p. 7). In the East, in the 1980s, the average factory manager was paid only about twice as much as the average factory worker. In West Germany in 1990, pay for a managing director averaged about 4.5 times that of an average factory worker (Ardagh, pp. 174, 374).

Inequality and Ethnic Minorities in West Germany

In one important respect, however, West Germany's relatively mild economic inequalities are significantly intensified. Many of those in unskilled, low-paying jobs are foreign workers—*Gastarbeiter* ("guest workers")—from Italy, Spain, Greece, Yugoslavia, or especially, Turkey, and they face prejudice and discrimination because of their ethnicity and darker skin.

Gastarbeiter first came to West Germany in the 1960s, when rapid economic growth led to labor shortages and the government of the Federal Republic negotiated agreements with poorer countries to supply temporary laborers. At first, single men came to Germany, intending to earn money and return home, but many sent for their families and settled permanently, working at menial jobs in mines and factories, in construction, and as sweepers and garbage collectors. By 1990, there were 4.8 million foreign workers in Germany (or approximately 13 percent of the West German population), about one-third of them Turkish. Foreign workers are concentrated in industrial cities; in Frankfurt, for example, 22 percent of the population are *Gastarbeiter.* Although recruitment of foreign workers ended in 1973, the foreign population continues to grow, because of its relatively high birth rate (Ardagh, pp. 276, 282; Nyrop, p. 110).

By law, *Gastarbeiter* are entitled to the same pay as Germans and they are fully entitled to the benefits of the welfare state, to which they contribute through taxes and payroll deductions, like other Germans. Although there are stories of exploitation of foreigners, by and large they are treated fairly by employers. There are incidents of violence against the *Gastarbeiter,* and particularly the Turks, but these are rare. More generally, however, the Turks today find themselves unwelcome and rejected in Germany. As Amity Schlaes explains, the very term *Gastarbeiter* "expresses the government's vain wish that these arrivals are here for a visit." German citizens will readily tell a visitor, "Germany is not an immigration country." In their view, having German blood makes you German, and long residence, or even birth in Germany, does not, if you are of foreign stock (Turner, p. 163; Ardagh, p. 276; Shlaes, pp. 19–20, 36).

Turkish workers have lower incomes, less skilled jobs, and higher unemployment rates that do other Germans (16.7 percent by 1983, twice the FRG average).

---

[1]In comparison, the richest quintile of Japanese received only 4.3 times as much as the poorest quintile. In Mexico, the richest fifth received 13.5 times as much income as the poorest fifth. And in the United States, in 1985, the richest fifth received just under 9 times as much income as the poorest. (See Table 1.3, p. 36.)

Their children tend to do poorly in school and rarely achieve admission to academic high schools or university. As unemployment has increased in Germany, outspoken prejudice against the Turks has increased also. Turkish workers tend to live in run-down inner-city neighborhoods, somewhat separated from other Germans. Germans don't invite Turks into their homes, although German children do learn to tolerate their foreign classmates.

In a society as much given to legal regulation as West Germany, it is significant that there are no laws against racial discrimination, other than in pay. Ads for jobs or apartments often say "only Germans," or "only Europeans," and bars often prohibit entry to Turks. By law, a German worker has preference over a foreigner for a job. Furthermore, it is difficult to become a citizen if you are not of German heritage; even children born in Germany are not automatically citizens. Germany has one of the lowest rates of granting citizenship of any western society (Ardagh, pp. 287, 288, 297).

Representative Democracy in West Germany

There is no characteristically "German" form of government. In the past century, Germans have lived under the most varied political orders—from the small, independent kingdoms of the early nineteenth century, to the great monarchy which Prussia dominated at the end of the nineteenth century, and then on to the Weimar parliamentary democracy which fell to Nazi dictatorship. When the governments of the two Germanys were created after World War II, there were precedents for almost any modern form of government. West Germany instituted **democratic** political institutions and East Germany developed an **authoritarian** government.

The West German government was created under the influence of the occupying forces of the United States and Britain, who were determined to establish a democracy—that is, a political system in which the citizens choose their leaders and participate in making government decisions and the government functions according to rules set down in a constitution, which also guarantees basic human rights. But West Germans themselves, horrified by Nazi carnage, reached back in their history to identify with a German democratic tradition. It was no accident that they chose for their flag the red, gold, and black bands first carried by the republican revolutionaries of 1848, which was also the flag of the Weimar Republic. West Germany, like all modern societies, is much too big to be a **direct democracy** in which all the citizens actually meet together and directly make the decisions which affect their lives. Instead, it is an **indirect democracy,** a **representative democracy** in which people express their preferences by voting for the candidates of competing political parties.

A Federation of States

The particular type of representative democracy adopted in West Germany is characteristically German. It reflects both Germany's tragic history and its present-day values. With typical German thoroughness and attention to detail, the West German political system was designed to make it difficult for a dictator like Hitler ever to seize power again. First of all, West Germany chose to avoid a centralized government like that of Nazi Germany. Instead, West Germany adopted a **federal system** (like that of the United States and Canada). It consisted of ten states, to which five additional states were added when Germany was reunified. Many of the states were based on old German principalities, which had united in past German confederations. In this federal system, the rights of the states limit the power of the central government. In Germany, the states control education, radio and TV, police, environmental regulation, cultural affairs, and local government and planning (Turner, p. 39; Ardagh, p. 86).

Every state elects its own parliament and its own prime minister and has an office, a kind of embassy, in the federal capital. All personal income taxes and corporate taxes are shared 50-50 between the states and the federal government, although federal law ensures that tax rates are the same in all states.

Parliamentary Government

West Germany also chose a parliamentary system of representative democracy, similar to the governments of other western European democracies. In a parliamentary system, the head of the government (in Germany, the chancellor) is elected by the upper house of parliament, not directly by the citizens. The vote takes place along party lines, so when a particular party or coalition of parties wins a majority of seats, its leader almost automatically becomes chancellor.

The upper house of the parliament (or *Bundestag*) is the nation's most powerful political institution. The lower house (the *Bundesrat*) is composed of delegates of the states. Representatives are elected to the *Bundestag* following an intricate system of **proportional representation** designed to frustrate the seating of small extremist parties, like the Nazi Party. Every German casts two votes for representatives: one for a district candidate, elected as an individual, and one for a party list of candidates. Half the seats go to district candidates and half to party list candidates, in proportion to their party's share of the vote. Any party that fails to win either three election districts or 5 percent of the party lists is denied representation (Dalton, pp. 281–285; Turner, pp. 40–41). In West Germany, power is carefully divided between the federal government and the states, between the upper and lower houses of parliament, and among the parties.

Political Parties

Finally, as specified in the constitution of the Federal Republic, the West German political system is fundamentally a **party system.** Political parties, distinguished by their differing political perspectives, compete for votes. In parliament they follow party discipline; that is, their members almost always vote as blocs. Political parties make the system orderly. When they vote for a party or its candidates, voters know what they are getting. The party system keeps the government responsible to voters; legislators know that if they do not act as they promised, voters can always turn to another party and vote them out of office (Dalton, pp. 249–250).

In West Germany since World War II there have been two major parties, the Christian Democratic Union and the Social Democratic Party; and two lasting minor parties, the Christian Social Union (which usually acts in coalition with the CDU) and the Free Democratic Party (which has allied itself with either of the two major parties). The CDU has been the party of the moderate right, advocating anticommunism and a commitment to capitalist economies. The SDP, the oldest German party, was traditionally committed to socialism and democracy, but since World War II, it has been a moderate left party, clearly anticommunist and oriented to a market economy, but with a strong belief in the welfare state (Dalton, pp. 251–276; Nyrop, pp. 264–273).

West Germans are also free to create other political organizations to make their opinions heard and to compete for political power. **Interest groups** speak for people who share common needs and problems. They lobby the government for desired legislation and policies. In the Federal Republic the "big four" interest groups are business, labor, the churches, and farmers, represented by organizations like the Federation of German Industries, the German Federation of Trade Unions, the Catholic Church and the Evangelical Church in Germany (an association of Protestant churches), and the German Farmers Association (Dalton, pp. 210–227).

Since the 1960s, new groups of political organizations have developed which often challenge the traditional interest groups. These new groups, known collectively as the New Politics movement include environmentalist organizations, the women's movement, and the peace movement. In 1980, people involved in these groups created a new party—the Green Party, which has since become an influential alternative party, represented in the *Bundestag* and in state parliaments. The Greens express younger Germans' serious concerns about pollution, nuclear weapons and nuclear power, militarism, gender inequality, and alienating work (Dalton, pp. 227–228, 266–269).

Constitutional Rights

The 1949 Basic Law (or constitution) which established the political system in West Germany, also granted citizens certain basic rights: freedom of speech and assembly, freedom of the press, equality before the law, religious freedom, and freedom from discrimination based on race, sex, religious or political beliefs, and the right to relief from military service on grounds of conscientious objection. All these rights had been lost under the Nazi regime, so restoring them was a very important step toward democracy. But ironically, the Nazi experience led the new German government to qualify some of these rights in order to protect the democracy. Thus, it is constitutional to ban parties that advocate the overthrow of democracy and this provision has been used against both Nazi and Communist parties. Similarly, the right of free speech cannot be used to attack democracy or to advocate Nazism. For example, publication of Hitler's book MEIN KAMPF is still banned in Germany today (Nyrop, p. 247). In recent years, West Germans have debated conscientiously about how far the right of free speech should license neo-Nazis who parade and publish anti-Semitic literature and wear Nazi symbols, and how much repression is necessary in order to protect democracy.

Authoritarian Government in East Germany

East Germany's government was created during the Soviet occupation after World War II. At first, the new political institutions paralleled those of West Germany.

There were five federated states, upper and lower houses of parliament, and a minister-president elected by a majority of the upper house (or People's Chamber). The Constitution of 1949 resembled West Germany's Basic Law, and guaranteed fundamental rights like freedom of assembly and speech, freedom of the press, religious freedom, the right to strike, and the right to emigrate.

But as early as 1947, these institutions of representative democracy became an empty shell, within which a second set of centralized and authoritarian political institutions developed. The political systems of East and West Germany became more and more unlike, but the GDR system was just as German as the FRG's. In the East, real power was highly centralized in one party, the Social Unity Party or SED, and within the Party, in the hands of the top SED leaders, the *Politburo*. Early on, the states ceased to have any separate powers, and they were replaced by administrative districts in 1952 (Turner, p. 101). Although basic civil rights were formally guaranteed, in actuality those rights were denied in a repressive **police state** that permitted no opposition to SED rule.

A Sham Democracy

Officially, the East German state was a parliamentary democracy with a total of five competing parties. In fact, four of the parties were really puppets of the SED, run by leaders acceptable to the ruling party and never permitted to challenge SED power. This was how it worked: East Germans did not get to choose between candidates or party slates when they voted. An organization called the National Front put together a single slate of candidates, representing all five parties and also the "mass organizations" like trade unions, farmers' cooperatives, women's and youth organizations. East Germans could vote only for or against this "unity slate," and the vote was always reported as overwhelmingly in favor of it.

In any case, the power of the People's Chamber was very limited. It met only about 6 times a year, for a day at a time and unanimously passed only about a dozen bills a year, all submitted to it on direction from the Central Committee of the SED. Even Jonathan Steele, a sympathetic observer, commented, "there is no chance of voters exerting any influence against SED policy" (Steele, p. 145). Western critics of Soviet-style socialism argued that the SED had no intention of allowing democracy, since they knew that if East Germans had a choice they would vote out the SED and get rid of the socialist regime. This is probably true: when East Germans were given a choice in 1989–1990 after the collapse of the Soviet Union and the fall of the Berlin Wall, they voted to join West Germany and adopt its political and economic systems.

The One-Party State

Real power in East Germany was exercised by the political institutions of the SED. At the top was the *Politburo,* the supreme party organization, composed of about twenty-five senior officials, ministers, and army officers, and headed by the general secretary. Below was the Central Committee, then the Party Congress, then the regional congresses, and at the bottom the local party organizations. In theory, the *Politburo* was elected by the Central Committee, which was elected by the Party Congress and so on, but in reality, the top levels were self-selecting and party members had no influence on their choice. **Centralism** was the official principle of government in the GDR. Decisions were to be made at the top, and lower-level organizations were expected to act on orders without question.

In East Germany, the leaders of the SED lived in a separate guarded suburb outside Berlin. They selected the individuals who would get special training at party schools to become party officials. All the people they worked with realized that the way to get ahead was to support the party leaders, not to challenge them. The party membership lacked access to the means for making their voices heard. For example, when the Party Congress issued a new Five-Year Plan, it was sent out to every branch of the party and state for discussion. Union locals met to discuss how the Plan would affect their work and to make suggestions. But union members were all full-time workers who met after work. They had no researchers or libraries or statisticians, and they were given only two weeks to discuss a proposed plan (Steele, p. 135). You can see that it would be very difficult for them to challenge a plan or even document any well-founded doubts. Party officials had an enormous advantage over them in resources, time, and power.

Democratic Centralism

Despite its centralization of power, SED leaders claimed that the GDR was, in fact, a democracy. It was not a parliamentary democracy like West Germany, but rather a new socialist kind of democracy they called **"democratic centralism."** The SED's leaders believed that a single party could integrate within itself all the different social groups so democracy would take place in debate within the party, not in competition among parties. SED leaders prided themselves on the high degree of political involvement among East Germans. They said political participation made East Germany more democratic than the western democracies, where citizens took little part in ongoing politics, most not even bothering to vote in elections every couple of years.

In East Germany, the government urged people to belong to the SED and other political parties, join mass organizations, run for office and join committees, and attend meetings—and large numbers of people did so. Approximately one in six East Germans over 18 (or about 2.3 million people) were SED members, and they belonged to over 84,000 local organizations. Nearly 100 percent of adults were trade union members. Hundreds of thousands more people were members of state legislatures or legislative committees, National Front committees, production councils, and PTAs. Millions joined youth and women's organizations (Burant, pp. 182, 187, 201; Dalton, p. 43).

GDR leaders proudly emphasized that people from all different classes participated in the SED and could rise to positions of power. The SED monitored the class background and current status of party members and described its membership as 56 percent working class (Steele, p. 142). They argued that the SED was democratic because all different classes were represented in it. In the West, people believed their society was democratic because many different views were represented in parliament, even though almost all representatives were middle class or upper class. In the East, it was relatively easy to join the party hierarchy, and in fact it was a major channel of upward mobility. But to rise to leadership, you had to be ideologically loyal. Thus, people from many classes were represented, but only one viewpoint—that of the SED—was allowed.

> *Gunter, a 53-year-old East German factory worker lived all his life under "democratic centralism." Since reunification, he has been introduced to western-style democracy, and he is critical of it. "In the GDR, a man like me or my son could hope to have a place in the life of the nation. In today's Germany, no one has a minute for you unless you drive a big car! Is this democracy? A democracy of the Mercedes? Everyone is free to have their say as long as they have money! Even the Socialists are Doktoren! When was the last time you saw a man with callused hands in the Bundestag? Honecker [past general secretary of the SED] was a fool, but he knew that in a democracy, everyone has a part."*

A Police State

The East German government demanded political mobilization and ideological loyalty from its citizens, but just to make sure there was no opposition, the government suppressed all dissent. A large secret police force, a network of informers, a guarded border, and an army prevented the expression of opposition to the SED or to socialism, and prevented the penetration of seditious ideas from outside East German borders. Any group larger than seven people needed official permission to meet (Ferree, p. 96).

Censorship. In East Germany, the newspapers, radio, and television were all state-owned and state-run. News reporting was considered part of the campaign to build socialism, so events within the GDR and outside that might cast the regime in a bad light were simply not reported. For example, when the worker movement Solidarity challenged the Communist Party in Poland in 1980, it was never mentioned in the GDR news media. Newspapers and radio gave lots of news about sports and the arts, but there was no reporting on crime or consumer shortages. Party congresses were reported in predictable boring detail, economic reports were always positive, and headlines like "Delegates Unanimously Praise Workers' Collectives" were so obviously canned that they defeated their own purposes. TV programs were similarly relentlessly upbeat. Since most East Germans could tune in to West German TV, they learned about censored news anyhow, and their faith in the GDR was undermined (Ardagh, pp. 391–392).

Prohibition of Travel. One of the things that angered East Germans most about their repressive regime was the ban on travel to the West. To leave East Germany or its Soviet-bloc neighbors you needed special government permission, seldom granted. Married couples were never permitted to exit at the same time and individuals, like athletes or musicians, permitted to tour the West were carefully watched by spies. Only old people were allowed to visit relatives in West Germany. But West Germans could visit the East, and could keep in touch with relatives by phone.

The Threat of Force. Ultimately, the SED kept its power in East Germany through the threat and use of force against its citizens. There were police, se-

cret police, border guards, a regular military, and volunteer militia units. Together these all added up to quite a large military meant exclusively for internal use.

Most sinister was the *Stasi,* the secret police, which in the very repressive days
of the 1950s and 1960s imprisoned and tortured dissidents without trial. By the
1980s the *Stasi* was simply in the business of spying on people, looking for dissent.
The secret police force was huge: it had a regular staff of 85,000, as many as half
a million paid informers—ordinary people who spied on their coworkers, neighbors, friends, or even spouses—and secret files on a third of all GDR citizens. Until the Wende, no one knew how big the *Stasi* was. People just had the feeling that
it was important to watch what you said all the time. When the true size of the *Stasi*
operations was revealed after 1989, people were horrified and furious.

In 1961 construction of the Berlin Wall completed the sealing of the border
between East and West. The entire border was fenced and guarded by 50,000 GDR
border police, who patrolled a mined no-man's-land and were trained to shoot anyone attempting to cross. East Germany's military was not large, but it was conspicuous. People were also aware of the threat of the Soviet army, which had been
brutally used to put down rebellions in East Germany in 1953 and in Hungary in
1956.

The Welfare State

When you read about the political and economic institutions of East Germany and
West Germany, you see how very different the two societies were. But in one very
important respect, both Germanys were similar. They were both **welfare states,** and
welfare institutions worked effectively and met with popular approval in both societies. In both East and West, the welfare state meant the same thing: it meant that
the government accepted responsibility for its citizens' social welfare. In the West,
this meant that the government pledged to guarantee citizens the right to certain
benefits and services, like health care and housing, even if they couldn't afford to
buy them on the free market. The East German welfare state was more extensive
than the West's but it was based on a similar belief that the government has an
obligation to provide for the well-being of its citizens. Both societies also took responsibility for making certain that all young people were able to get an education
that prepared them for a job.

The institutions of the welfare state date back long before the division of Germany. The welfare state began in the 1880s, under the rule of Kaiser Wilhelm I and
his prime minister, Otto von Bismarck, as a conservative response to the trade
union and socialist movements of the time. They instituted three historic compo-
nents of a universal welfare system: national health insurance, accident insurance,
and old-age/disability insurance. Unemployment insurance was added in 1927.

During the twentieth century other European countries followed Germany's
example, establishing similar welfare programs. In the United States, where the
obligation of the state to ensure the social welfare of its citizens is not fully accepted, only two of the usual welfare programs—old-age pensions and unemployment insurance—have been enacted.

The West German Welfare State

West Germany added to this basic welfare package. The government gives all parents a yearly family allowance for each child, regardless of income or marital status. There is also a program of rent allowances for low-income families, to make sure they can afford market rents and prevent homelessness. Finally, there is a small "welfare" component: allowances for people who for some reason cannot work (Nyrop, pp. 97–98).

West Germany's social insurance and welfare programs are expensive. Approximately one-third of the country's GNP is spent on health and welfare. Social programs are paid for by high income taxes, payroll taxes, and mandatory employer contributions. Health insurance, for example, is paid for by required contributions from employees and employers equal to about 6 percent of salary (Nyrop, 94; Glouchevitch, p. 111). (See Table 5.2.)

The East German Welfare State

In East Germany, the welfare state went even farther. As Jonathan Steele reported, in East Germany the state "takes responsibility for providing almost everything from stable consumer prices to a job for every school leaver. People expect the state's promises to be kept. They make higher claims on it than most people do in the West" (Steele, p. 13). Although the overall standard of living in the East was much lower than in the West, no East German was excluded from education or health care for lack of money. No one was homeless or jobless; no elderly people or single mothers were left without social and financial support.

East Germany provided the standard European universal welfare institutions: health insurance, accident and disability insurance, old-age pensions, unemployment insurance, and family allowances. Health care was readily available, without charge, from state-employed medical professionals, so patients neither laid out money in advance nor filed paperwork. The quality of health care was high and the atmosphere caring.

Family benefits were generous: women received six months' maternity leave at full pay for their first child, and a full year at reduced pay for subsequent children.

TABLE 5.2. Access to Health Care: Although Germans and Japanese go to the doctor more often than Americans, their societies spend less per capita on health care.

	National Legislation Requiring Health Insurance for Entire Population	Percent of Population Uninsured at Some Point in a Year, 1990	Per Capita Spending on Health (U.S. $), 1991	Average Number of Doctor Visits per Year, 1990
Germany	Yes	1	$1287	12
Japan	Yes	1	$1035	13
United States	No	26	$2566	5

Source: World Bank, *World Development Report 1993: Investing in Health.* New York: Oxford University Press, 1993.

Children and teachers from an East Berlin day-care center are out for an afternoon walk. Cars were scarce in East Germany, but high-quality, inexpensive day care was easily obtained by working mothers.

Years spent caring for children were credited in figuring pensions. Families received allowances for their children until they reached age 18. Newly married young couples were given free "starter loans," with repayment waived incrementally as children were born. Day care was inexpensive and readily available (Edwards, p. 46).

Many additional benefits were provided through the workplace and administered by the unions, including holidays in union hotels, factory hospitals and clinics, day-care centers, sports facilities, adult classes, libraries, discount shops, and housing (Steele, p. 131; Burant, p. 98).

Finally, an important element in the East German welfare state was management of wages and prices through the Plan, which made basic goods available to everyone at subsidized prices, at the cost of making luxuries scarce and expensive. Prices of basic foods like bread and milk and sausage, rents, gas and electric, and commuter fares were frozen. Even the prices of theater and concert tickets and restaurants were subsidized. Rents were especially low: about 4 to 5 percent of average family income. (To imagine what this means, figure that a family earning $500 a week would pay only $25 a week in rent.) Forty percent of government spending went to these subsidies (Burant, pp. 88–89).

Educational Institutions

Germany has a highly effective educational system that will be of real interest to students from other societies. Education is treated with great seriousness and thoroughness and students make a smooth transition to adult jobs. Only students who are admitted to academic high schools, get good grades, and pass rigorous entrance exams are permitted to attend university, but those who are admitted pay no tuition and are given allowances for living expenses so they needn't work while they are in school. Most people who don't go to college undertake apprenticeships, a German tradition and a respected alternative to university education. However, even those in technical and vocational education must show their grades to employers when they seek jobs, so everyone works hard in school.

> At 18, Georg Messer is in his final year of apprenticeship with the famous Konigsdorfer Shoe Company in Hamburg, training to be an Industriekaufmann, an office worker in an industrial firm. Georg felt lucky to get this apprenticeship; it was highly competitive. One thousand graduates applied for twenty-five places. Konigsdorfer chose young men and women who were socially skilled and presentable and whose records attested to their ability to work hard and carefully. Having served in twelve different departments at Konigsdorfer, Georg is finishing his apprenticeship in the Cost Accounting Department, working closely with his mentor and applying new computer models to develop prices for the spring shoe line. He uses his knowledge of international exchange rates, import-export tariffs, and the costs of materials and labor, learned in the one-day-a-week formal instruction (Berufsschule), which is part of his apprenticeship.
>
> We asked Georg if he is ever sorry he didn't go to Gymnasium (academic high school) and on to university. "No, not at all. Why should I be," he answered. "I was really getting tired of school by the time I was 15. This apprenticeship has let me out in the real world, and the one-day-a-week formal school makes sense, because I use what I learn in Berufsschule here at the factory. Did I tell you I've been offered a job, in the Cost Accounting Department? I can begin as soon as I take my qualifying exams. My bosses seem certain I'll pass. You know I'll have a responsible job with a real adult salary and plenty of room for advancement by the time I'm 18."

West German Education

Public education is controlled by the states in West Germany and there is some variation from state to state in curriculum and educational philosophy, but the basic system is the same throughout the country, and 95 percent of children attend public school. States try hard to assure all students an equal start in primary school. Primary schools are neighborhood schools and richer and poorer children often attend school together, because neighborhoods often have diverse populations. Teachers are paid by the state and salaries are standard, but school buildings and equipment are supplied by the locality and vary greatly in quality. There is no **tracking** (ability grouping) at the primary level: all the children are taught the same lessons in heterogeneous classes.

But at the end of the fourth grade (in some states sixth grade) German children face a crucial life transition. Based on their grades, their teachers' assessments, and their parents' wishes, they will transfer to one of three types of secondary schools. From here on, German schools are seriously tracked and the kind of secondary school one attends has lasting life consequences (Hamilton, pp. 73–74, 77–78).

TABLE 5.3. Postsecondary Education: More young adults attend college in the United States than in Germany or Japan.

	Students in Postsecondary Education (as a Percent of Those 20–24)†		Percent of University Students Who Are Female, 1988
	1965	1991	
East Germany	19	31*	47
West Germany	9	30*	38
Japan	13	31	24
United States	40	76	50
Mexico	4	16	34
Egypt	7	19	33

*Data for East and West Germany are for 1985.
†Postsecondary education includes vocational schools as well as community and four-year colleges and universities.
Sources: World Bank, *World Development Report 1994: Infrastructure for Development.* New York: Oxford University Press, 1994; World Bank, *World Development Report 1988: Opportunities and Risks in Managing the World Economy.* New York: Oxford University Press, 1988.

Three High School Tracks. Students considered to have the strongest academic ability go to academic high school (or *Gymnasium*) which they attend until age 19. It is roughly equivalent to American high school plus one or two years of college. In 1990, 31 percent of German students attended *Gymnasium.* Most of them were from middle-class families. Students whose grades are satisfactory, and who pass a rigorous entrance exam are admitted to university, and about 75 percent of those qualified go right on to further study ("A Profile of the German Education System," p. 21; Hamilton, p. 85; Ardagh, p. 249). (See Table 5.3.)

Twenty-eight percent of German students move from primary school to technical institutes (or *Realschule*). These are vocational schools which specialize in commercial or technical fields and also provide some academic education. Technical institutes go through tenth grade and when students graduate at 16 they go on either to apprenticeship or to a technical college *(Fachhochschule)* which trains for careers like nursing or accountancy. Those who don't go on to technical colleges get jobs as lab technicians, precision mechanics, secretaries, or personnel managers, and so forth (after completing apprenticeships in these jobs). *Realschule* educate a true cross section of the German population.

The largest and least academically qualified group of students (33 percent) attend vocational high school *(Hauptschule)* until age 15.[2] These schools prepare students for apprenticeship or work in manual, clerical, and semiskilled service jobs. They become construction workers, auto mechanics, file clerks, and salespeople in retail stores. The *Hauptschule* is usually a neighborhood school, often in the same building as the primary school, and its prestige is low. Students at *Hauptschule* are usually from working-class families (Hamilton, pp. 80, 85).

[2]Another 8 percent of German students attend comprehensive high schools, which are uncommon in Germany ("A Profile of the German Education System," p. 21).

Second Chances. In recent years, West Germany has modified its tracking system to allow more second chances to students who start out doing poorly, but later decide they want a university education. It is now possible for technical school students to switch over to the academic high school after graduation, though they often lose a year or two in making the switch. In some states as few as 2 percent do so, but in others up to 16 percent make the move up. Also, there are now adult-education courses which prepare people for college entrance later in life (Hamilton pp. 78–79; "A Profile of the German Education System," p. 21.)

Apprenticeship. The most impressive characteristic of German education is that in every track education is taken very seriously by both teachers and students, and at every level education culminates in marketable skills that qualify students for good, full-time jobs immediately upon graduation. For most students this is accomplished through a system of apprenticeship. More than 60 percent of all Germans 16 to 18 years old are apprentices who typically train for three years, spending four days a week in the workplace and one day a week in vocational school (Hamilton, p. 32). Apprenticeships are provided by German companies, which pay for the training.

Young people in Germany apprentice as auto mechanics and personnel managers, postal workers, computer programmers, graphic designers, copywriters, plumbers, railway conductors, shoe sales workers—for white-collar and blue-collar jobs in over 350 occupations. You might even think that German apprenticeships overtrain young people. Even relatively unskilled jobs are treated with the greatest seriousness. For example, shoe sales workers serve a full apprenticeship and learn about sales, sizing, cash-register operation, the process of shoe manufacture, and bookkeeping. Ordinary workers are very competent as a result, which adds to their status, and they are also qualified to advance to the next step of promotion. Every shoe salesperson has the knowledge necessary to be manager. More than half of all apprentices go to work for the company that trained them, but others move into jobs with companies not offering apprenticeships or into related occupations that don't have apprenticeships (Hamilton, pp. 35, 143–144). In Germany, the school-to-work transition is a smooth one; not just for an educated elite, but for students at every level of the educational system.

East German Education

The East German educational system was similar to that of the FRG. Consistent with East German values, it laid more emphasis on equality, on manual labor, and on ideological education. First of all, the East German system postponed the start of tracking to eleventh grade in order to provide a more equal start for all students. Also, the East German system laid even greater emphasis than did West Germany on technical and vocational education. Starting in seventh grade all children took vocational instruction, spending one day a week in practical work in factories or on farms. Even university-bound students in *Gymnasium* had to spend a full year training for a trade. Finally, East Germany sent only about one-third as many students to university as did West Germany. The number of students admitted to technical schools and universities was fixed according to labor force needs, so students, once accepted, could rely on getting jobs after graduation. Most students (86 percent in the 1980s) took apprenticeships and only about 8 percent attended the equivalent of *Gymnasium* and another 6 percent went to technical institutes (Glaessner, pp. 81–84; Childs, pp. 171–178; Ardagh, p. 248).

Typically, for East Germany, the whole educational system was highly centralized, and it devoted a great deal of its resources to ideological education, teaching Marxism-Leninism and Russian to all students. In the early decades, the government gave preference to children of manual workers in admission to university, but by the 1980s college students were mainly middle class. Ideological orthodoxy and activism in party-sponsored organizations were very important qualifications for university admission.

DEVIANCE AND SOCIAL CONTROL

In East Germany, because of collectivism, centralization, and police power, the state had tremendous power over individuals. The government was able to monitor what individuals did and said and use sanctions to ensure that people conformed. The government responded most severely to deviance it considered a political challenge to the SED or to socialism. A great deal of behavior seen elsewhere as private was defined as political in the GDR. For example, listening to rock music was considered a political act. In the West, in contrast, an emphasis on individualism, compartmentalization, and civil liberties shields individuals from state power, and leaves them freer of official social controls. Using state power against political deviance makes the West German government uncomfortable.

Totalitarian Social Controls

East Germany was often characterized by western critics as a **totalitarian state,** that is, a society in which the government intrudes into all aspects of public and private life, so that the individual is nowhere sheltered from state power. In a totalitarian state the government imposes its ideology through control of the media and education. It controls the police, the economy, and the ruling party. Through these institutions, the state exercises supreme power over individuals. In a totalitarian state there is no "independent public space" free of government control (Philipsen, p. 79).

Collectivism, Centralization, and Social Sanctions

It is important to understand that all formal East German social groups were in some way government-controlled. Some, like the party, the unions, the youth groups, and the Women's Federation were more tightly controlled, and others, like the work collectives and social clubs were more independent, but in every group there were party members pushing the party line and *Stasi* agents noting what people said and did. People were induced to participate in official organizations by means of powerful positive and negative social sanctions controlled by the SED.

Centralization meant that anything you did in one group could have consequences in every aspect of your life. People could not expect to be promoted at work unless they took leadership roles in basic organizations like the Youth Federation or Women's Federation (Scharf, pp. 141–142). Those who joined the party, enthusiastically gave their time to other voluntary groups, and voiced their belief in socialist ideology were more likely to be admitted to university, given responsible jobs and promotions, good apartments, even perhaps permission to travel to the West. You could lose these desirable rewards too. If your child defected to the West, you might lose your responsible job and get work only as a janitor; if you joined a church, your child might be turned down for the university; if you opposed the party line at work, you might never get a better apartment.

Adult Organizations. Adults were expected to join many official organizations—unions, of course, professional associations, sports leagues, the Women's Federation, volunteer social service groups, and possibly the SED or another party. Adult workers were also expected to participate in collectives in their place of work and about half did so. Collectives were social groups: they kept scrapbooks with pictures of members' families, records of members' health, and minutes of meetings. They went on picnics and trips and did weekend volunteer work maintaining the factory's summer camp and staging plays, concerts, or educational events (Steele, p. 136). Though East Germans felt coerced by this system, they also found personal satisfaction in it. People felt the work collectives, clubs, and volunteer groups were humane; they belonged and others cared about them.

Petra is a hospital radiologist in Potsdam. In the old days, before 1990, she was a union member, a member of the Democratic Women's Federation and the Society for German-Soviet Friendship. Further, as an SED member, she played a role in the party organization in her hospital. She had been a swimmer since primary school and retained her membership in the sports league. Petra was busy, managing her household and children in addition to attending meetings after work, but she enjoyed meeting people and valued the respect with which her friends and coworkers viewed her accomplishments. She felt like she was a participant in making her society run.

In 1990, Petra's younger brother Helmut had just begun work as a graphic artist. He belonged to the Arts Union, the Chamber of Technology, and the Free German Youth. Helmut worried about their cousin Dieter, a musician, who had not joined the Association of Composers and Musicians, and who had stopped going to meetings of the Free German Youth. Dieter had also pierced his nose and hung out in the bars downtown with other "punk" youth. He had completed an apprenticeship as a primary school music teacher, but somehow the school year began without Dieter being placed in a job.

Youth Organizations. Children and teenagers spent a great deal of their time in organizations controlled by the government. First of all, all children attended the same kind of government-controlled schools (there were no private schools). Ninety-nine percent of them joined the Young Pioneers, the official children's organization, and 75 percent went on to join the Free German Youth, the official youth group from which the SED recruited new members. Children spent a lot of time after school and on weekends in Pioneer activities like cleaning up public areas, collecting paper for recycling, or helping old people to shop, carry coal, or shovel snow. Thousands attended Pioneer camp each summer as well (Steele, p. 175).

Teenagers were attracted to youth clubs, which offered discos and hobby groups, and cheap vacations, all under the watchful eyes of party cadre. Boys were encouraged to join The Society for Sport and Technology, where they received military training in driving, navigation, flying and diving, radio technology, shooting, and parachuting. Once they finished school or apprenticeship, young people were pressed to join youth commissions or youth teams on their first job. Youth teams in the workplace had their own "plan" to fulfill (Edwards, pp. 124, 129, 130, 135, 141, 144). In its mobilization and indoctrination of children, the GDR resembled the Nazi state.

Women and Group Life. Throughout its fifty-year history the government of the GDR worked to bring women into the labor force, both for ideological and for political reasons. In ideological terms, Marxism teaches that "socially useful work" is an essential human activity and that no one can fully develop as a person without it. Paid work was politically desirable too, as a means of integrating women into East German society, making them part of the collectives, unions, and volunteer groups that were the fundamental social units. As early as 1950, the GDR began working to counter the Nazi belief that women belonged at home. By the 1980s, 88 percent of women aged 15 to 60 were either employed or in school, the highest percentage in any country in the world (Edwards, pp. 50, 78, 82). And East German women typically remained in the workforce throughout their childbearing years, supported by low-cost day-care centers, shorter hours, and time off for childbirth. Early in its history, East Germany was short of labor, so it helped to have women work. But by the 1980s, the GDR had trouble finding enough jobs for all its people. Still, women were urged to work—in response to political, not market priorities.

The Elderly. East Germany also tried to prevent isolation of elderly people. Old people were encouraged to continue at work, or maintain contact with their old collectives and unions, and to join old people's clubs or other clubs. Factories and primary schools were "twinned" with old people's homes or clubs, visited the elderly, did repairs for them, and ran trips and parties for them. Union committees also kept in touch with retired members. In turn, elderly people frequently visited schools or youth groups to give talks about the past, the Nazi era, and the building of socialism. A separate adult volunteer society ran old people's clubs, delivered meals on wheels, and provided home aides (Edwards, pp. 170–172, 193–196).

The Effectiveness of Social Controls

Social control in East Germany was focused on preventing political opposition to the SED and its style of socialism. The government was less concerned with deviance it defined as nonpolitical, except insofar as it saw all crime as political because it reflected poorly upon the merits of socialist society. Ordinary crime was handled in a style that was unmistakably both socialist and German. There was great emphasis on responding to deviance within worker- or neighborhood-based collectives. For example, factory managers were required to report to the police any workers "who show serious signs of developing a work-shy outlook, who try to obtain a livelihood in an unworthy way, who break work discipline through constant abuse of alcohol or who show by their social behavior that they need extra instruction" (quoted in Steele, p. 158).

Some deviance was handled within the factory itself. Workers elected conflict commissions of eight to ten members which acted as courts for disciplining fellow workers in cases of quarrels, insults, petty theft, or damage to factory property. These panels were taken seriously and were quite effective. They might require convicted individuals to apologize to another person or to the collective, to repair or pay for damage, be publicly reprimanded, or pay a fine. The party newspaper published conflict commission cases weekly. Local disputes commissions played the same role in residential neighborhoods, adjudicating cases involving quarrels, noise, drunk driving, or even child abuse. Offenders convicted by the regular courts were expected to return to their old jobs after imprisonment and be looked after and helped to go straight by their fellow workers (Steele, pp. 139, 140, 157).

East Germany kept an unusually large uniformed police force, and they maintained files on all citizens, regardless of whether or not they committed any crimes. But except in cases of "political crimes," the police operated in typically German legalistic fashion, processing crimes and complaints strictly by the book (Ardagh, p. 316).

Defining Political Deviance. East German statistics cannot be relied on for accuracy, but it seems likely that there were in fact relatively low crime rates. Political deviance was another matter entirely. East Germany's leaders understood that many people did not support the regime; they were, in one way or another, **dissidents.** Open dissidence was treated harshly. Dissidents and their families were blocked from universities, jobs, and apartments. They were watched and followed by the secret police, so others avoided them. In extreme cases they were jailed, or even expelled from the country. Even people who were not explicitly "political" but simply tried to "drop out" of conventional life were defined as antisocialist. Hippies, folk musicians, punk rockers, and unconventional artists were all viewed with suspicion. When rock music came to East Germany in the 1970s, the SED considered it harmful and threatening. Much rock was individualistic: it explored private, subjective feelings, and other rock was critical of government and society. As early as 1976 the SED decided that only carefully controlled rock music could be played in official discos by "disco moderators," who received special training in Marxism-Leninism and could be trusted. All other rock music performances were banned (Ramet, pp. 91–92).

But despite its tremendous power to sanction deviance, the East German government was caught in a dilemma. Leaders wanted both to suppress dissent and to give the appearance that there was no dissent, that East Germans enthusiastically supported the SED. In particular, SED leaders wanted to play down the amount of violence required to keep their regime in power. As much as possible, they wanted to avoid the open use of force. Above all, they wanted to avoid a recurrence of open revolt like the June 1953 rebellion, put down in such an ugly way by Soviet troops.

On the other hand, they weren't willing to let dissidents leave East Germany, because they were afraid that millions of people would do so, revealing the pervasiveness of discontent.

The government hoped that by involving all citizens, from early childhood, in government-controlled organizations, they could build willing support for the regime. Government and people engaged in a sort of silent struggle, with the government trying to control all aspects of its citizens' lives and the people trying to create private space shielded from state power. By trying to control so much of people's lives, the government turned every aspect of life into an arena of political struggle. Many people who were otherwise apolitical found themselves defined as dissidents and in opposition to the government. Many people retreated from the public realm to country cottages and gardens and the kitchen-table society of friends and family. Informal friendship circles were particularly important to young people. Among friends they listened to music, talked politics, defined individual identities, and participated in a youth culture which was outside of government control (Lemke, pp. 68–71).

In the mid-1970s, the SED, under the leadership of Erich Honecker, decided that it would be better to allow people selected safety valves for their discontent, rather than increase the level of repression. The SED selected two seemingly harmless outlets: television and the church. They decriminalized the watching of western TV, figuring that since so many of West Germany's serious-minded TV programs were devoted to social problems like poverty and drug abuse, watching western TV would decrease the attractiveness of the West. The SED also permitted the Protestant Church, harassed since the 1950s, to increase its level of activity. The church became the only institution independent of the state and it took on an enormously important role in opposing the East German regime (Ardagh, p. 384).

The Church and Dissent

East Germany is a traditionally Lutheran part of Germany and the Catholic Church is rather small and inactive there, so Honecker sought his rapprochement with the Lutheran Church, promising some degree of church independence in exchange for a pledge that the church would stay out of politics. Honecker hoped the church would attract discontented people and direct their energies into religion, not political opposition. As a result, the church came to offer "the only organized public alternative to the official value-system, and thus attracted many people not otherwise very religious" (Ardagh, p. 385). All kinds of deviants—homosexuals, punks, rebellious youth, rock musicians, peace activists, and would-be emigrants—were attracted to the church (Goeckel, pp. 211, 216–217).

The church hierarchy, pastors, and congregations constantly argued over the role of the church: How far should it go along with the state? How much should the church allow its premises to be used for dissent? This very discussion, which called into question the legitimacy of the government, was profoundly seditious, even when church authorities decided in the end to suppress political activity. The very existence of the church as an institution outside the hierarchies of the SED made the state nervous. Even in the 1980s, when the SED permitted the building of new churches, permitted religious programs on state radio, and permitted departments of theology to train ministers, the state still discriminated against church members and especially pastors. Their children were usually excluded from higher education. They were officially put in a special category, the *Sonderlinge*—literally "the peculiar"—with a very small admissions quota and active Christians were not permitted to become schoolteachers or government officials (Ardagh, p. 387; Darnton, p. 226).

In the late 1980s, as the domination of the SED weakened, the churches, somewhat reluctantly, became the natural focus of dissident activity. In many cities peace groups, environmentalist groups, and human rights groups began meeting in churches and they pressured church officials to allow and protect greater freedom of speech within the church. Concerts and church services arranged by these groups drew more and more people and became weekly events that spilled over into candlelight marches, demonstrations, and vigils. In the fall of 1989, as the regime crumbled, church services in small towns attracted crowds, and while praying for divine intervention, people began to speak out against the government. Following the pattern established in Leipzig and Berlin, village churches held weekly prayer meetings and candlelight marches, and the authorities, as they felt their power undermined, began to back off from confronting the demonstrators (Philipsen, pp. 141–150; Darnton, pp. 222–226). In this way, the churches, the only independent institutions, became the nurseries of dissident organization.

Deviance and Social Control in the Federal Republic

You can see a clear contrast: East Germany was a **collectivist** society that treated individuals as members of groups, but West Germany was (and remains) an **individualistic** society that sees individuals as autonomous actors, free to join groups or remain private. West Germans belong to fewer groups than East Germans and the groups they do belong to are under no centralized control.

Social Groups in an Individualistic Society

As Hall and Hall put it, in West Germany social institutions are compartmentalized. Politically, the nation is divided into states, and the federal government must share power with them. In business, work is divided among departments, which jealously guard their territory. Information is seldom shared freely among work groups (Hall and Hall, pp. 44–45). People keep their friends and their work separate, their school life and social life separate, and their friends and neighbors separate. How they behave in one social group will likely have little bearing on their treatment in another.

Children and School Life. West German schools were (and are still) quite narrowly focused on academic preparation. West Germans think schools are for learning, not for character building, team sports, or leadership development, which should be the responsibility of parents, churches, or voluntary groups like the Boy Scouts. School is held only between 8 A.M. and 1 P.M. and is devoted to academic classes. There might be a few classes or clubs in the afternoon, but most students go home for lunch, and then do many hours of homework or play team sports at local sports centers. Few schools have their own playing fields or swimming pools or even libraries or auditoriums where the whole school can assemble. Children often spend a great deal of time with friends or classmates, but their social life is outside the school. Similarly, while schools teach about democracy and the constitution and how the German government works, there are no student government organizations or even debating teams (Ardagh, pp. 241–243).

Women and Group Life. Short school days have had a major effect on women's lives in West Germany. Children don't start school until age 6 or 7 and there are few day-care centers or even kindergartens, and those that exist are privately run and relatively expensive. School, once begun, is only a half-day affair, and there is little after-school care available either. Then, of course, the shops close at 6:30, so someone has to be home to take care of children and shop in the afternoons (Marsh, p. 311). West German society assumes that it is the responsibility of individual families, not the society or government, to work out this problem. As a result, West German women are much less likely to work than East German women, and actually less likely to work than women in England or France or the United States.

Under 40 percent of West German women worked in the 1980s, and only a third of these women had children. They brought home only 18 percent of family income. Women tend to work for several years before marriage and childbearing, at which time they leave the labor force, reentering it only when their children are grown. As a result, there are few women in professional careers: only 5 percent of lawyers and 3.4 percent of senior civil servants are women, although 20 percent of doctors are female. In banking, business, and industry, only about 2 percent of all top positions are held by women. Mostly, women are found in less skilled jobs, primarily in traditionally female occupations like office work and sales, and they earn only about half as much as men. Even women in salaried jobs earn only two-thirds of men's pay. The unemployment rate is about twice as high for women as for men.

Married West German women are likely to spend many years during which their primary social focus is home and family, and they have few connections to social groups in the larger society. Many German women express discontent with these restricted roles. They are marrying later, having fewer children, or none at all, and a growing number of unmarried women are becoming mothers. Feminist groups have accused the Helmut Kohl government of trying to push women back into the home to ease unemployment and to raise the birth rate, though the government denies it (Ferree, p. 93; Ardagh, pp. 192–194; Nyrop, pp. 123–124; Craig, 1982, pp. 167–168).

Responses to Deviance

West Germans respond to deviance in ways that are both characteristic of parliamentary democracies and characteristically German. Because of the burden of their Nazi past, West Germans are fearful of any government intervention that smacks of totalitarianism. They don't want the government spying on people or controlling private organizations or limiting freedom of speech. But as Germans they value an orderly society and they expect people to conform closely to the law. As we have seen, West Germans take it upon themselves to correct other people's behavior—in the streets, in the neighborhoods, at work. Also, West Germans are notoriously litiginous—that is, they readily litigate, or bring lawsuits against each other. Neighborhood residents will sue a restaurant that stays open too late, or a homeowner who doesn't follow the rules for mowing the grass. At work, employees will use grievance procedures to contest mandatory overtime they think unjustified, or a missed promotion.

> *Johanna Silberschnitt still blushes with embarrassment and anger when she talks about the lawsuit her neighbors brought against her family for excessive noise. They tried, she protests, to observe all the rules about quiet hours and laundry hours and hallway neatness in their apartment house. "But when you have four boys under the age of 10, you have to expect some noise," she remarks. In the end, the courts upheld the Silberschnitts, but "though we won the battle, we lost the war," Johanna says. It was hard to face angry neighbors day after day, and teachers began to look at the older boys as troublemakers. Finally, her in-laws helped them with the down payment and they bought a house in a new development outside town. It's further from the shops and school, Johanna says, but it's worth it. "There is no one living beneath us hearing footsteps and there are a lot more young families in the neighborhood, so people understand."*

Political Deviance. West Germans have a harder time responding to organized political deviance. Activity by skinheads and neo-Nazis has been on the upswing ever since reunification. There are more young men seen in the streets with shaved heads and paramilitary gear, wearing Nazi symbols, and there have been many attacks on foreigners and handicapped people. Neo-Nazis have desecrated old Jewish cemeteries, set a synagogue on fire, and firebombed shelters for foreigners seeking political asylum. According to government figures, far-right groups committed 2285 acts of racial violence in 1992, more than 22 times the level of a decade ago, but still fewer than are committed yearly in Great Britain. There are eighty-two "right-wing extremist organizations and other groupings," according to government intelligence sources, with a total membership of about 22,000, but with probably no more than 1500 activists (Whitney, Oct. 21, 1993, pp. A1, A10).

There is disagreement among both Germans and outside observers about the seriousness of neo-Nazi violence. The extremist groups remain small, and their political party, the National Democratic Party, or NDP, has been losing support and last year failed to get enough votes to send any representatives to the *Bundestag*. Most West Germans are genuinely horrified by anything smacking of Nazism. In some cases they take individual action, helping a handicapped man attacked by skinheads, or throwing a known neo-Nazi out of a bar. In several cities, after neo-Nazi attacks thousands of Germans turned out in candlelight processions to show their opposition to intolerance and anti-Semitism. In the government's view, neo-Nazi groups are an ugly, but relatively minor problem, and while it has increased the security force devoted to keeping them under surveillance, it has not attempted to stamp out their activity, arguing that free speech must be protected. For example, when a gang of twenty-two neo-Nazis recently threw stones and shouted Nazi slogans at the site of the Buchenwald concentration camp, they were detained by police, but only one was arrested on possible charges of disturbing the peace and making threats (*The New York Times,* July 25, 1994, p. A4; Cowell, p. A4; Whitney, Jan. 19, 1993, p. A4; Ardagh, pp. 504–505).

Erich Kessel (age 22) lives in a run-down working-class community on the industrial out-skirts of Cologne. His mother works cleaning houses and his father is one of an increasing number of German workers who have been unemployed for years. His father yells at him all the time for leaving his apprenticeship: "You'll be nothing now; nothing, just like me. No one gives a damn for an ordinary worker; even the Ossis will spit on you!" Lately Erich has shaved his head, stopped going around the factories looking for regular work, and has been spending much of his time practicing martial arts with his skinhead friends. "It's all those foreigners who are ruining Germany," he says. "Hitler was right: there's red tide pouring out of the east—Poles and Russians and Ossis, taking all the good jobs and stealing our women, breeding a new race of Untermenschen [inferior people]. The government is plot-ting with NATO to let an international government take over Germany. Soon there'll be no more white people."

Last week Erich and his group surrounded a young Turkish woman on the street downtown. "Hitler would have known what to do with you," they shouted, punching and kicking her. People looked at them aghast, but no one tried to stop them, and by the time the police came they were far away. Last night things didn't go so smoothly. The firebomb they threw into an apartment house filled with Turkish workers exploded magnificently, but as Erich ran from the scene his aging motorcycle refused to start. When the police pulled him off the bike he was still cursing his stupid "Polish" machine. Now he's in jail, charged with attempted murder and very much alone. Even Helga, his girlfriend, turned up only once—and she bluntly told him he was disgusting and she never wanted to see him again!

SOCIAL CHANGE AND THE FUTURE

The story of the *Wende* (German reunification) is a wonderful example of how his-toric social change actually takes place. Years of quiet organizing by dissident groups suddenly blossomed into exhilarating collective action in the demonstra-tions that led to the fall of the Berlin Wall. But the pace of change slowed after that, and the discouraging process of institutionalizing a revolution began.

The *Wende* really began with Gorbachev, because he loosened the hold of the Soviet Union upon all its eastern European satellites. When Hungary moved toward democracy and opened its border with Austria, early in 1989, East Germans began fleeing through Hungary to the West. In the first nine months of 1989 alone, 130,000 East Germans defied their government by leaving the country.[3] Because it was unable to stop this flood of emigration, the government's authority was fatally undermined. Gorbachev himself made it clear that Soviet troops would no longer be available to prop up the SED. That emboldened more people to flee and it made the SED seem more vulnerable. In October 1989, SED chief Erich Honecker stepped down and new leaders began to reorganize the party.

[3] Almost 345,000 people left East Germany by the end of 1989, 2 percent of the country's remaining population. Those who left were mostly young, educated, and skilled, making their loss the more painful (Craig, 1994, p. 36). Many hospitals lost so many staff their operation was crippled.

Celebrating the fall of the Berlin Wall in 1989, these young German men are intoxicated with the excitement of making history. Emboldened by participating in mass demonstrations, they have actually climbed the Wall. Only days before, they would have been shot by East German police if they had dared to cross the no-man's-land which bordered the Wall.

In November 1989, millions of people demonstrated in East Berlin and Leipzig. They carried banners reading "No More Fear," "Socialism: Who Destroyed Its Meaning?" "Stop Privileges," and "Those Who Don't Move Don't Feel Their Chains." One said only "1789–1989." The crowds roared "We are the people." After that, events moved quickly. First, the whole ministry resigned, then troops and tanks rolled into the streets of East Berlin, only to be withdrawn; then the whole *Politburo* resigned. Finally, on November 9, an SED spokesman was holding a news conference and someone handed him a handwritten note. He read it off casually, perhaps inaccurately, and reporters announced that the Wall was officially opened! Then Berliners took matters into their own hands. Hundreds of thousands of people from both sides of Berlin converged on the Wall. They argued with the guards, who looked frightened, but didn't shoot, and then suddenly one guard opened a gate. The crowd surged through and suddenly there were thousands of people through the Wall, and then on top of it—dancing, hugging, drinking wine, exchanging flowers, hammering at the Wall, and destroying it with pickaxes. The crowd chanted, "We are ONE people."

Collective Behavior and Social Movements

The fall of the Berlin Wall was one of the great revolutionary moments of the twentieth century, a moment when events move so fast that a crowd, and even individuals in that crowd hold history in their hands. Just imagine: those young, frightened border guards could as easily have started shooting as opened the gate. They made history!

Sociologists who study spontaneous history making like this call the phenomenon **collective behavior.** Events on this scale don't happen often, because they require an unusual combination of conditions. First of all, they occur in response to preexisting grievances. People are likely to engage in collective behavior when they are convinced that the authorities won't listen to them any other way. Collective behavior happens most readily in an already existing crisis, when there are structural strains in the society and social controls have weakened. People have a feeling that the possible gains from collective action outweigh the risks that authorities will punish them. Even then, collective action may not occur unless two other prior conditions are present. People need some way to communicate with each other so they know other people share their grievances and will act with them. Then, there is usually some precipitating incident that focuses long-standing complaints.

In Berlin in 1989, demonstrations grew out of years of organizing activity by dissident groups. Dissidents, working mostly through the Protestant churches, organized the growing demonstrations and helped people voice beliefs about the need for change. Then the collapse of the SED precipitated action and many more people spontaneously joined in. In the crowd at the Wall people improvised norms and individual actors played a major role in the actual events.

When the Berlin Wall was opened on November 9, events began to move very quickly. Until then, the dissident movement had focused on demands for democracy—in a separate, socialist East Germany. But the masses of November 9 suddenly looked through the Wall and saw the prosperous West—a society that worked. "We are ONE people," they declared, and the rush to reunification was born. The dissidents who led the movement were horrified. But Helmut Kohl, the chancellor of West Germany, saw a unique opportunity. Hastily, he announced a plan for rapid reunification, figuring that it could take place only while Gorbachev was still in power. In March 1990, East Germans democratically elected a new parliament; by July, the economic union of the two countries was a reality; and on October 3, the two nations were officially joined as one again.

Institutional Change

Germans were euphoric: no one had ever expected Germany to be whole once more, nor had anyone anticipated the end of Soviet domination in the East. But euphoria was short-lived. It soon became clear that in forty years, West and East had become two very different societies, with contrasting values, different ways of thinking and interacting, as well as two incompatible economic systems. People realized that reunification would be difficult and very expensive. The East required new political institutions: new political parties, a new legal system, and new local governments at every level. It needed newly privatized economic institutions to replace the old state-owned structures. Schools, hospitals, and social welfare institutions had to be reorganized along western lines. And the terrible legacy of environmental damage had to be cleaned up. As institutions changed, East Germans had to reorient themselves to new roles and norms.

Reorganizing the Economy

The course of economic change was set by decisions taken early in the process of reunification. The governments of East and West Germany chose to merge the East into the Federal Republic as rapidly as possible, in part in an effort to stem the tide of emigration which was disruptive to West German society and damaging to the East as well.

The first step toward economic merger was the 1:1 currency union which took effect on July 1, 1990. Once East Germans had deutschmarks to spend, they bought western goods. A Trabant had cost 10,000 marks, but a far superior used BMW from the West cost 4000 marks. East German TVs cost 6000 marks, but West German TVs cost 4000 (Ardagh, p. 431). Without buyers for their goods, without the state subsidies which had kept them afloat, and without guaranteed markets in other Soviet satellite nations (now opening their own borders to western goods), East German factories were driven out of business. Within a year unemployment in the East reached 30 percent.

Privatization. Simultaneously with the currency union, the German government began a process of complete privatization of the East German economy. East German companies would immediately either be sold to private investors or shut down. The government created a new agency, the Public Trust (or *Treuhandanstalt*) to carry out privatization. The Public Trust's job was daunting. As one East German industrialist explained, "No one knew how to transform an economy from socialist central planning to a free market. There was no road map" (Siegfried Schlottig, quoted in Protzman, p. D1).

The *Treuhand* took over more than 13,000 formerly state-owned companies. The agency's work went slowly at first. After a year, only 600 companies had been sold and East Germans had begun to demonstrate against the Kohl government demanding an end to factory closings and better job retraining and replacement plans (Ardagh, pp. 433, 450). In truth, the agency faced enormous obstacles. Many factories were antiquated: they used old equipment and technologies long since discarded in the West. Production caused air and water and soil pollution at levels considered illegal and intolerable in the West. Potential buyers feared becoming responsible for the staggering costs of environmental cleanup. Many factories were overstaffed, so their productivity was low, typically only a third that of western plants. Any buyer would have to spend hundreds of millions of dollars in renovation costs.

Another problem blocked privatization: the "property question," as Germans called it. After the *Wende,* more than a million claims were made on land, companies, and buildings nationalized by the GDR after the war. Some claims, by Jewish owners, dated back to the Nazi era. The German legal process is thorough but slow, and no one wanted to buy a property on which unresolved claims were pending.

By 1995 privatization, however difficult, was almost complete. Perhaps a third of East German companies proved unsaleable and were shut down; other were sold after reorganization by the *Treuhand.* The agency spent $173 billion paying the debts of these companies and another $94 billion in restructuring their operations.

They took in $47 billion in sales, leaving a deficit of $170 billion which has been paid by West Germans through increased taxes. Buyers are committed to investing a further $112 billion in their new companies. There were 4.1 million people who worked in the companies taken over by the *Treuhand,* but today, only 1.5 million of their jobs still exist (Protzman, pp. D1, D2).

The Economic Situation Today. The German government has poured money into eastern Germany: at least $100 billion a year, so far mostly for retraining, industrial restructuring, unemployment benefits, and subsidized work. The subsidies will probably continue for another decade to rebuild the roads, railroads, communications networks, and public buildings. In every major eastern city cranes and bulldozers are seen everywhere, laying new sewers and power cables, restoring historic churches, and building new roads. This enormous investment is being paid for by a 7.5 percent income tax surcharge on western Germans.

In some ways, eastern Germans are better off than they were before 1989. Soon, they will have the world's most modern infrastructure—at western German expense. Their wages are higher and they are able to buy consumer goods undreamed of five years ago. In some relatively prosperous places like Leipzig, there is a boom in retailing and American-style shopping malls are ringing the city. But many eastern Germans feel worse off. They worry terribly about unemployment, which they have never experienced before.

Adopting Western Political Institutions

Superficially, political incorporation of eastern Germany into the Federal Republic has proceeded more smoothly than economic reunification. All the old political institutions of the GDR disbanded upon reunification and the East adopted the legal system, constitution, and political institutions of the Federal Republic. The traditional five states of eastern Germany, which had been abolished in the centralizing GDR, were reestablished. The old puppet political parties of the GDR, with two important exceptions, disappeared, and the major West German parties established themselves in the East. One exception was the CDU, Helmut Kohl's governing party, which had already existed as an eastern party, and therefore inherited a membership and some organization. The other party that continued in existence was the SED, which purged itself of its top leadership and then continued under a new name, the Party of Democratic Socialism (PDS). So it did not take long to create all the standard West German political bodies in the former GDR.

On a deeper level, however, the establishment of democratic institutions in eastern Germany remains problematical. After the fall of the Berlin Wall, the dissident organizations that had led the protests struggled to transform themselves into mass democratic parties to lead an independent GDR. For a few months, they met and debated intensely and joined together as the Round Table to negotiate with the departing SED and the West German government. But once it became clear that the two Germanys would reunify, the West German parties moved their operations into the East. They played a dominating role in all the 1990 elections. Don't forget that eastern Germans had no experience with competitive party politics. They were overwhelmed by the TV ads, the posters, the rallies with huge sound systems, the election parties with beer and traditional costumes. The infant dissident parties had no way to compete.

Political Alienation. East Germany had no democratic institutions for sixty years, and now it has new ones, not local products, but an imported package. It would be fair to say that this is what eastern Germans wanted: to have the whole successful West German package and not have to struggle through any more social experiments. But, unsurprisingly, they don't yet feel entirely connected to their imported institutions. This is evident in many aspects of political life. Few eastern Germans have joined the new political parties. For example, the Social Democratic Party, the second major party in the Federal Republic, had signed up fewer than 25,000 eastern Germans as members by 1992. Voter turnout has fallen since 1990 (Koch, p. 31). Eastern Germans revealed their political alienation in the 1994 *Bundestag* elections by voting against the Kohl coalition, which won only one eastern German state while gaining almost every state in western Germany.

Also, there has been a shortage of political leadership on the local level. Initially, many states and towns "twinned themselves" with counterparts in western states, which sent advisers, civil servants, and politicians on loan, some of whom ran for office in eastern states. In many cases this stimulated resentment of "know-it-all" westerners, though the alternative was relying on people who had been part of the old SED hierarchy, which made people just as angry (Ardagh, pp. 473–474). In 1995, for example, the city of Rostock actually advertised for a new mayor to replace a departing westerner (Kinzer, Mar. 13, 1995, p. A4).

The PDS. Most worrisome to many observers is the revival of fortunes of the PDS (the successor to the SED). In 1994, thirty PDS members were elected to the *Bundestag,* their support coming almost entirely from the eastern states, which gave the renamed Communist Party about 20 percent of its votes. In earlier elections the PDS took nearly 40 percent of the vote in east Berlin, emerging as the strongest local party there, and pointing up the strong political divisions between the eastern and western halves of that city. East Berliners later elected four PDS candidates to the *Bundestag.* PDS strength has been particularly evident on the local level, electing town councillors and even the mayor of a middle-sized city (Ash, p. 22; Kinzer, June 27, 1994, p. A3).

The reasons for the Communist resurgence are complex. Some old SED functionaries are still loyal to the party but, more importantly, the PDS has become the vehicle of eastern German protest, dramatizing the sense of loss eastern Germans feel as their old society is dismantled. It expresses eastern Germans' resentment of condescending *Wessis* ("westerners," as opposed to *Ossis,* "easterners"). The PDS attracts people who have been hurt by privatization, who miss the security of the old society, and it attracts young people who feel the new inequalities keenly. But much of the local vote for the PDS is a vote for particular individuals, who are locally respected as hard workers dedicated to their city, not a vote for the PDS.

Nevertheless, westerners are very fearful of the PDS revival (which echoes a revival of Communist parties in all the former Soviet-bloc nations).

Sending Women Back to the Home

Though it had many faults, East German society had one virtue appreciated by its citizens: there were many benefits to help parents, and especially mothers, raise their children while working outside the home. As we have seen, affordable day care was widely available, most children stayed in school for a full day and ate lunch at school, there was generous maternity leave (a year at 80 percent of full pay) and the state enforced and guaranteed child support by absent fathers. Abortions were legal and available through the national health insurance system (Duggan and Folbre, p. 23; Ferree, p. 94).

By 1989, 91 percent of East German women of working age were employed, and working women contributed 40 percent of average household income. They held an unusually large percentage of skilled factory jobs and professional jobs. Women were certainly not completely equal to men: they were concentrated in typically "feminine" occupations like education, nursing, and textile production, and they did most of the housework and child care, even when they worked full-time (Dolling, pp. 34–37; Nickel, pp. 50–51; Ferree, pp. 91, 93).

After reunification, eastern German women suddenly found themselves living on the western plan. The cost of day care doubled relative to income, and it is in short supply. Maternity leave now pays only 25 percent of full pay and the state no longer fully guarantees child support. School lets out before lunch and women are expected to be at home waiting for their children. Now two-thirds of unemployed eastern Germans are women. And women now cannot obtain unemployment benefits unless they can prove they already have child care arranged. Finally, abortion is now illegal in eastern Germany, as in western Germany, except in very limited circumstances (Nyrop, p. 123; Ferree, p. 93; Duggan and Folbre, p. 23). (See Table 5.4.)

Anomie in the Former East Germany

To fully understand the impact of rapid social change in East Germany we need to turn to the work of a famous French sociologist, the great Emile Durkheim. At

TABLE 5.4. Working Women and Children in Day Care and Kindergarten in Germany: East German women were more likely to work than West German women and their children were more likely to be in day care.

	Working Women as a Percent of All Women, 1985–1987	Children in Day Care as a Percent of Children under 3, 1989	Children in Kindergarten as a Percent of Children 3–6, 1989
West Germany	55.4	3.0	67.5
East Germany	83.2	80.2	97.1

Source: Einhorn, Barbara, *Cinderella Goes to Market: Citizenship, Gender and Women's Movements in East Central Europe.* London: Verso Press, 1993.

the end of the nineteenth century, Durkheim wrote about the harmful consequences of rapid change in modern societies. He said that in a period of profound change, such as a time of rapid economic modernization, an economic collapse, or a revolution, old standards of behavior, values, and beliefs become irrelevant and a state of **anomie** (or normlessness) prevails. Old social controls on individual behavior become ineffective; new ones don't yet exist and people feel directionless and lost. They may expect too much from the changed society and they often become depressed or aggressive. Rates of deviant behavior like suicide, violent crime, and drug and alcohol abuse climb rapidly.

Life in eastern Germany after reunification presents a classic example of anomie. At first, when the Wall came down, there was euphoria. People thought that with Germany reunified, all their problems would be solved. But then everything changed. Timothy Garton Ash explains,

> Nowhere in post-Communist Europe has the change in every aspect of life been so sudden and total as in east Germany. Not just the political, economic and legal system but the street signs, the banks, the post offices, the health insurance, the cars, the products in the shops, why even the bread has changed. (Ash, p. 22)

Socialism, a set of ideals which many people respected, even if they thought it had not been achieved, seemed to have been decisively defeated. People were asked to adopt a whole new way of life previously considered reprehensible. They were asked to act as individuals, to put consumer desires first, and to value private enterprise and profit making. Some people rapidly adapted, but for many others it was as if the world had turned upside down.

> *"There couldn't be a worse time to be a teacher," declares Charlotte Metz, a seventh-grade history teacher in the mining town of Cottbus. "I truly don't know what to teach my students. You know, I really believed in socialism. I taught my students Marxism-Leninism and I thought we were building the workers' state. I cried when the Wall came down. But then I saw pictures of the West. I even visited my relatives in Berlin, and it wasn't all poverty and crime and drug addiction as we had been told. But now look what reunification has done here: the mines are closed and almost all the men are out of work. That would never have happened in the GDR."*
>
> *"Teach your students both sides," Charlotte's husband interjects. "Let them make up their own minds." "I do . . . I try to," Charlotte replies, "but I can't teach any of it with conviction. I don't know what's true anymore or what's the right way to run our country. And there's something worse. My students don't want to know. Yesterday, when I started my lesson on the division of Germany, they put on their earphones. Yes, they actually pulled out their Walkmans and put on their earphones!"*

Many eastern Germans describe their state of anomie quite clearly. The Reverend Christian Führer, who was a leader of the dissident movement in Leipzig, explains, "People here feel a real schizophrenia. No one wants to go back to the days of dictatorship, but at the same time we're not really happy with the new system. It's full of challenges for which we are totally unprepared." Even people who are better off economically, Reverend Führer contends, "are worried about what is happening to our society. Brutal competition and the lust for money are destroying our sense of community. Almost everyone feels a level of fear or depression or insecurity" (Kinzer, Oct. 14, 1994, p. A14).

Birth Rates and Death Rates

Anomie in eastern Germany has had chillingly concrete social consequences. Since the fall of the Berlin Wall birth rates have fallen precipitously. By 1993, there were 60 percent fewer births than there had been in 1989. Rates fell most for married women in the prime childbearing years. Such a sharp decline is almost unprecedented in twentieth-century history, though something similar did happen in Berlin in the last years of World War II. The rate of abortions in eastern Germany has fallen too, by over 40 percent, and the number of people undergoing sterilization has increased more than tenfold. Marriage rates have fallen to the lowest level in the world today. "Many eastern couples are reluctant to have children, because they are unsure whether they will be able to survive in the newly competitive society," concluded *The New York Times* ("Living, and Dying, in a Barren Land," p. 54; Kinzer, Jan. 25, 1994, p. A3).

Even more disturbing has been the sharp rise in death rates in the former GDR. For women between the ages of 25 and 45, the death rate rose by nearly 20 percent between 1989 and 1991, and for men of the same age it rose 30 percent. Most astonishingly, for girls 10 to 14 the death rate rose 70 percent. These increases have not been the result of deterioration in health care. Medical care has probably improved in the eastern states since reunification, a fact reflected in lower death rates for babies and the elderly. And since longevity had been improving under communism, we are now seeing a sharp break with past trends. For men, death rates from cardiovascular disease, injuries, including suicide, and cirrhosis of the liver have been particularly high. For women, injuries and suicide stand out. Eastern German men in 1990 were 156 percent more likely to die of injuries or suicide than men in western Germany ("Living, and Dying, in a Barren Land," p. 54). (See Table 4.5, p. 199.)

The Future: Building New "Walls"?

> There is a new joke now in east Germany: "'We are one people,' says the easterner. 'So are we, says the westerner.'" (Whitney, Jan. 24, 1995, p. A3)

Five years after reunification, Germans worried about "the wall in our minds" that has replaced the real Berlin Wall in dividing the two Germanys. Eastern Germans feel resentful of *Wessis,* who have been so quick to condemn and discard everything eastern. Their resentment is intensified by feelings of inferiority and fear, when confronted with the successful West. They have begun to talk of being "colonized." Easterners feel sorry for themselves and feel they deserve help after all they suffered in forty years of communism. Many eastern Germans are suddenly nostalgic for their old society: "In the old days we didn't have a crime problem, we didn't have traffic jams, we didn't have trouble finding kindergarten places for our kids, and nobody had to worry about being thrown out of work," said one *Ossi* (Kinzer, Aug. 27, 1994, p. 2).

Many western Germans, in turn, resent the burden of the East, abruptly shouldered before they knew its full weight. They resent paying so much to modernize eastern Germany and they are particularly infuriated because the *Ossis* are self-pitying and angry rather than grateful. They tell stories about passive eastern Germans, unwilling to take responsibility for themselves (Koch, p. 26).

Looking toward the Future

Naturally, it is impossible to predict Germany's future. The tasks of reuniting the cultures of East and West, and of rebuilding the East economically are certainly not easy ones. Germany, like other European countries, is suffering from high unemployment rates and high taxes. But Germany has one great advantage: it is a very wealthy, technologically sophisticated, hard-working country. It is tempting to say that if anyone can take a deteriorated socialist economy and make it into a successful capitalist economy, the Germans can. Germans themselves see three different possibilities for the future, all of which distress at least some people.

"Colonization." Many eastern Germans fear that manufacturing will never revive in the East and they will be forced to choose between migration to western Germany and permanent dependence on welfare. They fear the eastern states will become a poor and dependent "colony" of the western states. Their worries were intensified by the recession of the early 1990s. While the German economy revived somewhat after 1994, it remains to be seen whether the eastern states will attract enough new investment to put their people back to work.

Westernization. Another possibility is that eastern Germany will simply become more and more like western Germany. East German culture will yield to the powerful force of consumer capitalism, and the eastern states will discard their distinctive values and their collective life, along with state-owned industries and the SED. In such a future, eastern Germany's old culture will become a souvenir. Perhaps the clearest symbol of this future is the "stretch Trabi" built by a Berlin mechanic who cut an old Trabant in half and welded the center of an American-made limousine between the front and back of the Trabant. People rent the vehicle for weddings and parties, so the scorned emblem of the old East Germany has become a status symbol available for money in the new unified Germany (Kinzer, Aug. 27, 1994, p. 2).

A "Red/Green Coalition." This is an interesting alternative future, currently exciting a good deal of speculation in Germany. This scenario sees eastern German culture surviving in a somewhat altered form and actually reshaping the culture and politics of the new Germany. Chancellor Helmut Kohl's party, the CDU, has held a majority in the *Bundestag* in coalition with its long-time partner the Free Democrats or FDP. But in recent elections, CDU/FDP margins have dwindled, with the FDP losing much of its strength. Both parties have done poorly in the new states of the former East Germany. At the same time the Green Party, in coalition with Alliance 90, the party derived from East German dissident organizations, has grown greatly in strength, doubling their share of the vote in some states. These events suggest that the Green Party might join in a majority coalition with the Social Democrats (the SDP), a "red/green coalition," which would reorient German politics toward the left, reflecting the socialist heritage of the GDR. In 1995, it was unclear which of these three futures was most probable.

Thinking Sociologically

1. Describe the values and institutions that made East Germany a socialist society.
2. Germany and Japan are both capitalist societies, but in some ways they are quite different. What differences do you see in their attitudes toward consumerism, leisure, and individualism? How do their economic institutions differ?
3. Do you live in a capitalist society? If so, is its style of capitalism similar or different in any way from Germany's or Japan's?
4. Germany, Japan, and the United States are the world's three biggest capitalist economies. Refer to Table 1.3 (p. 36) and compare how equally or unequally these three societies distribute income to their citizens.
5. In institutional structure, Germany, Japan, and Mexico all are representative democracies. What are some of the differences in the ways their political institutions work?
6. Compare the system of higher education in Germany with the system in your society. What advantages or disadvantages do you see in each?
7. Compare and contrast the ways that East Germany and West Germany defined and responded to deviance.
8. Explain why many people in eastern Germany have experienced anomie since reunification. Can you think of some examples of people experiencing anomie in your own society?
9. Turn to Table 5.3 (p. 247) and compare the percentages of 20- to 24-year-olds attending institutions of postsecondary education in West Germany and in the United States. Can you explain why Germans' incomes rival those of Americans even though many fewer Germans attend college or university?

For Further Reading

ARDAGH, JOHN, *Germany and the Germans.* New York: Penguin, 1991.
DARNTON, ROBERT, *Berlin Journal, 1989–1990.* New York: Norton, 1991.
EINHORN, BARBARA, *Cinderella Goes to Market: Citizenship, Gender and Women's Movements in East Central Europe.* London: Verso Press, 1993.
HALL, EDWARD T., AND MILDRED REED HALL, *Understanding Cultural Differences.* Yarmouth, ME: Intercultural Press, 1990.
HAMILTON, STEPHEN F., *Apprenticeship for Adulthood.* New York: Free Press, 1990.
MARCUSE, PETER, *Missing Marx: A Personal and Political Journal of a Year in East Germany, 1989–1990.* New York: Monthly Review Press, 1991.
RUESCHMEYER, MARILYN, AND CHRISTIANE LEMKE, eds., *The Quality of Life in the German Democratic Republic.* Armonk, NY: Sharp, 1989.
STEELE, JONATHAN, *Inside East Germany: The State That Came in from the Cold.* New York: Urizen Books, 1977.

Bibliography

ADORNO, THEODOR W., et al., *The Authoritarian Personality.* New York: Norton, 1950.
ARDAGH, JOHN, *Germany and the Germans.* New York: Penguin, 1991.
ASH, TIMOTHY GARTON, "Kohl's Germany: The Beginning of the End?" *The New York Review,* Dec. 1, 1994, pp. 20–26.

BERGNER, JEFFREY T., *The New Superpowers: Germany, Japan, the U.S. and the New World Order.* New York: St. Martin's Press, 1991.

BURANT, STEPHEN R., ed., *East Germany: A Country Study,* 3d ed., Area Handbook Series. Washington, DC: U.S. Government Printing Office, 1988.

BURUMA, IAN, *The Wages of Guilt: Memories of War in Germany and Japan.* New York: Farrar, Straus & Giroux, 1994.

CHILDS, DAVID, *The GDR: Moscow's German Ally.* London: Allen & Unwin, 1983.

COHEN, ROGER, "The Growing Burden of Germany's Unification," *The New York Times,* Mar. 8, 1993, pp. D1, D3.

COWELL, ALAN, "German Paradox: Alongside Healing, New Flames," *The New York Times,* May 8, 1995, p. A4.

CRAIG, GORDON A., *The Germans.* New York: Putnam, 1982.

————, "United We Fall," *New York Review of Books,* Jan. 13, 1994, pp. 36-40.

DAHRENDORF, RALF, *Society and Democracy in Germany.* New York: Doubleday Anchor, 1969.

DALTON, RUSSELL J., *Politics in West Germany.* Boston: Scott, Foresman, 1989.

DARNTON, ROBERT, *Berlin Journal, 1989–1990.* New York: Norton, 1991.

DEBARDELEBEN, JOAN, "The Future Has Already Begun," in Marilyn Rueschmeyer and Christiane Lemke, eds., *The Quality of Life in the German Democratic Republic.* Armonk, NY: Sharp, 1989, pp. 144–164.

DOLLING, IRENE, "Culture and Gender," in Marilyn Rueschmeyer and Christiane Lemke, eds., *The Quality of Life in the German Democratic Republic.* Armonk, NY: Sharp, 1989, pp. 22–47.

DUGGAN, LYNN, AND NANCY FOLBRE, "Women and Children Last," *The New York Times.* Jan. 8, 1994, p. 23.

EDWARDS, E. E., *GDR Society and Social Institutions.* New York: St. Martin's Press, 1985.

EINHORN, BARBARA, *Cinderella Goes to Market: Citizenship, Gender and Women's Movements in East Central Europe.* London: Verso Press, 1993.

FERREE, MYRA MARX, "The Rise and Fall of 'Mommy Politics': Feminism and Unification in (East) Germany," *Feminist Studies,* Vol. 19, No. 1, Spring 1993, pp. 89–115.

GANNON, MARTIN J., *Understanding Global Cultures.* London: Sage, 1994.

GERTH, H. H., AND C. WRIGHT MILLS, *From Max Weber: Essays in Sociology.* New York: Oxford University Press, 1958.

GLAESSNER, GERT-JOACHIM, "Technology Policy and Educational Transformations," in Marilyn Rueschmeyer and Christiane Lemke, eds., *The Quality of Life in the German Democratic Republic.* Armonk, NY: Sharp, 1989, pp. 77–94.

GLOUCHEVITCH, PHILIP, *Juggernaut: The German Way of Business.* New York: Simon & Schuster, 1992.

GOECKEL, ROBERT R., "Church and Society in the GDR," in Marilyn Rueschmeyer and Christiane Lemke, eds., *The Quality of Life in the German Democratic Republic.* Armonk, NY: Sharp, 1989, pp. 210–227.

GRASS, GUNTER, *Two States—One Nation?* New York: Harcourt Brace Jovanovich, 1990.

HALL, EDWARD T., AND MILDRED REED HALL, *Understanding Cultural Differences.* Yarmouth, ME: Intercultural Press, 1990.

HAMILTON, STEPHEN F., *Apprenticeship for Adulthood.* New York: Free Press, 1990.

HANCOCK, M. DONALD, *West Germany: The Politics of Democratic Corporatism.* Chatham, NJ: Chatham House, 1989.

HEILIG, GERHARD, THOMAS BUTTNER, AND WOLFGANG LUTZ, "Germany's Population: Turbulent Past, Uncertain Future," *Population Bulletin,* Vol. 45, No. 4, Dec. 1990, p. 1–46.

KELLER, MARYANN, *Collision: GM, Toyota, Volkswagen and the Race to Own the 21st Century.* New York: Doubleday, 1993.

KINZER, STEPHEN, "Where Is Optimism in Germany? Among the Bedraggled Easterners," *The New York Times,* Jan. 27, 1993, pp. A1, A10.

———, "$650 a Baby: Germany to Pay to Stem Decline in Births," *The New York Times,* Jan. 25, 1994, p. A3.

———, "Ex-Communists in Eastern Germany Gain in Voting," *The New York Times,* June 18, 1994, p. 4.

———, "German Neo-Communists, Surging, Capture a City Hall," *The New York Times,* June 27, 1994, p. A3.

———, "In 'East Germany,' Bad Ol' Days Now Look Good," *The New York Times,* Aug. 27, 1994, p. 2.

———, "State Voting in Germany Reveals Shift," *The New York Times,* Sept. 15, 1994, p. A5.

———, "A Wall of Resentment Now Divides Germany," *The New York Times,* Oct. 14, 1994, pp. A1, A14.

———, "Wanted: Mayor for 'Very Big' (Read Tough) Job," *The New York Times,* Mar. 13, 1995, p. A4.

KIRCH, HENRY, *The German Democratic Republic.* Westview Profile/Nations of Contemporary Europe. Boulder, CO: Westview Press, 1985.

KOCH, BURKHARD, "Post-Totalitarianism in Eastern Germany and German Democracy," *World Affairs,* Vol. 156, No. 1, Summer 1993, pp. 26–34.

KOLINSKY, EVA, "Everyday Life Transformed: A Case Study of Leipzig since German Unification," *World Affairs,* Vol. 156, No. 4, Spring 1994, pp. 159–174.

KRAMER, JANE, "Letter from West Germany," *The New Yorker,* Dec. 19, 1983, pp. 102–121.

LANDUA, DETLEF, "Germany after Unification: Still a Twofold Society," *International Journal of Comparative Sociology,* Vol. 34, No. 1–2, Jan./Apr. 1993, pp. 75–86.

LAQUEUR, WALTER, *Germany Today.* Boston: Little, Brown, 1985.

LEMKE, CHRISTIANE, "Political Socialization in the 'Micromilieu,'" in Marilyn Rueschmeyer and Christiane Lemke, eds., *The Quality of Life in the German Democratic Republic.* Armonk, NY: Sharp, 1989, pp. 59–73.

LEWIS, FLORA, *Europe: A Tapestry of Nations.* New York: Simon & Schuster, 1987.

"Living, and Dying, in a Barren Land," *The Economist,* Apr. 23, 1994, p. 54.

LONG, ROBERT EMMET, ed., *The Reunification of Germany,* The Reference Shelf. New York: Wilson, 1992.

MARCUSE, PETER, *Missing Marx: A Personal and Political Journal of a Year in East Germany, 1989–1990.* New York: Monthly Review Press, 1991.

MARSH, DAVID, *The Germans: A People at the Crossroads.* New York: St. Martin's Press, 1989.

MARX, KARL, AND FRIEDRICH ENGELS, *Manifesto of the Communist Party.* New York: International Publishers, 1948, 1966.

MERKL, PETER, *Germany: Yesterday and Tomorrow.* New York: Oxford University Press, 1965.

MEYER, KARL E., "Berlin's Lost Generation," *The New York Times,* Jan. 3, 1995, p. A18.

The New York Times, "Neo-Nazis Rampage at Buchenwald Site," July 25, 1994, p. A4.

NICKEL, HILDEGARD M., "Sex-Role Socialization in Relationships as a Function of the Division of Labor," in Marilyn Rueschmeyer and Christiane Lemke, eds., *The Quality of Life in the German Democratic Republic.* Armonk, NY: Sharp, 1989, pp. 48–58.

NYROP, RICHARD F., ed., *Federal Republic of Germany: A Country Study,* 2d ed., Area Handbook Series. Washington, DC: U.S. Government Printing Office, 1982.

PHILIPSEN, DIRK, *We Were the People: Voices from East Germany's Revolutionary Autumn of 1989.* Durham, NC: Duke University Press, 1993.

"A Profile of the German Education System," *American Educator,* Vol. 18, No. 1, Spring 1994, pp. 21–22.

PROTZMAN, FERDINAND, "East Nearly Privatized, Germans Argue the Cost," *The New York Times,* Aug. 12, 1994, pp. D1, D2.

RADEMAEKERS, WILLIAM, "The Oh So Good Life," in Robert Emmet Long, ed., *The Reunification of Germany.* New York: Wilson, 1992, pp. 8–12.

RAMET, PEDRO, "Disaffection and Dissent in East Germany," *World Politics,* Vol. 37, No. 1, Oct. 1984, pp. 85–111.

RUSSELL, JAMES W., *After the Fifth Sun.* Englewood Cliffs, NJ: Prentice-Hall, 1994.

SCHARF, C. BRADLEY, *Politics and Change in East Germany.* Boulder, CO: Westview Press, 1984.

SHLAES, AMITY, *Germany: The Empire Within.* New York: Farrar, Straus & Giroux, 1991.

STEELE, JONATHAN, *Inside East Germany: The State That Came in from the Cold.* New York: Urizen Books, 1977.

STERN, FRITZ, *Dreams and Delusions: The Drama of German History.* New York: Knopf, 1987.

———, "Freedom and Its Discontents," *Foreign Affairs,* Vol. 72, No. 4, Sept./Oct. 1993, pp. 108–125.

TURNER, HENRY ASHBY, JR., *The Two Germanies since 1945.* New Haven, CT: Yale University Press, 1987.

UNITED NATIONS, DEPARTMENT OF INTERNATIONAL AFFAIRS, "National Accounts Statistics: Compendium of Income Distribution Statistics," *Statistical Papers,* Series M, No. 79, 1985.

WHITNEY, CRAIG R., "Disabled Germans Fear They'll Be the Next Target," *The New York Times,* Jan. 19, 1993, p. A4.

———, "Germans Begin to Recognize Danger in Neo-Nazi Surge," *The New York Times,* Oct. 21, 1993, pp. A1, A10.

———, "Germans Find Unity May Mean Long-Term Change and Sacrifice," *The New York Times,* Dec. 26, 1993, pp. 1, 14.

———, "Kohl Dismisses Vote Setback but Faces Harder Time," *The New York Times,* Oct. 18, 1994, p. A3.

———, "Eastern Germany's Road to Modernity Leads to the Shopping Mall," *The New York Times,* Jan. 2, 1995, p. 5.

———, "Comfortable Germans, Slow to Change (Especially If It Means More Work)," *The New York Times,* Jan. 16, 1995, p. A6.

———, "Germans Five Years Later: Bitter and Still Divided," *The New York Times,* Jan. 24, 1995, p. A3.

WORLD BANK, *World Development Report 1993: Investing in Health.* New York: Oxford University Press, 1993

Index